Mastering Oracle PL/SQL: Practical Solutions

CONNOR MCDONALD, WITH CHAIM KATZ,
CHRISTOPHER BECK, JOEL R. KALLMAN, AND DAVID C. KNOX

Mastering Oracle PL/SQL: Practical Solutions
Copyright © 2004 by Connor McDonald, with Chaim Katz, Christopher Beck, Joel
R. Kallman, and David C. Knox

ISBN (pbk): 1-59059-217-4

Printed and bound in the United States of America 12345678910

Trademarked names may appear in this book. Rather than use a trademark symbol with every occurrence of a trademarked name, we use the names only in an editorial fashion and to the benefit of the trademark owner, with no intention of infringement of the trademark.

Technical Reviewers: Jakob Hammer-Jakobsen, Torben Holm, Thomas Kyte, Connor McDonald

Technical Editor: Tony Davis

Editorial Board: Steve Anglin, Dan Appleman, Gary Cornell, James Cox, Tony Davis, John Franklin, Chris Mills, Steven Rycroft, Dominic Shakeshaft, Julian Skinner, Martin Streicher, Jim Sumser, Karen Watterson, Gavin Wray, John Zukowski

Assistant Publisher: Grace Wong

Project Manager: Tracy Brown Collins

Copy Editors: Nancy Depper, Nicole LeClerc

Production Manager: Kari Brooks

Production Editor: Janet Vail

Proofreader: Patrick Vincent

Compositor: Gina M. Rexrode, Point n' Click Publishing, LLC

Indexer: Valerie Perry

Artist: Christine Calderwood, Kinetic Publishing Services, LLC

Cover Designer: Kurt Krames

Manufacturing Manager: Tom Debolski

Distributed to the book trade in the United States by Springer-Verlag New York, Inc., 175 Fifth Avenue, New York, NY, 10010 and outside the United States by Springer-Verlag GmbH & Co. KG, Tiergartenstr. 17, 69112 Heidelberg, Germany.

In the United States: phone 1-800-SPRINGER, email orders@springer-ny.com, or visit http://www.springer-ny.com. Outside the United States: fax +49 6221 345229, email orders@springer.de, or visit http://www.springer.de.

For information on translations, please contact Apress directly at 2560 Ninth Street, Suite 219, Berkeley, CA 94710. Phone 510-549-5930, fax 510-549-5939, email info@apress.com, or visit http://www.apress.com.

The information in this book is distributed on an "as is" basis, without warranty. Although every precaution has been taken in the preparation of this work, neither the author(s) nor Apress shall have any liability to any person or entity with respect to any loss or damage caused or alleged to be caused directly or indirectly by the information contained in this work.

The source code for this book is available to readers at http://www.apress.com in the Downloads section. You will need to answer questions pertaining to this book in order to successfully download the code.

Contents at a Glance

Contents

Foreword to the OakTable Press Series

Put simply, the OakTable network is an informal organization consisting of a group of Oracle experts who are dedicated to finding ever better ways of administering and developing Oracle-based systems. We have joined forces with Apress to bring you the OakTable Press series of Oracle-related titles.

The members of the network have a few things in common. We take a scientific approach to working with the Oracle database. We don't believe anything unless we've seen it thoroughly tested and proved. We enjoy "moving boundaries," innovating, finding new and better ways to do things. We like good whiskey. These, in essence, are the ideals that we want to bring to the OakTable Press series (well, apart from the last one, possibly). Every book in the series will be written by and/or technically reviewed by at least two members of the OakTable network. It is our goal to help each OakTable Press author produce a book that is rigorous, accurate, innovative, and fun. Ultimately, we hope that each book is as useful a tool as it can possibly be in helping make your life easier.

Who Are the OakTable Network?

It all started sometime in 1998 when a group of Oracle experts, including Anjo Kolk, Cary Millsap, James Morle, and a few others, started meeting once or twice a year, on various pretexts. Each would bring a bottle of Scotch or Bourbon and in return earn the right to sleep on the floor somewhere in my house.

We spent most of our time sitting around my dining table, with computers, cabling, paper, and other stuff all over the place, discussing Oracle, relaying anecdotes, and experimenting with new and better ways of working with the database. By the spring of 2002, the whole thing had grown. One evening, I realized that I had 16 world-renowned Oracle scientists sitting around my dining table. We were sleeping three or four to a room and even had to borrow the neighbor's shower in the mornings. Anjo Kolk suggested we call ourselves the "OakTable network" (after my dining table), and about 2 minutes later, http://www.OakTable.net was registered.

Today, a total of 42 people have been admitted to the OakTable network, with perhaps half of them working for Oracle (there's an up-to-date list on the website). A committee, consisting of James Morle, Cary Millsap, Anjo Kolk, Steve Adams, Jonathan Lewis, and myself, reviews suggestions for new members.

You can meet us at various conferences and user group events, and discuss technical issues with us or challenge the OakTable network with a technical question. If we can't answer your question within 24 hours, you get a T-shirt that says, "I challenged the OakTable—and I won," with the three last words printed in very, very small type! We still meet twice a year in Denmark: in January for the Miracle Master Class (2001: Cary Millsap, 2002: Jonathan Lewis, 2003: Steve Adams, and 2004: Tom Kyte), when one of the members will present for three days, and in September/October for the Miracle Database Forum, which is a three-day conference for database people.

Many projects and ideas have come out of the OakTable network, with some of them resulting in courses (such as the Hotsos Clinic), others resulting in new software products, and one that resulted in the OakTable Press series. We hope you'll enjoy the books coming out of it in the coming years.

Best,

Mogens Nørgaard
CEO of Miracle A/S (http://www.miracleas.dk/) and cofounder of the OakTable network

About the Authors

 **Connor McDonald**, lead author, has been working with Oracle since the early 1990s. His involvement with the Oracle database started with versions 6.0.36 and 7.0.12. Over the last 11 years he has worked with systems in Australia, the United Kingdom, Southeast Asia, Western Europe, and the United States. Connor is a member of the OakTable network and is a well-known personality both on the Oracle speaker circuit and in online Oracle forums. He hosts a hints and tips website (http://www.oracledba.co.uk) to share his passion for Oracle and as part of an endeavor to improve the way in which Oracle software is used within the industry.

Chaim Katz is an Oracle Certified Professional who has worked with Oracle products since Oracle version 4. He specializes in database administration and PL/SQL development and, over the years, he has written numerous articles for various Oracle technical journals. He has taught Logo to children and database systems at the college level. He lives in Montreal, Quebec, where aside from his 9-to-5 job in information systems, he likes to study the Talmud, play clarinet, and discuss eternal problems. He and his wife, Ruthie, are currently enjoying the challenges of raising a large family.

Christopher Beck, who holds a bachelor's degree in computer science from Rutgers University, has worked in the industry for 13 years. Starting off as a junior Ada software developer for a government contractor, he has spent the last 9 years with Oracle Corporation and is now a principal technologist. He specializes in core database technologies and Web application development. When he isn't working for Oracle or spending time with his wife and four young children, he's tinkering with Linux or playing a friendly online game of *Quake III Arena*.

Joel R. Kallman is a software development manager for Oracle Corporation. Over the past 14 years, he has focused on database and content management, from SGML databases and publishing systems to text and document management. He is currently managing the development of Oracle HTML DB, a solution that allows customers to easily build database-centric Web applications.

When the daily advances in computer technology aren't consuming all his time, Joel enjoys football, woodworking, investing, and working out at the local "Y." Joel is a proud alumnus of The Ohio State University, where he received his bachelor's degree in computer engineering. He and his wife, Kristin, reside in Powell, Ohio.

David C. Knox is the chief engineer for Oracle's Information Assurance Center. He joined Oracle Corporation in June 1995. While at Oracle, he has worked on many security projects for various customers, including the U.S. Department of Defense (DoD), intelligence agencies, state and local governments, financial services organizations, and healthcare organizations. His computer security expertise derives not only from working knowledge and experience with Oracle's security products and database security, but also from his academic studies in the areas of multilevel security, cryptography, LDAP, and PKI. David earned a bachelor's degree in computer science from the University of Maryland and a master's degree in computer science from Johns Hopkins University.

About the Technical Reviewers

Jakob Hammer-Jakobsen was born in 1965. He earned his master's degree in 1992 and has been working with Oracle since 1986 (starting with Oracle version 5). He has worked primarily as developer of business systems on Oracle (and other databases), but over the last 5 years he's moved to the DBA segment as well. Jakob has taught all kinds of Oracle-related courses worldwide; his most recent course was "Developing Java Portlets." He is an Oracle Certified Developer and a member of OakTable.net. Other organizations he's worked for include the Department of Higher Education, University of Roskilde; Denmark's International Student Foundation (housing); Tom Pedersen International (the original distributor of Oracle in Europe); Oracle Denmark; Miracle Australia; and Miracle Denmark.

Torben Holm is a member of the OakTable network. He has been in the computer business as a developer since 1998, as a staff sergeant in the Royal Danish Airforce. He has been working with Oracle since 1992—his first 4 years as system analyst and application developer (Oracle 7 and Forms 4.0/Reports 2.0 and DBA), then 2 years as developer (Oracle6/7, Forms 3.0 and RPT, and DBA). He then worked 2 years in Oracle Denmark in the Premium Services group as a senior principal consultant, where he performed application development and DBA tasks. He worked as an instructor in PL/SQL, SQL, DBA, and WebDB courses. For the last 3 years, Torben has worked for Miracle A/S (http://www.miracleas.dk/) as application developer and DBA. He is Developer 6*i* Certified (and partly 8*i* Certified, for what it's worth—he didn't have the time to finish that certification). His "main" language is PL/SQL.

Tom Kyte is VP, Core Technologies at Oracle Corporation, and he has over 16 years of experience designing and developing large-scale database and Internet applications. Tom specializes in core database technologies, application design and architecture, and performance tuning. He is a regular columnist for *Oracle Magazine* and is the Tom behind the AskTom website (http://asktom.oracle.com/), where technical professionals can come to get answers to their questions. He's also the author of *Effective Oracle by Design*, an Oracle best practices book, and *Expert One-on-One Oracle*, a book that describes how to architect systems using core Oracle technologies, and he's the coauthor of *Beginning Oracle*, a book aimed at new Oracle developers.

Acknowledgments

First, I want to acknowledge the wonderful help afforded to me over the years by the OakTable network. I've never met a group of people who are so generous with their time and knowledge (and vast knowledge it is indeed!). It's a privilege to be associated with them. In particular, I want to thank Tom Kyte, Jonathan Lewis, and Dave Ensor, all of whom inspired me to explore Oracle more deeply, and Mogens Nørgaard, an OakTable network "founder," for his amazing hospitality and whiskey! Thanks also to my editor, Tony Davis, toward whom my emotions have oscillated between gratitude and wanting to knock him senseless, which pretty much means he's doing his job well.

I would also like to thank the companies I've worked with that use Oracle. There is no better way of exploring the power of PL/SQL and other Oracle technologies than to be challenged with solving problems and optimizing the use of the Oracle infrastructure.

Most important, I want to thank my wife, Gillian, for her support and tolerance of the time I spend exploring Oracle—time I should be spending with her! Exploring technology often means being locked away for hours or days in a dark room in front of a computer screen, but knowing that you've got the most beautiful and wonderful woman in the world just a few steps away in the next room makes finding inspiration easy.

—Connor McDonald

I would like to thank Tony Davis at Apress for sticking with me through this process, even though my submissions were always very late. Sorry again, Tony. I would also like to thank my wife, Marta, for her constant encouragement and support. Ti amo.

—Christopher Beck

I would first like to thank my wife, Sandy, for supporting me in writing this book. I would have never been able to do it without her allowing me to work on this project during "vacation." I would also like to acknowledge my colleagues at Oracle—Tom Kyte and Patrick Sack, in particular—for their technical perspectives and valuable input. I would also like to thank my editor, Tony Davis; my fellow authors; and the technical reviewers, all of whom have helped to make this book a success.

—David C. Knox

Introduction

I went to an online bookstore recently, typed **PL/SQL** in the Search box, and got 38 results back, excluding this book. Thirty-eight books! As far as I could see, none of them was listed alongside the Harry Potter books as worldwide top-sellers, so what on earth would inspire a group of authors to come together to produce the thirty-ninth book on this topic?

The reason is that, despite the plethora of available books, we still encounter a great deal of poor quality or antiquated PL/SQL code in Oracle applications. From a personal perspective, I've worked with Oracle systems around the world, and although the applications, architectures, and methodologies have been very diverse, I've found two common themes in almost all of these systems. Either they steer away from Oracle-specific functionality altogether, or they use it in a haphazard and less-than-optimal fashion. Nowhere is this more evident than in the use of PL/SQL, which has been less "used" and more "abused" in many of the systems that I've encountered.

At least part of the problem is that the majority of PL/SQL books are only about syntax. They'll show you how to code PL/SQL so that it will compile and execute on your systems (some books extend themselves to giving guidelines for good naming standards and coding structure). But, as with any programming language, there's a big difference between just using the language and using it well. The key to building successful applications is the ability to take your syntax knowledge and apply it intelligently to build programs that are robust, efficient, and easily maintained. This is the motivation for our book and its title. We don't want to make you a PL/SQL programmer—we want to make you a *smart* PL/SQL programmer.

What Does This Book Cover?

This book offers a wealth of tips, techniques, and complete strategies for maximizing the benefits of PL/SQL within your organization. By the end of this book, you'll be as convinced as we are that PL/SQL isn't just a useful tool—it's an integral part of any Oracle application you'll ever develop.

We'll demonstrate techniques that are applicable for all versions of Oracle, from 8*i* to 10*g*. The vast majority of the examples in this book were tested using Oracle9*i* R2, and all you'll need to run them is SQL*Plus.

The following is a chapter-by-chapter breakdown that summarizes some of the key topics we'll cover:

- **Setting Up.** The next section of this book shows you how to set up an effective SQL*Plus environment and how to get up and running with the performance tools that we use throughout the book, namely AUTOTRACE, SQL_TRACE, TKPROF, and RUNSTATS.

- **Chapter 1: Efficient PL/SQL.** This chapter defines what we mean by "efficient PL/SQL" and introduces the book's pervading theme of *demonstrability*—that is, the need to prove conclusively that your code meets performance targets under *all* reasonable conditions. It demonstrates why PL/SQL is almost always the right tool for programming within the database, but it also explores situations in which PL/SQL might not be appropriate, by presenting a few innovative uses of SQL as a means to avoiding procedural code altogether.

- **Chapter 2: Package It All Up**. Packages are much more than just a "logical grouping of procedures." They offer numerous advantages, from overloading and encapsulation to protection from dependency and recompilation issues. This chapter clearly demonstrates these advantages and also discusses interesting uses for some of the Oracle-supplied packages.

- **Chapter 3: The Vexed Subject of Cursors.** There is much debate and contention surrounding the issue of explicit versus implicit cursors. This chapter demonstrates why you might not need explicit cursors as often as you may think. It also looks at effective uses of cursor variables and cursor expressions in distributed applications.

- **Chapter 4: Effective Data Handling.** This chapter shows you how to maximize the integration between the data structures in the database and the data structures in your PL/SQL program, leading to code that is more robust and resilient to change. It also looks at how to make effective use of collections in passing data in bulk from your program to the database and vice versa.

- **Chapter 5: PL/SQL Optimization Techniques.** This chapter provides a number of ready-made solutions to some commonly encountered problems in PL/SQL development. It shows you how to avoid some of the hidden overheads and highlights "gotchas" that can trip up the unwary.

- **Chapter 6: Triggers.** This chapter covers fundamental trigger concepts and effective uses for some of the various types of triggers available. It also delves into the relatively new topic of Oracle Streams and shows how to use them to implement a centralized data audit trail.

- **Chapter 7: DBA Packages.** This chapter provides a "DBA toolkit"—a set of packages that can be used to automate recurring administrative activities, such as performance diagnosis and troubleshooting, backup and recovery, and monitoring the database for faults.

- **Chapter 8: Security Packages.** This chapter looks at the use of PL/SQL packages and triggers to implement effective security mechanisms in the database. It covers fundamental issues such as use of the invoker and definer rights models, package construction, and schema design, and then it moves on to present specific solutions for such issues as auditing database activity and protecting your source code.

- **Chapter 9: Web Packages.** This chapter investigates a set of built-in database packages, collectively known as the PL/SQL Web Toolkit, which allow developers to present dynamic Web pages from directly within the database. It covers issues such as use of cookies, management of tables and files, and how to invoke a Web Service directly from within a PL/SQL stored procedure.

- **Chapter 10: PL/SQL Debugging.** Few people get it right first time, so this chapter presents a range of techniques for effective debugging of your PL/SQL code, from the simple use of DBMS_OUTPUT to more complex packages such as DBMS_APPLICATION_INFO and UTL_FILE. It culminates with the development of DEBUG, a sophisticated custom debugging utility.

- **Appendix A: Building DEBUG.** This appendix presents the full code listing for the DEBUG utility used in Chapter 10.

Who Should Read This Book?

This book is targeted primarily toward the DBA or developer charged with the implementation of effective data handling, security, and database administration mechanisms in the Oracle database. However, it will also have great appeal to *any* developer whose applications rely on an Oracle database and who needs a sound understanding of how to use PL/SQL effectively.

If you're brand new to PL/SQL, then you'll want to take some time to get familiar with the language before tackling this book. It's not for the total beginner. But once you're up and running, we believe you'll find our book an invaluable guide for ensuring that the PL/SQL solutions you build are robust, perform well, and are easy to maintain.

—Connor McDonald

Setting Up

In this section we'll describe how to set up an environment capable of executing the examples in this book. We'll cover the following topics:

- How to set up the SCOTT/TIGER demonstration schema

- How to configure the SQL*Plus environment

- How to configure AUTOTRACE, a SQL*Plus facility that shows you either how Oracle performed a query or how it will perform the query, along with statistics regarding the processing of that query

- How to set up to use SQL_TRACE, TIMED_STATISTICS, and TKPROF, two parameters and a command-line tool that will tell you what SQL your application executed and how that SQL performed

- How to set up and use the RUNSTATS utility

Note that we provide only basic setup instructions here for the various performance tools, so that you may quickly configure your environment to run to the examples in this book. For full instructions and information on how to interpret the data that these tools provide, we refer you to the Oracle documentation set or to a relevant book, such as Thomas Kyte's *Expert One-on-One Oracle* (Apress, ISBN: 1-59059-243-3).

Setting Up the SCOTT/TIGER Schema

Many of the examples in this book draw on the EMP/DEPT tables in the SCOTT schema. We recommend that you install your own copy of these tables in some account other than SCOTT to avoid side effects caused by other users using and modifying the same data. To create the SCOTT demonstration tables in your own schema, simply perform the following:

1. From the command line, run cd [ORACLE_HOME]/sqlplus/demo.

2. Log into SQL*Plus as the required user.

3. Run @DEMOBLD.SQL.

The DEMOBLD.SQL script will create and populate five tables for you. When it's complete, it exits SQL*Plus automatically, so don't be surprised when SQL*Plus disappears after running the script. If you would like to drop this schema at any time to clean up, you can simply execute [ORACLE_HOME]/sqlplus/demo/demodrop.sql.

The SQL*Plus Environment

The examples in this book are designed to run in the SQL*Plus environment. SQL*Plus provides many useful options and commands that we'll make frequent use of throughout this book. For example, a lot of the examples in this book use DBMS_OUTPUT in some fashion. In order for DBMS_OUTPUT to work, the following SQL*Plus command must be issued:

```
SQL> set serveroutput on
```

Alternatively, SQL*Plus allows us to set up a LOGIN.SQL file, a script that is executed each and every time we start a SQL*Plus session. In this file, we can set parameters such as SERVEROUTPUT automatically. An example of a LOGIN.SQL script is as follows (you can edit it to suit your own particular environment):

```
define _editor=vi

set serveroutput on size 1000000

set trimspool on
set long 5000
set linesize 100
set pagesize 9999
column plan_plus_exp format a80
```

Furthermore, we can use this script to format our SQL*Plus prompt so that we always know who we're logged in as and on which database. For example, as you work through this book, you'll encounter prompts of the following format:

```
scott@oracle9i_test>
```

This tells you that you're logged into the SCOTT schema on the ORACLE9I_TEST database. The following is the code in the LOGIN.SQL script that achieves this:

```
column global_name new_value gname
set termout off
select lower(user) || '@' ||
```

```
global_name from global_name;
set sqlprompt '&gname> '
set termout on
```

This login script will only be run once, on startup. So, if you login on startup as SCOTT and then change to a different account, this won't register on your prompt:

```
SQL*Plus: Release 8.1.7.0.0 - Production on Sun Mar 16 15:02:21 2003

(c) Copyright 2000 Oracle Corporation.  All rights reserved.

Enter user-name: scott/tiger

Connected to:
Personal Oracle8i Release 8.1.7.0.0 - Production
With the Partitioning option
JServer Release 8.1.7.0.0 - Production

scott@ORATEST> connect tony/davis
Connected.
scott@ORATEST>
```

The following CONNECT.SQL script will solve this:

```
set termout off
connect &1
@login
set termout on
```

Then you simply run this script (which connects, and then runs the login script) every time you want to change accounts:

```
scott@ORATEST> @connect tony/davis
tony@ORATEST>
```

To get SQL*Plus to run the login script automatically on startup, you need to save it in a directory (put CONNECT.SQL in the same directory) and then set the SQLPATH environment variable to point at that directory. If you're working on Windows, navigate to the Start button, select Run, and type **regedit**. Navigate to HKEY_LOCAL_MACHINE/SOFTWARE/ORACLE and find the SQLPATH file (mine was in HOME0). Double-click it and set the path to the directory where you stored the scripts (for example, C:\oracle\ora81\sqlplus\admin).

*Setting Up AUTOTRACE in SQL*Plus*

Throughout the book it will be useful for us to monitor the performance of the queries we execute. SQL*Plus provides an AUTOTRACE facility that allows us to see the execution plans of the queries we've executed and the resources they used. The report is generated after successful SQL DML. This book makes extensive use of this facility. There is more than one way to configure the AUTOTRACE facility, but the following is a recommended route:

1. Access cd $ORACLE_HOME/rdbms/admin.

2. Log into SQL*Plus as any user with CREATE TABLE and CREATE PUBLIC SYNONYM privileges.

3. Run @UTLXPLAN to create a PLAN_TABLE for use by AUTOTRACE.

4. Run CREATE PUBLIC SYNONYM PLAN_TABLE FOR PLAN_TABLE, so that everyone can access this table without specifying a schema.

5. Run GRANT ALL ON PLAN_TABLE TO PUBLIC, so that everyone can use this table.

6. Exit SQL*Plus and change directories as follows:
    cd $ORACLE_HOME/sqlplus/admin.

7. Log into SQL*Plus as a SYSDBA.

8. Run @PLUSTRCE.

9. Run GRANT PLUSTRACE TO PUBLIC.

You can test your setup by enabling AUTOTRACE and executing a simple query:

```
SQL> set AUTOTRACE traceonly
SQL> select * from emp, dept
  2    where emp.deptno=dept.deptno;


14 rows selected.

Execution Plan
----------------------------------------------------------
   0      SELECT STATEMENT Optimizer=CHOOSE
   1    0   MERGE JOIN
```

```
2    1       SORT (JOIN)
3    2          TABLE ACCESS (FULL) OF 'DEPT'
4    1       SORT (JOIN)
5    4          TABLE ACCESS (FULL) OF 'EMP'
```

```
Statistics
----------------------------------------------------------
         0  recursive calls
         8  db block gets
         2  consistent gets
         0  physical reads
         0  redo size
      2144  bytes sent via SQL*Net to client
       425  bytes received via SQL*Net from client
         2  SQL*Net roundtrips to/from client
         2  sorts (memory)
         0  sorts (disk)
        14  rows processed
```

```
SQL> set AUTOTRACE off
```

For full details on the use of AUTOTRACE and interpretation of the data it provides, see Chapter 11 of *Oracle9i Database Performance Tuning Guide and Reference* in the Oracle documentation set or Chapter 9 of *SQL*Plus User's Guide and Reference.*

Performance Tools

In addition to using AUTOTRACE, we make use of various other performance tools throughout the book. We'll present brief setup instructions in this section.

TIMED_STATISTICS

The TIMED_STATISTICS parameter specifies whether Oracle should measure the execution time for various internal operations. Without this parameter set, there is much less value to the trace file output. As with other parameters, you can set TIMED_STATISTICS either on an instance level (in INIT.ORA) or on a session level. The former shouldn't affect performance, so it's generally recommended. Simply add the following line to your INIT.ORA file and then the next time you restart the database, it will be enabled:

```
timed_statistics=true
```

On a session level, you would issue this:

```
SQL> alter session set timed_statistics=true;
```

SQL_TRACE and TKPROF

Together, the SQL_TRACE facility and the TKPROF command-line utility enable detailed tracing of the activity that takes place within the database. In short, SQL_TRACE is used to write performance information on individual SQL statements down to trace files in the file system of the database server. Under normal circumstances, these trace files are hard to comprehend directly. For that purpose, you use the TKPROF utility to generate text-based report files from the input of a given trace file.

SQL_TRACE

The SQL_TRACE facility is used to trace all SQL activity of a specified database session or instance down to a trace file in the database server operating system. Each entry in the trace file records a specific operation performed while the Oracle server process is processing a SQL statement. SQL_TRACE was originally intended for debugging, and it's still well suited for that purpose, but it can just as easily be used to analyze the SQL activity of the database for tuning purposes.

Setting Up SQL_TRACE

SQL_TRACE can be enabled for either a single session or a whole database instance. It is, however, rarely enabled at a database level, because that would cause serious performance problems. Remember that SQL_TRACE writes down every SQL statement processed down to a log file, with accompanying I/O activity.

To enable tracing for the current session, you should issue ALTER SESSION, as shown here:

```
SQL> alter session set sql_trace=true;
```

Enable tracing for a session at a selected interval and avoid having tracing in effect for long periods of time. To disable the current trace operation, you execute the following:

```
SQL> alter session set sql_trace=false;
```

Controlling the Trace Files

The trace files generated by SQL_TRACE can eventually grow quite large. A few global initialization parameters, set in INIT.ORA for the database instance or session settings, affect the trace files. If enabled, SQL_TRACE will write to a file in the operating system directory indicated by the USER_DUMP_DEST initialization parameter. You should note that trace files for USER processes (dedicated servers) go to the USER_DUMP_DEST directory. Trace files generated by Oracle background processes such as the shared servers used with MTS and job queue processes used with the job queues will go to the BACKGROUND_DUMP_DEST. Use of SQL_TRACE with a shared server configuration isn't recommended. Your session will hop from shared server to shared server, generating trace information in not one but in many trace files, rendering it useless.

Trace files are usually named

```
ora<spid>.trc,
```

where *<spid>* is the server process ID of the session for which the trace was enabled. On Windows, the following query may be used to retrieve your session's trace file name:

```
SQL> select c.value || '\ORA' || to_char(a.spid,'fm00000') || '.trc'
  2    from v$process a, v$session b, v$parameter c
  3   where a.addr = b.paddr
  4     and b.audsid = userenv('sessionid')
  5     and c.name = 'user_dump_dest';
```

On Unix, this query can be used to retrieve the session's trace file name:

```
SQL> select c.value || '/' || d.instance_name || '_ora_' ||
  2                 to_char(a.spid,'fm99999') || '.trc'
  3    from v$process a, v$session b, v$parameter c, v$instance d
  4   where a.addr = b.paddr
  5     and b.audsid = userenv('sessionid')
  6     and c.name = 'user_dump_dest';
```

The size of the trace files is restricted by the value of the MAX_DUMP_FILE_SIZE initialization parameter set in INIT.ORA for the database instance. You may also alter this at the session level using the ALTER SESSION command, for example:

```
SQL> alter session set max_dump_file_size = unlimited;
Session altered.
```

TKPROF

The TKPROF utility takes a SQL_TRACE trace file as input and produces a text-based report file as output. It's a very simple utility, summarizing a large set of detailed information in a given trace file so that it can be understood for performance tuning.

Using TKPROF

TKPROF is a simple command-line utility that is used to translate a raw trace file to a more comprehensible report. In its simplest form, TKPROF can be used as shown here:

```
tkprof <trace-file-name> <report-file-name>
```

To illustrate the joint use of TKPROF and SQL_TRACE, we'll set up a simple example. Specifically, we'll trace the query we used previously in our AUTOTRACE example and generate a report from the resulting trace file. First, we log onto SQL*Plus as the intended user and then execute the following code:

```
SQL> select c.value || '\ORA' || to_char(a.spid,'fm00000') || '.trc'
  2      from v$process a, v$session b, v$parameter c
  3    where a.addr = b.paddr
  4        and b.audsid = userenv('sessionid')
  5        and c.name = 'user_dump_dest';

C.VALUE||'\ORA'||TO_CHAR(A.SPID,'FM00000')||'.TRC'
-----------------------------------------------------------
C:\oracle\admin\oratest\udump\ORA01528.trc

SQL> alter session set timed_statistics=true;

Session altered.
```

```
SQL> alter session set sql_trace=true;

Session altered.

SQL> select * from emp, dept
  2    where emp.deptno=dept.deptno;

SQL> alter session set sql_trace=false;

SQL> exit
```

Now, we simply format our trace file from the command line using TKPROF, as follows:

```
C:\oracle\admin\oratest\udump>tkprof ORA01528.TRC tkprof_rep1.txt
```

Now we can open the TKPROF_REP1.TXT file and view the report. We don't intend to discuss the output in detail here, but briefly, at the top of the report we should see the actual SQL statement issued. Next, we get the execution report for the statement. This report is illustrated for the three different phases of Oracle SQL processing: parse, execute, and fetch. For each processing phase, we see the following:

- The number of times that phase occurred

- The CPU time elapsed for the phase

- The real-world time that elapsed

- The number of physical I/O operations that took place on the disk

- The number of blocks processed in "consistent-read" mode

- The number of blocks read in "current" mode (reads that occur when the data is changed by an external process during the duration of the statement processing)

- The number of blocks that were affected by the statement

The execution report is as follows:

call	count	cpu	elapsed	disk	query	current	rows
Parse	1	0.01	0.02	0	0	0	0
Execute	1	0.00	0.00	0	0	0	0
Fetch	2	0.00	0.00	0	2	8	14
total	4	0.01	0.02	0	2	8	14

Following the execution report, we can see optimizer approach used and the user ID of the session that enabled the trace (we can match this ID against the ALL_USERS table to get the actual username):

```
Misses in library cache during parse: 0
Optimizer goal: CHOOSE
Parsing user id: 52
```

Additionally, we see the number of times the statement wasn't found in the library cache. The first time a statement is executed, this count should be 1, but it should be 0 in subsequent calls if bind variables are used. Again, watch for the absence of bind variables—a large number of library cache misses would indicate that.

Finally, the report displays the execution plan used for this statement. This information is similar to that provided by AUTOTRACE, with the important difference that the number of actual rows flowing out of each step in the plan is revealed to us:

```
Rows     Row Source Operation
-------- -------------------------------------------------------
      14 MERGE JOIN
       5 SORT JOIN
       4 TABLE ACCESS FULL DEPT
      14 SORT JOIN
      14 TABLE ACCESS FULL EMP
```

For full details on use of SQL_TRACE and TKPROF, and interpretation of the trace data, see Chapter 10 of *Oracle9i Database Performance Tuning Guide and Reference.*

RUNSTATS

RUNSTATS is a simple test harness that allows comparison of two executions of code and displays the costs of each in terms of the elapsed time, session-level statistics (such as parse calls), and latching differences. The latter of these, latching, is the key piece of information that this tool provides.

> **NOTE** The RUNSTATS tool was originally built by Tom Kyte, the man behind the http://asktom.oracle.com website. Full information and an example usage of RUNSTATS can be found at http://asktom.oracle.com/~tkyte/runstats.html. In Chapter 4 we provide a useful customization of this tool that makes use of collections.

To run this test harness, you must have access to V$STATNAME, V$MYSTAT, and V$LATCH. You must be granted *direct* SELECT privileges (not via a role) on SYS.V_$STATNAME, SYS.V_$MYSTAT, and SYS.V_$LATCH. You can then create the following view:

```
SQL> create or replace view stats
  2  as select 'STAT...' || a.name name, b.value
  3         from v$statname a, v$mystat b
  4        where a.statistic# = b.statistic#
  5       union all
  6       select 'LATCH.' || name,  gets
  7           from v$latch;

View created.
```

All you need then is a small table to store the statistics:

```
create global temporary table run_stats
( runid varchar2(15),
  name varchar2(80),
  value int )
on commit preserve rows;
```

The code for the test harness package is as follows:

```
create or replace package runstats_pkg
as
    procedure rs_start;
    procedure rs_middle;
    procedure rs_stop( p_difference_threshold in number default 0 );
end;
/
```

```
create or replace package body runstats_pkg
as

g_start number;
g_run1  number;
g_run2  number;

procedure rs_start
is
begin
    delete from run_stats;

    insert into run_stats
    select 'before', stats.* from stats;

    g_start := dbms_utility.get_time;
end;

procedure rs_middle
is
begin
    g_run1 := (dbms_utility.get_time-g_start);

    insert into run_stats
    select 'after 1', stats.* from stats;
    g_start := dbms_utility.get_time;

end;

procedure rs_stop(p_difference_threshold in number default 0)
is
begin
    g_run2 := (dbms_utility.get_time-g_start);

    dbms_output.put_line
    ( 'Run1 ran in ' || g_run1 || ' hsecs' );
    dbms_output.put_line
    ( 'Run2 ran in ' || g_run2 || ' hsecs' );
    dbms_output.put_line
    ( 'run 1 ran in ' || round(g_run1/g_run2*100,2) ||
      '% of the time' );
    dbms_output.put_line( chr(9) );
```

```
insert into run_stats
select 'after 2', stats.* from stats;

dbms_output.put_line
( rpad( 'Name', 30 ) || lpad( 'Run1', 10 ) ||
  lpad( 'Run2', 10 ) || lpad( 'Diff', 10 ) );

for x in
( select rpad( a.name, 30 ) ||
         to_char( b.value-a.value, '9,999,999' ) ||
         to_char( c.value-b.value, '9,999,999' ) ||
         to_char( ( (c.value-b.value)-(b.value-a.value)), '9,999,999' ) data
    from run_stats a, run_stats b, run_stats c
   where a.name = b.name
     and b.name = c.name
     and a.runid = 'before'
     and b.runid = 'after 1'
     and c.runid = 'after 2'
     and (c.value-a.value) > 0
     and abs( (c.value-b.value) - (b.value-a.value) )
           > p_difference_threshold
   order by abs( (c.value-b.value)-(b.value-a.value))
) loop
    dbms_output.put_line( x.data );
end loop;

dbms_output.put_line( chr(9) );
dbms_output.put_line
( 'Run1 latches total versus runs -- difference and pct' );
dbms_output.put_line
( lpad( 'Run1', 10 ) || lpad( 'Run2', 10 ) ||
  lpad( 'Diff', 10 ) || lpad( 'Pct', 8 ) );

for x in
( select to_char( run1, '9,999,999' ) ||
         to_char( run2, '9,999,999' ) ||
         to_char( diff, '9,999,999' ) ||
         to_char( round( run1/run2*100,2 ), '999.99' ) || '%' data
    from ( select sum(b.value-a.value) run1, sum(c.value-b.value) run2,
                  sum( (c.value-b.value)-(b.value-a.value)) diff
             from run_stats a, run_stats b, run_stats c
            where a.name = b.name
              and b.name = c.name
              and a.runid = 'before'
```

```
                           and b.runid = 'after 1'
                           and c.runid = 'after 2'
                           and a.name like 'LATCH%'
                       )
        ) loop
            dbms_output.put_line( x.data );
        end loop;
    end;

    end;
    /
```

Using RUNSTATS

To demonstrate the information that we can get out of RUNSTATS, we'll compare the performance of a lookup on a normal heap table (HEAP) and an index-organized table (IOT). We'll consider three scenarios:

- Full table scan on small tables

- Primary key lookup on moderate tables

- Secondary index lookup on moderately sized tables

Full Scan on Small Tables

First we create our tables and indexes:

```
SQL> create table HEAP
  2      as select * from DUAL;

Table created.

SQL> create table IOT ( dummy primary key)
  2      organization index
  3      as select * from DUAL;

Table created.
```

Now we analyze both tables to ensure consistency in our results:

```
SQL> analyze table HEAP compute statistics;

Table analyzed.

SQL> analyze table IOT compute statistics;

Table analyzed.
```

Next we perform a preliminary run to massage the cache:

```
SQL> declare
  2       x varchar2(1);
  3    begin
  4       for i in 1 .. 10000 loop
  5         select dummy into x
  6         from   HEAP;
  7       end loop;
  8    end;
  9  /

PL/SQL procedure successfully completed.

SQL> declare
  2       x varchar2(1);
  3    begin
  4       for i in 1 .. 10000 loop
  5         select dummy into x
  6         from   IOT;
  7       end loop;
  8    end;
  9  /

PL/SQL procedure successfully completed.
```

We then take a snapshot of our statistics before we run our tests:

```
SQL> exec RUNSTATS_PKG.rs_start;

PL/SQL procedure successfully completed.
```

Now we run our lookup code for the HEAP table:

```
SQL> declare
  2      x varchar2(1);
  3    begin
  4      for i in 1 .. 10000 loop
  5        select dummy into x
  6        from    HEAP;
  7      end loop;
  8    end;
  9  /

PL/SQL procedure successfully completed.
```

And now another snapshot:

```
SQL> exec RUNSTATS_PKG.rs_middle

PL/SQL procedure successfully completed.
```

And then we run our lookup code for the IOT table:

```
SQL> declare
  2      x varchar2(1);
  3    begin
  4      for i in 1 .. 10000 loop
  5        select dummy into x
  6        from    IOT;
  7      end loop;
  8    end;
  9  /

PL/SQL procedure successfully completed.
```

Then we take our final snapshot and get our comparative statistics:

```
connor@ORATEST> exec RUNSTATS_PKG.rs_stop;
Run1 ran in 130 hsecs
Run2 ran in 74 hsecs
run 1 ran in 175.68% of the time
```

Name	Run1	Run2	Diff
LATCH.checkpoint queue latch	1	2	1
STAT...calls to kcmgas	1	0	-1

```
STAT...cleanouts and rollbacks        1          0        -1
STAT...immediate (CR) block cl        1          0        -1
STAT...parse time cpu                 1          0        -1
      <output cropped>...
LATCH.library cache              20,211     20,089      -122
STAT...redo size                  2,472      1,740      -732
STAT...table scan blocks gotte   10,000          0   -10,000
STAT...table scan rows gotten    10,000          0   -10,000
STAT...table scans (short tabl   10,000          0   -10,000
STAT...no work - consistent re   10,009          2   -10,007
STAT...buffer is not pinned co   10,014          3   -10,011
LATCH.undo global data           40,007          4   -40,003
STAT...calls to get snapshot s   50,011     10,002   -40,009
STAT...consistent gets           50,027     10,012   -40,015
STAT...db block gets            120,014         18  -119,996
STAT...session logical reads    170,041     10,030  -160,011
LATCH.cache buffers chains      340,125     20,113  -320,012

Run1 latches total versus runs -- difference and pct
      Run1      Run2      Diff       Pct
   400,570    40,285  -360,285   994.34%

PL/SQL procedure successfully completed.
```

Not only do we get faster execution times with the IOT, but we also get a massive reduction on the amount of latching performed in the database, suggesting that use of an IOT in this scenario would provide a much more scalable solution. For *small* table scans, IOTs are better because they don't have the overhead of reading the segment header block a number of times.

Note that the preceding test was run on an Oracle 8.1.7 database. If we repeat the test on an Oracle9*i* R2 database, we see the following:

```
Run1 ran in 145 hsecs
Run2 ran in 88 hsecs
run 1 ran in 164.77% of the time

Run1 latches total versus runs -- difference and pct
    Run1       Run2      Diff      Pct
 113,812     73,762   -40,050   154.30%
```

So the latching difference is much less marked, but the IOT is still worth considering for a full scan on small tables.

Primary Key Lookup on Moderate Tables

For this test we drop our existing HEAP and IOT tables and re-create them as follows:

```
create table HEAP ( r primary key, padding)
    as select rownum r, rpad(rownum,40) padding
    from all_objects;

create table IOT ( r primary key, padding)
    organization index
    as select rownum r, rpad(rownum,40)
    from all_objects;
```

The SQL in our lookup code simply changes from

```
select dummy into x
    from    [HEAP | IOT];
```

to

```
select padding into x
    from    [HEAP | IOT]
    where   r = i;
```

With this modification, we perform the tests just as before. The following results were obtained on an 8.1.7 database:

```
Run1 ran in 101 hsecs
Run2 ran in 96 hsecs
run 1 ran in 105.21% of the time

Run1 latches total versus runs -- difference and pct
     Run1       Run2      Diff      Pct
    50,297     40,669    -9,628   123.67%
```

As we expected, the results here are closer, but the IOT still performs less latching and runs slightly faster then the HEAP.

Secondary Lookup on Moderate Tables

For this test we drop our existing HEAP and IOT tables and re-create them as follows:

```
create table HEAP ( r primary key, c , padding)
  as select rownum r, mod(rownum,5000), rpad(rownum,40) padding
 from all_objects;

create table IOT ( r primary key, c , padding)
  organization index
  as select rownum r, mod(rownum,5000), rpad(rownum,40) padding
  from all_objects;

create index HEAP_IX on HEAP ( c);
create index IOT_IX on IOT ( c);
```

The SQL in our lookup code becomes

```
select max(padding) into x
from    [HEAP|IOT]
where   c = i;
```

The following results were obtained on an 8.1.7 database:

```
Run1 ran in 93 hsecs
Run2 ran in 94 hsecs
run 1 ran in 98.94% of the time

Run1 latches total versus runs -- difference and pct
    Run1      Run2      Diff     Pct
   75,554    75,430    -124 1   00.16%
```

Here, the degree of latching is very similar, and the HEAP performs marginally the better of the two. IOTs don't have a ROWID, so to read via a secondary index, Oracle typically must read the secondary index and then read via the primary key.

Overall, we hope that this section has demonstrated how useful RUNSTATS can be in benchmarking a number of different solutions.

CHAPTER 1

Efficient PL/SQL

IN THIS CHAPTER, WE DISCUSS PL/SQL efficiency. We have deliberately avoided the term "performance" because efficiency is more than just performance. We'll define exactly what *we* mean by "efficient PL/SQL" and explain how to ensure that the PL/SQL you build meets that definition.

When used intelligently, PL/SQL can build applications that perform well, are resilient to change over time, and scale to large user populations. We contend that PL/SQL should be your language of choice for database-centric application development. Therefore, when you're deploying Oracle within your organization, you should encourage the use of PL/SQL as an integral component of the applications that you develop.

Why Use PL/SQL?

Before covering the important issues surrounding PL/SQL efficiency, let's address the question that we've often been asked by developers over the years: "Do I need to use PL/SQL at all?"

Ever since organizations began their obsession with getting their applications off the mainframe in the late 1980's—moving first to client-server applications and then to Web-based solutions—the application *data* (stored in an Oracle database) has been getting "further away" from the application code itself.

As a consequence, when stored procedures first appeared in the Oracle server back in version 7, they were generally marketed as a solution for improving client/server applications over slow networks. Rather than making lots of discrete database calls from a client application, we could bundle those calls inside a PL/SQL stored procedure that resided on the server, issue a single call from the client application, and thus reduce our dependency on the speed of the network.

This is a terrible underselling of the value of PL/SQL (and let's face it, underselling a feature is something we generally don't expect from Oracle). Worse, it led to the idea that if you didn't intend to run an application across a wide area network, you didn't need PL/SQL. But as this book will demonstrate time and time again, not using PL/SQL in an Oracle project is equivalent to coding with one hand tied behind your back. Nevertheless, the first battle you're likely to face on a project will not be ensuring that you use PL/SQL efficiently, but convincing management to use it at all!

Often, the arguments against using PL/SQL during application development include:

- It locks you into using Oracle.

- "It doesn't do anything I could not do in *<insert your favorite 3GL here>*."

Launching into a tirade about the foolhardiness of building applications that purport to be truly database independent is outside the scope of the book, but avoiding PL/SQL in an Oracle application could well be a death knell for that project. And although it is true that the functionality of PL/SQL is reproducible in most 3GLs, the second argument demonstrates an ignorance of the two key benefits of using PL/SQL.

PL/SQL is Close to the Data

Very, very close, in fact. PL/SQL is inextricably part of the database. As you will see in Chapter 4, "Effective Data Handling," we can forge strong links between variable and data structures used in PL/SQL programs and the equivalent structures in the database.

Also, as will be demonstrated in Chapter 2, "Package It All Up," PL/SQL is aware of structural changes in the database and can provide insulation from those changes. You can track the dependencies between PL/SQL programs and other database objects but not need to perform any code maintenance when those database objects are changed.

The Simplest Option is Often the Best

If you compare the amount of code required in PL/SQL to process SQL with that required in any other language, PL/SQL usually wins. Any time you can use less code to achieve the same result is a good thing in terms of development time and ongoing maintenance. Consider the following examples, taken from the standard documentation, that show the difference between using PL/SQL and ProC to retrieve a BLOB from one table and insert it into another. First, the PL/SQL version (all eight lines of it!).

```
PROCEDURE insert_blob_proc IS
  Blob_loc  BLOB;
BEGIN
  SELECT ad_photo INTO Blob_loc
  FROM Print_media
  WHERE product_id = 3106 AND ad_id=13001;
```

```
   INSERT INTO Print_media VALUES  (2056, 12001, Blob_loc);
END;
```

And now the ProC version.

```c
#include <oci.h>
#include <stdio.h>
#include <sqlca.h>

void Sample_Error()
{
   EXEC SQL WHENEVER SQLERROR CONTINUE;
   printf("%.*s\n", sqlca.sqlerrm.sqlerrml, sqlca.sqlerrm.sqlerrmc);
   EXEC SQL ROLLBACK WORK RELEASE;
   exit(1);
}

void insertBLOB_proc()
{
   OCIBlobLocator *Lob_loc;

   EXEC SQL WHENEVER SQLERROR DO Sample_Error();
   /* Initialize the BLOB Locator: */
   EXEC SQL ALLOCATE :Lob_loc;

   EXEC SQL SELECT ad_photo INTO :Lob_loc
      FROM Print_media WHERE product_id = 2268 AND ad_id = 21001;

   /* Insert into the row where product_id = 3106 and ad_id = 13001: */
   EXEC SQL INSERT INTO Print_media
      VALUES (3106, 13001, :Lob_loc);

   /* Release resources held by the locator: */
  EXEC SQL FREE :Lob_loc;
}

void main()
{
   char *samp = "pm/pm";
   EXEC SQL CONNECT :pm;
   insertBLOB_proc();
   EXEC SQL ROLLBACK WORK RELEASE;
}
```

The lower level OCI version of the code is even lengthier than the ProC one. Similarly, with many languages that can access a database, there are several mechanisms available on which SQL can be run and the results retrieved. More often than not, the mechanism that provides the quickest or simplest coding path is not the one that provides optimal efficiency. For example, in Java, the `Statement` and `PreparedStatement` classes are readily available for processing SQL statements. For the majority of applications, the most efficient way to write JDBC applications that access Oracle is to use the `PreparedStatement`. (You'll see the reason for this in the "Achieving Efficiency" section, later in this chapter.) However, this requires more code from the developer, and not surprisingly, developers often take the shortest distance between two points and code with the `Statement` method.

With PL/SQL, the quick and simple coding solution for the processing of SQL also turns out to be the optimal way. You have to go out of your way to force PL/SQL to process SQL in a way that is not optimal. We'll be exploring this point later in this chapter. But first, we need to define what we mean by efficiency.

What is Efficient PL/SQL?

If (or hopefully, after you have read this book, *when*) you are convinced of the benefits of PL/SQL, the next logical task is to ensure that any PL/SQL code you develop runs efficiently.

There are a myriad of books on the market that espouse best practices for efficient PL/SQL. However, many of these texts propose that efficiency comes from good standards and consistent coding styles, for example, a set of naming standards for such constructs as variables, cursor definitions, and so on. It certainly is true that adhering to such standards will improve the consistency and readability and thus reduce the maintenance effort required during the coding life-cycle. However, it takes a leap of faith to assume that this will magically result in PL/SQL code that is efficient. Having well-structured methodologies and standards gives you an efficient *environment* for coding PL/SQL, but this by no means guarantees that you will create efficient *code*. So let's state in advance that this chapter (indeed, this book) is not about having good naming standards or consistent coding practices within your development team. These are important components of a successful development project (for any language, not just PL/SQL), but building efficient PL/SQL is a related but different topic.

What do we mean by efficiency? Assuming that your code meets it functional requirement, our general philosophy is that PL/SQL code can be considered *efficient* if it satisfies three general conditions.

- **Performance**: It runs within an acceptable elapsed time.

- **Impact**: It does not break (or degrade in an unacceptable fashion) any other components in your system.

- **Demonstrability**: You can prove (or demonstrate) that under all reasonable conditions, the code will not violate the Performance or Impact conditions. Put simply, you tried to break it and you couldn't.

The order here is important. You must prove that your code can meet the elapsed time requirement before you move on to the impact analysis. Let's take a look at these broad guidelines in a bit more detail.

Performance

Ask a PL/SQL developer what efficient code is, and the standard response will be "it runs fast." After all, this seems like common sense—if your code runs as fast as possible, what more could be asked of you? But how fast is fast enough?

The problem with this philosophy is that it is impossible to define an end goal. How do you know that the program can't run just a little bit faster? Given the vast number of features that appear in each new release of Oracle, for any given PL/SQL program, there is probably always some adjustment you could make to squeeze a little more performance out of it. A perfect example of this is the native compilation features in 9*i*. It is probably true that any PL/SQL program that contains some procedural logic (as opposed to being just a wrapper around some simple SQL) would run faster if it were natively compiled as opposed to the interpreted nature of PL/SQL (which is the default). But is it worth it? Natively compiled PL/SQL means that you have an external file system directory that needs to be backed up as part of your standard backup procedures. Also, there are overheads when mixing interpreted and natively compiled PL/SQL units, so you may need to look at natively compiling *every* PL/SQL unit in the database including those delivered in the standard database installation scripts (`catproc.sql` and so on). And after the effort of converting to a natively compiled database, did the gains justify the additional license costs of that C compiler you had to install? Can you quantify the gains you achieved anyway?

Trying to get PL/SQL to run as fast as it can is a waste of resources, namely your own! The question you have to ask yourself is not "Is it running as fast as possible?" but "Does it run within an acceptable elapsed time?" There is a subtle difference between the two. You will notice that we have not quantified what "acceptable" is because only you or your users can define the appropriate limits for each PL/SQL unit. If the code is designed for processing the nightly set of batch interfaces, it may not need to run sub-second; it simply needs to finish within the boundaries defined by the nightly batch window. However, if the code needs to (for example) return a description for a product item to a field on the user's data entry screen, a quick turnaround time is vital. Even more vital is that these limits are defined *before* the code is written.

Once the elapsed time criteria have been defined and accepted, *you cannot consider your code to be performance efficient until that target has been reached.*

This is true even if the reason the target wasn't reached is not "your fault." Oracle professionals (both DBAs and developers) sometimes have a tendency to "pass the performance buck." For example, consider a PL/SQL program that has to complete in three minutes but part of its function is to query data from a remote Oracle database, which can only be accessed via very slow network. As a result, the PL/SQL program takes seven minutes to run. The typical response to this sort of performance problem is "The program is fine, it's a network issue." We argue that because this program fails the elapsed time requirement, it is therefore *inefficient*. It's unfortunate for the developer that there is a network problem, but that's just plain tough luck! Maybe the importance of the functionality of the program will yield a network upgrade, or alternatively, it might take a whole suite of other mechanisms (snapshots, queuing, materialized views, and so on) to yield a solution in which the program can run in its required three minutes. The fact remains that until it can be demonstrated that the proposed solution runs in three minutes, the solution is inefficient and *should not be implemented*. The definition of performance is not how much CPU a process uses or how many disk operations are required—it is a measure of acceptable response-time.

Impact

Here is where factors such as CPU, memory, and concurrency become a consideration. A PL/SQL program that runs at breakneck speed (or simply just satisfies the performance requirement) is not of much use if it disrupts another required system function in some way. A PL/SQL program could violate this requirement in a number of ways. For example:

- It could lock all the rows in a table while it runs, thus halting end-users from doing their day-to-day tasks.

- It could consume too many system resources (CPU, memory, and so on), thus causing response time problems in unrelated parts of the system, or crashing the system entirely.

- It might fail to meet its concurrency requirements. If 100 users are expected to use this PL/SQL module concurrently, but it dies a slow death as soon as 10 users try to execute it at once, then as fast as it is, it is useless.

Demonstrability

To use an Australian colloquialism, I am a bit of a "rev head." In a nutshell, this means I like driving my car fast, although four years of living in central London nearly broke me of the habit. The optimal time for driving fast tends to be about four o'clock in the morning, when there is no one else on the road. All I need is one long empty lane on the local freeway and I'm in heaven. Of course, does this mean that having a one-lane freeway is a guarantee of being able to drive fast? Definitely not. In fact, if I drive on the same freeway between 7am and 9am during the working week, it would be quicker if I got out of the car and walked!

It is common sense that what you can do when you are the only car on the road is a far cry from what you can do when there are a lot of cars on the road. But amazingly, we tend to put that same common sense on the shelf when it comes to developing (and more importantly, testing) applications. Many systems have failed under the assumption that if a program runs fine in isolation, it will run fine on a live system.

This is the key aspect of demonstrability. It is easy to wave off discussions about efficiency as just plain common sense: ("Of course I know that you want my code to run fast and not cause problems. I'm not stupid."). But there is more to efficiency than that. Developer testing strategies tend to fall into one of three categories.

- You *hope* the program will satisfy its performance and impact requirements.

- You *know* the program satisfies its performance and impact requirements but only under the conditions you've tested. (This is the most common testing strategy used by most developers.)

- You have busted your gut trying to come up with ways to break the thing and you can't!

The last of these is a coarse way of describing the true concept of demonstrability—having a definitive set of tests that prove both the functionality and efficiency of the program under *all reasonable conditions*. Tests that *prove* that the code will scale to the required number of users, tests that *prove* that performance goals are met under all conditions (during the rush hour, not just at 4AM on the open highway).

Consider the following (true) example taken from a site that was experiencing problems with one of its online systems. We will see shortly that the efficiency problems were actually caused by a design flaw, but this was only revealed once we attempted to demonstrate that the code met all its efficiency requirements.

One of the requirements for the online system was that all new customers needed to be able to track their own personal details once they had registered over the Internet. The initial specification was that customers were given a unique numeric ID and a pin number (effectively a numeric password) that would allow them to authenticate with the system. However, the requirement changed on the premise that two numeric IDs would be too much to remember for any customer, so the customer pin number would actually *be* the unique ID for that customer. Therefore, we wanted a table that would uniquely record customers by using a random numeric number as the primary key.

The resulting solution was that a random number generator would produce a random ID, and then the customers table would be probed to see if that ID already existed. If the customer did exist, another random number would be generated until a unique customer record was inserted. Let's look at a possible solution for the stated requirements. First we have the table that stores the unique ID for each customer.

```
SQL> create table customers (
  2    pin_number number(6) )

Table created.
SQL> alter table customers
  2    add constraint customers_pk
  3    primary key (pin_number);

Table altered.
```

The customers table contains a primary key, pin_number, that will hold the unique customer identifier. Next, we create a procedure that obtains a random number, generated by the built-in dbms_random package, and inserts it into the customers table.

```
SQL> create or replace
  2    procedure gen_customer is
  3      v_new_cid customers.pin_number%type;
  4    begin
  5      loop
  6        begin
  7          v_new_cid := round(dbms_random.value(1000000,9999999));
```

The variable, v_new_cid, contains the random number to be assigned for this new customer record. We then attempt to insert this into the customers table.

```
  8          insert into customers
  9          values (v_new_cid);
 10          exit;
```

Of course, if that random number is already in use, a constraint violation will occur and the dup_val_on_index exception will be raised. We simply catch this and loop around to try another random number.

```
11      exception when dup_val_on_index then
12         null;
13      end;
14   end loop;
15 end;
16 /
```

Procedure created.

This solution looks fairly simple. Let's put it through its paces and add a customer. We'll use the standard set timing on facility in SQL*Plus to record some executions times.

```
SQL> set timing on
SQL> begin
  2     gen_customer;
  3     commit;
  4  end;
  5  /
```

PL/SQL procedure successfully completed.

Elapsed: 00:00:00.02

No problems there; a customer record added in virtually no time at all. Let's scale up the test and simulate the creation of 100,000 customers.

```
SQL> set timing on
SQL> begin
  2     for i in 1 .. 100000 loop
  3        gen_customer;
  4     end loop;
  5     commit;
  6  end;
  7  /
```

PL/SQL procedure successfully completed.

Elapsed: 00:00:34.08

Voila! We can insert 100,000 customers in 30 seconds, and because it's unlikely that this many people are all going to try to register at once, we can be pretty confident that the program is fine from a performance perspective. However, the linchpin of demonstrability is not trying to get code to work, but trying to break it.

Of course, in this example, it doesn't take a rocket scientist to see where the problems are. Assuming that pin numbers are always positive, the column definition of pin_number tells us a maximum of 999,999 customers is expected. Table 1-1 shows what happens when we reach our maximum customer mark.

Table 1-1. Benchmark for Customer Registration

ROW INSERTION TEST	TIME TAKEN TO GENERATE
Rows 100,000 to 200,000	38 seconds
Rows 300,000 to 400,000	53 seconds
Rows 600,000 to 700,000	123 seconds

This makes sense—as more and more customer rows are created, the likelihood of a randomly generated pin number already being in use becomes higher, so we need to iterate more and more times through our random number generator before finding a unique pin number. With each additional customer, the process will continue to consume more and more CPU per customer and get slower and slower. Consider the poor customer who happens to be the one-millionth person to register (or at least attempt to). They will wait forever trying to obtain a pin number. Randomness and uniqueness are mutually exclusive—if the occurrence of something (in this case a pin number) is genuinely random, we can never be sure of uniqueness. We did not even have to extend the test to ensure lots of *concurrent* customers can register—we demonstrated that the system starts to exhibit performance issues with just one customer trying to register (presuming many others have already done so).

This is what I like to call the "Let's hope it's not a success" approach to coding. That is, it's quite possible that the solution just implemented will work well as long as you don't attract too many customers. But of course, we implemented this system in the hope of doing precisely the opposite. It's a no-win situation. The more customers you get, the worse the system will treat them.

The solution was to compose a longer customer ID, the first six digits generated by a sequence (an object that is inherently designed to be associated with uniqueness), and the second six digits generated randomly.

First we need a sequence that contains six digits, so we will make it start from 100,000. Our table will also need to be able to house a larger pin number.

```
SQL> alter table CUSTOMERS modify PIN_NUMBER number(12);

Table altered.

SQL> create sequence cust_seq cache 1000
  2   start with 100000;

Sequence created.
```

Then we amend our procedure to insert a pin number that is comprised of the next value from our sequence, appended to a random six-digit number. The code is smaller as well because by using a sequence, uniqueness is guaranteed, thus obviating the need for the dup_val_on_index checking.

```
SQL> create or replace
  2   procedure gen_customer is
  3     v_new_cid customers.pin_number%type;
  4   begin
  5       insert into customers
  6       values (cust_seq.nextval*100000+
  7               round(dbms_random.value(100000,999999)));
  8   end;
  9   /

Procedure created.
```

Repeating our tests show that we sacrificed a little of the initial performance (due to the larger amount of data being inserted) for the sake of consistent and predictable results right up to the maximum number of expected customers, as shown in Table 1-2.

Table 1-2. Repeated Benchmark for Customer Registration

ROW INSERTION TEST	TIME TAKEN TO GENERATE
Rows 0 to 100,000	55 seconds
Rows 100,000 to 200,000	55 seconds
Rows 300,000 to 400,000	59 seconds
Rows 600,000 to 700,000	59 seconds
Rows 900,000 to 999,999	61 seconds

With this simple change, we have definitively proved that one million customers can be handled, and that the millionth customer will be able to register just as efficiently as any other. We have thus demonstrated that the program works under the expected customer volume conditions. The next test ensures that if we have many customers *concurrently* trying to register, performance does not suffer. We can simulate concurrent users with the dbms_job scheduling facility. For example, consider the following anonymous PL/SQL block (which creates 10,000 customers):

```
begin
   for i in 1 .. 10000 loop
     gen_customer;
   end loop;
```

```
    commit;
end;
```

If we want to execute this simultaneously across 20 concurrent sessions, we simply submit it 20 times using dbms_job. First, we ensure that at least 20 concurrent job processes are allowed.

```
SQL> alter system set job_queue_processes = 20;

System altered.
```

Because we cannot directly view the output from database jobs using dbms_output, we will create a custlog table to hold the elapsed time for each of the job executions.

```
SQL> create table CUSTLOG ( elapsed_centiseconds number);

Table created.
```

We then submit our PL/SQL job within the dbms_job framework. We have altered the anonymous block that is submitted to capture the elapsed time into the custlog table.

```
SQL> declare
  2      j number;
  3      job_string varchar2(1000) :=
  4          'declare
  5              s number := dbms_utility.get_time;
  6          begin
  7            for i in 1 .. 10000 loop
  8              gen_customer;
  9            end loop;
 10            insert into custlog values (dbms_utility.get_time-s);
 11            commit;
 12          end;';
 13  begin
 14  for i in 1 .. 20 loop
 15    dbms_job.submit(j,job_string);
 16  end loop;
 17  end;
 18  /

PL/SQL procedure successfully completed.
```

The jobs will not commence until a `commit` is issued. Once the jobs have completed, we can view the `custlog` table to check the elapsed time of each submitted job.

```
SQL> select * from custlog;

ELAPSED_CENTISECONDS
--------------------
               10785
               10878
               11172
               11116
               11184
               11450
               11347
               11701
               11655
               11897
               11726
               12055
               11962
               12028
               12373
               11859
               11995
               11905
               12547
               11977

20 rows selected.
```

We averaged approximately 115 seconds for each of the jobs and the number of rows created in the `customers` table is 200,000. Given that these tests were performed on a single CPU laptop, these results are comparable with the 55-60 seconds per 100,000 rows results we obtained earlier.

Achieving Efficiency

For our programs to be efficient, they must fall within our elapsed time requirements and not cause critical damage to any other part of the system or its resources. We also must be able to demonstrate that this efficiency can be maintained under most or all anticipated conditions.

For the remainder of this chapter, we present some basic guidelines to achieving efficient PL/SQL along with code to demonstrate how this efficiency is achieved. We're not even going to try to cover everything here. After all, this whole book is basically about writing and using PL/SQL in an efficient manner. At this point, we're going to focus on three simple, high-level guidelines for achieving efficiency.

- Minimize the amount of work the database has to do when parsing the SQL you want to execute. In a sense, this is not a PL/SQL issue because it is by no means limited to executing SQL from PL/SQL. It applies to execution of SQL from any language (Java, Visual Basic, and so on). However, it is possibly the number one cause of nonscalability in Oracle applications, so it must be discussed.

- Understand PL/SQL's features and functionality and know how to correctly exploit them so you never have to reinvent the wheel.

- Never use PL/SQL to do the job of SQL.

Bind Variables and the Cost of Parsing

One of the reasons I am so passionate about PL/SQL is that it is naturally scalable to high degrees of concurrency and hence, large user populations. But as with any tool, if you abuse it, it will bite back!

Scalability is of course an integral part of PL/SQL efficiency, namely satisfying our second condition for efficiency—ensuring that a program does not impact other parts of the system. One of the single biggest scalability inhibitors when building Oracle-based applications is ignorance of the steps Oracle must take to execute a SQL statement. Many developers are familiar with tools such as EXPLAIN PLAN to ensure that the execution time of an SQL is optimal, but unbeknown to most developers, there is an additional cost that must be taken into consideration; you must check that a SQL statement is valid *before* it is executed. Notice that I used the general term "Oracle-based applications" here. This is not just an issue that applies to writing efficient PL/SQL. Any application that is built on Oracle (and intended to scale to large user populations)—be it a Java/JDBC application or a Visual Basic/ODBC application—that does not take into account the costs of processing a SQL statement before it is executed, *will not scale*.

To understand why parsing is so important (or more accurately, so expensive), imagine the following scenario. Your boss walks into your office and asks you to write a program that will be used by many other programs in the department. She tells you it's a simple little program—all it has to do is to decide if a given character string is valid SQL for an Oracle database. That basic task will take an enormous amount of complexity; you will need to know every possible allowable SQL keyword, the sequences and combinations in which they make sense, where the whitespace is allowed, what impact any comments may have, and you haven't even started checking the objects referenced in the query yet. That is a lot of work to do for every single SQL statement that gets passed to your program for checking. However, one simple enhancement could be to keep a log of SQL statements that have been processed at some stage in the past. If a SQL statement is presented for checking more than once, you need merely consult the log to see if it is valid.

Of course, if every SQL statement from each application program were different, this log would be of little benefit. In fact, over time, your centralized log of SQL statements is probably going to get quite large—searching through it to see if an SQL statement is already present could in itself take a reasonable amount of CPU. You would probably optimize this process even further by asking the other application developers in the department to code a similar logging facility within their own application code so that they only need to call your syntax-checking program once for each unique SQL their program needs.

Oracle works in the same way: the centralized log from the example is the shared pool. This process of checking all aspects of an SQL statement prior to its execution is known as *parsing* and it consumes a large amount of CPU. Every new SQL presented to the database must be parsed to ensure that it is valid before it can be executed. Hence, the fewer *new* SQL statements that are presented to the system, the better your systems will scale and perform. The impact of parsing can be especially severe when high levels of concurrency are required.

If we present a brand new SQL statement to Oracle, a "hard parse" will be performed, that is, the entire set of syntax and validity checks for the SQL is undertaken. If we present an SQL statement to Oracle and ask for it to be parsed, but it has already been hard parsed, a "soft parse" will be performed. But the ideal situation would be for applications to parse their own SQL statements only once, and remember that they do not need to be parsed again.

To minimize the number of different SQL statements that are parsed by the database, make intelligent use of bind variables. A bind variable is simply a mechanism through which you can create a placeholder for a literal value within an SQL statement. Obviously at the moment of execution, an appropriate value must be supplied for that placeholder (otherwise the SQL statement would not make sense), but a lot of work takes place before a SQL statement can be executed.

Where do the bind variables fit into the parsing picture? As we mentioned previously, an appropriate value for any placeholder must be present before a statement is executed, but Oracle can perform the parsing work on a SQL statement *before* those values are substituted. Thus, for any series of SQL statements that differ only by the value of the literal values within them, it should be possible to reduce the parsing overhead by replacing those literal values with bind variables.

Failure to Use Bind Variables

We can easily prove the impact of not using bind variables with the following tests. We'll use the dbms_sql built-in package for our examples because each call to dbms_sql describes each phase of SQL statement processing.[1] We will perform queries to a table, people, in which a single row lookup is done via a primary key.

```
SQL> create table people( pid primary key )
  2    organization index
  3    as select rownum from all_objects
  4    where rownum <= 10000;

Table created.
```

First, to get a measure for the cost of parsing, let's consider the case where a string to get each person is simply built by concatenation. Each query will be along the lines of

```
select pid from people where pid = 123;
select pid from people where pid = 124;
...etc....
```

Every SQL statement will be regarded as brand new by the SQL engine. We will run 10,000 different queries to the person table, each SQL simply getting the details for the particular person row.

```
SQL> create or replace
  2    procedure literals is
  3      c number;
  4      p number;
  5      x number;
  6      x1 number;
  7    begin
  8      for i in 1 .. 10000 loop
```

When using dbms_sql, we must first open a cursor using the OPEN_CURSOR function for the query we are about to execute. We then parse the text of the statement using the parse procedure. We then execute the statement and fetch the row from the cursor. When we are finished with each statement, we close its cursor with the close procedure.

---

1. I would like to acknowledge OakTable member, Jonathan Lewis, for providing the motivation and background for this example.

```
 9       c := dbms_sql.open_cursor;
10       dbms_sql.parse(c,
11         'select pid from people '||
12         'where pid = '||i, dbms_sql.native);
13       x := dbms_sql.execute(c);
14       x1 := dbms_sql.fetch_rows(c);
15       dbms_sql.close_cursor(c);
16    end loop;
17  end;
18  /
```

```
Procedure created.
```

The SQL*Plus timing facility yields the total elapsed time, but we want to distinguish between the time spent executing each of the SQL statements in the procedure and the time spent parsing. For this, we need to use the sql_trace facility.

```
SQL> set timing on

SQL> alter session set sql_trace = true;

Session altered.

SQL> exec literals;

PL/SQL procedure successfully completed.

Elapsed: 00:00:29.68

SQL> alter session set sql_trace = false;

Session altered.
```

Without any further investigation, it's quite possible that a developer would be satisfied with this result. After all, we ran 10,000 queries in 30 seconds. When we run Tkprof[2] on the raw trace data, the summary produces a startling result.

---

2. For details about how to use the tracing facilities and the trace formatter tool Tkprof, consult Chapter 10 of the Performance Tuning Guide and Reference in the standard Oracle documentation set.

OVERALL TOTALS FOR ALL RECURSIVE STATEMENTS

call	count	cpu	elapsed	disk	query	current	rows
Parse	10081	25.72	26.96	0	310	0	0
Execute	10134	1.70	1.63	0	0	0	0
Fetch	10492	0.76	0.86	0	20488	0	10425
total	30707	28.19	29.45	0	20798	0	10425

We chose the total for the *recursive* statements because each of the queries to the people table will be a child of the main procedure, literals.

The 10,000 queries needed only 2.49 seconds (that is, 1.63 + 0.86) to execute and fetch the rows, but before that could be done, we needed 26.96 seconds just to do the preparatory work. Parsing the queries took 10 times the effort of actually running them! This is an extreme (but sadly common in the real-world) example of the cost of running distinct SQL for every statement, and dramatically demonstrates the cost of parsing. Notice also that virtually all this parsing time was heavy-duty CPU work (28.19 out of 29.45 seconds).

Nevertheless, the CPU cost is *not* the main problem here. Let's look at what happens when we run four versions of the literals procedure in four concurrent sessions on a machine with four CPUs. Even though we've seen that the parsing is expensive in terms of CPU, with four CPUs, we should be able to run the four programs in approximately the same elapsed time as the single case on a single CPU.

The literals procedure was slightly altered to include a unique tag for each SQL, so that each procedure in the four concurrent sessions will be executing unique SQL.

```
SQL> create or replace
  2   procedure literals(tag number) is
  3     c number;
  4     p number;
  5     x number;
  6     x1 number;
  7   begin
  8     for i in 1 .. 10000 loop
  9        c := dbms_sql.open_cursor;
 10        dbms_sql.parse(c,
 11          'select pid t'||tag||' from people '||
 12          'where pid = '||i, dbms_sql.native);
 13        x := dbms_sql.execute(c);
 14        x1 := dbms_sql.fetch_rows(c);
 15        dbms_sql.close_cursor(c);
```

```
16      end loop;
17    end;
18    /
```

We then ran "literals(1)" in the first session, "literals(2)" in the second, and so on. The elapsed times were as follows (remember these were run concurrently, not one after the other):

```
SQL> exec literals(1);
Elapsed: 00:00:31.70
SQL> exec literals(2);
Elapsed: 00:00:32.05
SQL> exec literals(3);
Elapsed: 00:00:31.43
SQL> exec literals(4);
Elapsed: 00:00:32.21
```

What happened here? Remember that when we ran just the single literals procedure, it took 29.68 seconds. Because we have 4 CPUs, theoretically, each CPU should have run flat out and returned control to the user after just *under* 30 seconds. Somewhere we lost a second or so. To see where time is lost for a session, we need to consult the V$SESSION_EVENT view to see the wait statistics.

> **NOTE** For a full description of the benefit of wait statistics, refer to the revolutionary *Yet Another Performance Profiling Method* by Anjo Kolk, Shari Yamaguchi, and Jim Viscusi at oraperf.veritas.com.

Whereas we would like either the CPU or disks to be active processing our requests, the wait statistics indicate the time where work could not be done. In each session we ran

```
SQL> select sid, event, time_waited
  2  from v$session_event
  3  where sid = …
  4  and event = 'latch free';
```

Where the SID was the unique session ID for each of the 4 sessions that ran the test. When the results were tabled, the following was observed:

```
SID       EVENT         TIME_WAITED
-------   -----------   -----------
    43  latch free             79
    44  latch free             72
    45  latch free             69
    46  latch free             87
```

Oracle has to protect access to the important memory structures to ensure that while one session is parsing, no other session can modify any of those memory structures on which parsing is dependent. We can see that approximately 0.8 seconds per session (3 percent) got wasted on the "latch free" event; that is, the sessions spent time waiting for their turn to access the common resources required to parse a SQL statement.

> **NOTE** If you are using Oracle 9.2, there is a bug with session-level events—the SID value is incorrect by 1. Thus the wait event statistics for a session with (for example) SID=42 as viewed from V$SESSION will be found as SID=41 in V$SESSION_EVENT. This problem is fixed in version 10 and 9.2.0.4

Parsing doesn't just cost you vital CPU time, it stops other sessions from getting access to resources that they need, namely, the library and dictionary cache. You cannot solve this with more hardware—parsing stops you from getting the return you should be getting on the hardware you already have.

Bind Variables to the Rescue

Let's return to our example scenario from earlier in this section. We want to maximize the chances of an SQL statement being found in our log of previously processed SQL statements. In order to achieve that, we need to use bind variables. With a small change to the literals procedure, we can create a new procedure, binding, which takes advantage of bind variables.

```
SQL> create or replace
  2  procedure binding is
  3    c number;
  4    p number;
  5    x number;
  6    x1 number;
  7  begin
```

```
 8    for i in 1 .. 10000 loop
 9      c := dbms_sql.open_cursor;
10      dbms_sql.parse(c,
11        'select pid from people '||
12        'where pid = :b1', dbms_sql.native);
```

Notice that the SQL statement that we parse never actually changes. It is only *after* we have parsed the statement that we assign a value to the bind variable. This is the key difference here. From the point of view of hard parsing, in this procedure we are running 10,000 identical SQL statements. We'll see shortly how this makes a large difference to how Oracle will process the statement.

```
13        dbms_sql.bind_variable(c,':b1',i);
14        x := dbms_sql.execute(c);
15        x1 := dbms_sql.fetch_rows(c);
16        dbms_sql.close_cursor(c);
17      end loop;
18    end;
19    /
```

```
Procedure created.
```

We then run and trace the execution as per the previous test

```
SQL> alter session set sql_trace = true;

Session altered.

SQL> exec binding

PL/SQL procedure successfully completed.

SQL> alter session set sql_trace = false;

Session altered.
```

A look at the trace file seems to show that we are still parsing (the parse count is still 10,000), but somehow the performance is dramatically improved.

```
select pid
from
 people where pid = :b1
```

call	count	cpu	elapsed	disk	query	current	rows
Parse	10000	0.99	1.02	0	0	0	0
Execute	10000	1.17	1.26	0	0	0	0
Fetch	10000	0.77	0.56	0	20000	0	9999
total	30000	2.93	2.85	0	20000	0	9999

So the routine is still performing lots of parses—after all, we called the dbms_sql.parse routine 10,000 times, so the figures make sense. To explain where the performance benefit was obtained, we need to look at the session-level statistics. To do so, first we create a view that makes it easy to obtain session-level statistics.

```
SQL> create or replace
  2   view V$MYSTATS as
  3   select s.name, m.value
  4   from v$mystat m, v$statname s
  5   where s.statistic# = m.statistic#;

View created.

SQL> grant select on V$MYSTATS to public;

Grant succeeded.

SQL> create or replace public synonym V$MYSTATS for V$MYSTATS;

Synonym created.
```

Now we can look at the statistics that correspond to parsing on the system.

```
SQL> select * from v$mystats
  2   where name like 'parse%';

NAME                               VALUE
---------------------------------- ----------
parse time cpu                       107
parse time elapsed                   137
parse count (total)                10019
parse count (hard)                     2
parse count (failures)                 0
```

The key statistic is "parse count (hard)." Although in our binding procedure we asked Oracle to parse a SQL statement 10,000 times, Oracle performed this very expensive task only twice—once for the execution of the binding procedure, and once for the first SQL statement parsed. The remaining 9,999 calls to parse did not require a full parse because the SQL statement is unchanged between executions. We *reused* the parsing information. This is soft parsing—an explicit parse call was issued but the SQL code found in the shared pool could be reused. That is the beauty of bind variables—the likelihood of an individual SQL statement being reused is far greater. We can do even better than that—as we saw in the binding procedure, the SQL statement we parsed did not change for each iteration of the loop. So if the SQL does not change between executions, we do not need to parse it again at all, and we can take the parse call out of the loop altogether, yielding the following revised solution.

```
SQL> create or replace
  2  procedure binding is
  3    c number;
  4    p number;
  5    x number;
  6    x1 number;
  7  begin
  8    c := dbms_sql.open_cursor;
  9    dbms_sql.parse(c,
 10      'select pid from people '||
 11      'where pid = :b1', dbms_sql.native);
```

Notice the subtle difference here. The parse call is performed only once and is no longer within the loop.

```
 12    for i in 1 .. 10000 loop
 13      dbms_sql.bind_variable(c,':b1',i);
 14      x := dbms_sql.execute(c);
 15      x1 := dbms_sql.fetch_rows(c);
 16    end loop;
 17    dbms_sql.close_cursor(c);
 18  end;
 19  /

Procedure created.
```

When we execute and trace the execution of this new version, the trace file shows even better performance.

```
select pid
from
 people where pid = :b1
```

call	count	cpu	elapsed	disk	query	current	rows
Parse	1	0.00	0.00	0	0	0	0
Execute	10000	0.65	0.39	0	0	0	0
Fetch	10000	0.27	0.26	0	20000	0	9999
total	20001	0.92	0.66	0	20000	0	9999

We only have a single parse call now. By simply reducing the amount of parsing, performance has been improved from an initial 30 seconds to less than 1 second. Many developers simply refuse to believe me when I tell them that Oracle can run 10,000 SQL queries in less than one second.

The examples just shown are carefully crafted to use the dbms_sql package to process SQL. One of the best things about PL/SQL is that it's easy to adopt the best practices of minimal parsing and bind variables. Let's recode the example using conventional static SQL.

```
SQL> create or replace
  2  procedure EASY_AS_THAT is
  3    x1 number;
  4  begin
  5    for i in 1 .. 10000 loop
  6      select pid into x1
  7      from people
  8      where pid = i;
  9    end loop;
 10  end;
 11  /
```

```
Procedure created.
```

When we execute this, the trace file looks identical to the (optimal) results of the previous example. PL/SQL automatically uses bind variables for any PL/SQL variables, and minimizes parsing for static SQL. Oracle expects you to program using bind variables, and consequently PL/SQL makes it very easy for us to use them. As we said at the start, this is a strong argument for using PL/SQL in your applications. It naturally lends itself to building high-performance, scalable Oracle applications.

If the only language you use for working with Oracle is PL/SQL, you will probably be unaware that this is not generally the case with other 3GL languages.

You will often have a lot more work to do to ensure appropriate usage of bind variables. Let's pick up again on the point made earlier in the chapter about Java, and the use of the JDBC Statement and PreparedStatement. In JDBC, the easiest way to process a SQL statement is to use a statement object. It is quite common to see code such as the following, which does not use bind variables:

```
Statement stmt = conn.createStatement();
for (int i = 0; i < 10000; i++) {
  ResultSet rs = stmt.executeQuery("select pid from people where pid = " + i );
  stmt.close();
}
```

As we proved, this code will not scale. It is much more effective to put in a little more coding effort and use PreparedStatement and bind variables, as follows:

```
PreparedStatement ps;
for (int i = 0; i < 10000; i++) {
  pstmt = conn.prepareStatement("select pid from people where pid = ?" );
  pstmt.setInt(1, i);
  ResultSet rs = pstmt.executeQuery();
  pstmt.close();
  }
}
```

A few more lines of code are required to avoid the parsing cost. However, even this is not the whole story. The code achieves a result equivalent to the example that performs an unnecessary amount of *soft* parsing. Each and every time, we open pstmt, execute our SQL, and then close it again. To eliminate this, for each new SQL statement, we should parse only once and execute as many times as necessary. In Java, we do this using the singleton pattern, as follows:

```
static PreparedStatement pstmt;
  ...
  if (pstmt == null) {
   pstmt = conn.prepareStatement("select pid from people where pid = ?" );
  }
  for (int i = 0; i < 10000; i++) {
    pstmt.setInt(1, i);
    pstmt.execute();
  }
```

Doing it the right way in JDBC takes quite a bit of thought and significantly more code.

We do not want to drift too far away from PL/SQL here, but it's hard to over-state the importance of this issue. If you were to act on every other tip we provide in this book about creating efficient PL/SQL except building your application to use bind variables, chances are your work will have been in vain and your application will not scale. We'll revisit the costs of parsing when we cover dynamic SQL in Chapter 5, "PL/SQL Optimization Techniques."

Use the PL/SQL Features Available

In this section, we would like to focus in on a particular aspect of the PL/SQL features, which is often expressed by the cliché "Don't reinvent the wheel." We prefer to extend the cliché to be "Don't reinvent a wheel that is typically more compli-cated, slower, and sometimes just plain wrong."

The power of PL/SQL is of course not lost on Oracle, which delivers a lot of powerful functionality using PL/SQL, which you should know about and exploit within your own applications. We'll come back to this again in Chapter 2, "Package It All Up," when we look at some of the Oracle supplied packages, but it is useful to cover a few simple examples here, in order to illustrate the point.

Use the Provided Error Handling Facilities

Consider the following procedure, update_emp. It accepts as parameters an employee number and the factor by which we will be decreasing their salary. A simple SQL statement then effects the change.

```
SQL> create or replace
  2   procedure UPDATE_EMP(p_empno number, p_decrease number) is
  3   begin
  4      update EMP
  5      set SAL = SAL / p_decrease
  6      where   empno = p_empno;
  7   end;
  8   /

Procedure created.
```

To decrease the salary of employee 7379 by a factor of 2, we would simply call the procedure as follows:

```
SQL> exec UPDATE_EMP(7369,2);

PL/SQL procedure successfully completed.
```

It doesn't take a university degree to see where this procedure could encounter some problems—we simply pass a value of 0 for the p_decrease parameter.

```
SQL> exec UPDATE_EMP(7369,0);
BEGIN UPDATE_EMP(7369,0); END;
*
ERROR at line 1:
ORA-01476: divisor is equal to zero
ORA-06512: at "UPDATE_EMP", line 3
ORA-06512: at line 1
```

But it is at this point that many developers take an incorrect approach to enhancing the code to make it more robust. The processing of errors within PL/SQL is based around the exception handler model, namely, capturing errors as they occur and either taking remedial action or propagating the error back to the calling environment. However, developers regularly avoid using the exception-handling facilities by attempting to anticipate every possible error, and thus ensuring that a PL/SQL program always succeeds. For example, we can erroneously extend the update_emp procedure to return a Boolean variable indicating whether the call was successful. To set this variable, we check for the validity of the p_decrease parameter before performing the update.

```
SQL> create or replace
  2    procedure UPDATE_EMP(p_empno number, p_decrease number,
  3    p_success out boolean) is
  4    begin
  5    if p_decrease = 0 then
  6    p_success := false;
  7    else
  8    update EMP
  9    set SAL = SAL / p_decrease
 10    where empno = p_empno;
 11    p_success := true;
 12    end if;
 13    end;
 14    /

Procedure created.
```

It is impossible to anticipate every error that could occur in a PL/SQL program. To attempt to do so merely adds complexity to the code, and may even cause issues with data integrity—something that we will revisit when we cover transaction management within PL/SQL in Chapter 4, "Effective Data Handling."

Binary Operations

To use the available PL/SQL features, first learn which features are available. (If you are thinking this is a polite way of saying: "Go reread those manuals," you're correct.) For example, if we need to perform the logical numeric operations, AND, OR, and XOR, with a little bit of arithmetic, the following PL/SQL function can be built for binary AND. We will not delve too deeply into the specifics of how it works because as we will see imminently, creating such a function is a wasted effort.

```
SQL> create or replace
  2  function binary_and(x number, y number) return number is
  3    max_bin number(22) := power(2,64);
  4    l_x number := x;
  5    l_y number := y;
  6    result number := 0;
  7  begin
  8    for i in reverse 0 .. 64 loop
  9      if l_x >= max_bin and l_y >= max_bin then
 10        result := result + max_bin;
 11      end if;
 12      if l_x >= max_bin then
 13        l_x := l_x - max_bin;
 14      end if;
 15      if l_y >= max_bin then
 16        l_y := l_y - max_bin;
 17      end if;
 18      max_bin := max_bin/2;
 19    end loop;
 20    return result;
 21  end;
 22  /

Function created.
```

This is a wasted effort because such a function *already exists*, namely the BITAND function. This is perhaps a special case, and a developer could possibly be excused for building his own version because although the BITAND function existed as far back as version 7 (and probably before), Oracle didn't document its existence until version 8.1.7. Performance-wise, there is no comparison. Comparing 50,000 executions of the home-grown BITAND PL/SQL function to its native counterpart using the SQL*Plus timing facility shows the dramatic difference.

```
SQL> declare
  2     x number;
  3   begin
  4     for i in 1 .. 50000 loop
  5       x:= binary_and(i,i+1);
  6     end loop;
  7   end;
  8   /
```

PL/SQL procedure successfully completed.

Elapsed: 00:00:07.07

```
SQL> declare
  2     x number;
  3   begin
  4     for i in 1 .. 50000 loop
  5       x:= bitand(i,i+1);
  6     end loop;
  7   end;
  8   /
```

PL/SQL procedure successfully completed.

Elapsed: 00:00:00.01

Filling in the Blanks

It's difficult in SQL to generate result sets of data that don't necessarily exist in the database at all. For example, for the requirement to generate a list of database objects created in the last two weeks by day, every day must be listed even if no objects were created. The conventional workaround to this problem is a "filler" table—an example of which you'll see in the next section of this chapter. We can demonstrate this to produce the required list of recently created objects. First we create a table, src, which contains the digits 1 to 9999 as rows. (The name "src" was chosen because this table will serve as an arbitrary source of rows.)

```
SQL> create table SRC ( x number ) pctfree 0;

Table created.

SQL> insert into SRC
```

```
  2  select rownum
  3  from all_objects
  4  where rownum < 10000;
```

9999 rows created.

Now we'll create a copy of the ALL_OBJECTS view in a table T1 with the created column truncated down to remove the time component from the date.

```
SQL> create table T1 as
  2  select trunc(created) created
  3  from all_objects;
```

Table created.

By joining to the src table, we can report the objects created in the last two weeks, even if no objects were created on a particular day. A simple outer-join serves the purpose.

```
SQL> select trunc(sysdate)-14+x created, count(created) no_of_obj
  2  from t1, src
  3  where trunc(sysdate)-14+x = t1.created(+)
  4  and x <= 14
  5  group by trunc(sysdate)-14+x
  6  /
```

CREATED	NO_OF_OBJ
30/MAY/03	0
31/MAY/03	0
01/JUN/03	0
02/JUN/03	0
03/JUN/03	0
04/JUN/03	0
05/JUN/03	0
06/JUN/03	0
07/JUN/03	0
08/JUN/03	0
09/JUN/03	41
10/JUN/03	4
11/JUN/03	6
12/JUN/03	8

Once again, understanding what facilities are available in PL/SQL could lead to a solution that does not require an additional table, which also resolves the issue of how many rows in src are enough. The pipeline function facility that is new to version 9 can also be used as a mechanism for artificially generating as many rows as we see fit. (See Chapter 5 for a full description of pipelined functions.[3]) First we need to create a nested table collection type (because all pipelined functions must return such a datatype).

```
SQL> create or replace
  2    type date_list is table of date;
  3    /
```

```
Type created.
```

Next we create a pipelined function that pipes back rows ranging from a provided starting date (parameter p_start_date) up to any limit we specify (parameter p_limit).

```
SQL> create or replace
  2    function pipe_date(p_start date, p_limit number)
  3    return date_list pipelined is
  4    begin
  5      for i in 0 .. p_limit-1 loop
  6        pipe row (p_start + i);
  7      end loop;
  8      return;
  9    end;
 10    /
```

```
Function created.
```

Instead of using the src table, we can now call our pipeline function PIPE_DATE to artificially create as many rows as we desire. In this case, we only require 14 rows back from the function. Our query now looks like this.

```
SQL> select column_value, count(created) no_of_obj
  2    from t1, table(pipe_date(trunc(sysdate)-14,14))
  3    where column_value = t1.created(+)
  4    group by column_value
  5    /
```

---

3. We've retained the use of the src table in upcoming sections for those readers using version 8 (who will not be able to take advantage of pipeline functions).

COLUMN_VA	NO_OF_OBJ
29/MAY/03	0
30/MAY/03	0
31/MAY/03	0
01/JUN/03	0
02/JUN/03	0
03/JUN/03	0
04/JUN/03	0
05/JUN/03	0
06/JUN/03	0
07/JUN/03	0
08/JUN/03	0
09/JUN/03	41
10/JUN/03	4
11/JUN/03	6

We can also assist the optimizer by telling it how many rows we will be returning from our pipeline function. We can use the CARDINALITY hint to assist Oracle with its optimization. In the example just shown, we can tell the optimizer that there will be 14 rows returned as follows:

```
SQL> select /*+ CARDINALITY(t 14) */ column_value, count(created) no_of_obj
  2  from t1, table(pipe_date(trunc(sysdate)-14,14)) t
  3  where column_value = t1.created(+)
  4  group by column_value
  5  /
```

Don't Use PL/SQL to Do the Job of SQL

PL/SQL is often used excessively. The very first sentence of the PL/SQL Users Guide and Reference book that comes as part of the Oracle 9.2 documentation is "PL/SQL, Oracle's procedural extension of SQL...." PL/SQL was designed as (and always has been) an *extension* to SQL, that is, a tool that can be used *when SQL cannot do the job requested.*

To demonstrate, let's look at a fictitious example that would appear to be tailor-made for PL/SQL. We will re-create the ubiquitous emp and dept tables for our example so that we can populate them with some larger sample data sizes.

```
SQL> drop table EMP;

Table dropped.
```

```
SQL> drop table DEPT;

Table dropped.

SQL> create table EMP (
  2    EMPNO        NUMBER(8),
  3    ENAME        VARCHAR2(20),
  4    HIREDATE     DATE,
  5    SAL          NUMBER(7,2),
  6    DEPTNO       NUMBER(6) );

Table created.

SQL> create table DEPT (
  2    DEPTNO       NUMBER(6),
  3    DNAME        VARCHAR2(20) );

Table created.
```

We add primary keys to the tables, which will in turn index the empno and deptno columns respectively in these tables.

```
SQL> alter table EMP add constraint EMP_PK
  2    primary key (EMPNO);

Table altered.

SQL> alter table DEPT add constraint DEPT_PK
  2    primary key (DEPTNO);

Table altered.
```

Before proceeding, we will re-create the src table from the previous section to hold 200,000 rows of nonsensical data. We'll use this table as a source of data to populate other tables in this example. We don't care what is in the table rows, just that there are at least 200,000 of them. If your system already has such a table, you can use that one in any of the following examples. Alternatively, if you are using version 9 or above, you can use the pipeline function solution presented in the previous section.

```
SQL> create table SRC ( x varchar2(10));

Table created.
```

```
SQL> begin
  2   for i in 1 .. 200000 loop
  3     insert into SRC values ('x');
  4   end loop;
  5   end;
  6   /

PL/SQL procedure successfully completed.

SQL> commit;

Commit complete.
```

Let's now populate the emp table with 500 employees by using the rownum pseudo-column to generate names and date of hiring, dbms_random to generate some random salaries, and ensure that the department (deptno) ranges between 1 and 10.

```
SQL> insert into EMP
  2   select rownum,
  3          'Name'||rownum,
  4          sysdate+rownum/100,
  5          dbms_random.value(7500,10000),
  6          dbms_random.value(1,10)
  7   from SRC
  8   where rownum <= 500;


500 rows created.
```

We now do a similar exercise with the dept table, simply adding 10 rows with a deptno ranging from 1 to 10.

```
SQL> insert into DEPT
  2   select rownum, 'Dept'||rownum
  3   from SRC
  4   where rownum <= 10;

10 rows created.
```

Now there are 500 employee records, each assigned to one of 10 departments. The reason for creating this example is that the CEO is disgusted at the vast difference between the salaries of the highest income earners in each department versus the pittance that the low incomes earners currently receive. (As we said, it is a fictitious example!)

The CEO wants to balance the distribution of salaries within each department so that there is less of a discrepancy. After a detailed analysis, a module specification has been produced as follows:

Please code a module report_sal_adjustment that runs in less than three seconds and fetches each employee record from the emp tables and performs the following:

1. Determine the average salary for this employees department.

2. If the employee's salary differs by more than 20 percent of the average salary, add a row to the emp_sal_log table with the employee number, name, department name, hiring date, and the amount that the current salary differs from the average salary.

3. If this employee's salary is the lowest in the department, flag this employee by setting the min_sal column in emp_sal_log to "Y," otherwise set this column to "N."

Based on the module specifications you have probably seen over the years, this would rate as a fairly good one, and strangely enough, herein lies the fundamental problem. Procedural specifications yield procedural solutions.

In an attempt to make the module specification easy and straightforward to follow, it has been written in a way that lends itself to a procedural solution. The specification outlines a number of discrete steps to be taken for each employee in the organization. Let's look at a solution that represents a direct mapping of the specification to our database. First we will need a table called emp_sal_log in which to record the results of our report.

```
SQL> create table EMP_SAL_LOG (
  2    ENAME        VARCHAR2(20),
  3    HIREDATE     DATE,
  4    SAL          NUMBER(7,2),
  5    DNAME        VARCHAR2(20),
  6    MIN_SAL      VARCHAR2(1) );

Table created.
```

Now let's look at a PL/SQL program that satisfies the requirements of the specification. We'll break it into sections that align with the module specification that was used to build the program.

```
SQL> create or replace
  2  procedure report_sal_adjustment is
```

We will need some variables to store the average and minimum salaries for each department, as well as the department name for an employee.

```
  3      v_avg_dept_sal emp.sal%type;
  4      v_min_dept_sal emp.sal%type;
  5      v_dname        dept.dname%type;
```

We will have a cursor to allow us to loop through each employee in the EMP table.

```
  6      cursor c_emp_list is
  7          select empno, ename, deptno, sal, hiredate
  8          from emp;
  9  begin
```

Here is where the real work begins. We start fetching through our cursor, picking up each employee row in turn. Using this employee's department number, we can determine the average salary for this department (module specification component #1)

```
 10      for each_emp in c_emp_list loop
 11          select avg(sal)
 12          into   v_avg_dept_sal
 13          from   emp
 14          where  deptno = each_emp.deptno;
```

Now we compare the employee's salary with the average salary for his or her department. If it's more than 20 percent away from the average, we want to log a row in the emp_sal_log table (module specification component #2). Before we can do that, however, we need to look up the name of the employee's department, at which point we may as well pick up the lowest salary for the department as well because we will need that shortly to satisfy module specification component #3.

```
 15      if abs(each_emp.sal - v_avg_dept_sal ) / v_avg_dept_sal > 0.20 then
 16          select dept.dname, min(emp.sal)
 17          into   v_dname, v_min_dept_sal
 18          from   dept, emp
```

```
19          where   dept.deptno = each_emp.deptno
20          and     emp.deptno = dept.deptno
21          group by dname;
```

Before we insert a record into the emp_sal_log table, we need to know if this employee has the lowest salary for this department. Comparing the minimum department salary we just picked up with the employee's salary allows us to set the min_sal flag in emp_sal_log.

```
22          if v_min_dept_sal = each_emp.sal then
23            insert into emp_sal_log
24            values ( each_emp.ename, each_emp.hiredate,
25                        each_emp.sal, v_dname, 'Y');
26          else
27            insert into emp_sal_log
28            values ( each_emp.ename, each_emp.hiredate,
29                        each_emp.sal, v_dname, 'Y');
30          end if;
31        end if;
32      end loop;
33    end;
34    /
```

```
Procedure created.
```

A couple of executions (not shown) confirm that the procedure satisfies the functional requirements, so let's look at how efficient it is. When run against the sample data that was generated earlier (that is, 500 employees and 10 departments), all appears well.

```
SQL> exec report_sal_adjustment

PL/SQL procedure successfully completed.

Elapsed: 00:00:00.03
```

Magic! It ran in less then three seconds (one of the requirements of our module specification) so our code is ready for deployment into production! And depending on the size of the company, this might be a perfectly adequate solution. But what happens when we scale this up to a larger number of employees. This company (or a company that we might be hoping to sell this solution to) might have thousands of employees. To test the efficiency of the solution under various scenarios (after all, we want to *demonstrate* that our code is efficient), a simple SQL*Plus script can be used to test the performance with varying employee and departmental populations. Follow the REM lines in the script to see how it works.

```
rem   REPTEST.SQL
rem   ————
rem   Takes as input two parameters, the first being
rem   the number of employees, the second the number
rem   of departments.  Employees are assigned at random
rem   to departments, and salaries are randomised between
rem   7500 and 10000
rem
set termout off

rem Number of employees will be passed as the first parameter,
rem number of departments as the second.  We want to assign these
rem values to two SQL Plus substitution variables called NUM_EMPS
rem and NUM_DEPTS respectively

col x new_value num_emps
col y new_value num_depts

rem Select the values from DUAL to complete the assigment

select &1 x, &2 y from  dual;

rem Now we erase the contents of the EMP table and DEPT table
rem in preparation for population with sample data

truncate table EMP reuse storage;
truncate table DEPT reuse storage;

rem Now we load up the EMP table just like we did in the
rem previous example, using the SRC table to generate as
rem many rows as we require

insert into EMP
select rownum,
        'Name'||rownum,
        sysdate+rownum/100,
        dbms_random.value(7500,10000),
        dbms_random.value(1,&num_depts)
from SRC
where rownum <= &num_emps;
```

```
rem We do a similar exercise with the DEPT table to load
rem the required number of department rows

insert into DEPT
select rownum, 'Dept'||rownum
from SRC
where rownum <= &num_depts;

rem And for good measure, we will calculate optimizer
rem statistics on the two tables, because no-one should
rem be using the rule based optimizer anymore

analyze table emp compute statistics;
analyze table dept compute statistics;

rem We truncate our results table in preparation for the test
truncate table EMP_SAL_LOG;


rem And now, here is the real testing portion of the script
rem We will run the procedure 3 times, and report an average
rem execution time across the 3 executions.  To do this, we
rem use the DBMS_UTILITY.GET_TIME function to give start and
rem end timings for the test - the delta of these two times
rem is the total time elapsed (in centiseconds).  Dividing
rem by 100 and then by 3, gives us the average execution
rem time in seconds.
set serverout on
set termout on
declare
  x number := dbms_utility.get_time;
begin
  for i in 1 .. 3 loop
    report_sal_adjustment;
  end loop;
  dbms_output.put_line('Average run time: '||
          round((dbms_utility.get_time-x)/3/100,2));
end;
/
```

Now we can simply generate any size employee/department base for our test and get the average run time for the procedure based on three executions. Let's look at the output:

```
SQL> @c:\reptest 500 50
Average run time: .3

PL/SQL procedure successfully completed.

SQL> @c:\reptest 1000 100
Average run time: .93

PL/SQL procedure successfully completed.

SQL> @c:\reptest 1500 150
Average run time: 1.87

PL/SQL procedure successfully completed.

SQL> @c:\reptest 2000 200
Average run time: 3.3

PL/SQL procedure successfully completed.

SQL> @c:\reptest 2500 250
Average run time: 4.96

PL/SQL procedure successfully completed.
```

The developer's apparently fast piece of code scales very poorly. In fact, running a large number of tests shows that the elapsed time increases exponentially with a linear increase in the employee numbers. Given that the program was supposed to run within three seconds, we can see that (on the hardware used for testing) we have a 1900 employee limit on the solution. After this, our solution no longer works because it takes longer than three seconds.

Luckily, we caught this flaw in our testing, so the poor developer is marched into the office and told to improve the performance of his code. Here is where the second fundamental problem occurs.

Improving a Procedural Solution Yields another Procedural Solution

If you want to make things run faster, you need to do less work. Our developer observes that most of the work appears to be queries to the emp table, so if he can avoid that, he can improve performance. As a first cut, he can merge the two queries that look up average and minimum salaries:

```
SQL> create or replace
  2  procedure report_sal_adjustment2 is
  3    v_avg_dept_sal emp.sal%type;
  4    v_min_dept_sal emp.sal%type;
  5    v_dname        dept.dname%type;
  6    cursor c_emp_list is
  7      select empno, ename, deptno, sal, hiredate
  8      from emp;
  9  begin
 10    for each_emp in c_emp_list loop
```

Here we can pick up the department name and minimum salary at the same time we get the average salary.

```
 11        select avg(emp.sal), min(emp.sal), dept.dname
 12        into   v_avg_dept_sal, v_min_dept_sal,v_dname
 13        from   dept, emp
 14        where  dept.deptno = each_emp.deptno
 15        and    emp.deptno = dept.deptno
 16        group by dname;
```

The rest of the code is unchanged.

```
 17        if abs(each_emp.sal - v_avg_dept_sal ) / v_avg_dept_sal > 0.20 then
 18          if v_min_dept_sal = each_emp.sal then
 19            insert into emp_sal_log
 20            values ( each_emp.ename, each_emp.hiredate,
 21                       each_emp.sal, v_dname, 'Y');
 22          else
 23            insert into emp_sal_log
 24            values ( each_emp.ename, each_emp.hiredate,
 25                       each_emp.sal, v_dname, 'Y');
 26          end if;
 27        end if;
 28    end loop;
 29  end;
 30  /
Procedure created.
```

We adjust the REPTEST.SQL script to now call the new report_sal_adjustment2 procedure. Running this through for similar employee and department numbers yields the results shown in Table 1-3.

Table 1-3. Results of Changes to REPORT_SAL_ADJUSTMENT

EMPLOYEES	DEPARTMENTS	ELAPSED TIME
500	50	0.27
1000	100	0.86
1500	150	1.68
2000	200	3.03
2500	250	4.64

We can see that performance has improved by approximately 10 percent, which raises the employee ceiling to around 2000, but that's hardly a massive gain. What if there are 50,000 employees in the organization?

Encouraged by the gains on the first bout of tuning, our developer can explore further alternatives. We have seen that running less SQL against the emp table seems to make things run faster. Perhaps an even more efficient solution will be to pre-fetch all the average department salaries into a memory-based lookup table so no additional SQL will be required. Being a savvy developer who always keeps up with the latest and greatest PL/SQL functionality, he knows that this can be achieved using a collection. With some additional code, we arrive at a new solution.

```
SQL> create or replace
  2   procedure report_sal_adjustment3 is
```

Now we need some type definitions to hold an array (or list) of departmental details, namely the average salary, the minimum salary, and the department name. This is done in two sections—a record to hold each row of details, and an array of those records.

```
  3      type dept_sal_details is record (
  4        avg_dept_sal emp.sal%type,
  5        min_dept_sal emp.sal%type,
  6        dname          dept.dname%type );
  7      type dept_sals is table of dept_sal_details
  8            index by binary_integer;
  9      v_dept_sal dept_sals;
 10      cursor c_emp_list is
 11        select empno, ename, deptno, sal, hiredate
 12        from emp;
```

We have a new cursor to retrieve the department summary details—this will be the source of the entries we will add to our PL/SQL table.

```
13    cursor c_dept_salaries is
14      select avg(sal) asal, min(sal) msal, dname, dept.deptno
15      from dept, emp
16      where emp.deptno = dept.deptno
17      group by dname, dept.deptno;
18  begin
```

As a preliminary step, we collect the departmental summary detail and add it to our PL/SQL table. Because the deptno is numeric, it can also serve as the index for our PL/SQL table.

```
19    for i in c_dept_salaries loop
20      v_dept_sal(i.deptno).avg_dept_sal := i.asal;
21      v_dept_sal(i.deptno).min_dept_sal := i.msal;
22      v_dept_sal(i.deptno).dname        := i.dname;
23    end loop;
24    for each_emp in c_emp_list loop
```

In our main processing loop, we no longer need to do any more lookups to the dept table. We simply reference the appropriate information from the PL/SQL table (v_dept_sal).

```
25      if abs(each_emp.sal - v_dept_sal(each_emp.deptno).avg_dept_sal ) /
26          v_dept_sal(each_emp.deptno).avg_dept_sal > 0.20 then
27        if v_dept_sal(each_emp.deptno).min_dept_sal = each_emp.sal then
28          insert into emp_sal_log
29          values ( each_emp.ename, each_emp.hiredate,
30                      each_emp.sal, v_dept_sal(each_emp.deptno).dname, 'Y');
31        else
32          insert into emp_sal_log
33          values ( each_emp.ename, each_emp.hiredate, each_emp.sal,
34                      v_dept_sal(each_emp.deptno).dname, 'Y');
35        end if;
36      end if;
37    end loop;
38  end;
39  /
```

Procedure created.

At the cost of a little more code complexity, we have managed to reduce our code to a single pass through the dept table and a single pass through the emp table. Look at the impressive results we get through testing through the REPTEST.SQL script (after adjusting it to run report_sal_adjustment3).

Table 1-4. Further Refinements to REPORT_SAL_ADJUSTMENT

EMPLOYEES	DEPARTMENTS	ELAPSED TIME
500	50	0.03
1000	100	0.05
5000	500	0.24
25000	2500	1.24
50000	5000	2.74

We have improved performance significantly. More importantly, the scalability now appears to be linear as opposed to exponential. However, with this solution, a new problem lurks under the covers. Storing the departmental information obviously consumes some memory. To observe just exactly how much memory is being chewed up, we need to look at the session statistics using the V$MYSTATS view we defined earlier. After running the test with 5,000 departments, let's look at how much memory was consumed by this session.

```
SQL> col value format 999,999,999
SQL> select * from v$mystats
  2  where name = 'session pga memory max'
  3  /

NAME                                         VALUE
----------------------------------------    ------------
session pga memory max                       3,669,024
```

Our session used nearly 4 megabytes of memory. But we can now handle more than 50,000 employees within our time constraints. Problem solved…well, not really.

A solution exists that is even more efficient and has none of the associated memory overhead. In adding greater levels of complexity to the procedural solution, our developer has been getting further and further from the optimal result. We did not need all that complexity in our PL/SQL—we didn't need PL/SQL at all! The problem can be resolved with SQL using analytic functions. (Note that you will need to use Oracle 9 for this routine to compile as presented. If you have version 8, the insert statement will need to run as dynamic SQL; that is, wrapped within the EXECUTE IMMEDIATE command.)

```
SQL> create or replace
  2  procedure report_sal_adjustment4 is
  3  begin
  4    insert into emp_sal_log
  5    select e.empno, e.hiredate, e.sal, dept.dname,
  6      case when sal > avg_sal then 'Y'
```

```
 7      else  'N'
 8        end case
 9    from (
10      select empno, hiredate, sal, deptno,
11        avg(sal) over ( partition by deptno ) as avg_sal,
12        min(sal) over ( partition by deptno ) as min_sal
13      from emp ) e, dept
14    where e.deptno = dept.deptno
15    and abs(e.sal - e.avg_sal)/e.avg_sal > 0.20;
16  end;
17  /
```

Procedure created.

And that's it! Our procedure has been reduced to a single SQL statement. No lookup tables, no complicated code, just simple SQL. And when we benchmark it using the REPTEST.SQL script, we get the following astounding scalability results shown in Table 1-5.

Table 1-5. *Optimal* REPORT_SAL_ADJUSTMENT

EMPLOYEES	DEPARTMENTS	ELAPSED TIME
500	50	0.01
5000	500	0.08
50000	5000	0.83
100000	10000	1.71

Analytic Functions

If you are unfamiliar with the syntax shown in the report_sal_adjustment4 procedure, you have been missing out on one of Oracle's greatest database achievements. These analytic functions, which have been available since version 8.1.6, increase in functionality and power with each release. Unfortunately, they are not widely known because they were initially proposed primarily for data warehousing queries for such requirements as moving averages and regression statistics. As such, they are documented in the Data Warehousing guide (one of the standard manuals in the Oracle documentation set). Unfortunately, this manual isn't typically consulted except for those Oracle customers who are implementing warehouses. That is a great pity—analytic functions can achieve many remarkable things on any database.

Every major release of Oracle adds more diversity and more complexity to the SQL command set. As a consequence, there will (or should be) more tasks that can be achieved with standard SQL and not PL/SQL. One classic case of this that is worth a specific mention is the processing of results in a join (or view containing a join). We have lost count of the number of times we have seen a PL/SQL module built because the module specification ran along the lines of:

"A view V is based on tables, X, Y, and Z. Update the rows in table X for rows in the view V where (some criteria)."

A PL/SQL module is built because the general consensus among developers is that "you cannot update a join view." This was true way, way back in version 7.1, but for many years now, there is an entire class of views in Oracle that are allowed to be directly updated as though they were tables. Oracle even provides a data dictionary object (DBA_UPDATEABLE_COLUMS) that tells you exactly whether a view or part thereof is a candidate for DML.

Consider the following example module specification:

Increase the bonus by 10 percent for all employees who appear in the view YEARLY_BONUS.

Where this view is defined as

```
create or replace view YEARLY_BONUS as
select emp.empno, emp.ename, dept.dname, emp.bonus
from EMP, DEPT
where emp.hiredate < sysdate + 1
and emp.deptno = dept.deptno
```

A PL/SQL solution that queries the view and then updates the underlying table is relatively easy to code.

```
create or replace
procedure XXX is
begin
for i in ( select empno from yearly_bonus ) loop
    update emp
  set bonus = bonus * 1.1
  where empno = i.empno;
end;
/
```

But the *best* solution is even more unremarkable:

```
update yearly_bonus set bonus = bonus * 1.1;
```

Which of course you could simply wrap within a PL/SQL procedure if required. *That is all you need!* In fact, even if there is not a view defined at all, you can *still* avoid any complex processing. You could simply code

```
update ( select emp.ename, dept.dname, emp.bonus
         from EMP, DEPT
         where emp.hiredate < sysdate + 1
         and emp.deptno = dept.deptno)
set bonus = bonus * 1.1;
```

As long as you satisfy the requirements for updating a join view (See "Modifying a Join View" in the Application Developer fundamentals guide), you do not need, and you should not use PL/SQL.

Choose SQL Innovation Over PL/SQL

The hardest thing about using SQL instead of PL/SQL is convincing yourself that something *can* be coded in SQL when PL/SQL might seem the natural choice. Here are a few examples where SQL can be used but it does not appear obvious to do so. It is of course by no means the definitive set of ways in which SQL can be used instead of PL/SQL, and you will not find a manual anywhere which tells you when a SQL solution can be used instead of PL/SQL. The key is that you need to think outside the box when confronted with a problem that does not appear to be readily solvable with pure SQL.

Displaying a Calendar

PL/SQL combined with DBMS_OUTPUT.PUT_LINE seems to be the only way to display the calendar for the current month (or any month for that matter) because there isn't any obvious function within SQL to generate it. But with the common technique of using decode to pivot rows into columns, we can in fact generate a calendar purely with SQL. First, we will define a substitution variable mdate that holds the value of the date for which the calendar month will be generated.

```
SQL> col dte new_value mdate
SQL> select '23-JUN-03' dte from dual;

DTE
---------
23-JUN-03
```

And now a little SQL can be used to generate the month. We retrieve n rows from our src table where n is the number of days in the month, and then use a little date arithmetic to align the results into the appropriate day column.

```
SQL> select
  2        max(decode(dow,1,d,null)) Sun,
  3        max(decode(dow,2,d,null)) Mon,
  4        max(decode(dow,3,d,null)) Tue,
  5        max(decode(dow,4,d,null)) Wed,
  6        max(decode(dow,5,d,null)) Thu,
  7        max(decode(dow,6,d,null)) Fri,
  8        max(decode(dow,7,d,null)) Sat
  9   from
 10   ( select rownum d,
 11              rownum-2+to_number(
 12                   to_char(trunc(
 13                      to_date('&mdate'),'MM'),'D')) p,
 14            to_char(trunc(to_date('&mdate'),'MM')
 15              -1+rownum,'D') dow
 16     from SRC
 17     where rownum <= to_number(to_char(
 18           last_day(to_date('&mdate')),'DD')))
 19   group by trunc(p/7)
 20  /

SUN   MON   TUE   WED   THU   FRI   SAT
---   ----  ----  ----  ----  ----  -----
                                      1
  2     3     4     5     6     7     8
  9    10    11    12    13    14    15
 16    17    18    19    20    21    22
 23    24    25    26    27    28    29
 30

6 rows selected.
```

Such SQL could then easily be folded away within a view to provide a calendar for any desired month.

Calculating the Median Value

The median has always been a classical problem to solve within a relational database because historically, although databases are fine at *returning* a rowset in order, they have been poor at *processing* a rowset in order, which is a prerequisite for calculating the median. A typical algorithm for calculating the median might look like:

- Determine the count of the rows in the rowset and call it n.

- If n is odd, fetch rows in ascending order until you get to row [n/2+1], this is the median.

- If n is even, fetch rows in ascending order until you get to row [n/2].

- The mean of this row and the next are the median.

However, a quick scan of the data-warehousing guide reveals a far easier solution, once again using an analytic function (this one being new to version 9).

```
SQL> select percentile_cont(0.5)
  2   within group (order by sal desc ) median_sal
  3   from   emp;


MEDIAN_SAL
----------
      1550
```

More importantly, we still can observe the performance benefits of using SQL instead of PL/SQL when we test against a table larger than the standard emp. We've loaded 1,000,000 rows into the emp table, and then created two PL/SQL procedures—one that implements the median using the conventional algorithm listed earlier in this section, and another with the median calculated using the PERCENTILE_CONT function.

```
SQL> set timing on
SQL> exec median_using_old_method
6044.5

PL/SQL procedure successfully completed.
Elapsed: 00:00:05.05
SQL> exec median_using_percentile
6044.5

PL/SQL procedure successfully completed.
Elapsed: 00:00:01.00
```

On this system, using the percentile function is five times faster when the size of the underlying table is large.

Conditional Table Lookup

A common (but from a design perspective, hideous) occurrence in databases is a single column representing several different attributes, each of which requires lookup to a *different* reference code table. Such systems are often the result of migration of a file-based database to a relational model. For example, a specification to print salary options might read:

List all persons in the staff table plus their salary calculated as follows:

- A part-time worker salary is the FIXED_PRICE from the part_time_package table

- A contractor salary is the HRS * HRLY_RATE from the contract_package table

- A permanent salary is the ANNUAL_SAL + BONUS from the perm_package table

Within the staff table, the class_type column indicates whether a staff member is a part-time, contract, or permanent employee. Let's set up the required tables to investigate the options for a solution. First we will re-create the emp and dept tables with the sample data that comes with the database software distribution.

```
SQL> @$ORACLE_HOME/sqlplus/demo/demobld.sql
Building demonstration tables.  Please wait.
Demonstration table build is complete.
```

Then create some additional tables required for the example.

```
SQL> create table STAFF (
  2     staffno      number,
  3     name         varchar2(30),
  4     class_type   number,
  5     class_id     number);

Table created.

SQL> create table part_time_package (
  2     id number,
  3     fixed_price number );
```

```
Table created.

SQL> create table contract_package (
  2       id number,
  3       hrly_rate number,
  4       hrs number );

Table created.

SQL> create table perm_package (
  2       id number,
  3       annual_sal number,
  4       bonus number );

Table created.
```

We will then seed these tables with sample data, once again using the src table to give us an arbitrary number of rows.

```
SQL> insert into part_time_package
  2   select rownum, rownum*130
  3   from SRC where rownum < 6;

5 rows created.

SQL> insert into contract_package
  2   select rownum, rownum*10, rownum*30
  3   from SRC where rownum < 6;

5 rows created.

SQL> insert into perm_package
  2   select rownum, rownum*10000, rownum*500
  3   from SRC where rownum < 6;

5 rows created.

SQL> insert into staff
  2   select empno, ename, mod(rownum,3)+1, mod(rownum,5)+1 from emp;

14 rows created.
```

At first glance, a PL/SQL solution seems called for because the determination of which table to look up is driven by the *data* in another. A PL/SQL solution is presented as follows, the comments within it describe how we look up various tables dependent on the value of the staff member's CLASS_TYPE.

```
SQL> create or replace
  2  procedure SHOW_SAL is
  3    v_sal number;
  4  begin
  5   for i in ( select * from staff ) loop
  6    --
  7    -- Part time employee so we need to look up
  8    -- the PART_TIME_PACKAGE table
  9    --
 10     if i.class_type = 1 then
 11       select fixed_price
 12       into   v_sal
 13       from   part_time_package
 14       where  id = i.class_id;
 15    --
 16    -- For contractors, we need to look up
 17    -- the CONTRACT_PACKAGE table
 18    --
 19     elsif i.class_type = 2 then
 20       select hrs * hrly_rate
 21       into   v_sal
 22       from   contract_package
 23       where  id = i.class_id;
 24    --
 25    -- For permanent employees, we need to look up
 26    -- the PERM_PACKAGE table
 27    --
 28     elsif i.class_type = 3 then -- permanent
 29       select annual_sal + bonus
 30       into   v_sal
 31       from   perm_package
 32       where  id = i.class_id;
 33     end if;
 34     dbms_output.put_line(rpad(i.name,20)||lpad(v_sal,10));
 35   end loop;
 36  end;
 37  /

Procedure created.
```

Using this procedure, we can now display the salary options for each staff member, as outlined in the module specification.

```
SQL> exec show_sal;
ALLEN                   1200
WARD                   31500
MARTIN                   520
BLAKE                   7500
CLARK                  10500
SCOTT                    260
KING                    2700
TURNER                 42000
ADAMS                    650
JAMES                    300
FORD                   21000
MILLER                   390

PL/SQL procedure successfully completed.
```

A static SQL solution can be built even for this problem—in fact, it quite closely resembles the PL/SQL code and uses the CASE statement and the scalar subquery functionality available in 8*i* onward.

```
SQL> select s.name,
  2     case class_type
  3     when 1 then (
  4        select fixed_price
  5        from   part_time_package
  6        where  id = s.class_id )
  7     when 2 then (
  8        select hrs * hrly_rate
  9        from   contract_package
 10        where  id = s.class_id )
 11     when 3 then (
 12        select annual_sal + bonus
 13        from   perm_package
 14        where  id = s.class_id )
 15     end sal
 16  from staff s;
```

NAME	SAL
ALLEN	1200
WARD	31500
MARTIN	520
BLAKE	7500
CLARK	10500
SCOTT	260
KING	2700
TURNER	42000
ADAMS	650
JAMES	300
FORD	21000
MILLER	390

New Oracle 10g Features

The importance of staying up to date with the features available is no more apparent than in the many extensions to SQL that are available in version 10*g*. This raises the bar even higher for what can be achieved with pure SQL. Note in particular the new MODEL clause functionality that yields a new suite of facilities to probe and manipulate a SQL result set.

As a very basic example of what can be achieved with the new MODEL functionality, first we will create some sample data for a fictitious scenario in which we measure the probability that a lab animal produces a favorable result in a range of different experiments.

```
SQLSQL> create table SAMPLES (
  2    lab_id          varchar2(10),
  3    animal          varchar2(10),
  4    experiment_id   number,
  5    probability     number );
```

Table created.

```
SQLSQL> set feedback off
SQLSQL> insert into SAMPLES values ('OXFORD','RATS',1,0.993);
SQLSQL> insert into SAMPLES values ('OXFORD','RATS',2,0.93);
SQLSQL> insert into SAMPLES values ('OXFORD','RATS',3,0.91);
SQLSQL> insert into SAMPLES values ('OXFORD','MICE',1,0.91);
SQLSQL> insert into SAMPLES values ('OXFORD','MICE',2,0.99);
SQLSQL> insert into SAMPLES values ('OXFORD','MICE',3,0.90);
```

```
SQL> insert into SAMPLES values ('HARVARD','RATS',1,0.993);
SQL> insert into SAMPLES values ('HARVARD','RATS',2,0.93);
SQL> insert into SAMPLES values ('HARVARD','RATS',3,0.91);
SQL> insert into SAMPLES values ('HARVARD','MICE',1,0.91);
SQL> insert into SAMPLES values ('HARVARD','MICE',2,0.99);
SQL> insert into SAMPLES values ('HARVARD','MICE',3,0.90);
SQL> set feedback on
```

What is the probability that a given animal returns a favorable result across all tests? We need the *product* of each probability by lab and animal for experiments 1, 2, and 3. With Oracle 10*g*, this answer can be discovered with the MODEL clause.

```
SQL> SELECT lab_id, animal, experiment_id, s
  2  FROM samples
  3  SPREADSHEET PARTITION BY (lab_id)
  4    DIMENSION BY (animal, experiment_id)
  5    MEASURES (probability s) IGNORE nav
  6  (s['MICE',-1]=s['MICE',1]*s['MICE',2]*s['MICE',3],
  7    s['RATS',-1]=s['RATS',1]*s['RATS',2]*s['RATS',3]);
```

LAB_ID	ANIMAL	EXPERIMENT_ID	S
OXFORD	RATS	1	.993
OXFORD	RATS	2	.93
OXFORD	RATS	3	.91
OXFORD	MICE	1	.91
OXFORD	MICE	2	.99
OXFORD	MICE	3	.9
HARVARD	RATS	1	.993
HARVARD	RATS	2	.93
HARVARD	RATS	3	.91
HARVARD	MICE	1	.91
HARVARD	MICE	2	.99
HARVARD	MICE	3	.9
OXFORD	*RATS*	*-1*	*.8403759*
OXFORD	*MICE*	*-1*	*.81081*
HARVARD	*RATS*	*-1*	*.8403759*
HARVARD	*MICE*	*-1*	*.81081*

16 rows selected.

The rows with an experiment ID of −1 show the result required. Although a full discussion of the MODEL facilities in Oracle 10*g* is outside the scope of this book (and the example demonstrates only a tiny fraction of the flexibility offered by this new functionality), it further reduces the number of areas where PL/SQL is adopted because a SQL solution cannot be found.

Is a PL/SQL Solution Ever Justified?

If a SQL solution exists, is there ever a reason for using a slower PL/SQL equivalent? There is possibly one circumstance when this may be the case. Although processing a large DML operation is going to be more efficient with SQL than its PL/SQL equivalent, it also is an all-or-nothing process. If that SQL operation fails due to an *unforeseeable* error, the time taken to roll back the change may be unacceptable. (The reason for the emphasis on "unforeseeable" will be revealed shortly). If the DML operation is restartable, that is, it can logically be broken into discrete chunks of work, using PL/SQL can provide some insulation by turning an all-or-nothing operation into a smaller set of piecemeal tasks. Even in these cases, more often than not, the underlying SQL can also be broken up into similar small units of work thus obviating the need for PL/SQL. Possibly what is springing to most readers minds at this point is the common practice of using PL/SQL to avoid consuming excessive undo by issuing regular commits within a processing loop, but this is *most definitely not* a justification for using PL/SQL over SQL. Failing due to insufficient undo (or temporary) space is not an unforeseeable error and is catered to by either using the resumable transaction features available in version 9, or even better, configuring the appropriate amount of undo/temporary space for the task.

To summarize, if you are responsible for developing PL/SQL programs, always take the time to check out the latest SQL features in your Oracle version before leaping into PL/SQL code. A SQL solution will typically be faster and simpler to understand and maintain than a PL/SQL alternative. Remember (just like the PL/SQL manual says) it is an *extension* to SQL, not an alternative.

Conclusion

What we've tried to stress throughout this chapter is that building PL/SQL applications that are efficient is not difficult to do. This is indeed one of the great beauties of PL/SQL—the coding actions that are typically simplest are usually also the optimal way to code your applications.

It is only when you try to fight against these native features that PL/SQL goes bad. The number of occasions that you need to take a convoluted or complex approach to delivering functionality within PL/SQL is far lower than you might think, especially if you stay informed and up to date on the PL/SQL features that become available with each new release of the database.

Whichever PL/SQL feature you are taking advantage of, it is vital that you test and re-test the efficiency of anything you build. Being able to *prove* the performance and scalability of a PL/SQL program is just as important as the performance and scalability itself. There are many programming environments around that make it very difficult to track where efficiency problems are, and developers are forced to build their own sophisticated instrumentation facilities. With the simple timing and tracing facilities we have taken advantage of within this chapter, however, and the more advanced debugging APIs that are used by various third party PL/SQL development tools, there is no excuse for not taking to time to ensure that your PL/SQL code is as efficient as possible.

CHAPTER 2

Package It All Up

VIRTUALLY EVERY APPLICATION development language has some concept of subprograms. Typically they are called "procedures," "functions," "routines," or "sections," but they all are indicative of a logical or modular grouping of code segments within a program. Similarly, PL/SQL, which is a derivative of Ada, also has the concept of subprograms, but the package mechanism is a wonderful extension to this model, as we will demonstrate in this chapter.

We'll cover the functionality that packages offer over and above merely grouping program units together, and we'll look at how this functionality makes your code more resilient to the changes that occur over time to the database structure. We will also look at why developers have steered away from packages in the past and consider the circumstances under which you may want to avoid using packages. Finally, we'll look at a few of the packages that Oracle supplies with the database to demonstrate that it is always worthwhile to check out the available functionality before embarking on a custom solution.

Basic Benefits of Packages

The main reason packages are not more widely adopted is that users are unaware of the benefits they offer. Most of the applications that use PL/SQL are a mixture of procedures and functions, with the occasional package thrown in. In fact, many a training manual, book, and even the standard Oracle documentation imply that packages are simply a convenient way of grouping PL/SQL components together. The "typical" package example provided in training documentation is something along the lines of

```
create or replace
package emp_maint is
   procedure hire_emp(p_empno number, p_name varchar2);
   procedure fire_emp(p_empno);
   procedure raise_salary(p_empno number, p_salary number);
end;
/
```

The package body implements the underlying code for each of the modules in the package specification.

```
create or replace
package body emp_maint is
  procedure hire_emp(p_empno number, p_name varchar2) is
  begin
      insert into emp …
  end;

  procedure fire_emp(p_empno) is
  begin
   delete from emp …
  end;

  procedure raise_salary(p_empno number, p_salary number) is
  begin
    update emp …
  end;
end;
/
```

There is nothing explicitly *wrong* with using packages in this way.[1] However, such examples give the impression that use of packages is merely a cataloguing convenience. However, with only a little editing of the example, we can highlight some of the true benefits of using packages.

```
create or replace
package emp_maint is
  cursor annual_review_candidates return emp%rowtype;
  v_last_empno_used number;
  procedure hire_emp(p_empno number, p_name varchar2);
  procedure fire_emp(p_empno number);
  procedure raise_salary(p_empno number, p_salary number);
  procedure hire_emp (p_empno number, p_name varchar2,
            p_hiredate date, p_sal number);
end;
/

create or replace
package body emp_maint is

  cursor annual_review_candidates return emp%rowtype is
    select * from emp where hiredate > trunc(sysdate,'YYYY');
```

---

1. In past versions of Oracle, if the resulting package was extremely large, there could be problems. See the "It's a Package, Not a Library" section later in this chapter for more details.

```
    v_pkg_execution_count number := 0;

  procedure hire_emp(p_empno number, p_name varchar2) is
  begin
     insert into emp …
  end;

  procedure fire_emp(p_empno number) is
  begin
   delete from emp …
  end;

  procedure raise_salary(p_empno number, p_salary number) is
  begin
    update emp …
  end;

  procedure check_sal_limit(p_empno number) is
  begin
     …
  end;

  procedure hire_emp(p_empno number, p_name varchar2,
              p_hiredate date, p_sal number) is
  begin
   check_sal_limit(p_empno);
     insert into emp..
  end;

begin
  select empno into v_last_empno_used
  from EMP
  where hiredate = ( select max(hiredate)
                        from emp )
  and rownum = 1;
end;
/
```

In the following sections, we'll discuss the highlighted code in this amended package and demonstrate the true power of package use.

Package Overloading

You'll notice that within our revised emp_maint package, there are now *two* procedures named hire_emp. The first allows us to enter a new employee based on their employee number and name.

```
procedure hire_emp(p_empno number, p_name varchar2);
```

The second requires that we also supply the employee's date of hiring and initial salary.

```
procedure hire_emp(p_empno number, p_name varchar2,
          p_hiredate date, p_sal number);
```

Packages allow multiple procedures and functions to have the same name, but each instance of the procedure can take a different parameter set. At execution time, the number of parameters passed and their datatypes will determine which version of hire_emp is to be executed.

You may be thinking that a viable alternative would be to create a standalone procedure with the additional parameters coded as optional.

```
procedure hire_emp(p_empno number, p_name varchar2,
          p_hiredate date default null, p_sal number default null);
```

However, you would then need to add code that caters to the case in which the p_hiredate or p_sal parameter value is supplied, but not *both*. Package overloading allows implicit enforcement of the parameters that must be supplied. Overloading also yields an effective mechanism for adding functionality to your applications in a low risk manner. Consider if you had deployed the first hire_emp procedure (the one that takes only employee name and employee number as parameters) throughout hundreds of programs within your enterprise. Say you wanted to build new programs that require new logic (where the additional salary and hire date parameters are allowed). Without overloading, you would need to find every occurrence of the existing hire_emp package to make appropriate code alterations. With overloading, the new four-parameter version can be added without difficulty—the new application programs will pick up the new version while existing programs will still successfully use the original two-parameter version.

Public and Private Package Variables

In our definition of emp_maint, we now have a public variable.

```
v_last_empno_used number;
```

And a private variable.

```
v_pkg_execution_count number := 0;
```

Packages give greater flexibility in defining the scope of the variables contained within them. Any variable declared in the package specification (in other words, in the create package section) is a *public* variable. Once instantiated, public variables maintain their values for the duration of an entire session.

> **NOTE** Recall that a conventional local variable declared within a procedure and any value it may hold is lost as soon as the procedure is completed.

For example, if we called one of the procedures within the emp_maint package, which assigned a value of 1000 to the package variable v_last_empno, this variable and its value would remain accessible to any other procedures and programs within that connected session, even after the execution of the procedure is completed. Even though a session cannot see any other session's package variables, public package variables are often referred to as "global" variables because they exist for the duration of the session connection.

> **TIP** If persistence is not desired, you can override this behavior by using the serially_reusable pragma.

A private package variable is any variable that is declared in the package body. In other words, a variable that is not defined locally to any one of the package body procedures. Private variables are available only to the other procedures within the package. Like public variables, private variables are persistent for the duration of a user session—their values are retained between package calls.

Public and private variables are ideal for implementing any functionality to record session level detail such as cumulative totals, counters, and the like.

Initialization

You may have noticed that the package body itself has its own PL/SQL block. This is the **initialization** section.

```
create or replace
package body emp_maint is
...
...
...
begin
  select empno into v_last_empno_used
  from EMP
  where hiredate = ( select max(hiredate)
                           from emp )
  and rownum = 1;
end;
```

When *any* component of a package is first referenced or executed, the code in the initialization section is processed only once. In our emp_maint example, we determine the employee number for the most recently hired person and store that data in v_last_empno, which is then available for the remainder of the session. This would not be possible with a standalone procedure because there is no persistence of variables once the procedure is completed.

Information Hiding

Details can be hidden within the package body. This is described as **encapsulation**. There are two such examples in the emp_maint package. The first is the check_sal_limit procedure.

```
procedure check_sal_limit(p_empno number) is
begin
  ...
end;
```

We can assume that the check_sal_limit procedure contains sensitive pay scale information so we do not want people to be aware of that source code. Furthermore, even with the source code hidden, it would not be appropriate for this routine to be called except from within the hire_emp procedure, when an initial salary is passed in for scrutiny. If check_sal_limit were a standalone procedure, controlling access to it would be extremely difficult. Having it defined only within the package body guarantees the security level we need—it cannot be run except by other routines within the package.

Similarly, the cursor annual_review_candidates shows that with packages, we can make the *usage* of a cursor available to the calling environment while keeping the *definition* of that cursor private. In the package specification, we simply declare the existence of the cursor.

```
cursor annual_review_candidates return emp%rowtype;
```

We then fully define it within the package body.

```
cursor annual_review_candidates return emp%rowtype is
  select * from emp where hiredate > trunc(sysdate,'YYYY');
```

Anyone with the appropriate privileges (that is, execution rights on the package) can get a list of the employees who are due for their annual review, but the underlying query is kept secure. The cursor can be used as per any normal cursor definition, not just within the emp_maint package. For example, a second procedure, designed for processing the annual review details, might get a list of annual review candidates.

```
procedure process_annual_review is
begin
 for i in emp_maint.annual_review_candidates loop
   ( processing )
   end loop;
 end;
```

Notice that in order to take advantage of this facility, an explicit cursor is required. Believe it or not, this is one of the very few times when you *must* use explicit cursor definitions in PL/SQL. Of course, if there were no use for them at all, Oracle would not have invented them in the first place, but consult Chapter 3 for more information about why explicit cursors are perhaps overused in PL/SQL applications.

Standalone Procedures and the Dependency Crisis

The benefits obtained from information hiding, persistent public and private variables, and the initialization section are all inextricably linked to the separation of packages into public and private components. This separation also gives rise to the most significant advantage of packages over standalone procedures: insulation from what we call the "dependency crisis."

Within Oracle (or any other environment), knowing the interrelationships between objects is vital for assessing the scope of impact when one or more of those objects is to be altered. Oracle exposes these relationships in the USER_DEPENDENCIES view, shown as follows:

```
SQL> desc user_dependencies
 Name
 -----------------------------------------------
 NAME
 TYPE
 REFERENCED_OWNER
 REFERENCED_NAME
 REFERENCED_TYPE
 REFERENCED_LINK_NAME
 SCHEMAID
 DEPENDENCY_TYPE
```

For example, we can view the dependencies for our emp_maint package as follows:

```
SQL> select name, type,
  2   referenced_name, referenced_type
  3   from user_dependencies
  4   where name = 'EMP_MAINT'
  5   /
```

NAME	TYPE	REFERENCED_NAME	REFERENCED_TYPE
EMP_MAINT	PACKAGE	STANDARD	PACKAGE
EMP_MAINT	PACKAGE BODY	STANDARD	PACKAGE
EMP_MAINT	PACKAGE	EMP	TABLE
EMP_MAINT	PACKAGE BODY	EMP	TABLE
EMP_MAINT	PACKAGE BODY	EMP_MAINT	PACKAGE

```
8 rows selected.
```

Looking at each row in turn, we can see the following dependencies:

- The emp_maint *package* depends on the standard package (from which all PL/SQL is based).

- The emp_maint *package body* also depends on the standard package.

- The emp_maint *package* depends on the emp table (because the cursor annual_review_candidates refers to it).

- The emp_maint *package body* depends on emp table (because we insert/delete/update and query it).

- The emp_maint *package body* depends on its own package specification.

Thus the USER_DEPENDENCIES view consists of a hierarchical tree of parent-child pairs that describes the relationship between objects within the database. Hierarchical tables are typically queried using Oracle's CONNECT-BY clause, but check the following information before embarking down that route.

Querying Dependencies Using CONNECT-BY Clause

If you try to query USER_DEPENDENCIES using the CONNECT-BY clause in versions of Oracle prior to 9, you will typically get an SQL error because CONNECT-BY is not supported on joins. Even in version 9, elaborate hierarchical queries to USER_DEPENDENCIES typically run slowly because of the underlying complexity in the view definition. To overcome this, you can take advantage of the delivered script $ORACLE_HOME/rdbms/admin/utldtree.sql to populate a tree-structure of dependencies. For example, to see a tree of dependencies for the table emp in the MCDONAC schema, use the following:

```
SQL> exec deptree_fill('TABLE','MCDONAC','EMP');

PL/SQL procedure successfully completed.

SQL> select * from ideptree;

DEPENDENCIES
-----------------------------------------
TABLE MCDONAC.EMP
    PACKAGE BODY MCDONAC.PKG1
    PROCEDURE MCDONAC.P1
        PROCEDURE MCDONAC.P2
            PROCEDURE MCDONAC.P3
                PROCEDURE MCDONAC.P4
TRIGGER MCDONAC.EMP_DEPT_CNT_TRIGGER
```

To demonstrate the difference between procedures and packages in terms of the dependency tree within the database, we'll create a few standalone procedures that have some fairly basic dependencies. First we'll create procedure, P1, which will count the rows in table emp.

```
SQL> create or replace
  2  procedure P1 is
  3    v_cnt number;
  4  begin
```

```
5    select count(*)
6    into   v_cnt
7    from   emp;
8  end;
9  /
```

Procedure created.

Next, we create three more procedures: P2, P3, and P4. Each one simply calls the previous one.

```
SQL> create or replace
  2  procedure P2 is
  3  begin
  4    P1;
  5  end;
  6  /
```

Procedure created.

```
SQL> create or replace
  2  procedure P3 is
  3  begin
  4    P2;
  5  end;
  6  /
```

Procedure created.

```
SQL> create or replace
  2  procedure P4 is
  3  begin
  4    P3;
  5  end;
  6  /
```

Procedure created.

Now we can look at the dependency information from USER_DEPENDENCIES view.

```
SQL> select name, type,
  2  referenced_name, referenced_type
  3  from user_dependencies
  4  /
```

NAME	TYPE	REFERENCED_NAME	REFERENCED_TYPE
P1	PROCEDURE	STANDARD	PACKAGE
P1	PROCEDURE	EMP	TABLE
P2	PROCEDURE	P1	PROCEDURE
P3	PROCEDURE	P2	PROCEDURE
P4	PROCEDURE	P3	PROCEDURE

This is exactly as we would expect: P1 depends on the emp table and STANDARD database package (which is the core component of PL/SQL itself). Procedure P2 depends on P1, P3 depends on P2, and P4 on P3. The importance of the dependency information is that it controls the scope of recompilation required when a parent object (in other words, an object that another object depends on) is altered. To further explain this, we'll make a simple alteration to P1 and gauge its impact on the other procedures. Initially, all our procedures have a status of VALID, as listed in the USER_OBJECTS dictionary view.

```
SQL> select object_name, status
  2  from user_objects
  3  where object_name in ('P1','P2','P3','P4');
```

OBJECT_NAME	STATUS
P4	VALID
P3	VALID
P2	VALID
P1	VALID

We now implement a simple change to the P1 procedure. Any change will do (that is, any change that involves re-creating P1). In this case, we add a clause to the SQL query so that we count only employees with a positive employee number.

```
SQL> create or replace
  2  procedure P1 is
  3    v_cnt number;
  4  begin
  5    select count(*)
  6    into   v_cnt
  7    from   emp
  8    where  empno > 0;
  9  end;
 10  /
```

```
Procedure created.
```

We then requery the USER_OBJECTS view to assess the impact of this change.

```
SQL> select object_name, status
  2  from user_objects
  3  where object_name in ('P1','P2','P3','P4');


OBJECT_NAME      STATUS
------------      ----------
P4               INVALID
P3               INVALID
P2               INVALID
P1               VALID
```

Procedure P1 is fine (after all, we have just successfully compiled it), but *all* the procedures that are dependent on P1 now require recompilation. Oracle automatically attempts to recompile a procedure if it is called. For example, if we run the (currently invalid) procedure P3, it will work successfully.

```
SQL> exec p3;

PL/SQL procedure successfully completed.
```

Now we look at the status of each of our procedures after P3 was executed.

```
SQL> select object_name, status
  2  from user_objects
  3  where object_name in ('P1','P2','P3','P4');


OBJECT_NAME      STATUS
------------      ----------
P4               INVALID
P3               VALID
P2               VALID
P1               VALID
```

We can see that procedure P2 must be recompiled before P3 can be recompiled and finally executed. P4 remains invalid because it is yet to be called. This sets you up for a maintenance nightmare—it could be days, weeks, or months before P4 is called again, and what if it refuses to compile? Informing the end users that there is a flaw in one of their programs that has been lying around undetected for months and an emergency fix is needed will not be a pleasant task.

One way to avoid this scenario is to write a script that cycles through user_objects repeatedly and manually recompiles all invalid objects. You could also use the utl_recomp package (available in version 10g) for a procedural mechanism.

Similarly, you might think that a little bit of recompilation here and there is not going to cause you any great problems, but consider a project of more realistic size in which you may have hundreds or thousands of interwoven PL/SQL modules. Let's extend the example to model a system that contains several hundred PL/SQL procedures. We'll start with a simple procedure, P0, that does nothing and so will not be dependent on anything except the core standard package.

```
SQL> create or replace
  2  procedure p0 is
  3  begin
  4    null;
  5  end;
  6  /

Procedure created.
```

Rather than write 100 individual procedure modules, we'll use a little bit of PL/SQL to dynamically generate more PL/SQL procedures. The following processing loop creates 50 procedures, named prc_0001 to prc_0050, each of which simply calls P0.

```
SQL> declare
  2      x varchar2(32767);
  3      y varchar2(32767);
  4  begin
  5    for i in 1 .. 50 loop
  6      execute immediate
  7      'create or replace procedure prc_'||to_char(i,'fm0000')||
  8      ' is begin p0; end;';
```

The next processing loop creates 50 more procedures, named prc_0051 to prc_0100. Each of these procedure calls each of the 50 procedures, prc_0001 to prc_0050, which we created in the previous step.

```
  9        x := x || 'prc_'||to_char(i,'fm0000')||'; ';
 10    end loop;
 11    for i in 51 .. 100 loop
 12      execute immediate
 13      'create or replace procedure prc_'||to_char(i,'fm0000')||
 14      ' is begin '||x||' end;';
```

Finally, we create a single procedure, prc_main, which calls each of the 50 procedures prc_0051 to prc_0100.

```
15      y := y || 'prc_'||to_char(i,'fm0000')||'; ';
16    end loop;
17    execute immediate
18      'create or replace procedure prc_main '||
19      ' is begin '||y||' end;';
20  end;
21  /
```

```
PL/SQL procedure successfully completed.
```

We have only 102 procedures, but we have already created a massive dependency chain.

```
SQL> select name, type,
  2  referenced_name, referenced_type
  3  from user_Dependencies
  4  where name like 'PRC_____'
```

NAME	TYPE	REFERENCED_NAME	REFERENCED_TYPE
PRC_0066	PROCEDURE	PRC_0023	PROCEDURE
PRC_0067	PROCEDURE	PRC_0023	PROCEDURE
...			
...			

2600 rows selected.

All it takes is a small change to a highly nested standalone procedure to create a massive recompilation overhead. Let's change the P0 procedure.

```
SQL> create or replace
  2  procedure P0 is
  3    x number;
  4  begin
  5    x := 1;
  6  end;
  7  /
```

```
Procedure created.
```

Because all other procedures rely on P0 either directly or indirectly, every procedure has become invalid.

```
SQL> select object_name, status
  2  from user_Objects
  3  where object_name like 'PRC%'
  4  /

OBJECT_NAME               STATUS
-------------             -------
PRC0001                   INVALID
PRC0002                   INVALID
PRC0003                   INVALID
...

PRC_MAIN                  INVALID

101 rows selected.
```

In this extreme case, your entire PL/SQL project must be recompiled either manually or by letting Oracle do the work on an as used basis, as described earlier.

The Cost of Recompilation

Keep in mind that recompilation is resource intensive. We can monitor some session-level statistics that will compare the difference between running prc_main under normal conditions versus when the massive recompilation is required. To record the resource costs, we will take a before and after snapshot of the V$MYSTATS[2] view. The deltas between these two snapshots will show the various components of resource usage. We store our first snapshot in table x1.

```
SQL> create table x1 as select * from v$mystats;

Table created.
```

Now we run prc_main. Due to the change we just made to P0, all the prc_xxxx procedures will be recompiled on the fly.

```
SQL> exec prc_main;

PL/SQL procedure successfully completed.
```

Now we take a second snapshot of session-level statistics and store these in table x2.

---

2. See chapter 1 for instructions on how to create the V$MYSTATS view.

```
SQL> create table x2 as select * from v$mystats;

Table created.
```

Next, we re-run prc_main. All the dependent procedures (as well as prc_main) have now been recompiled, so this will be a normal execution.

```
SQL> exec prc_main;

PL/SQL procedure successfully completed.
```

We take a final snapshot of statistics in table x3.

```
SQL> create table x3 as select * from v$mystats;

Table created.
```

The difference between the statistics in tables x2 and x1 represents the resource cost for running prc_main with a full recompilation, and the difference between the statistics in tables x3 and x2 represents normal operation (no recompilation). The simple SQL shown in the following listing presents the data side-by-side.

```
SQL> select x2.name, x3.value-x2.value NORMAL_RUN,
  2        x2.value-x1.value WITH_RECOMP
  3    from x1, x2, x3
  4   where x2.name = x1.name
  5     and x3.name = x2.name
  6   order by 3;
```

(some selected results shown)

NAME	NORMAL_	RUN WITH_RECOMP
parse count (hard)	1	103
sorts (memory)	2	103
workarea executions - optimal	5	207
recursive cpu usage	2	1394
CPU used by this session	3	1401
parse time cpu	1	1439
parse time elapsed	1	1476
opened cursors cumulative	20	1535
enqueue releases	17	1635
enqueue requests	17	1635

parse count (total)	18	5068
consistent gets - examination	19	5284
execute count	22	10372
consistent gets	50	10853
redo entries	37	30539
db block gets	43	46627
recursive calls	273	57059
session logical reads	93	57480
db block changes	56	60250
table scan rows gotten	2	75550
redo size	7748	7017416

We will not address each row in isolation, but it is relatively easy to see that all the critical performance areas of an Oracle database (parsing, redo, CPU usage, and enqueue requests) take a significant hit under recompilation. Even Oracle has recognized the massive cost of recompilation by adding enhancements in version 10*g* whereby invalidations are minimized under certain scenarios, such as synonym manipulation.

NOTE Savvy administrators may have noticed the appearance of the new event, 10520, which is used when applying patchsets in versions 8*i* and 9*i* when the entire PL/SQL infrastructure is reloaded via the standard PL/SQL installation script catproc.sql. When event 10520 is set and a PL/SQL module is replaced, the incoming source is checked against the existing source in the data dictionary. If they are identical (that is, the source has not changed), compilation is skipped and thus invalidation of dependent objects does not occur. But this does not assist in the more general case in which a non-PL/SQL object (a table, view, and the like) is altered—all dependent PL/SQL modules will be marked for recompilation.

Breaking the Dependency Chain

The division between package specification and package body allows us to break the dependency linkages and avoid the need to worry about excessive recompilation problems. Let's return to our first simple example with four procedures: P1, P2, P3, and P4. We'll put each one in its own package and repeat the tests. Procedure P1 will be placed into package PKG1, procedure P2 into package PKG2 and so on.

```
SQL> create or replace package PKG1 is
  2     procedure P1; end;
  3   /

Package created.

SQL> create or replace package body PKG1 is
  2     procedure P1 is
  3       v_cnt number;
  4     begin
  5       select count(*)
  6       into   v_cnt
  7       from   emp;
  8     end;
  9   end;
 10   /

Package body created.

SQL> create or replace package PKG2 is
  2     procedure P2; end;
  3   /

Package created.

SQL> create or replace package body PKG2 is
  2     procedure P2 is
  3     begin
  4       PKG1.P1;
  5     end;
  6   end;
  7   /

Package body created.

SQL> create or replace package PKG3 is
  2     procedure P3; end;
  3   /

Package created.

SQL> create or replace package body PKG3 is
  2     procedure P3 is
  3     begin
```

```
  4       PKG2.P2;
  5     end;
  6   end;
  7   /
```

Package body created.

```
SQL> create or replace package PKG4 is
  2       procedure P4; end;
  3   /
```

Package created.

```
SQL> create or replace package body PKG4 is
  2       procedure P4 is
  3       begin
  4          PKG3.P3;
  5       end;
  6   end;
  7   /
```

Package body created.

Thus from a functional perspective, the four new packages perform identically to our original four procedures. Now we will make the same simple SQL modification to procedure P1 (now PKG1.P1) so that we count only employees with a positive employee number.

```
SQL> create or replace package body PKG1 is
  2       procedure P1 is
  3        v_cnt number;
  4       begin
  5        select count(*)
  6        into    v_cnt
  7        from    emp
  8        where   empno > 0;
  9       end;
 10   end;
 11   /
```

Package body created.

When we look at the status of the four packages, we get a very interesting result.

```
SQL> select object_name, object_type, status
  2  from user_objects
  3  where object_name in ('PKG1','PKG2','PKG3','PKG4');

OBJECT_NAME      OBJECT_TYPE       STATUS
-------------    ---------------   -------
PKG4             PACKAGE           VALID
PKG4             PACKAGE BODY      VALID
PKG3             PACKAGE           VALID
PKG3             PACKAGE BODY      VALID
PKG2             PACKAGE           VALID
PKG2             PACKAGE BODY      VALID
PKG1             PACKAGE           VALID
PKG1             PACKAGE BODY      VALID
```

Everything is valid! There is no recompilation needed at all. Any stored program that references a package depends only upon the package *specification*, thus changes to the package *body* do not cause dependency chain violations. This simple separation, achieved by simply moving to packages for all your production code, provides insulation from massive dependency chains, which are of course typical in any project of reasonable size.

Avoiding a Single Dependency Point

Although having thorough control of the dependency hierarchy is an admirable goal, sometimes it can be difficult to avoid having one or two packages upon which everything in your application depends. One apposite example of this is the practice of storing common application constants in a single package for use by all other PL/SQL components.

> **CAUTION** Too often this practice is based on the misplaced assumption that storing reference codes in a database table will somehow be inherently less efficient than using a PL/SQL variable. However, there are some valid reasons for maintaining a set of global variables within PL/SQL, such as storing application error codes and messages for use within all PL/SQL programs in your application.

A typical package of global variables could look something like this.

```
create or replace
package globals is
  g_gender_m constant char(1) := 'M';
  g_gender_f constant char(1) := 'F';
  g_error_msg_misc constant varchar2(80)
                := 'An unknown error has occurred';
  g_error_msg_gender constant varchar2(80)
                := 'Gender must be '|| g_gender_m|| ' or '|| g_gender_f;
  …
  …
end;
```

If you have a very well specified and controlled application environment, having a globals package of this nature can be a very efficient means of managing application constants. The emphasis here is on *well specified* because the likelihood of changes to the contents of the globals package over time should be quite low (or at least well managed and controlled). However, many projects don't have that luxury, and additions to the globals package can occur on an ad hoc basis.

Of course, the problem with frequent change to a package such as globals is that there is a high probability that every single PL/SQL module within your system will have a dependency on one or more of these global variables. After all, that is why you create such a package in the first place. To be able to reference the variables, they must be declared within the package *specification*, and thus the addition of a new global variable could easily invalidate *all* the application PL/SQL.

Solving this problem is not trivial. We still recommend that the best solution is one of the following:

- Ensure that the package is not being used where a database table would be more appropriate

- Increase the level of control and management so that global variable changes are made rarely

Let's explore some options you could possibly consider to lessen your exposure to a massive invalidation crisis. First, we'll create a globals package in the normal way so we can compare the conventional implementation with some variants.

```
SQL> create or replace
  2  package globals is
  3     g_1 constant number(5) := 1;
  4     g_2 constant number(5) := 1;
```

```
  5    g_3 constant number(5) := 1;
  6  end;
  7  /
```

Package created.

These global package variables will typically be referenced from other parts of the application, or they may even be used within SQL. To cater for each possibility, we create two functions that represent such typical usage of a global variable. First, a function that simply references one of the global variables.

```
SQL> create or replace
  2  function use_g1 return number is
  3  begin
  4     return globals.g_1;
  5  end;
  6  /
```

Function created.

Now we create a second function that uses the global variables within an SQL statement.

```
SQL> create or replace
  2  function use_g2 return number is
  3    x number;
  4  begin
  5    select globals.g_3 into x
  6    from dual
  7    where globals.g_2 = globals.g_2;
  8    return x;
  9  end;
 10  /
```

Function created.

The baseline benchmark test we will run calls each of the functions many times and records some execution time statistics. To do this, we will use the DBMS_UTILITY.GET_TIME function. This returns the number of centiseconds elapsed from some arbitrary epoch. By itself, this figure is useless. However, recording its value before and after a testing event allows us to observe the duration of that event to the nearest centisecond.

To test the access of a global variable, we will run the test a million times and record the elapsed time. To test the access of a global variable within a SQL statement, we will run the test 50,000 times (to keep the total duration of the test down to an acceptable level).

```
SQL> declare
  2     d number;
  3     s number;
  4   begin
  5     s := dbms_utility.get_time;
  6     for i in 1 .. 1000000 loop
  7       d := use_g1;
  8     end loop;
  9     dbms_output.put_line((dbms_utility.get_time-s)/100||' seconds for usage');
 10     s := dbms_utility.get_time;
 11     for i in 1 .. 50000 loop
 12       d := use_g2;
 13     end loop;
 14     dbms_output.put_line((dbms_utility.get_time-s)/100||' seconds for usage in SQL');
 15   end;
 16   /
1.42 seconds for usage
5.61 seconds for usage in SQL

PL/SQL procedure successfully completed.
```

For the standard implementation, performance is very good. Let's add a new global variable.

```
SQL> create or replace
  2   package globals is
  3     g_1           number(5) := 1;
  4     g_2           number(5) := 1;
  5     g_3           number(5) := 1;
  6     g_new_global  number(5) := 1;
  7   end;
  8   /

Package created.
```

As usual, we gauge the impact of this by querying the USER_OBJECTS view.

```
SQL> select object_name, status
  2   from user_objects
  3   where object_name in ('USE_G1','USE_G2');
```

```
OBJECT_NAME                          STATUS
--------------                       -------
USE_G2                               INVALID
USE_G1                               INVALID
```

The functions that use the global variables have become invalid. What we would like to achieve is an alternative implementation that performs as well as the standard solution but is resilient to changes to the globals package.

Option 1: Use a Context

Contexts first appeared in version 8.1 and were part of the Virtual Private Database (VPD) feature.

> **TIP** The VPD is covered in more detail in Chapter 11 of the Oracle *Application Developer Fundamentals Guide*

Contexts are used within VPD to provide values for a predetermined set of attributes that belong to a particular context definition. And of course, that is precisely what a set of global variables is, so we can explore the use of contexts to store global variables. Like a public package variable (or set of them), a context is bound to a particular session. (There are a number of extensions to the scope and usage of contexts within versions 9 and 10 of Oracle that we will not cover here.)

First, we create a context, glob, which is associated with the procedure, set_values, which we can then use to modify the attributes of the glob context.

> **NOTE** You must have the create any context privilege to run this code.

```
SQL> create or replace
  2   context glob using pkg_security.set_values;

Context created.
```

Now we create the set_values procedure within package pkg_security. We simply use the set_context procedure in the built-in dbms_session package to define three attributes for our context: g_1, g_2, and g_3, with values of 1, 2, and 3 respectively. Thus the glob context holds the same name-value pairs as our previous globals package. Next, we create pkg_security.

```
SQL> create or replace
  2  package PKG_SECURITY is
  3  procedure set_values;
  4  end;
  5  /

Package created.

SQL> create or replace
  2  package body PKG_SECURITY is
  3  procedure set_values is
  4  begin
  5    dbms_session.set_context('glob','g_1',1);
  6    dbms_session.set_context('glob','g_2',2);
  7    dbms_session.set_context('glob','g_3',3);
  8  end;
  9  /

Package body created.
```

The set_values procedure must be executed before any reference to the glob context within will succeed. A logon trigger would be a prudent means of ensuring that the globals are available for any new database session.

We now create our standard two functions that use our context attributes. Again, the first one simply references an attribute value (via the SYS_CONTEXT function).

```
SQL> create or replace
  2  function use_g1 return number is
  3  begin
  4    return sys_context('glob','g_1');
  5  end;
  6  /

Function created.
```

The second function uses the value in a SQL statement.

```
SQL> create or replace
  2  function use_g2 return number is
  3    x number;
  4  begin
  5    select sys_context('glob','g_3') into x
  6    from dual
  7    where sys_context('glob','g_2') = sys_context('glob','g_2');
  8    return x;
  9  end;
 10  /

Function created.
```

And now we will repeat the benchmark tests (after first setting our context values).

```
SQL> exec set_values

PL/SQL procedure successfully completed.
```

Our first attempt at testing this didn't finish within 15 minutes so we abandoned it and conducted a smaller test. We had to reduce the number of executions from 1,000,000 all the way down to 50,000.

```
SQL> declare
  2      d number;
  3      s number;
  4  begin
  5    s := dbms_utility.get_time;
  6    for i in 1 .. 50000 loop
  7      d := use_g1;
  8    end loop;
  9    dbms_output.put_line((dbms_utility.get_time-s)/100||' seconds for usage');
 10    s := dbms_utility.get_time;
 11    for i in 1 .. 50000 loop
 12      d := use_g2;
 13    end loop;
 14    dbms_output.put_line((dbms_utility.get_time-s)/100||' seconds for usage in SQL');
 15  end;
 16  /
8.48 seconds for usage
7.1 seconds for usage in SQL

PL/SQL procedure successfully completed.
```

The performance is similar whether you use a global variable (and hence a context) in an SQL statement or the globals package. However, by simply referencing a global in a package, we suffer a large negative performance impact—the results suggest that this approach is more than 20 times slower.

A little investigation into the definition for the base PL/SQL package standard reveals the reason for the performance hit. In $ORACLE_HOME/rdbms/admin/stdbody.sql, the source reveals the following definition for SYS_CONTEXT:

```
function SYS_CONTEXT(namespace varchar2, attribute varchar2)
   return varchar2 is
c varchar2(4000);
BEGIN
   select sys_context(namespace,attribute) into c from sys.dual;
   return c;
end;
```

It would appear that every call to SYS_CONTEXT from PL/SQL results in a recursive query to the database. This probably eliminates contexts as a source for (frequent use) global variables within PL/SQL because they are only performant when used from within SQL. And if SQL is the only place you are referencing globals, those globals should be stored in a database table!

On the positive side, using context provided insulation from dependency chain problems. Now we add a new name-value pair to hold a fourth global variable.

```
SQL> create or replace
  2  package body PKG_SECURITY is
  3  procedure set_values is
  4  begin
  5    dbms_session.set_context('glob','g_1',1);
  6    dbms_session.set_context('glob','g_2',2);
  7    dbms_session.set_context('glob','g_3',3);
  8    dbms_session.set_context('glob','g_new_global',3);
  9  end;
 10  /

Package body created.
```

We can see that our functions have not been adversely affected:

```
SQL> select object_name, status
  2  from user_objects
```

```
3  where object_name in ('USE_G1','USE_G2');
```

```
OBJECT_NAME                          STATUS
-------------------                  -------
USE_G2                               VALID
USE_G1                               VALID
```

Option 2: Varchar2 Associative Arrays

Starting in version 9.2, Oracle allows associative arrays (formerly known as "index by" tables) to be indexed by a varchar2 datatype. Thus, a character string can be used to uniquely identify an entry within an array of values. This means that we can use the name of a global variable as the index into a PL/SQL table of global variable values. In its simplest form, we could create an associative array as a package specification variable. However, this would immediately create the dependency issues already covered, so we will create a function defined in the specification to return the appropriate value from the associative array, and hide the definition and population of array values within the package body. Our package specification thus simply contains the declaration of a function to return the global variable value.

```
SQL> create or replace
  2  package new_globals is
  3     function g(gname in varchar2) return number;
  4  end;
  5  /
```

Package created.

Our package body is where all the work takes place. We define a type, num_tab, which is indexed by a varchar2. This index will be the name of the global variable that we want to reference. Our function will return the value of the array entry indexed by the passed global variable name. We also take advantage of the initialization section of the package body so that all the global variable values are assigned only once—when the package is referenced for the first time.

```
SQL> create or replace
  2  package body new_globals is
  3
  4     type num_tab is table of number
  5            index by varchar2(30);
  6
```

```
 7      n num_tab;
 8
 9      function g(gname in varchar2) return number is
10      begin
11        return n(gname);
12      end;
13
14    begin
15      n('g_1') := 1;
16      n('g_2') := 1;
17      n('g_3') := 1;
18    end;
19    /
```

Package body created.

Now we rerun our benchmark. First we re-create our test functions to access the function within the globals package just created.

```
SQL> create or replace
  2  function use_g1 return number is
  3  begin
  4    return new_globals.g('g_1');
  5  end;
  6  /
```

Function created.

```
SQL> create or replace
  2  function use_g2 return number is
  3    x number;
  4  begin
  5    select new_globals.g('g_3') into x
  6    from dual
  7    where new_globals.g('g_2') = new_globals.g('g_2');
  8    return x;
  9  end;
 10  /
```

Function created.

Next we run our standard benchmark test to capture execution times. (We were able to use 1,000,000 executions when referencing the global variable.)

```
SQL> declare
  2      d number;
  3      s number;
  4   begin
  5    s := dbms_utility.get_time;
  6    for i in 1 .. 1000000 loop
  7      d := use_g1;
  8    end loop;
  9    dbms_output.put_line((dbms_utility.get_time-s)/100||' seconds for usage');
 10    s := dbms_utility.get_time;
 11    for i in 1 .. 50000 loop
 12      d := use_g2;
 13    end loop;
 14    dbms_output.put_line((dbms_utility.get_time-s)/100||' seconds for usage in SQL');
 15   end;
 16   /
4.11 seconds for usage
11.36 seconds for usage in SQL

PL/SQL procedure successfully completed.
```

A promising result! However, is our solution also resilient from dependency issues? Let's add another global variable to the initialization section in the package body.

```
SQL> create or replace
  2   package body new_globals is
  3
  4      type num_tab is table of number
  5             index by varchar2(30);
  6
  7    n num_tab;
  8
  9      function g(gname in varchar2) return number is
 10      begin
 11        return n(gname);
 12      end;
 13
 14   begin
 15     n('g_1') := 1;
 16     n('g_2') := 1;
 17     n('g_3') := 1;
 18     n('g_new_global') := 1;
```

```
19   end;
20   /
```

Package body created.

Next, look at the status of our testing functions.

```
SQL> select object_name, status
  2   from user_Objects
  3   where object_name in ('USE_G1','USE_G2');
```

```
OBJECT_NAME                      STATUS
--------------------             -------
USE_G2                           VALID
USE_G1                           VALID
```

It appears that ⌐   ⌐y issues are covered as well. Is the associative
array the answ⌐   ⌐? Possibly, but there are some drawbacks to
the appro⌐   le example, all the global variables
return   This is hardly likely to be the case in a
                              lication. There will be strings, dates,
                              ⌐renced as global constants. This
                              ultiple associative arrays, one for
                              ⌐present. Because packaged func-
                              by their return datatype, you
                              ⌐type. For example, to handle
                              ckage may look like the

```
pac
  fur.                                    ..umber;
  funci                                 . date;
  functic              ∠) return varchar2;
end;
```

Thus, any   ⌐ion must explicitly know the datatype of the global
variable it is see⌐   ⌐his might not be such a bad thing, but it introduces additional complexity into the implementation.

To summarize, there is no perfect solution to handling of globals within your
application. It's a balancing act between your requirements—reducing the
dependency issues versus maintaining adequate control over the ongoing additions and changes to those global variables. Ultimately as always, you should
benchmark your alternatives carefully.

Enabling Recursion

Traversal of trees, management of linked list structures, backtracking algorithms, and many similar classical computing problems are often more easily coded with recursive techniques than a sequential coding approach. Although a full discussion on recursion is beyond the scope of this chapter, it is worth noting (within the context of packages) that using standalone procedures prohibit you from using any mutually recursive routines. They simply will not compile.

```
SQL> create or replace
  2   procedure A(p number) is
  3   begin
  4     if p < 5 then
  5         B(p+1);
  6     end if;
  7   end;
  8   /

Warning: Procedure created with compilation errors.

SQL> create or replace
  2   procedure B(p number) is
  3   begin
  4     if p < 5 then
  5         A(p+1);
  6     end if;
  7   end;
  8   /

Warning: Procedure created with compilation errors.

SQL> alter procedure B compile;
alter procedure B compile
*
ERROR at line 1:
ORA-04020: deadlock detected while trying to lock object MCDONAC.B


SQL> alter procedure A compile;
alter procedure A compile
*
ERROR at line 1:
ORA-04020: deadlock detected while trying to lock object MCDONAC.A
```

However, using packages allows forward references, thus opening the possibilities for recursion. If we embed the two procedures just shown within a package, mutual recursion becomes possible.

```
SQL> create package RECURSION  is
  2      procedure A(p number);
  3      procedure B(p number);
  4  end;
  5  /


Package created.

SQL> create or replace
  2  package body RECURSION  is
  3
  4  procedure A(p number) is
  5  begin
  6    if p < 5 then
  7        B(p+1);
  8    end if;
  9  end;
 10
 11  procedure B(p number) is
 12  begin
 13    if p < 5 then
 14        A(p+1);
 15    end if;
 16  end;
 17
 18  end;
 19  /


Package body created.
```

Why Have People Avoided Packages?

So far, everything we've said about packages is positive. You have all the facilities of standalone procedures plus the additional benefits of code encapsulation, insulation from change, greater control over the scope of variables, and initialization. There are no negatives with using packages. Is it just purely ignorance that has kept so many developers away from packages?

In early versions of Oracle, packages received some bad press for a variety of reasons, most of which were attributable to their usage and the way that this usage wreaked havoc with shared pool memory management on the server. Let's explore a couple of the poor usage habits that have historically dogged packages.

Ignorance of the Benefits of Separation

Most of the benefits of packages discussed in this chapter are a direct consequence of the separation between package specification and package body. These benefits are lost if the two are treated as one. Common mistakes in this regard are as follows:

- Recompiling both specification and body for any change that is made. If you have not changed the package specification, do *not* reload it into the database every time the package body is changed. Doing so eliminates the insulation from dependency.

- Storing the package specification and package body in a single text file. Look in the $ORACLE_HOME/rdbms/admin directory and you'll see that all the supplied Oracle packages are delivered in separate files—one file for the specification, one for the body.

In a perfect world, package specifications would never change. That has long been one of the primary goals for any language that supports encapsulation of the functionality offered to the calling environment.

It's a Package, Not a Library

Many developers were first exposed to packages (or PL/SQL, for that matter) through Oracle's client-server tools (Forms, Reports, and Graphics), all of which used a local PL/SQL engine as the runtime environment. The dependency tree benefits of packages were not particularly well documented and in any event, early releases of Forms required that every PL/SQL unit in a module be recompiled (even if it was already valid) before an executable fmx file was produced. Therefore, it didn't really matter how many dependencies a PL/SQL unit had— they all had to be compiled each time anyway.

Therefore, many developers treated packages as a convenience more than anything else, merely as a means for grouping logically related PL/SQL program units. This didn't cause major problems on the client software development environments, but it was an approach that was carried over into the server-based

PL/SQL platform. As such, it was common to see enormous packages with generic names such as common, tools or utils, each serving as a catch-all for hundreds of small routines.

The problem with this approach was that in early releases of Oracle 7, packages (or any PL/SQL program unit) were loaded entirely into memory when any reference was made to one of their components, and that memory had to be a single contiguous chunk.

Because the shared pool is typically made up of a large number of small pieces of memory (see the following sidebar), loading a large package into a contiguous memory space could easily put a system under enormous strain. Hundreds or thousands of objects would need to be flushed out of the shared pool in least-recently used order to make space for the package. Imagine a large bucket filled to the brim with tennis balls numbered from 1 to 1,000, and you must find space for an incoming basketball by removing tennis balls in numerical order—that should give you an idea of the amount of work required in shared pool memory management to load a single package.

Compounding the problem, there was no guarantee of success in this operation because you could conceivably flush out all chunks of memory that were freeable and still not have a big enough chunk of free space because you may not have been flushing out *contiguous* chunks of memory. Systems could easily be brought to a standstill while this operation took place.

As a consequence, many developers and DBAs began to equate packages with the ubiquitous error message "ORA-4031:unable to allocate bytes of shared memory."

More About the Shared Pool

Although it is outside the scope of this book to go into detail about the makeup of the shared pool, the following query (which you must run while connected as SYSDBA) will demonstrate that for normal use within a typical database, the shared pool is comprised of a large number of small chunks of memory.

```
SQL> select bytes chunk_size, count(*) no_of_chunks from
  2  (
  3    select power(10,trunc(ln(ksmchsiz)/ln(10)))||' to '||
  4      (power(10,trunc(ln(ksmchsiz)/ln(10))+1)-1) chunk_size
  5    from x$ksmsp
  6    where ksmchcls != 'perm' )
  7  group by bytes
  8  /
```

CHUNK_SIZE	NO_OF_CHUNKS
10 to 99	2487
100 to 999	16548
1000 to 9999	4573
10000 to 99999	15
100000 to 999999	18
1000000 to 9999999	7

This query shows the number of free and in-use memory chunks in the shared pool within a logarithmic distribution.

Since version 7.3 of Oracle, the problems associated with loading PL/SQL units into the shared pool have largely been resolved. The management of PL/SQL program units can be likened to demand paging; that is, the execution code for a PL/SQL program unit is loaded on an on-demand basis and in chunk sizes no larger than 4k.

This can be demonstrated by creating a large package and seeing whether the entire package code is loaded if just a small routine from that package is executed. We will create a package where the source code is comprised of 300 small procedures.

```
package MEMTEST is
   procedure X1;
   procedure X2;
   ...
   procedure X300;
end;
```

Each procedure assigns the number 1 to a numeric variable, y. Rather than type the source by hand, we will use some PL/SQL to dynamically create the large package and its body.

```
SQL> declare
  2    x varchar2(32767);
  3  begin
  4    for i in 1 .. 300 loop
  5      x := x || ' procedure X'||i||';';
  6    end loop;
  7    execute immediate
  8      'create or replace package MEMTEST is '||x||' end;';
  9    x := replace(x,';',' is y number; begin y := 1; end;');
```

```
10    execute immediate
11      'create or replace package body MEMTEST is '||x||' end;';
12    end;
13    /
```

PL/SQL procedure successfully completed.

Now we'll flush the shared pool to clear out any existing evidence of the memtest package, execute just one of the procedures in the package, and recheck the contents on the shared pool.

```
SQL> alter system flush shared_pool;
```

System altered.

```
SQL> exec memtest.x1;
```

PL/SQL procedure successfully completed.

Next we look at the V$SGASTAT view to determine the amount of memory in use for PL/SQL code (the procedure we just executed).

```
SQL> select * from v$sgastat
  2 where name like 'PL/SQL MPCODE';
```

POOL	NAME	BYTES
shared pool	PL/SQL MPCODE	80980

Approximately 80K are in use. That may seem like a lot, but remember that to run any PL/SQL program, components of the standard package (which defines PL/SQL itself) must also be loaded. If our memtest package code was loaded entirely into memory, presumably any references to other procedures in package memtest should already be present. However, as we execute different procedures, we can see the amount of code loaded into shared pool memory increases with each execution. Next we execute procedure X2 within the memtest package.

```
SQL> exec memtest.x2;
```

PL/SQL procedure successfully completed.

```
SQL> select * from v$sgastat
  2 where name like 'PL/SQL MPCODE';
```

```
POOL           NAME             BYTES
-----------    ---------------  ----------
shared pool  PL/SQL MPCODE      85612

SQL> exec memtest.x10;

PL/SQL procedure successfully completed.

SQL> select * from v$sgastat
  2   where name like 'PL/SQL MPCODE';

POOL           NAME             BYTES
-----------    ---------------  ----------
shared pool PL/SQL MPCODE       90652

SQL> exec memtest.x100;

PL/SQL procedure successfully completed.

SQL> select * from v$sgastat
  2   where name like 'PL/SQL MPCODE';

POOL           NAME             BYTES
-----------    ---------------  ----------
shared pool  PL/SQL MPCODE      95284
```

We stress that just because large packages do not place the system under the memory and latching strain that they have in the past, it does not imply that we should create systems comprised of just a few massive packages. Each version of Oracle tends to raise the limits on the maximum allowed size of a PL/SQL unit, but we should not forget the other maxims of maintainability, modularity, and perhaps most importantly, common sense, when composing our packages.

When Not to Use Packages

There is one scenario for which a package is not the preferred solution for a PL/SQL stored program: any PL/SQL function that will be a candidate for a function-based index. In these cases, the protection from the dependency chain that packages afford can cause problems. Let's demonstrate the issue with an example. First, we will create and populate a table on which we will create a function-based index.

```
SQL> create table x ( x number, y varchar2(30));

Table created.

SQL> insert into x
  2 select rownum, 'xxxxx'||rownum
  3 from SRC
  4 where rownum < 10000;

9999 rows created.
```

We will be indexing the table, x, with a function-based index where that function is defined within a package. The next step is to create a package to hold such a function. For a function to be used within a function-based index, it must be defined as deterministic. Doing this will tell Oracle that this function will always return a consistent (in other words, unchanging) result for multiple executions with a specific parameter value.

```
SQL> create or replace
  2   package FBI is
  3      function ix(p varchar2) return varchar2 deterministic;
  4   end;
  5   /

Package created.
```

Our function will be very simple—it will return whatever value is passed to it.

```
SQL> create or replace
  2   package body FBI is
  3      function ix(p varchar2) return varchar2
  4        deterministic is
  5      begin
  6         return p;
  7      end;
  8   end;
  9   /

Package body created.
```

Now we can use this package function to build an index on our table, x. For the optimizer to use this (or any) function-based index, we also need to collect optimizer statistics for the table and index once created.

```
SQL> create index x1 on x ( FBI.ix(y));

Index created.

SQL> analyze table x estimate statistics

Table analyzed.
```

To prove that the index will be used, we can enable the SQL*Plus autotrace facility to display execution plans for any SQL that we run.

```
SQL> set autotrace on
SQL> select *
  2  from x
  3  where FBI.ix(y) = 'xxxxx123';

X                 Y
------            ---------
123               xxxxx123

Execution Plan
----------------------------------------------------------------
   0        SELECT STATEMENT Optimizer=CHOOSE (Cost=2 Card=1 Bytes=12)
   1    0    TABLE ACCESS (BY INDEX ROWID) OF 'X' (Cost=2 Card=1 Bytes=12)
   2    1      INDEX (RANGE SCAN) OF 'X1' (NON-UNIQUE) (Cost=1 Card=1)
```

No problems so far. The function-based index is being used as anticipated. Obviously, if we were to change the package function, we would need to rebuild our index to pick up the new values being returned from the function. Nevertheless, one of the selling points of packages is that to change the underlying implementation of one of its components, only the *package body* needs to be changed. We'll alter just the package body to append the value abc to the return value.

```
SQL> create or replace
  2  package body p1 is
  3    function ix(p varchar2) return varchar2
  4      deterministic is
  5    begin
  6      return p||'abc';
  7    end;
  8  end;
  9  /
```

```
Package body created.
```

Oracle is *not* aware that the function code has been altered because the dependency chain is based on the package specification, not the body. As a result, the values stored in the index are effectively "out of sync" with the function upon which it is based. This could lead to the nasty situation of getting different results from a query dependent on how the optimizer decides to run the query. If we re-run the SQL from above, and we allow the optimizer to use the index as per the previous execution plan, we obtain a row in the result.

```
SQL> select *
  2  from x
  3  where p1.ix(y) = 'xxxxx123';


X                Y
--------    ----------
123         xxxxx123
```

The fact that we have obtained a row reveals the problem here—there is no row in the table for which column Y has a trailing abc, so no rows should be returned. If the same query is re-executed but we force the optimizer to not use the index, then we get the correct result, namely, no rows being returned:

```
SQL> select /*+ FULL(x) */ *
  2  from x
  3  where p1.ix(y) = 'xxxxx123';


no rows selected
```

Until the index is rebuilt, it will yield incorrect results. Of course, if the package *specification* had also been re-created, the function-based index would have been marked as unusable (that is, the funcidx_status column in user_indexes would be set to disabled), and the index would need to be rebuilt. But in an application development environment where package bodies *only* are being altered and recompiled (to ensure dependency problems are avoided), it is risky to assume that someone will take the time to check whether any functions in that package are used within indexes. For this reason, PL/SQL functions used in indexes are best created as standalone routines.

Delivered Packages

Another positive aspect that will result from embracing packages throughout your applications is that the development team may start to focus on the functionality that is delivered *for free* with the PL/SQL packages that are supplied with the Oracle software.

Take a moment to run a query to see the PL/SQL packages that are delivered under the SYS account and you will get some startling results. The following query was performed on a version 9.2 database:

```
SQL> select object_name
  2  from dba_objects
  3  where owner = 'SYS'
  4  and object_type = 'PACKAGE';

OBJECT_NAME
----------------------------------
CONNECTIONINTERFACE
CURSORMANAGERINTERFACE
DATABASEINTERFACE
DATAPROVIDERINTERFACE
DATATYPEIDCONSTANTS
DBMSOBJG
DBMSOBJG2
DBMSOBJGWRAPPER
DBMSOBJG_DP
DBMSZEXP_SYSPKGGRNT
DBMS_ALERT
DBMS_APPCTX
DBMS_APPLICATION_INFO
...


XSLPROCESSOR
XSLPROCESSORCOVER
XSLSTYLESHEETCOVER

357 rows selected.
```

Over 300 packages! Even though not all of them are intended for developers, the ones that are for developers are very well documented in the standard Oracle documentation. One of the manuals we always head to first when a new version of Oracle is released is the *Supplied PL/SQL Packages and Types Reference*. Within any company, certain functionality often pops out as being common across several Oracle projects. When that functionality becomes common across many companies, Oracle will "jump on the bandwagon" and deliver it as a native feature in the database. Each new release of Oracle delivers more PL/SQL built-in functions that you do not (and should not) have to build for yourself.

A definitive guide to all the packages delivered by Oracle is easily a book in its own right. In this book, we simply use these built-in packages as and where appropriate. For example, in the *Security Packages* chapter, we use the built-in dbms_fga package for fine-grained auditing. In the *Web Packages* chapter, we use utl_http to make HTTP requests directly from an Oracle database, and in the *Debugging* chapter, we investigate various built-in packages for effective debugging (alongside our own custom solution).

In the next section, we will look at a few delivered package solutions because they highlight two very important points:

- They are solutions to common requirements. We have seen developers spend hours (or days or weeks) building solutions because they didn't know that Oracle supplied a package that was perfect for the job.

- If you take the time to explore the supplied packages, you can often discover effective alternative uses for them that Oracle might not have originally intended.

Code Path Tracing Made Easy

Being able to debug your application code is vital to the success of any project. For many 3GL languages, the developer is responsible for tracking where the code is currently executing. The most typical solution to this requirement is the implementation of a stack. For example, a solution of this type in PL/SQL could look as follows:

```
SQL> create or replace
  2  package stack is
```

We define an associative array to represent a stack of modules.

```
  3    type module_list is
  4      table of varchar2(80)
  5      index by binary_integer;
  6
```

We then define the standard operations that we perform on a stack—pushing an item onto the stack and popping an item off the top of the stack.

```
  7    procedure push(module_name varchar2);
  8    procedure pop;
  9    procedure show_stack;
```

```
10
11   end;
12   /
```

Package created.

The underlying stack operations are trivial to implement with associative arrays because the array itself maintains a count of the entries within it.

```
SQL> create or replace
  2   package body stack is
  3
  4     m module_list;
  5
  6   procedure push(module_name varchar2) is
  7   begin
  8     m(m.count+1) := module_name;
  9   end;
 10
 11   procedure pop is
 12   begin
 13     m.delete(m.count);
 14   end;
 15
 16   procedure show_stack is
 17   begin
 18     for i in 1 .. m.count loop
 19       dbms_output.put_line(rpad('-',i,'-')||m(i));
 20     end loop;
 21   end;
 22
 23   end;
 24   /
```

Package body created.

Now that we have a generic stack facility within PL/SQL, we can use it within our applications programs to manage tracking our execution paths. As we enter a new procedure, we add its name to the stack, and when we exit the procedure, we remove its name from the stack. To demonstrate, the following three procedures use the stack to record the execution of each procedure:

```
SQL> create or replace
  2   procedure p1 is
```

```
  3   begin
  4     stack.push('P1');
  5     stack.show_stack;
  6     stack.pop;
  7   end;
  8   /

Procedure created.

SQL> create or replace
  2   procedure p2 is
  3   begin
  4     stack.push('P2');
  5     p1;
  6     stack.pop;
  7   end;
  8   /

Procedure created.

SQL> create or replace
  2   procedure p3 is
  3   begin
  4     stack.push('P3');
  5     p2;
  6     stack.pop;
  7   end;
  8   /

Procedure created.
```

Now, when we execute procedure P3, the call to show_stack within procedure P1 outputs the stack of procedure calls.

```
SQL> exec p3;
-P3
 --P2
  ---P1

PL/SQL procedure successfully completed.
```

There are two major problems with this. First, every PL/SQL program that we want to participate in the stack tracing must be coded so that it pushes its name onto the stack at its entry point, and also removes its name from the stack *for every possible exit point* in the procedure. Every possible error must be accounted for, and all it takes is a single PL/SQL module to miss a call to the stack management for the stack to be corrupted. Second, and this is a more fundamental point, the functionality is already provided by Oracle! We can recode procedure P1 as the following:

```
SQL> create or replace
  2  procedure p1 is
  3  begin
  4    dbms_output.put_line(
  5      substr(dbms_utility.format_call_stack,1,255));
  6  end;
  7  /

Procedure created.
```

The FORMAT_CALL_STACK function within the delivered dbms_utility package returns the call stack as a character string. No special stack package is required, and there is no requirement to have special code within every single PL/SQL program developed. Executing the revised P3 procedure demonstrates the output from DBMS_UTILITY.FORMAT_CALL_STACK.

```
SQL> exec p3;
----- PL/SQL Call Stack -----
  object            line   object
  handle          number   name
700000003f56250        3   procedure SCOTT.P1
700000003f4c3c0        4   procedure SCOTT.P2
700000003f47e38        4   procedure SCOTT.P3
700000003f44e98        1   anonymous block
```

We also get the added benefits of the actual line number at which each PL/SQL module called another. Admittedly, a little string manipulation would be required to parse the output string, but this is small price to pay for such a convenient facility.

And while you are developing debugging utilities that take advantage of the DBMS_UTILITY.FORMAT_CALL_STACK function, you can get more benefits from other built-in packages, such as the dbms_application_info package, which we'll discuss in detail in the *Debugging* chapter.

Other Useful Routines

There are a number of other useful tools within the dbms_utility package that allow you to obtain information about your system architecture. We have already seen how the DBMS_UTILITY.GET_TIME function can return the number of centiseconds from arbitrary epoch. Let's take a quick look at a few others.

Dependency Information

This procedure (which does not appear in the documentation) provides a neat listing of all the dependency information associated with a database object.

```
SQL> exec dbms_utility.get_dependency('TABLE',user,'EMP');
-
DEPENDENCIES ON SCOTT.EMP
----------------------------------------------------------
*TABLE SCOTT.EMP()
*    PACKAGE BODY SCOTT.PKG()
-
DEPENDENCIES ON SCOTT.EMP
----------------------------------------------------------
*TABLE SCOTT.EMP()
*    PACKAGE BODY SCOTT.PKG()

PL/SQL procedure successfully completed.
```

Platform and Version Information

These programs return the version and operating system port for the database. For example, on a laptop running version 9204 of the database, the following tests were performed:

```
SQL> variable b1 varchar2(64)
SQL> variable b2 varchar2(64)
SQL> exec dbms_utility.db_version(version=>:b1,compatibility=>:b2);

PL/SQL procedure successfully completed.

SQL> print b1
```

```
B1
--------------------------------------------------
9.2.0.4.0

SQL> print b2

B2
--------------------------------------------------
9.2.0.0.0

SQL> select dbms_utility.port_string from dual;

PORT_STRING
--------------------------------------------------
IBMPC/WIN_NT-8.1.0
```

From these results, it would appear that the port string is useful to determine on the platform, but certainly version information should not be trusted from the resultant string.

Retrieving DDL

Suppose you have a table (or any database object) in the database for which you would like to see the underlying DDL. This may sound like a simple enough task but unfortunately, given the increasing flexibility and functionality that arrives with each release of Oracle, it is actually more difficult than you might imagine.

Many developers or administrators have tackled this problem by using scripts to probe the data dictionary. In fact, a quick search on Google reveals a myriad of such solutions, one of which is reproduced as follows. This sample is designed to regenerate the create table statement used for each of the tables within the current schema.

```
SELECT DECODE(T1.COLUMN_ID,1,'CREATE TABLE ' ||
T1.TABLE_NAME ||   ' (',' ') A,
 T1.COLUMN_NAME B,  T1.DATA_TYPE ||
DECODE(T1.DATA_TYPE, 'VARCHAR2',  '('||
TO_CHAR(T1.DATA_LENGTH)||')', 'NUMBER','('||
TO_CHAR(T1.DATA_PRECISION)||
',' ||TO_CHAR(T1.DATA_SCALE)||')',
 'CHAR','('||TO_CHAR(T1.DATA_LENGTH)||')')||
DECODE(T1.COLUMN_ID,MAX(T2.COLUMN_ID), ');',',') C
FROM USER_TAB_COLUMNS T1, USER_TAB_COLUMNS T2
```

```
WHERE   T1.TABLE_NAME = T2.TABLE_NAME
GROUP BY T1.COLUMN_ID, T1.TABLE_NAME, T1.DATA_TYPE,
 T1.DATA_LENGTH, T1.DATA_SCALE, T1.COLUMN_NAME, T1.DATA_PRECISION
ORDER BY T1.COLUMN_ID;
```

Such a script does generate some meaningful output, but the resultant DDL misses a number of important elements such as the storage clause, the constraints, the object datatypes, the handling of index-organized, clustered, or partitioned tables, and many other elements that may be used for a table definition. It's a good starting point, but certainly not a definitive or complete solution. Maybe the best bet is therefore to head over to an Oracle site and get an official version of such a script. The following script was found on the Metalink support site.

```
DECLARE
    cursor cur0 is
        select table_name,TABLESPACE_NAME,PCT_FREE,PCT_USED,
                   INI_TRANS,MAX_TRANS,
                   INITIAL_EXTENT,NEXT_EXTENT,PCT_INCREASE
        from    user_tables
        order by table_name;

    cursor cur1 (t_name varchar2) is
        select table_name, column_name, data_type, data_length,
               data_precision, data_scale, nullable
        from    user_tab_columns
        where   table_name = t_name
        order by column_name;

    tab_name      varchar2(40);
    tabsp_name varchar2(40);
    mpct_free   number;
    mpct_used    number;
    mini_trans number;
    mmax_trans number;
    mini_ext    number;
    mnext_ext   number;
    mpct_inc    number;
    col_name      varchar2(40);
    ct               number := 0;
    line_ct       number := 0;

BEGIN
    delete from  AAA;
```

```
for cur0_rec in cur0 loop
    tab_name := cur0_rec.table_name;
    tabsp_name := cur0_rec.TABLESPACE_NAME;
    mpct_free := cur0_rec.PCT_FREE ;
    mpct_used := cur0_rec.PCT_USED;
    mini_trans := cur0_rec.INI_TRANS;
    mmax_trans := cur0_rec.MAX_TRANS;
    mini_ext := cur0_rec.INITIAL_EXTENT ;
    mnext_ext := cur0_rec.NEXT_EXTENT ;
    mpct_inc := cur0_rec.PCT_INCREASE ;
    insert into AAA(f1, line)
    values(line_ct, 'create table '|| tab_name || '(' );
    line_ct := line_ct + 1;

    ct := 0;
    for cur1_rec in cur1(tab_name) loop
        ct := ct + 1;
        if ct = 1 then
            insert into  AAA(f1, line )
            values (line_ct ,
                '    '|| cur1_rec.column_name||'    '||
                cur1_rec.data_type||
                decode(cur1_rec.data_type, 'VARCHAR2','('||
                to_char(cur1_rec.data_length)||')',
                'NUMBER',decode(cur1_rec.data_precision, null,'',
                '('||to_char(cur1_rec.data_precision)||
                decode(cur1_rec.data_scale, null, ')', ','||
                to_char(cur1_rec.data_scale)||')' )  ), '')||
                decode(cur1_rec.nullable, 'Y', '', '   NOT NULL') );
            line_ct := line_ct + 1;
        else
            insert into  AAA(f1, line)
            values (line_ct, '  ,'|| cur1_rec.column_name||'    '||
                cur1_rec.data_type||
                decode(cur1_rec.data_type, 'VARCHAR2','('||
                to_char(cur1_rec.data_length)||')',
                'NUMBER',decode(cur1_rec.data_precision, null,'',
                '('||to_char(cur1_rec.data_precision)||
                decode(cur1_rec.data_scale, null, ')', ','||
                to_char(cur1_rec.data_scale)||')' ) ), '')||
                decode(cur1_rec.nullable, 'Y', '', '   NOT NULL') );
            line_ct := line_ct + 1;
        end if;
```

```
      end loop;
      insert into AAA (f1, line )
      values(line_ct, ')' );
      line_ct := line_ct + 1;
      insert into AAA (f1, line )
      values (line_ct, ' PCTFREE ' || mpct_free || ' PCTUSED ' || mpct_used ) ;
        line_ct := line_ct + 1;
      insert into AAA (f1, line )
      values (line_ct, ' INITRANS ' || mini_trans || ' MAXTRANS ' || mmax_trans);
      insert into AAA (f1, line )
      values (line_ct, ' TABLESPACE '||tabsp_name );
      line_ct := line_ct + 1;
      insert into AAA (f1, line )
      values(line_ct, ' STORAGE ( INITIAL ' || mini_ext || ' NEXT '
                  || mnext_ext || ' PCTINCREASE ' || mpct_inc || ');' );
        line_ct := line_ct + 1;
      insert into AAA (f1, line )
      values(line_ct, 'REM -------------NEXT TABLE ------------ ');
      line_ct := line_ct + 1;
      commit;
   end loop;
END;
/
```

Although this script looks impressive and yields more of the finer details, it still doesn't cover everything. Storage clauses are taken care of, but the moment a new feature arrives, the script will need to be corrected. For example, the script has no support for generating the DDL for a partitioned table.

Once again, taking the time to look for a predelivered package yields the best solution. A simple call to the GET_DDL function within the dbms_metadata package returns the DDL as a character large object (CLOB). For example, to obtain the DDL for the emp table within the SCOTT schema, we need only issue a simple select statement, shown as follows.

```
SQL> select dbms_metadata.get_ddl('TABLE','EMP','SCOTT')
  2  from dual;

  CREATE TABLE "SCOTT"."EMP"
   (    "EMPNO" NUMBER(4,0),

        "ENAME" VARCHAR2(10),
        ...
        CONSTRAINT "PK_EMP" PRIMARY KEY ("EMPNO")
```

```
      USING INDEX PCTFREE 10 INITRANS 2 MAXTRANS 255
      STORAGE(...) TABLESPACE "USERS"  ENABLE,
              CONSTRAINT "FK_DEPTNO" FOREIGN KEY ("DEPTNO")
              REFERENCES "SCOTT"."DEPT" ("DEPTNO") ENABLE
      ) PCTFREE 10 PCTUSED 40 INITRANS 1 MAXTRANS 255
  NOCOMPRESS LOGGING STORAGE(...) TABLESPACE "USERS"
```

It is that simple. There are also a number of transformations that you can make to the DDL that is returned. For example, if you want to omit the storage parameters, you can simply set the appropriate transformation variable as follows:

```
begin
  DBMS_METADATA.SET_TRANSFORM_PARAM(
      DBMS_METADATA.SESSION_TRANSFORM,
      'STORAGE',
      false);
end;
```

The DDL is not limited to tables. You can get the DDL for just about anything in the database. For example, the user definitions are easily retrieved with the following:

```
SQL> select dbms_metadata.get_ddl('USER','SCOTT')
  2  from dual;

CREATE USER "SCOTT"
IDENTIFIED BY VALUES 'F894844C34402B67'
DEFAULT TABLESPACE "USERS"
TEMPORARY TABLESPACE "TEMP"
```

See the *PL/SQL Supplied Packages Guide* for a complete list of the different objects for which you can retrieve the defining DDL. It's far easier than writing a suite of scripts to do the task.

An Interesting Use for DBMS_ROWID

Most developers are aware of the dbms_rowid package, which consists of a number of utilities to manipulate rowids, but many may think it is no big deal. After all, rowid manipulation is something that is rarely if ever required in the application development life cycle. However, something that *is* part of application development is resolving locking (or *enqueue*) problems, and the dbms_rowid package can be very useful in assisting here. To demonstrate, let's consider two separate sessions, each attempting to remove rows from the emp table. The first session adds 10 percent to the salaries of all our long-term employees (anyone who was hired before September 19, 1981, in this case).

```
SQL> update emp
  2   set sal = sal * 1.1
  3   where hiredate < to_date('08/SEP/1981','DD/MON/YYYY');

6 rows updated.
```

Our second session closes department 20, and all employees in this department are relocated to department 30.

```
SQL> update emp set deptno = 30 where deptno = 20;
(waiting...)
```

We have a locking problem but because we are updating multiple rows, it is not immediately apparent which row(s) are causing the problem. This is where dbms_rowid becomes very useful. First, we examine V$SESSION view, which identifies the explicit row that is causing the problem. The row prefixed columns are populated when a session is waiting for an enqueue, so we can check for those sessions that are waiting on an enqueue on the emp table.

```
SQL> select row_wait_obj#, row_wait_file#,
  2          row_wait_block#, row_wait_row#
  3   from    v$session
  4   where   row_wait_obj# in (
  5     select data_object_id
  6     from    user_objects
  7     where   object_name = 'EMP');
```

ROW_WAIT_OBJ#	ROW_WAIT_FILE#	ROW_WAIT_BLOCK#	ROW_WAIT_ROW#
49627	7	138	0

Armed with this information, we can now use the dbms_rowid package to isolate precisely the row that is causing the problem.

```
SQL> select *
  2   from emp
  3   where rowid = dbms_rowid.rowid_create(1,49627,7,138,0);
```

EMPNO	ENAME	MGR	HIREDATE	SAL	DEPTNO
7369	SMITH	7902	17/DEC/80	880	20

Of course, it would take very little effort for a DBA to set this kind of activity in a simple script so that developers could always easily locate rows involved in an enqueue problem. This is much better than developers having to take the more drastic action of terminating their database sessions until the problem disappears.

Background Tasks

Consider the case in which a database task (for example, report generation) may take 30 seconds to complete. We don't want to lock up the requesting user's terminal/PC while that request is executed; we would like the user to be able to request the report and then continue on with other tasks. A commonly implemented (but generally flawed) approach to solving this problem is to use database pipes. Because of the length of the code, we won't include the entire solution here, but we will summarize the pseudo-code for such a solution.

Foreground Process:

1. Pack a pipe message with the task to be run in the background.

2. Send the pipe message in pipe P1.

3. Wait for a return message on a different pipe P2 to ensure the sent message was received.

4. Return control to the user.

Background Processor:

1. Wait for a message on pipe P1.

2. When a message is received, remove it from pipe P1.

3. Send acknowledgment on pipe P2.

4. Run commands as specified in the message (or have some sort of indication of what was done).

5. Resume waiting on pipe P1.

A number of complexities in this solution that are not immediately apparent from the algorithm just shown are:

- You need to ensure that the background processor is running.

- You need to ensure that foreground processes don't wait forever in case the background processor failed or is busy on another task.

- Pipes are nontransactional, so if the foreground process requests a background task as part of a transaction, the task will execute even if the foreground process later issues a rollback.

If the last item above is a "back breaker," the resolution is not trivial. You might consider using transactional database alerts, but task requests can be dropped because the implementation of database alerts only guarantees that one (not all) message is received by a background processor that has registered interest.

Of course a better solution is to use a database table that stores the requests, and have the background processor read from this table. Even this approach requires some careful forethought. For example, if we want to increase the number of concurrent background processors, we will need to build in some locking intelligence to ensure that no task is executed either more than once or not at all.

We are amazed at the number of sites where such a solution exists, painstakingly built and tested from scratch by a development team when once again, *the functionality is already delivered for free*. The Job Queue facility has been available since version 7 but it is under utilized because it is mistakenly considered to be purely for tasks that run on a fixed schedule. Using a job queue to perform a background task is as simple as setting the following foreground task:

```
dbms_job.submit(:job, 'task_to_be_performed;');
```

That's all there is to it! The task request is automatically transactional—if you issue a rollback, the job will not be run. You can have up to 36 background processors in version 8, and 1,000 in version 9. You can add, subtract, stop, and start the background processors at any time without affecting a foreground process's ability to submit tasks. Any errors are logged in trace files, and you get some restartability features if a job fails.

Launching processes asynchronously with transactional processes is a fantastic means of adding functionality to your database. For example, you could use job queues to delete a file only when a transaction is actually committed. First we create a table, list_of_files, which contains the filename and directory where that file is located.

```
SQL> create table LIST_OF_FILES (
  2     fname varchar2(30),
  3     fdir  varchar2(30)) ;
```

```
Table created.

SQL> insert into LIST_OF_FILES
  2      values ('demo.dat','/tmp');

1 row created.
```

We can now create a trigger on that table that will submit a job to run the `utl_file.fremove` procedure (which deletes files) when a user deletes a row. Because jobs are transactional, the deletion of the file will take place only if the user commits the action.

```
SQL> create or replace
  2    trigger DEL_FILE
  3    before delete on LIST_OF_FILES
  4    for each row
  5    declare
  6      j number;
  7    begin
  8      dbms_job.submit(j,'utl_file.fremove('''||
  9            :old.fdir||''','''||:old.fname||''');');
 10    end;
 11    /

Trigger created.
```

Let's see this in action. We inserted a row previously for the file /tmp/demo.dat. We can see that this file exists on our system.

```
SQL> !ls /tmp/demo.dat
/tmp/demo.dat
```

We now delete this row from the table.

```
SQL> delete from list_of_files;

1 row deleted.
```

If we had deleted the file immediately from within the trigger, we would have been stuck if the user issued a rollback. The row would be reinstated to the table, but the file would be gone. But because the deletion was wrapped as a database job, it does not start until we commit. We can see that our file still exists.

```
SQL> !ls /tmp/demo.dat
/tmp/demo.dat
```

When the changes are committed, the background job will execute shortly thereafter and the file will be removed.

```
SQL> commit;

Commit complete.

SQL> !ls /tmp/demo.dat
ls: 0653-341 The file /tmp/demo.dat does not exist.
```

> **NOTE** You can see additional examples of the usefulness of DBMS_JOB in Chapter 6, *Triggers*.

The list of functionality delivered for free goes on and on. We stress again, when a new version of Oracle is released, take the time to check out what PL/SQL packages are provided. They might save you a bundle of time and energy.

Summary

We recommend that every PL/SQL program you write (except the function-based index example discussed earlier) be defined as a package. Even if a routine appears to be entirely self-contained and thus unlikely to be affected by dependency or recompilation issues, the one fact that never changes in the application development business is that applications change. If a self-contained program performs a useful function, it's probably a case of *when,* not *if,* someone will write a program that calls it, and thus introduce the more complicated dependencies that make packages worth their weight in gold. The extra effort of just a few extra keystrokes to code a package instead of a standalone procedure or function is well worth it.

CHAPTER 3

The Vexed Subject of Cursors

IN CHAPTER 1, WE CAUTIONED against using PL/SQL when a SQL solution would be appropriate. Of course, if every possible functional requirement could be written in SQL, PL/SQL never would have been created by Oracle in the first place. When you have satisfied yourself that PL/SQL *is* required to meet a functional requirement, any access to the database will, of course, involve the use of cursors.

Cursors are remarkably simple things. You ask the database to prepare some results, you retrieve those results, and then you tell the database that you are finished with those results. However, this is a chapter born out of frustration with seeing the hoops developers often jump through to make cursors much more complicated than they are. In this chapter, we'll look at:

- Side by side performance analysis of implicit and explicit cursors

- Why you probably don't need to use explicit cursors in a lot of your code

- The usefulness of cursor variables when dealing with applications that may not reside on the database server

- Cursor expressions, which allow you to return a nested cursor from within a SQL statement

Implicit vs. Explicit Cursors

When you issue a SELECT INTO statement (that is, an *implicit* cursor) in PL/SQL, there are three possible outcomes:

- The result set contains a single row and the SELECT succeeds

- The result set contains no rows (or more accurately, there is *no* result set) and the NO_DATA_FOUND exception is raised

- The result set contains two rows or more and the TOO_MANY_ROWS exception is raised

As most developers know, when you fetch from a cursor, you retrieve a single row from the result set. It would therefore seem that for the PL/SQL engine to know when to raise the TOO_MANY_ROWS exception, it must fetch *twice* from the implicit cursor to check for the presence of a second row in the result set. It was this hypothesis that led to the theory that you will find in many textbooks: explicit cursors are best practice in terms of performance.

The argument was that an implicit cursor would (theoretically) issue:

- Open cursor

- Fetch row

- Fetch again (to check for TOO_MANY_ROWS)

- Close cursor

An explicit cursor would be more efficient because the PL/SQL developer has full control and thus can code only a single fetch. This is a fairly compelling argument, and in the very early releases of PL/SQL, the argument had some merit.

However, as far back as Oracle version 7.1, the concept of pre-fetching was introduced. Put simply, when pre-fetching is used in a call to fetch a row from a cursor, the next row is retrieved within the same call. It's akin to the read-ahead mechanism that can be found on modern disk drives and file systems. The database anticipates that, more often than not, you will want to get that next row anyway. This is a godsend for the implicit cursor in PL/SQL because a single fetch call is all that is required to fully evaluate the appropriate response to the calling program, namely, return the single row fetched or raise one of the NO_DATA_FOUND or TOO_MANY_ROWS errors, *both* being determinable from that single fetch.

The passion with which the explicit versus implicit cursor issue has been debated over the last few years is quite astounding. A quick search on Google reveals such comments as:

"The day I find a developer at any company where I consult using anything other than explicit for pulling records in a loop, they will no longer be on the project. And the other DBAs in my group agree."

"SELECTs should always be performed with explicit cursors. I have yet to find a single instance when an implicit cursor will work better than an explicit one."

"There is something that goes on behind the scenes that seems to make implicit cursors a bad choice."

If nothing else, this indicates that developers are passionate about their code, although interestingly the people who sit on the "explicit is faster than implicit" side of the fence also seem very reluctant to provide any hard evidence for their claims. Whenever a debate gets heated, the best way to settle the argument is to put together a thorough suite of tests—which we provide now to demonstrate that implicit cursors are just as good, and in some cases faster, than explicit cursors.

Single Row Fetching

First, we create the most efficient table possible for scanning—a single block, index-organized table. We use this for the performance test so that the cost of querying this table is minimized, and therefore the cost of opening, fetching, and closing[1] the cursor is the focus.

```
SQL> create table one_row_tab ( x primary key )
  2  organization index as select 1 from dual;

Table created.
```

Now we can build a procedure that performs 50,000 iterations of an implicit cursor and its explicit cursor equivalent.

```
SQL> create or replace
  2  procedure implicit is
  3     dummy number;
  4  begin
  5     for i in 1 .. 50000 loop
  6        select 1
  7        into    dummy
  8        from    one_row_tab;
  9     end loop;
 10  end;
 11  /

Procedure created.

SQL> create or replace
  2  procedure explicit is
  3     cursor explicit_cur is
```

---

1. As most readers know, PL/SQL does not close cursors as a performance feature (REF cursors are an exception to this rule). However, this is true for both explicit and implicit cursors so this anomaly will not bias the results of the tests.

```
 4        select 1
 5        from    one_row_tab;
 6     dummy number;
 7  begin
 8     for i in 1 .. 50000 loop
 9        open explicit_cur;
10        fetch explicit_cur
11        into dummy;
12        close explicit_cur;
13     end loop;
14  end;
15  /
```

Procedure created.

Our PL/SQL modules are now at the proverbial starting line—let's see who wins the race.

```
SQL> exec implicit;

PL/SQL procedure successfully completed.

Elapsed: 00:00:04.02
SQL> exec explicit;

PL/SQL procedure successfully completed.

Elapsed: 00:00:05.07
```

These tests were repeated several times with iterations varying from 50,000, as displayed, up to 1,000,000, and in all instances, the implicit cursor code is approximately 20 percent faster than its explicit equivalent. The reason for this is that PL/SQL is an interpreted language, so the smaller the volume of code required to fulfill a particular purpose, the faster that code will run. There is nothing wrong with the explicit cursor version, and in real applications, the difference is unlikely to be as great. But whatever the circumstances, the implicit cursor performs slightly better, yields code that is more compact, and in our opinion, is also easier to read and comprehend.

Explicit Cursors Fight Back

As an interesting digression from these tests, another contributor to a public forum proposed the following rebuttal to the argument that implicit cursors were faster than explicit cursors. The contributor proposed that because of the PL/SQL performance feature that automatically reuses cursors, the OPEN and CLOSE commands could be placed outside the iteration loop. According to this theory, the following code would be the best solution:

```
SQL> create or replace
  2   procedure explicit2 is
  3     cursor explicit_cur is
  4        select 1
  5        from   one_row_tab;
  6     dummy number;
  7   begin
  8     open explicit_cur;  - placed before loop
  9     for i in 1 .. 50000 loop
 10        fetch explicit_cur
 11        into dummy;
 12     end loop;
 13     close explicit_cur; - placed after loop
 14   end;
 15   /

Procedure created.

SQL> exec explicit2

PL/SQL procedure successfully completed.

Elapsed: 00:00:00.00
```

Wow! Very impressive. The explicit cursor might be back in the race. There is only one small problem with the code—it's entirely wrong! It doesn't work. Yes, it's true that PL/SQL can reuse cursors, but this is a performance feature built into the PL/SQL engine itself, not some mechanism through which we can alter our own PL/SQL code. The error in the code can be demonstrated easily enough. The procedure issues a SELECT statement against a single row table, so it should successfully return a single row for each of the 50,000 iterations. We added some debugging code, displayed as follows, to output the line "I worked" whenever a fetch succeeded.

```
SQL> create or replace
  2   procedure explicit2 is
  3     cursor explicit_cur is
  4        select 1
  5        from   one_row_tab;
```

```
 6    dummy number;
 7  begin
 8    open explicit_cur;
 9    for i in 1 .. 50000 loop
10        fetch explicit_cur
11        into dummy;
12        if explicit_cur%found then
13            dbms_output.put_line('I worked');
14        end if;
15    end loop;
16    close explicit_cur;
17  end;
18  /
```

Procedure created.

Thus, the string "I worked" should be displayed 50,000 times. But when the procedure is executed, we see the following:

```
SQL> set serverout on
SQL> exec  explicit2
I worked

PL/SQL procedure successfully completed.

Elapsed: 00:00:00.00
```

In fact, only the *very first* of the 50,000 iterations succeeded. All the others iterations had no work to do—which, of course, explains the "performance boost."

Explicit Cursors Fight Back Again

Given the passionate comments from the top of this section, it is to be expected that fans of the explicit cursor are not going to give up the fight easily. Armed with the information that the implicit cursor requests two rows in a single fetch, it is possible to concoct the following test that "proves" explicit cursors are faster.

```
SQL> create table EXPLICIT_IS_BEST
  2    ( x number, y char(100));

Table created.
```

```
SQL> insert into EXPLICIT_IS_BEST
  2  select rownum, 'padding'
  3  from all_objects
  4  where rownum < 10001;

10000 rows created.
```

We created a table with 10,000 rows, the first row having a value of 1 for column X. The Y column is merely some padding to ensure that the table occupies plenty of space on disk. Let's now re-create the procedure IMPLICIT and EXPLICIT to retrieve the row from the EXPLICIT_IS_BEST table, where X = 1. As with the previous procedure, we will then perform the retrieval 50,000 times to observe any significant performance differences.

```
SQL> create or replace
  2  procedure implicit is
  3     dummy number;
  4  begin
  5     for i in 1 .. 50000 loop
  6         select 1
  7         into    dummy
  8         from    explicit_is_best
  9         where   x = 1;
 10     end loop;
 11  end;
 12  /

Procedure created.

SQL> create or replace
  2  procedure explicit is
  3     cursor explicit_cur is
  4         select 1
  5         from    explicit_is_best
  6         where   x = 1;
  7     dummy number;
  8  begin
  9     for i in 1 .. 50000 loop
 10         open explicit_cur;
 11         fetch explicit_cur
 12         into dummy;
 13         close explicit_cur;
 14     end loop;
 15  end;
 16  /
```

123

```
Procedure created.
```

We then run our procedure to find out who wins in this special test.

```
SQL> exec implicit

PL/SQL procedure successfully completed.

Elapsed: 00:06:41.00
SQL> exec explicit

PL/SQL procedure successfully completed.

Elapsed: 00:00:05.04
```

The explicit cursor seems to have regained the performance crown. The reason for the slowdown in the implicit case is that the table must be entirely scanned in order to find a second row for the result set (a search that ends in vain). By contrast, the explicit cursor code is interested only in the first row and searches no further.

This result is based on good luck more than any genuine performance benefit. Rows in an Oracle (heap) table are not stored in any particular order. We can never be sure that the row where X = 1 will always be at the "top" of the table (that is, present in just the first few blocks). In fact, a simple DELETE and INSERT of that row has a dramatic impact on our tests. Let's replace the row where X = 1.

```
SQL> delete from explicit_is_best
  2   where x= 1;

1 row deleted.

SQL> insert into explicit_is_best
  2   values (1,'padding');

1 row created.

SQL> commit;

Commit complete.
```

It appears that we have made no change to the table, but a query to the table shows that the row we re-inserted has not been reinstated to the same position—it's been added to the first block that Oracle considers available, in this case, the last block in the table.

```
SQL> select x
  2  from    explicit_is_best;

        X
-----------
        2
        3
        4
        5
        6
        7
       ...
       ...
     9998
     9999
    10000
        1

10000 rows selected.
```

What has this done to our tests? Let's re-execute the procedures and find out.

```
SQL> exec implicit

PL/SQL procedure successfully completed.

Elapsed: 00:06:41.00
SQL> exec explicit

PL/SQL procedure successfully completed.

Elapsed: 00:06:42.72
```

Suddenly the explicit cursor procedure has dropped its performance back to just slightly slower than that of the implicit equivalent. Only when we are lucky enough to search for a single row that happens to be located in the first few blocks of the table does the explicit cursor have an advantage.

Re-read the previous sentence—we are *only interested in a single row*. In fact, the implicit cursor has not been coded correctly. Ask any developer how to code a query that returns only the first row that matches the provided predicates and she will reply with

```
select …  from …  where …  and rownum = 1
```

Let's change the implicit cursor procedure to look for the value of X=2 (which is still within the first block of the table) and we will add a ROWNUM = 1 predicate to the SQL to answer the same question as the explicit cursor code.

```
SQL> create or replace
  2  procedure implicit is
  3    dummy number;
  4  begin
  5    for i in 1 .. 1000 loop
  6       select 1
  7       into   dummy
  8       from   explicit_is_best
  9       where  x = 2 and rownum = 1;
 10    end loop;
 11  end;
 12  /

Procedure created.

SQL> exec implicit;

PL/SQL procedure successfully completed.

Elapsed: 00:00:04.05
```

Once again, when we compare this result to the original explicit cursor procedure test (which took 5.04 seconds), we can see that implicit cursors still perform best.

Multi-Row Processing

The examples just shown demonstrate that implicit cursors are just as good, if not better, than explicit cursors for the case of retrieving a single row. They are also just as useful for fetching sets of rows using the implicit cursor syntax within a FOR loop. There has never been much usage of SQL directly within a cursor FOR loop mainly because Oracle never took the time to explain that it could be done. We prefer coding cursor loops in this way because we do not have to scan up to the declaration section of the code to check the definition—the SQL is right there. Here is a simple example of an implicit cursor within a FOR loop.

```
SQL> begin
  2  for i in ( select ename from emp ) loop
  3     dbms_output.put_line(i.ename);
```

```
   4   end loop;
   5   end;
   6   /
SMITH
ALLEN
...
JAMES
FORD
MILLER

PL/SQL procedure successfully completed.
```

Even if you prefer this style of code, with the SQL defined right where it's being used within the cursor, you may be concerned about the ability to use cursor attributes such as SQL%ROWCOUNT and SQL%FOUND. These and other attributes are not available to implicit cursors used within a FOR loop. How do we handle coding requirements such as the number of rows processed or whether any rows existed in the result set at all? Does their usage imply that we must resort to explicit cursors? No. Let's address each of these requirements in turn.

Row Counts

The two most common reasons why the row count from a cursor might be used are as follows:

- To provide a grand total of rows processed when we are finished with the cursor

- To provide a row number as we fetch each row from the cursor

When using explicit cursors, the %ROWCOUNT cursor attribute is not available once the cursor loop is exited. For example, if you attempt to amend the previous example to output the count of rows, once the loop has finished, an error occurs.

```
SQL> declare
   2     cursor c is select ename from emp ;
   3   begin
   4     for i in c loop
   5        null;
   6     end loop;
   7     dbms_output.put_line(c%rowcount);
   8   end;
```

```
  9   /
declare
*
ERROR at line 1:
ORA-01001: invalid cursor
ORA-06512: at line 7
```

To use it to calculate a grand total you need to assign a scalar variable for each row fetched from the cursor. There is no advantage to doing this over using an implicit cursor and simply incrementing a scalar variable, as follows:

```
SQL> declare
  2      cnt pls_integer := 0;
  3   begin
  4     for i in (select ename from emp) loop
  5       cnt := cnt + 1;
  6     end loop;
  7     dbms_output.put_line(cnt);
  8   end;
```

Similarly, to obtain a row number for each fetched row, once again it is just as easy to use a scalar variable and increment it for each loop iteration. Alternatively, the query itself can include the ROWNUM variable to yield a row number for each fetched row.

Existence Checks

A typical example of an existence check specification reads as follows:
"See if a record that satisfies <some criteria> exists. If so, then <take some action>."

The use of explicit cursors for such existence checks often arises from blindly following a procedural specification, or to put it another way, from giving up on SQL too quickly. By way of an example, say our existence check was
"See if anyone was hired in the last month."
Then, a poor SQL implementation might look as follows:

```
SQL> select count(*)
  2   from    emp
  3   where   hiredate > trunc(sysdate,'MM');
```

This is poor SQL because we don't need a *count* of employees; it is inefficient to count all the records in a result set just to verify that at least one exists.

Therefore, many developers quickly revert to a PL/SQL solution, using an explicit cursor and the %FOUND attribute to perform a single fetch.

```
SQL> create or replace
  2   function IS_EMP_THERE return varchar2 is
  3     cursor C is
  4       select 1 from emp
  5       where  hiredate > trunc(sysdate,'MM');
  6     r number;
  7     v varchar2(3);
  8   begin
  9     open C;
 10     fetch C into r;
 11     if C%FOUND then
 12         v :=  'YES';
 13     else
 14         v := 'NO';
 15     end if;
 16     close C;
 17     return v;
 18   end;
 19   /

Function created.
```

Although it is indeed true that a single fetch is more efficient than counting all records for a result set, this solution violates one of our core efficiency guidelines, presented in Chapter 1, "Efficient PL/SQL"—don't use PL/SQL when there is an SQL solution available. If the specification asks for an existence check, SQL has precisely the syntax we need.

```
select count(*)
from    dual
where exists (select null from emp where hiredate > trunc(sysdate,'MM'))
```

The result of which will be either 1 (an appropriate record exists) or 0 (no record exists), with no PL/SQL required at all.

Exception Handling

Cursor attributes are also often used within the exception handling section of a PL/SQL program. In the vast majority of cases, their use there is not required. Consider the following example of a procedure that closes its cursors in the event of an error. It loops through each record in the EMP table and calculates a bonus amount for the organization. Because the calculation includes a division by the salary amount, we might encounter a division by zero error.

```
SQL> create or replace
  2  procedure PROCESS_EMP is
  3    cursor C is
  4      select empno, sal, comm
  5      from   emp;
  6    v_bonus number := 10000;
  7  begin
  8    for i in c loop
  9      v_bonus := v_bonus + i.comm / i.sal;
 10    end loop;
 11  exception
 12    when zero_divide then
 13      if C%ISOPEN then
 14        close C;
 15      end if;
 16  end;
 17  /

Procedure created.
```

It might be argued that we need to use an explicit cursor so that we could close it if an error occurs. This is not the case. Any cursor defined locally within the procedure declaration section will automatically be logically closed as soon as the procedure terminates (either successfully or in error). The only time such a check may be required is if the cursor is held open throughout a session, for example, if that cursor is defined within a package specification.

TOP-N Processing

We can extend our previous existence check example to the more generic case, namely the erroneous use of explicit cursors to retrieve the top value (or top n values) from a set of rows. The argument from the explicit cursor camp is that if you need just the first row from an ordered result set, declaring an explicit cursor for that result set and then fetching the first row would be an efficient means of doing so. Thus an explicit cursor procedure that returned the value of column X corresponding to the highest value of column Y would be coded as follows. I've included 500 iterations in the loop so we can benchmark our solutions.

```
SQL> create or replace
  2  procedure explicit is
```

```
 3     cursor explicit_cur is
 4         select x
 5         from    explicit_is_best
 6         order by y desc;
 7     dummy number;
 8  begin
 9     for i in 1 .. 500 loop
10         open explicit_cur;
11         fetch explicit_cur
12         into dummy;
13         close explicit_cur;
14     end loop;
15  end;
16  /
```

Procedure created.

The equivalent code for the implicit cursor requires slightly more complicated SQL because it requires use of an inline view.

```
SQL> create or replace
  2  procedure implicit is
  3     dummy number;
  4  begin
  5     for i in 1 .. 500 loop
  6         select x into dummy
  7         from ( select x
  8                  from explicit_is_best
  9                  order by y desc )
 10         where rownum = 1;
 11     end loop;
 12  end;
 13  /
```

Procedure created.

It's often assumed that this must be more resource intensive, so let's see if this assumption is correct. Once again, we test the responsiveness of each solution.

```
SQL> exec implicit;
```

PL/SQL procedure successfully completed.

```
Elapsed: 00:00:09.09
SQL> exec explicit;

PL/SQL procedure successfully completed.

Elapsed: 00:00:23.06
```

The implicit cursor solution wins handsomely this time. A savvy reader might suggest that the example just shown is cheating somewhat in favor of the implicit cursor procedure. The implicit cursor contains a ROWNUM clause wrapped around an inline view that contains an ORDER BY clause, and when Oracle encounters SQL statements of this type, it can employ a performance optimization that is not available to the SQL used in the explicit cursor procedure.

In a sense this is true, but resorting *by default* to explicit cursors will tend to keep you away from a possible implicit cursor option that uses SQL to get the result, not cursor processing. Of course, if we convert the explicit cursor procedure to define a cursor with the same SQL statement as used within the implicit procedure version, we have two procedures that run an identical SQL—one with an explicit cursor and one with an implicit cursor. In which case, as proved by our previous discussions in this chapter, an implicit cursor will always perform as well as or better than its explicit counterpart.

Conclusions

In this section, we have not tried to prove that you should not use explicit cursors anywhere in your code. Indeed, there are times when they are essential and you'll see some references to them throughout this book—for example when performing bulk collection in Chapter 4, "Effective Data Handling."

Implicit cursors do not have some magical property that makes them intrinsically better than explicit cursors. What we *have* proved, however, is that implicit cursors result in code that is more compact and that will, in the vast majority of cases, perform just as well or better than their explicit cursor counterparts.

In addition, implicit cursors are easier to comprehend and less likely to be misused in the way that explicit cursors are (as we have demonstrated with the examples in this section).

Cursor Management Across Architectures

Not surprisingly, any application backed with a database store delivers most of its functionality either by retrieving data from the database, modifying existing data, or creating new data.

In times gone by, the user interface, the application code, and the database all coexisted on a common infrastructure (that is, typically a mainframe computer with a single architecture such as CICS-COBOL). However, today's applications are deployed on a diverse array of architectures running on a multitude of servers. This has implications for the way data retrieved from the database is processed. Under the centralized philosophy, all components of an application have direct access to the database store—now data must be passed between different servers and across different software architectures, each possibly with different interfaces for receiving that data and returning sets of data.

Cursor Variables

This is where cursor variables, (also referred to as REF cursors) come into play with PL/SQL. They provide a consistent means through which query result sets can be passed between application components. The application components need not necessarily be PL/SQL programs; cursor variables can be passed between software architectures such as Java programs, Oracle client programs such as Forms Developer Suite, and within the ProC or OCI programming interfaces.

Whereas a normal cursor within PL/SQL is fixed, that is, bound to a static SQL definition, a cursor variable is not associated with any particular query; it simply points to a cursor result set. The result set never moves—the cursor variable, which points to it, can be passed around between PL/SQL programs or more commonly between PL/SQL and a client application. Of course, the most efficient means of passing a large result set between application components is not to pass it at all—you just pass a pointer to where that data is.

Consider the following example. First, we'll create a function that returns a cursor variable.

```
SQL> create or replace
  2  function emp_list return sys_refcursor is
  3    rc sys_refcursor;
  4  begin
  5    open rc for select * from emp;
  6    return rc;
  7  end;
  8  /

Function created.
```

> **NOTE** The SYS_REFCURSOR type is new to version 9. If you are running version 8, you will need to include the line type sys_refcursor is ref cursor before you define the RC variable.

And now we can create a procedure, LIST_EMPS, which will use that cursor variable to list data from the EMP table. Notice that we have not defined any cursor in the following procedure—it simply contains its own ref cursor, which will point to the cursor within the EMP_LIST function we just created.

```
SQL> create or replace
  2    procedure list_emps is
  3      e   sys_refcursor;
  4      r   emp%rowtype;
  5    begin
  6      e := emp_list;
  7      loop
  8        fetch e into r;
  9        exit when e%notfound;
 10        dbms_output.put_line(r.empno||','||r.hiredate);
 11      end loop;
 12      close e;
 13    end;
 14    /
```

Procedure created.

Now we can execute our LIST_EMPS procedure to output the employee detail.

```
SQL> exec list_emps;
7369,17/DEC/80
7499,20/FEB/81
7521,22/FEB/81
7566,02/APR/81
7654,28/SEP/81
7698,01/MAY/81
7782,09/JUN/81
7788,19/APR/87
7839,17/NOV/81
7844,08/SEP/81
7876,23/MAY/87
7900,03/DEC/81
7902,03/DEC/81
7934,23/JAN/82
```

```
PL/SQL procedure successfully completed.
```

At this point you may be thinking that this is not a very big deal. This, of course, could just as easily have been done with a normal static cursor. But consider now a second usage of the same cursor variable, this time from SQL*Plus (which also supports local cursor variables).

SQL> variable x refcursor

```
SQL> declare
  2     r   emp%rowtype;
  3   begin
  4     :x := emp_list;
  5     loop
  6       fetch :x into r;
  7       exit when :x%notfound;
  8       dbms_output.put_line(r.empno||','||r.hiredate);
  9     end loop;
 10     close :x;
 11   end;
 12   /
7369,17/DEC/80
7499,20/FEB/81
7521,22/FEB/81
7566,02/APR/81
7654,28/SEP/81
7698,01/MAY/81
7782,09/JUN/81
7788,19/APR/87
7839,17/NOV/81
7844,08/SEP/81
7876,23/MAY/87
7900,03/DEC/81
7902,03/DEC/81
7934,23/JAN/82

PL/SQL procedure successfully completed.
```

Therein lies the power of the feature. In this second example, both a client program (SQL*Plus) and a server based PL/SQL routine have been able to share access to a result set. An even simpler example shows that a client program (such as SQL*Plus) can even be responsible for fetching from the cursor variable once it has been opened by the EMP_LIST function. The PRINT command, when used against a cursor variable, fetches all rows from the cursor and outputs them to the screen.

```
SQL> exec :x := emp_list;

PL/SQL procedure successfully completed.

SQL> print x
```

EMPNO	ENAME	JOB	MGR	HIREDATE	SAL
7369	SMITH	CLERK	7902	17/DEC/80	800
7499	ALLEN	SALESMAN	7698	20/FEB/81	1600
7521	WARD	SALESMAN	7698	22/FEB/81	1250
7566	JONES	MANAGER	7839	02/APR/81	2975
7654	MARTIN	SALESMAN	7698	28/SEP/81	1250
7698	BLAKE	MANAGER	7839	01/MAY/81	99999
7782	CLARK	MANAGER	7839	09/JUN/81	2450
7788	SCOTT	ANALYST	7566	19/APR/87	3000
7839	KING	PRESIDENT		17/NOV/81	5000
7844	TURNER	SALESMAN	7698	08/SEP/81	1500
7876	ADAMS	CLERK	7788	23/MAY/87	1100
7900	JAMES	CLERK	7698	03/DEC/81	950
7902	FORD	ANALYST	7566	03/DEC/81	3000
7934	MILLER	CLERK	7782	23/JAN/82	1300

The cursor variable was defined on the client, opened on the server, and the results fetched from the client. We did not have to build a result set on the server and pass the entire set back to the client (SQL*Plus)—the client had direct access to the cursor. Anywhere that you have a client application that supports cursor variables (Java, Pro*C, and so on), that client program can get access to cursor result sets without requiring the entire result set to be retrieved, stored, and passed back to it.

Cursor Expressions

Any PL/SQL variable that you define within your programs can be included in the SQL queries you write within those PL/SQL programs. For example, it's simple to reference the variable, V_BONUS, when calculating the maximum salary in the following anonymous block.

```
SQL> declare
  2    v_bonus number := 10000;
  3    v_max_sal number;
  4  begin
  5    select max(sal)+v_bonus
```

```
6    into   v_max_sal
7    from   emp;
8  end;
9  /
```

PL/SQL procedure successfully completed.

We have just seen in the previous section that we now have variables that are in fact pointers to a result set, but they are still just variables. The anonymous block just shown shows that we include a variable in a result set returned from a query. Can we do the same if that variable is a cursor variable? Yes, we can. This is known as a **cursor expression**—again, a feature new to version 9. A simple example of a cursor expression within a query can be written as follows:

```
select deptno, dname,
       cursor(select empno, ename
              from emp
              where deptno = d.deptno)
from dept d;
```

The third column in the query result set is a cursor in its own right. You can fetch from the parent result set (the DEPT table) and, for each row fetched, a nested cursor is automatically opened on the EMP table, which you can fetch from as well. Running this example in SQL*Plus illustrates how this is performed. Within SQL*Plus, as each row is fetched from the DEPT table, SQL*Plus will automatically fetch and display the rows from the nested cursor expression as well.

```
SQL> select deptno, dname,
  2          cursor(select empno, ename
  3                 from emp
  4                 where deptno = d.deptno)
  5  from dept d;

    DEPTNO   DNAME          CURSOR(SELECTEMPNO,E
---------- -------------- --------------------
        10   ACCOUNTING     CURSOR STATEMENT : 3

CURSOR STATEMENT : 3

    EMPNO   ENAME
  ------- --------
     7782  CLARK
     7839  KING
     7934  MILLER
```

```
        20 RESEARCH        CURSOR STATEMENT : 3

CURSOR STATEMENT : 3

    EMPNO  ENAME
    ------ ----------
     7369  SMITH
     7566  JONES
     7788  SCOTT
     7876  ADAMS
     7902  FORD

        30 SALES           CURSOR STATEMENT : 3
```

Once again, you might be thinking that this is not that impressive and that you could just implement this functionality with a join between EMP and DEPT. There is a subtle difference here. Consider a client application program that needs to implement a slightly more complicated requirement, as follows:

- Fetch a list of departments from the DEPT table

- For only *some* of the departments (dependent on some external application criteria)

  - Get a list of employees for that department

  - Get a list of customers for that department

This cannot be done with a join because you have two one-to-many relationships (from department to employees, and from department to customers). Without cursor expressions, an application would have to build the following solution (in pseudo-code):

```
open dept_cursor
for each row in dept_cursor
  open emp_cursor
  for each row in emp_cursor
    print details
  close emp_cursor

  open cust_cursor
  for each row in cust_cursor
    print details
  close cust_cursor
```

For any application performing this code on an application server, this could yield a large number of network trips to and from the database server, continuously opening and closing cursors. Use of cursor expressions allows for all the cursor processing to be controlled within a single call. We can demonstrate this using SQL*Plus as the client application that wants to obtain the results in a single call. First we create a function, DEPT_EMP_CUST, to return a cursor variable containing the parent cursor on the DEPT table, with the EMP and CUSTOMER cursor expressions nested within it.

```
SQL> create or replace
  2  function dept_emp_cust return sys_refcursor is
  3    rc sys_refcursor;
  4  begin
  5    open rc for
  6    select deptno, dname,
  7           cursor(select empno, ename
  8                    from emp
  9                   where deptno = d.deptno) emps,
 10           cursor(select custid, custname
 11                    from customers
 12                   where purchasing_dept = d.deptno) custs
 13    from dept d;
 14    return rc;
 15  end;
 16  /

Function created.
```

Then, using the same SQL*Plus functionality we saw previously, we can open the cursor variable with a locally defined cursor variable, X, and then print from X to obtain all the rows from DEPT, as well as fetching the rows from the nested cursor expressions.

```
SQL> variable x refcursor
SQL> exec :x := dept_emp_cust;

PL/SQL procedure successfully completed.

SQL> print x
```

```
    DEPTNO  DNAME           EMPS                   CUSTS
----------  --------------  --------------------   --------------------
        10  ACCOUNTING      CURSOR STATEMENT : 3   CURSOR STATEMENT : 4

CURSOR STATEMENT : 3

    EMPNO ENAME
    ------- ----------
     7782 CLARK
     7839 KING
     7934 MILLER


CURSOR STATEMENT : 4

   CUSTID CUSTNAME
   ------- ---------
        7 Cust7
        9 Cust9
       14 Cust14
```

<more rows>

A single function call yields a ref cursor that in turn contains two nested cursors to print out department, employee, and customer details.

This is not to say that you should include cursor expressions within your SQL on a casual basis. Remember that each row retrieved from the driving table in the query will yield a second query execution, that of the SQL within the cursor expression. For example, using the standard SQL*Plus AUTOTRACE facilities[2], we can examine the vast difference in work done between two similar queries, one that contains a reference to a cursor expression and one that does not. First, we consider the query without a cursor expression.

```
SQL> set arraysize 50
SQL> set autotrace on statistics
SQL> select empno, deptno   -- no cursor expression here
  2   from emp
  3   /
```

---

2. The Introduction to this book gives basic set up details for AUTOTRACE. For a full description, see Chapter 9 of the *SQL*Plus Users Guide and Reference*.

```
Statistics
----------------------------------------------------
         0  recursive calls
         0  db block gets
      1249  consistent gets
       244  physical reads
         0  redo size
    603709  bytes sent via SQL*Net to client
     11488  bytes received via SQL*Net from client
      1001  SQL*Net roundtrips to/from client
         0  sorts (memory)
         0  sorts (disk)
     50000  rows processed
```

Now we will create an empty table that we will fetch from a cursor expression. The table is empty so the only overhead we will measure will be the nested cursor processing and not the processing of any rows that could be returned from the nested cursor.

```
SQL> create table IX ( x number primary key )
  2  organization index;

Table created.

SQL> analyze table IX estimate statistics;

Table analyzed.

SQL> select empno, cursor(select x from ix)
  2  from emp
  3  /
```

```
Statistics
----------------------------------------------------
    250070  recursive calls
         0  db block gets
     75112  consistent gets
         0  physical reads
         0  redo size
  13102130  bytes sent via SQL*Net to client
   7577901  bytes received via SQL*Net from client
     75000  SQL*Net roundtrips to/from client
         0  sorts (memory)
```

```
     0  sorts (disk)
 50000  rows processed
```

Notice the massive jump in recursive calls and the amount of logical I/O performed—the "consistent gets" figure jumped from 1249 to 75112! Obviously, some extra work is to be anticipated, but given that we know that the cursor expression will not fetch any rows from our empty IX table, this does seem like an extreme increase. Possibly related to this is the fact that cursor expressions also seem to restrict the ability to retrieve more than one row when a single fetch is performed. SQL*Plus supports array fetching, so let's see what happens when we execute a query to retrieve 200 rows using an array size of 50, with and without cursor expressions. The following results were obtained from the TKPROF-formatted trace file for the query that does *not* use cursor expressions.

```
select *
from
 emp where rownum < 200
```

call	count	cpu	elapsed	disk	query	current	rows
Parse	1	0.00	0.03	0	0	0	0
Execute	1	0.00	0.00	0	0	0	0
Fetch	5	0.00	0.26	2	11	24	**199**
total	7	0.00	0.30	2	11	24	199

We can see the array fetching in action here—only five fetches were required to obtain 200 rows. However, we do not appear to be using array fetching when we include the cursor expression.

```
select empno,
       cursor(select x
              from ix) from emp where rownum < 200
```

call	count	cpu	elapsed	disk	query	current	rows
Parse	1	0.01	0.00	0	0	0	0
Execute	1	0.00	0.00	0	0	0	0
Fetch	101	0.11	0.07	0	104	0	199
total	103	0.12	0.08	0	104	0	199

We will see array fetching fully in the next chapter. For the time being, it's important that you simply realize that the inability to use array fetching could be a performance inhibitor for your applications. Thus, we need to take care when using cursor expressions because it seems that the best we can do is two rows per fetch.

Summary

As we stated at the beginning of this chapter, cursor processing should not be a topic that generates so much discussion and confusion in PL/SQL programming (or any language that processes data from an Oracle database, for that matter).

Once you have mastered processing cursors within your PL/SQL programs, scrutinize cursor variables and cursor expressions where you are building applications that sit outside of the database. There are efficiency benefits to be had just by passing the pointer to a result set between application layers rather than passing the data that a result set comprises, especially if that data is large.

Cursor processing is of course part of the much broader topic of data management in PL/SQL. In the next chapter, we will delve further into this topic and discuss some of the enhancements that you can make to your cursor processing to take advantage of array fetching.

CHAPTER 4

Effective Data Handling

LIKE MANY IT PROFESSIONALS OF my generation, I began programming with COBOL on mainframes. One thing that I always found odd about COBOL was its incredibly relaxed rules on datatypes (especially after having the importance of structured data typing beaten into me through the long years of university education). When processing a file with COBOL, a sequence of bytes read from a file could be treated as a character string, a date, a number, even binary data—as long as I could overlay the bytes successfully into a working storage definition then the COBOL compiler was happy. In fact, it was not uncommon to see definitions along the lines of

```
YEAR-END-STRING  PIC X(8)
YEAR-END-NUM REDEFINES  YEAR-END-STRING  PIC 99999999
```

This syntax means that the stored value of the YEAR-END variable can be treated as either a string or a numeric datatype, depending on the application requirement. This flexibility comes at a cost. Corruptions in data are discovered only when a variable is used inappropriately, and not necessarily when the initial assignment to that variable was made. In the example just shown, we could just as easily assign "HELLO" to the string variable (YEAR-END-STRING) only to have a crash when we try to reference that variable as a numeric field (YEAR-END-NUM). Nothing explicitly ties a COBOL program to the data that it references—you just need to code and hope for the best (at least, that's what I did!).

The tighter the relationship between the data structures in the database and the data structures in your PL/SQL program, the more robust and resilient to changes your applications will become. In this chapter, I will discuss the importance of having a thorough understanding of how best to establish that relationship.

Taking Control of Your Datatypes

PL/SQL offers extensive and strict control over data structures. I say "offers" extensive control because it's amazing how many applications don't take advantage of this control. In any well-built Oracle application, a lot of effort is put into ensuring that the appropriate datatypes and business rules are defined within the database. For any column in a database table, we typically define

- Its datatype

- Its maximum allowable length (and precision if appropriate)

- Some constraint on the allowable values. This could be implemented directly via a check constraint or indirectly via a referential integrity constraint or trigger

Within the database, we don't simply dictate that someone's salary must be numeric, we also create rules that define precisely what a salary means for our application. For example, we would specify that it is numeric, must be positive, cannot be more than x, has a precision of two decimal places, and so on. Databases that do not have these controlled definitions are typically criticized and the architect scorned by his peers.

However, the existence of similar poor practices in PL/SQL code tends not to attract the same sort of criticism. For example, it's common to see code along the lines of

```
declare
  v_salary   number;
  v_surname varchar2(2000);
```

Although this code assigns a suitable datatype to a variable, it does not achieve any of the controls that we would demand if these variables were database columns. Do we *really* expect that someone's salary could extend to over billions of dollars, or that their surname could be nearly a page long? Of course not. Clearly, the variables should be defined with an appropriate precision and scale. In fact, with PL/SQL, we can do even better, as we will now explore.

Using the %TYPE Attribute

The vast majority of PL/SQL variables bear a direct relationship to an underlying database column, and as most developers will be aware, the %TYPE attribute can be used to make this relationship explicit within the code. It is a pity that the manuals downplay the importance of %TYPE attribute.

> *"…If the database definition of (database column) changes, the datatype of (variable) changes accordingly at run time."—PL/SQL User's Guide*

This is true, but the manuals do not emphasize the fact that this helps make your PL/SQL future proof. In a perfect world, on day one of a production system, the data model and its implementation would satisfy both the current and future requirements of both the business and the users of that system. However, it is an unfortunate fact of life that the first enhancement requests start to filter in from the user community about 42 seconds after your system has gone live.

It is not too difficult to adapt your relational database design to reflect changing business or user requirements. This is one of the attractions of the relational model. With just a few keystrokes, we can insert, delete, or update metadata that defines how the system should operate, or we can perform more "traumatic" operations such as adding attributes (for example, new columns to existing tables) or adding entirely new relationships (new tables and new integrity rules) to the data model.

Why then do we see application upgrade projects running into months and years (and millions of your local currency)? Typically, it is because of all of the *coding* changes that result from a "simple" change to the data model. Using the %TYPE attribute protects you from such changes. Let's take a look at a classic example: the enlargement of a column's allowable length over time.

As a preliminary step, we re-create the standard demo tables in our own schema.

```
SQL> @$ORACLE_HOME/sqlplus/demo/demobld.sql
Building demonstration tables.  Please wait.
Demonstration table build is complete.
```

Next, we build two procedures that perform an identical purpose; they simply retrieve the highest salary from the EMP table. The second one uses the %TYPE attribute for the salary variable and the first one doesn't.

```
SQL> create or replace
  2  procedure WITHOUT_TYPE is
  3    v_salary number(7,2);
  4  begin
  5    select max(sal)
  6    into v_salary
  7    from emp;
  8  end;
  9  /

Procedure created.

SQL> create or replace
  2  procedure WITH_TYPE is
  3    v_salary emp.sal%type;
```

```
4  begin
5    select max(sal)
6    into v_salary
7    from emp;
8  end;
9  /
```

Procedure created.

Employee SMITH, who has EMPNO = 7369, has hit the proverbial salary gold mine, and is about to get a raise to one million dollars. To handle this, first we need to increase the size of the SAL column in the EMP table, before updating SMITH's details.

```
SQL> alter table EMP modify sal number(10,2);
```

Table altered.

```
SQL> update EMP set sal = 1000000
  2  where EMPNO = 7369;
```

1 row updated.

Let's try to obtain the highest salary within the organization using our WITH-OUT_TYPE procedure.

```
SQL> exec WITHOUT_TYPE;
BEGIN WITHOUT_TYPE; END;

*
ERROR at line 1:
ORA-06502: PL/SQL: numeric or value error: number precision too large
ORA-06512: at "WITHOUT_TYPE", line 4
ORA-06512: at line 1
```

As expected, the larger size of this new salary in the EMP table broke the procedure. It will need to be edited so that the V_SALARY variable can handle the larger possible values. However, if we had taken the care to use the %TYPE attribute, no such code revision would be necessary. We can see that our procedure WITH_TYPE has no such problems.

```
SQL> exec WITH_TYPE

PL/SQL procedure successfully completed.
```

Also, using %TYPE within a procedure immediately establishes the dependency mechanisms between the code and the underlying table, which assists in impact analysis. Used in conjunction with packages, as described in Chapter 2, "Package It All Up," you get the benefits of dependency tracking without the costs of excessive recompilation.

Although using %TYPE to insulate your code from column-level changes is good practice, what if a variable, or a number of common variables, do not have any relationship to a database table column. Use of the %TYPE attribute is still relevant in these cases. Consider the following snippet of code in which we have four variables, each defined as a 30-character string:

```
procedure MY_PROC(p_input varchar2) is
  v1 varchar2(30);
  v2 varchar2(30);
  v3 varchar2(30);
  v4 varchar2(30);
begin
  v1 := p_input;
  …
end;
```

This code may run smoothly in production until that one fateful day when someone tries to pass a package variable MY_PKG.GLOB_VAR to the procedure, in which the package has been defined as

```
package MY_PKG is
  glob_var varchar2(40);
end;

SQL> exec MY_PROC(my_pkg.glob_var);
BEGIN MY_PROC(my_pkg.glob_var); END;

*
ERROR at line 1:
ORA-06502: PL/SQL: numeric or value error: character string buffer too small
ORA-06512: at "MY_PROC", line 33
ORA-06512: at line 1
```

A quick look at the source code reveals that V1 is the problem variable. Some further analysis (that is, by looking at the source for package MY_PKG) reveals that the length of the variable, V1, needs to be increased to 40 characters in order to avoid this particular instance of the error. It then only takes a few seconds to fix the code and recompile the procedure. However, questions remain.

- Why was the possibility of error not identified before it happened? That is, if MY_PKG.GLOB_VAR is regularly being passed to MY_PROC, either the error has *always* been a possibility or the size of GLOB_VAR has been altered without a corresponding fix being applied to MY_PROC.

- Do variables V2, V3, and V4 also need to be increased in length?

- How do I stop this error from happening again?

We can use the %TYPE attribute to establish the linkages between variables within a PL/SQL application. The procedure MY_PROC can be re-coded directly referencing the MY_PKG.GLOB_VAR variable definition.

```
create or replace
procedure MY_PROC(p_input varchar2) is
  v1 my_pkg.glob_var%type;
  v2 my_pkg.glob_var%type;
  v3 my_pkg.glob_var%type;
  v4 my_pkg.glob_var%type;
begin
...
end;
```

This binds the type of the local variables to that of the package variable MY_PKG.GLOB_VAR. Now MY_PROC and MY_PKG share a dependency, which ensures that the problem will not recur. If we make a change to MY_PKG, increasing the size of GLOB_VAR to (for example) 60 characters

```
SQL> create or replace
  2   package MY_PKG is
  3     glob_var varchar2(60) := rpad('x',60);
  4   end;
  5   /

Package created.
```

the MY_PROC procedure will automatically adjust its variables to match, and no error will be encountered upon execution.

```
SQL> exec MY_PROC(my_pkg.glob_var);

PL/SQL procedure successfully completed.
```

Centralizing Datatype Control Using Packages

Revisiting the last example, there is no readily available information (other than the source code itself) that records the fact that MY_PROC depends on the type definition for MY_PKG.GLOB_VAR. Although you could probe the USER_DEPENDENCIES view, it would simply show that MY_PROC depends on the MY_PKG package, but not *precisely* why it does. To overcome this shortfall, an effective mechanism to centralize the control of datatypes in your PL/SQL programs is to use a package to define the types and subtypes that you will make available to all developers. The previous MY_PROC example could be reworked by defining a package whose purpose is to hold all types within an application. We will call this package APPLICATION_TYPES.

```
SQL> create or replace
  2  package APPLICATION_TYPES is
  3     subtype short_varchar2 is varchar2(40);
  4  end;
  5  /

Package created.
```

Our MY_PROC procedure and MY_PKG package no longer define their own types—they reference the types defined within the APPLICATION_TYPES package.

```
SQL> create or replace
  2  procedure MY_PROC(p_input application_types.short_varchar2) is
  3     v1 application_types.short_varchar2;
  4     v2 application_types.short_varchar2;
  5     v3 application_types.short_varchar2;
  6     v4 application_types.short_varchar2;
  7  begin
  8     null;
  9  end;
 10  /

Procedure created.

SQL> create or replace
  2  package MY_PKG is
  3     glob_var application_types.short_varchar2 := rpad('x',40);
  4  end;
  5  /

Package created.
```

If we need to alter what is meant by a SHORT_VARCHAR2, a change to the definition within package APPLICATION_TYPES will ripple through to all other modules. However, be careful when implementing this level of control because *every* PL/SQL module will probably be dependent on this package. If your application development cycle consists of adding and changing type definitions on an ad hoc basis, you return the dependency problems described in Chapter 2 when addressing global variables. If you have a disciplined and well-defined application development environment, this may be an option you want to explore.

Avoiding Implicit Datatype Conversion

There are also performance benefits to be had by ensuring that all appropriate variables are strongly typed. The PL/SQL engine is very hospitable to developers in terms of its handling of datatypes (a bad thing in my opinion). Try to assign a string to a numeric variable, and Oracle will silently attempt to convert it to a number and complete the assignment. Throw a date at a VARCHAR2 variable and it is automatically converted to a string.

Besides the fact that this is not such a good programming practice, datatype conversions have an overhead that is measurable. Consider an example of what is probably the most commonly observed lazy practice: conversion of strings to dates. Using the before-and-after timing facilities via DBMS_UTILITY.GET_TIME, we can build a procedure that will time how long it takes to perform 1,000,000 datatype conversions.

```
SQL> create or replace
  2  procedure data_type_test is
  3    x date;
  4    y varchar2(12) := '01-MAR-03';
  5    t number := dbms_utility.get_time;
  6  begin
  7    for i in 1 .. 1000000 loop
  8      x := y;  -- implicit char to date
  9    end loop;
 10    dbms_output.put_line((dbms_utility.get_time-t)||'cs');
 11  end;
 12  /

Procedure created.
```

We enable server output, and then run the benchmark.

```
SQL> set serverout on
SQL> exec data_type_test
771cs (In fact this was averaged over 5 executions)
```

This is an impressive result. It means that the lowly laptop on which we are running this test can squeeze out some 140,000 datatype conversions per second. Obviously some of the 7.7 seconds of elapsed time was consumed by the PL/SQL code itself and not the datatype conversion. What proportion of the 7.7 seconds is attributable to datatype conversion? The next test will tell us. We recreate the procedure to perform the identical workload, but no datatype conversions are required because the datatypes align.

```
SQL> create or replace
  2  procedure data_type_test is
  3    x date;
  4    y x%type := to_date('01-MAR-03');
  5    t number := dbms_utility.get_time;
  6  begin
  7    for i in 1 .. 1000000 loop
  8      x := y;
  9    end loop;
 10    dbms_output.put_line((dbms_utility.get_time-t)||'cs');
 11  end;
 12  /

Procedure created.
```

And then we run this more correct version.

```
SQL> exec data_type_test
31cs   (In fact this was averaged over 5 executions)
```

Wow! 96 percent of the execution time was consumed solely to perform datatype conversion. Datatype conversion, although very fast, is still expensive in terms of CPU resources.

An Aside on Loop Counter Variables

One interesting result that came out of testing datatype conversions was the apparent error in the PL/SQL manuals about loop iteration variables. The manual states that the loop counter variable (shown as "i" in the following examples) is of type INTEGER. We are assigning the variable I to a variable X, which is also defined as INTEGER, so if we are to believe the manual, the following procedure is optimal and no data conversion should be necessary:

```
SQL> create or replace
  2  procedure num_test_as_integer is
```

```
 3     x integer;
 4     t number := dbms_utility.get_time;
 5   begin
 6     for i in 1 .. 10000000 loop
 7       x := i;
 8     end loop;
 9     dbms_output.put_line((dbms_utility.get_time-t)||'cs');
10   end;
11   /
```

Procedure created.

```
SQL> exec num_test_as_integer
```
500cs (averaged over 5 executions)

Let's now repeat the test, but this time, the variable X will be defined as the PLS_INTEGER datatype.

```
SQL> create or replace
  2   procedure num_test_as_pls is
  3     x pls_integer;
  4     t number := dbms_utility.get_time;
  5   begin
  6     for i in 1 .. 10000000 loop
  7       x := i;
  8     end loop;
  9     dbms_output.put_line((dbms_utility.get_time-t)||'cs');
 10   end;
 11   /
```

Procedure created.

If this procedure runs faster than the previous one, there is a high probability that the loop iteration variable is in fact of type PLS_INTEGER:

```
SQL> exec num_test_as_pls
```
319cs (averaged over 5 executions)

At this point, we suspect that loop variables are probably of type PLS_INTEGER. We can provide more concrete evidence by altering the loop counter to range beyond the acceptable limits for the PLS_INTEGER datatype.

```
SQL> begin
  2     for i in power(2,31) .. power(2,31)+10 loop
```

```
   3        null;
   4      end loop;
   5    end;
   6    /
begin
*
ERROR at line 1:
ORA-01426: numeric overflow
ORA-06512: at line 2
```

Hence we can be confident that the loop counter is a PLS_INTEGER and not an INTEGER datatype, as indicated by the manuals.

From Fields to Rows—Using %ROWTYPE

Disciplined usage of the %TYPE attribute in your PL/SQL code ensures that field (or column) changes within the database will be automatically catered to within your PL/SQL applications. What if we add or remove entire columns from a table? Any PL/SQL programs that fetch or manipulate entire rows of information may start to fail. Another powerful feature of PL/SQL is the ability to insulate a program from these even more significant database changes by defining variables using the %ROWTYPE attribute. Consider the following SQL code snippet:

```
select *
into var1, var2, ..., varN
from table
where <some criteria>
```

We could use the %TYPE attribute for each of the variables VAR1, VAR2, and so on, to insulate us from datatype changes in the table columns, but what if the table undergoes some structural modification, such as the addition or removal of a column? The code, executed in virtually any language except PL/SQL, will definitely break.

PL/SQL offers the %ROWTYPE variable attribute as a simple solution to this problem. It immediately insulates a PL/SQL program from a myriad of database changes. Consider a procedure, WITH_ROWTYPE, which retrieves a row from a simple table T.

```
SQL> create table T (
   2    c1 number,
   3    c2 number );

Table created.
```

```
SQL> insert into T values (1,2);

1 row created.

SQL> create or replace
  2   procedure WITH_ROWTYPE is
  3     r   T%ROWTYPE;
  4   begin
  5     select *
  6     into   r
  7     from   T
  8     where  rownum = 1;
  9   end;
 10   /

Procedure created.
```

The variable, R, is referred to as a **record**, whereby each field in the record matches that of the underlying table. First, let's make sure that our procedure works based on the current definition of table T.

```
SQL> exec WITH_ROWTYPE

PL/SQL procedure successfully completed.
```

Let's see what happens when we start altering the table definition.

```
SQL> alter table T add c3 number;

Table altered.

SQL> exec WITH_ROWTYPE;

PL/SQL procedure successfully completed.
```

Our procedure still works. Although it is true that there are possibly some code changes that still might be required from a functionality perspective, at least it has not created an error in the application. In version 9, columns can even be renamed but our procedure will still remain valid.

```
SQL> alter table T rename column C1 to C01;

Table altered.
```

```
SQL> exec WITH_ROWTYPE;

PL/SQL procedure successfully completed.
```

It keeps working, even after an event as drastic as dropping a column.

```
SQL> alter table T drop column C2;

Table altered.

SQL> exec WITH_ROWTYPE;

PL/SQL procedure successfully completed.
```

Use of %ROWTYPE makes our PL/SQL programs very robust. Not even database views exhibit such powerful resilience. Let's drop and re-create the T table, and then define a view V based on this table.

```
SQL> drop table T;

Table dropped.

SQL> create table T (
  2    c1 number,
  3    c2 number);

Table created.

SQL> create or replace
  2  view V as select * from T;

View created.
```

Now we add a column to the underlying table T.

```
SQL> alter table T add c3 number;

Table altered.
```

Adding a column to the underlying table invalidates the view and forces its recompilation.

```
SQL> alter view V compile;

View altered.
```

Now let's look at our view and table.

```
SQL> desc V
 Name                                 Null?    Type
 ----------------------------------- -------- -------------
 C1                                            NUMBER
 C2                                            NUMBER


SQL> desc T
 Name                                 Null?    Type
 ----------------------------------- -------- -------------
 C1                                            NUMBER
 C2                                            NUMBER
 C3                                            NUMBER
```

The new column is simply missing when the view is recompiled. The reason for this is that a view, defined as SELECT * FROM TABLE, is stored in the database at view creation time as:

```
select col1, col2, …, colN from table
```

The view does not pick up the new column because the view text is not stored as SELECT * in the database. Because of this, you probably should never use SELECT * view definitions. Consider the possible consequences if you were to drop the underlying table and re-create it with the same column names but in a different sequence.

Of course, cynical readers may point out that some of the benefits of using %ROWTYPE variables are diluted as soon as you start to make references to the individual fields within the variable. For example, if we extend our earlier WITH_ROWTYPE procedure to transfer the results from the T table to another table

```
SQL> drop table T;

Table dropped.

SQL> create table T (
  2      c1 number,
  3      c2 number );

Table created.
```

```
SQL> insert into T values (1,2);

1 row created.

SQL> create table T1 as select * from T;

Table created.

SQL> create or replace
  2  procedure WITH_ROWTYPE is
  3    r  T%ROWTYPE;
  4  begin
  5    select *
  6    into   r
  7    from   T
  8    where  rownum = 1;
  9
 10    insert into T1
 11    values (r.c1, r.c2);
 12  end;
 13  /

SQL> exec WITH_ROWTYPE

PL/SQL procedure successfully completed.
```

No problems there, but now we have lost the insulation from changes to the underlying tables because of the references to the individual items within the %ROWTYPE variable. If we add a column to the table T, the procedure will fail on the INSERT statement, as the following sequence demonstrates:

```
SQL> alter table T add c3 number;

Table altered.

SQL> alter table T1 add c3 number;

Table altered.

SQL> exec WITH_ROWTYPE
BEGIN WITH_ROWTYPE; END;

    *
```

```
ERROR at line 1:
ORA-06550: line 1, column 7:
PLS-00905: object WITH_ROWTYPE is invalid
ORA-06550: line 1, column 7:
PL/SQL: Statement ignored
```

For versions 7 and 8 of Oracle, the only solution is to explicitly reference the table columns in the INSERT clause. This stops the procedure from failing, but a possibly worse scenario results: if you added a column to a table, the procedure will silently omit adding values for it during insert operations. However, the new record-based DML features, available in version 9.2 onward, offer an excellent solution to all of these issues.

Record-Based DML Features

Although it has always been possible in PL/SQL to SELECT a row into a %ROWTYPE variable, it is now also possible to use a %ROWTYPE variable within INSERT and UPDATE statements. We can recode the WITH_ROWTYPE procedure to use the new record-based DML for the INSERT statement. (We re-created and repopulated the tables T and T1 as per the previous example.)

```
SQL> create or replace
  2  procedure WITH_ROWTYPE is
  3    r  T%ROWTYPE;
  4  begin
  5    select *
  6    into   r
  7    from   T
  8    where  rownum = 1;
  9
 10    insert into T1
 11    values r;
 12  end;
 13  /

Procedure created.
```

Let's see what happens when a column is added to table T and a corresponding column is added to table T1.

```
SQL> alter table T add c5 number;

Table altered.
```

```
SQL> alter table T1 add c5 number;
```

```
Table altered.
```

The procedure still works, without modification.

```
SQL> exec WITH_ROWTYPE
```

```
PL/SQL procedure successfully completed.
```

Altering the procedure slightly, we can demonstrate record-based DML for an UPDATE statement. An entire record can be updated without referencing any of the individual fields.

```
SQL> create or replace
  2  procedure WITH_ROWTYPE is
  3    r  T%ROWTYPE;
  4  begin
  5    select *
  6    into   r
  7    from   T
  8    where  rownum = 1;
  9
 10    update T1
 11    set row = r
 12    where rownum = 1;
 13  end;
 14  /
```

```
Procedure created.
```

There is of course no equivalent record-based DML for a DELETE statement because a DELETE always removes the entire record anyway.

> **NOTE** The flexibility of record-based DML comes at a cost. In the next chapter, we will discuss some of the issues to be aware of when using record-based DML.

From Records to Objects

Log on to most databases and run SELECT * FROM DBA_TYPES and you will rarely see any types beside those that are used by the predelivered schemas within the database (such as those in use for the Spatial and Text options). The moment the familiar terms "columns" and "rows" are replaced with "collections," "varrays," and the like, Oracle developers often revert to the attitude of "I'm not interested—I'm not an object-oriented person."

Since object features first appeared in version 8.0, there has been general aversion to using them, possibly due to the FUD factor (fear, uncertainty, doubt) or maybe due to the lack of software tools that could successfully integrate with them. SQL*Plus works fine with objects but not too many applications are built in SQL*Plus nowadays! A presenter at the OracleWorld2002 conference in San Francisco eloquently described the general feeling toward objects: "Is anyone in this audience daft and stupid enough to be using objects in the database?"

The motivation for such comments is that Oracle is first-and-foremost a relational database, and a little investigation reveals that the storage of objects is done in a relational manner anyway. For example, let's create an object type, and then create a table that contains a column with that object as a datatype.

```
SQL> create or replace  type STOLEN_ITEMS as object (
  2      firstname       varchar2(30),
  3      surname         varchar2(30),
  4      date_of_birth   date,
  5      incident_date   date,
  6      item_count      number(4),
  7      items_retrieved varchar2(1)
  8  )
  9  /

Type created.

SQL> create table CRIMES (
  2      person_id number(10),
  3      crime_details stolen_items );

Table created.
```

What has Oracle done in the background to allow the storage of this datatype? If we query the DBA_TAB_COLUMNS view, we see only the column names used in the table creation statement, but let's take a closer look at a *definition* of the DBA_TAB_COLUMNS view.

```
SQL> set long 50000
SQL> select text
  2  from dba_views
  3  where view_name = 'DBA_TAB_COLUMNS'
  4  /


TEXT
-------------------------------------------------------------------------
select OWNER, TABLE_NAME,
       COLUMN_NAME, DATA_TYPE, DATA_TYPE_MOD, DATA_TYPE_OWNER,
       DATA_LENGTH, DATA_PRECISION, DATA_SCALE, NULLABLE, COLUMN_ID,
       DEFAULT_LENGTH, DATA_DEFAULT, NUM_DISTINCT, LOW_VALUE, HIGH_VALUE,
       DENSITY, NUM_NULLS, NUM_BUCKETS, LAST_ANALYZED, SAMPLE_SIZE,
       CHARACTER_SET_NAME, CHAR_COL_DECL_LENGTH,
       GLOBAL_STATS, USER_STATS, AVG_COL_LEN, CHAR_LENGTH, CHAR_USED,
       V80_FMT_IMAGE, DATA_UPGRADED
  from DBA_TAB_COLS
 where HIDDEN_COLUMN = 'NO'
```

DBA_TAB_COLUMNS simply references DBA_TAB_COLS for columns that are not hidden. And that is the key here. Probing the DBA_TAB_COLS for all columns, not just those that are not hidden, reveals how Oracle has in fact created the table behind the scenes.

```
SQL> select column_name, hidden_column, data_type
  2  from DBA_TAB_COLS
  3  where table_name = 'CRIMES'
  4  /


COLUMN_NAME                      HID  DATA_TYPE
------------------------------   ---  -------------
PERSON_ID                        NO   NUMBER
CRIME_DETAILS                    NO   STOLEN_ITEMS
SYS_NC00003$                     YES  VARCHAR2
SYS_NC00004$                     YES  VARCHAR2
SYS_NC00005$                     YES  DATE
SYS_NC00006$                     YES  DATE
SYS_NC00007$                     YES  NUMBER
SYS_NC00008$                     YES  VARCHAR2
```

Our object datatype has been expanded out into its component columns to create a conventional relational structure. Because the storage of objects is implemented with relational structures anyway, proponents of a purely relational model ask, "Why don't we just do it ourselves and have full control over the implementation?"

I readily confess that until recently, I was not convinced of the advantages of using an Oracle database to store objects. This is possibly because my programming and database background commenced before objects became the "next big thing." Although I have no doubts about the *theoretical* benefits of an object-oriented approach to both coding and the underlying data structures, the vast majority of software tools in the marketplace still only work effectively on relational data, and the fact remains that most end-users still view their data in a relational way. However, with version 9.2 and 10*g*, the implementation of objects is closer to what an object-oriented purist may desire: subtypes that can inherit methods and attributes from their parent types, evolution of type definitions over time, user control over constructor methods, and introduction of abstract types. All this suggests that objects are here for the long haul.

Object Types

Whatever your point of view on storing objects in an Oracle database, I need to stress the important distinction between objects *stored* in the database and object types *defined* in the database. An object type *describes* how an object will be defined, whereas as object is an actual *instantiation* of an object type.

Even if you never store objects in the database, object types provide the ability to represent more structured datatypes within PL/SQL programs, as well as being a vital part of the bulk collection facilities, which will be described shortly. Object types add to the power and flexibility of the PL/SQL language, thus they should be a vital part of any PL/SQL developers skill set.

The various object types available within Oracle can be broadly categorized into two areas.

- **Records**: Any logical grouping of scalar variables. This includes the %ROW-TYPE variables described earlier in this chapter, records with explicitly defined fields using the RECORD syntax in PL/SQL, and records with explicitly defined fields using the CREATE TYPE AS OBJECT syntax in SQL.

- **Collections**: Any ordered list of items. An item can be anything from a simple scalar variable to a complex object (including other collections).

It is the collections category of objects that is relevant to the remainder of this chapter, in terms of their importance in storing and processing SQL result-sets within PL/SQL variables. It is not my intention to simply rehash the syntax for using collections from the standard documentation—the best way to demonstrate the power of collections within PL/SQL is to step through a complete example and prove how effective they can be.

Extending Runstats with Collections

In this section, we will build an extension of the RUNSTATS[1] utility, a tool originally built by Tom Kyte, the man behind the acclaimed http://asktom.oracle.com Web site. We have already seen numerous examples comparing the execution times between two PL/SQL alternatives, but Tom's tool extends this to show the difference in the cost of executing two different code solutions in terms of the elapsed time, session level statistics, and latching differences.

Such a tool is naturally vital when benchmarking two different solutions to the same problem. Once again, we come back to our familiar mantra of demonstrability, that is, *proving* that one solution is better than another. Although more often than not, elapsed time is the critical factor in deciding the appropriateness of a solution, using the RUNSTATS tool yields other important information about a coding strategy such as the number of calls made to the database to achieve the result and the amount of serialization that the code requires—both of which may be more important than response time if the solution is destined for a highly concurrent environment.

Set up and usage of the original version of RUNSTATS is described in the "Setting Up" section at the start of this book, but concisely, the usage is to first take an initial snapshot of various session and system level statistics.

```
SQL> exec runstats_pkg.rs_start;
```

Next we run our first possible code solution. We then take another snapshot of the same statistics.

```
SQL> exec runstats_pkg.rs_middle;
```

Next, we run our alternative code solution. We take a final snapshot, which calculates and presents a comparison of the two approaches tested.

```
SQL> exec runstats_pkg.rs_stop;
```

The output of the standard RUNSTATS routine is in two sections.

```
Total Elapsed Time
Run1 ran in 123 hsecs
Run2 ran in 456 hsecs
run 1 ran in 26.9% of the time
```

---

1. You can find the runstats utility at http://asktom.oracle.com/~tkyte.

```
Latching / Statistical differences
                                Run1      Run2       Diff
LATCH.shared pool             12,543    39,543     27,000
LATCH.library cache           25,787    49,023     23,236
...
STAT...db block gets           4,123     8,432      4,309
STAT...consistent gets       123,432   354,392    230,960
STAT...physical reads          1,453     4,243      2,790
...
```

A very impressive tool! We get an easy-to-read tabular display of the cost of each tested piece of code, in terms of various system statistics and latching overhead. Although the tool covers the majority of testing scenarios that developers encounter, I wanted to extend the tool for so it could

- Test more than two different coding solutions.

- Have more flexibility in the format of the output so I could treat the output like a SQL result set, and thus have different ordering options or only show rows that exhibit certain criteria.

- Use collections rather than database tables to store the snapshot of the statistics. In this manner, the tool could be easily installed and used on various sites without requiring a lot of DBA intervention.

I will step through my implementation and then use it to demonstrate how collections can effectively extend the power of PL/SQL.

Customizing Runstats

First, we create a view that captures a snapshot of the session statistics and latch details (this is no different from Tom's original version). Whichever account you use to create this view on your own system, you will need SELECT access on the V$STATNAME, V$MYSTAT, V$LATCH, and V$TIMER performance views.

```
SQL> create or replace view stats
  2   as select 'S:' || a.name name, b.value
  3          from v$statname a, v$mystat b
  4         where a.statistic# = b.statistic#
  5         union all
  6         select 'L:' || name,  gets
  7          from v$latch
  8         union all
  9         select 'E:Elapsed', hsecs from v$timer;

View created.
```

The rows denoted by the prefix S: contain statistical information for this particular session. Rows denoted by the prefix L: are for database-wide latching activity (unfortunately, there are no session-level latching statistics), and the E: row is a marker to a current point in time. If we select from the view STATS, we get a point-in-time view of the session-level statistics and system-wide latching information.

```
SQL> select * from stats;

NAME                             VALUE
-----------------------------    -------
S:logons cumulative                  1
S:logons current                     1
S:opened cursors cumulative        359
...
L:latch wait list                    0
L:event range base latch             0
L:post/wait queue                   12
...
E:Elapsed                       453411

489 rows selected.
```

Note that, like Statspack, all these figures are taken at a point in time, so it is only the *difference* between multiple snapshots from the STATS view that makes sense for analysis.

In our version of RUNSTATS, rather than inserting this snapshot into a database table, we will be storing it within a collection. Each time this view is queried, we need to associate a snapshot ID with the results so that one resultset can be distinguished from another. Two object types are required to reflect that structure in a PL/SQL datatype. The first, STATS_LINE, represents a single line of output from the STATS view.

```
SQL> create or replace type stats_line as object
  2  ( snapid number(10),
  3      name varchar2(66),
  4      value int );
  5  /

Type created.
```

The NAME and VALUE columns will come from the STATS view, and the SNAPID will distinguish between different snapshots from that view. The second type is a collection that allows for the entire view resultset to be stored within a single object.

```
SQL> create or replace type stats_array as
  2   table of stats_line;
  3   /
```

Type created.

Hence, we can now take a snapshot of the STATS view and store it within a single variable, with the following code:

```
declare
  v_snap_id number := 0;
  s stats_array := stats_array();
begin
  v_snapid := v_snapid + 1;
  for i in ( select * from stats) loop
    s.extend;
    s(s.count) := stats_line(v_snapid, i.name,i.value );
  end loop;
end;
```

We will return to this PL/SQL code shortly when we place it within our complete RUNSTATS package.

As per the original RUNSTATS version, once several snapshots have been taken, we need to process them and be able to send the output back to the caller. For example, if we are comparing three different coding strategies, we will be taking a snapshot from the STATS view four times (once at the start, and once after each execution), so the output we want to see is

Name	Run1	Run2	Diff2	Pct2	Run3	Diff3	Pct3
E:Elapsed	100	105	5	5%	120	20	20%
S:consistent gets	200	230	30	15%	250	50	25%
etc							

where DIFF2 would be the difference between RUN1 and RUN2, DIFF3 is the difference between RUN1 and RUN3, and so forth. This makes it simple to assess which code run is optimal. But we would also like to be able to probe the report as though it were an SQL resultset so we can ask more sophisticated questions like "Which stats had a percentage difference between RUN3 and RUN1 of more than 20%?"

In the same way that we defined object types to capture the results of a query to the STATS view, we need to define object types to be able to report the output to the calling environment. First, we'll create an object type to hold a single line of the previous output.

```
SQL> create or replace
  2  type run_stats_line as object (
  3      tag varchar2(66),
  4      run1  int,
  5      run2  int,
  6      diff2 int,
  7      pct2  int,
  8      run3  int,
  9      diff3 int,
 10      pct3  int,
 11      run4  int,
 12      diff4 int,
 13      pct4  int,
 14      run5  int,
 15      diff5 int,
 16      pct5  int,
 17      run6  int,
 18      diff6 int,
 19      pct6  int);
 20  /

Type created.
```

We assume no more than six separate coding tests, but it would be simple to extend this to meet your specific requirements. In fact, if you are a developer who experiments with more than six different solutions to a problem, please come work for me!

Next, we need an object type to hold an array of output lines.

```
SQL> create or replace type run_stats_output
  2  as table of run_stats_line;
  3  /

Type created.
```

And now it's just a matter of bringing these types together with some code to expose the facility to the public.

RS Package Specification

Our new version of RUNSTATS is called RS.

```
SQL> create or replace package rs as
  2        procedure snap(reset boolean default false);
  3        function display return run_stats_output ;
  4        function the_stats return stats_array;
  5        s stats_array := stats_array();
  6        v_snapid integer := 0;
  7   end;
  8   /
```

```
Package created.
```

Let's take a look at the content of the package specification in more detail.

s stats_array := stats_array();

This defines an empty but initialized array to contain our snapshots. The variable does not need to be part of the package spec (it could be private within the package body), but we left it in the spec so a curious developer could easily look up specific values within the array.

```
v_snapid integer := 0;
```

The variable simply holds a count of the number of snapshots taken.

```
procedure snap
```

This procedure will query the STATS view and store it within a STATS_ARRAY object. I included a reset Boolean variable so that we can use the same procedure to start a fresh set of snapshots. Thus, typical usage of the procedure would be

```
snap(true);    -- to start a fresh set of snapshots
<benchmark test 1>
snap;
<benchmark test 2>
snap;
etc
```

```
function display return run_stats_output
```

This will process the array of snapshots taken and cycle through the data to produce the output just described. Obviously, this routine does the "muscle work" to translate the raw data into a meaningful comparison of the coding tests for which we have taken snapshots. The benefit of returning the output as a collection is that any function that returns a collection can be queried via standard SQL using the TABLE() operator. Such functions are (naturally enough) called table functions.

```
function the_stats return stats_array;
```

This function was included for completeness. It allows a developer to display the raw data for all of the snapshots taken.

RS Package Body

The package body is where all the work takes place. Let's take a look at each major component within the source code.

The following code allows us to take a snapshot of the STATS view and store it within a single variable:

```
SQL> create or replace package body rs as
  2
  3   procedure snap(reset boolean default false) is
  4   begin
  5     if reset then
  6       s := stats_array();
  7       v_snapid := 0;
  8     end if;
  9     v_snapid := v_snapid + 1;
 10     for i in ( select * from stats) loop
 11       s.extend;
 12       s(s.count) := stats_line(v_snapid, i.name,i.value );
 13     end loop;
 14   end;
```

This is basically the same as the code presented earlier, but we added the RESET parameter to allow for a new set of snapshots to be built. For each row in the STATS view, we extend the S array and associate the snapshot ID with the name, value pairs.

> **NOTE** This code could be made more efficient using the bulk facilities described later in this section. Because we haven't covered them in the text yet, we don't use them here.

The two tables driving this query demonstrate how easy it is to treat PL/SQL object types as relational structures.

```
15
16  function display return run_stats_output is
17    output run_stats_line :=
18      run_stats_line(null,
19            null,null,null,null,
20            null,null,null,null,
21            null,null,null,null,
22            null,null,null,null);
23    ret run_stats_output := run_stats_output();
24    base_val number;
25  begin
26    for i in ( select hi.snapid, lo.name, lo.value, hi.value-lo.value amt
27                from ( select * from table(the_stats) ) lo,
28                     ( select * from table(the_stats) ) hi
29                where lo.name = hi.name
30                and lo.snapid = hi.snapid -1
31                order by 2,1) loop
```

The TABLE() construct translates the object collection into a SQL result set.

Recall that each snapshot does not give any details about a coding test; only the *difference* between one snapshot and the subsequent one is useful. The difference (the AMT column) between one snapshot and the previous one is shown by the output from the query in the cursor FOR loop. For example, if we take the SQL from the source code and run it standalone, we can see the following output is from two coding tests (that is, three snapshots taken).

```
SQL> select hi.snapid, lo.name, hi.value-lo.value amt
  2                from ( select * from table(rs.the_stats) ) lo,
  3                     ( select * from table(rs.the_stats) ) hi
  4                where lo.name = hi.name
  5                and lo.snapid = hi.snapid -1
  6                order by 2,1
  7  /

    SNAPID NAME                                       AMT
---------- ------------------------------     ----------
         2 E:Elapsed                                2672
         3 E:Elapsed                                1291
         2 L:cache buffers chains                  49967
         3 L:cache buffers chains                  57323
         2 L:cache buffers lru chain               16555
         3 L:cache buffers lru chain                 869
```

The first row in the output (with `SNAPID=2`) represents the difference between snapshot 1 and snapshot 2, that is, the statistics and elapsed time for the first coding test (which is bounded by snapshots 1 and 2). The second row (with `SNAPID=3`) represents the difference between snapshots 2 and 3, that is, the second coding test, and so forth.

The output from the cursor-loop also explains how the remainder of the processing works. Each time we encounter a row where the `SNAPID` is 2, it is time to add a new row in the output resultset (except in the case of the very first row).

```
32      case i.snapid
33      when 2 then
34          if output.tag is not null then
35            ret.extend;
36            ret(ret.count) := output;
37          end if;
38          base_val := i.amt;
39          output.tag := i.name;
40          output.run1 := i.amt;
```

For all of the rows where `SNAPID` is greater than 2, we add the appropriate values to the current line of output. In this way, we incrementally fill a line for output.

```
41      when 3 then
42          output.run2 := i.amt;
43          output.diff2 := i.amt - base_val;
44          output.pct2 := i.amt / greatest(base_val,1) * 100;
45      when 4 then
46          output.run3 := i.amt;
47          output.diff3 := i.amt - base_val;
48          output.pct3 := i.amt / greatest(base_val,1) * 100;
49      when 5 then
50          output.run4 := i.amt;
51          output.diff4 := i.amt - base_val;
52          output.pct4 := i.amt / greatest(base_val,1) * 100;
53      when 6 then
54          output.run5 := i.amt;
55          output.diff5 := i.amt - base_val;
56          output.pct5 := i.amt / greatest(base_val,1) * 100;
57      when 7 then
58          output.run6 := i.amt;
59          output.diff6 := i.amt - base_val;
60          output.pct6 := i.amt / greatest(base_val,1) * 100;
61        end case;
62      end loop;
```

When we have finally looped through all the rows from all the snapshots, we send back RET, which is the array of output lines.

```
63     ret.extend;
64     ret(ret.count) := output;
65     return ret;
66  end;
67
68  function the_stats return stats_array is
69  begin
70     return s;
71  end;
72
73  end;
74  /
```

Package body created.

> **NOTE**   This package body will not compile under 8*i* due to usage of the CASE operator. You will need to convert this to a standard set of IF-THEN-ELSE statements for versions of Oracle earlier than version 9.

We can now query the DISPLAY function using the TABLE() operator in the same way that was done with the THE_STATS function from within the package.

To demonstrate our new package RS, we will revisit our example from Chapter 1 in which we compared the execution times of a PL/SQL program that used PL/SQL tables to process EMP and DEPT records (REPORT_SAL_ADJUSTMENT3) and one that used pure SQL to achieve the same thing (REPORT_SAL_ADJUSTMENT4).

We'll now conduct a more thorough investigation of the performance of these two packages, using the RS package.

```
SQL> exec rs.snap(true);

PL/SQL procedure successfully completed.

SQL> exec REPORT_SAL_ADJUSTMENT3    -- test code #1

PL/SQL procedure successfully completed.

SQL> exec rs.snap
```

```
PL/SQL procedure successfully completed.

SQL> exec REPORT_SAL_ADJUSTMENT4     -- test code #2

PL/SQL procedure successfully completed.

SQL> exec rs.snap

PL/SQL procedure successfully completed.
```

Because we are retrieving the output with standard SQL, the output can be manipulated in any desired fashion with the conventional WHERE clause and ORDER BY predicates and so on. For example, we can display only those results in which the percentage difference between the two tests (PCT2) is greater than zero.

```
SQL> select tag, run1, run2, diff2, pct2
  2  from table(rs.display)
  3  where run1 > 0
  4  and pct2 > 0
  5  order by run1
  6  /
```

TAG	RUN1	RUN2	DIFF2	PCT2
L:shared pool	37	36	-1	97
L:library cache	45	43	-2	96
L:SQL memory manager workarea	69	4	-65	6
S:recursive cpu usage	133	100	-33	75
S:CPU used by this session	229	101	-128	44
S:CPU used when call started	229	101	-128	44
E:Elapsed	234	147	-87	63
S:bytes sent via SQL*Net to cl	242	242	0	100
S:bytes received via SQL*Net f	351	351	0	100
S:buffer is not pinned count	50253	253	-50000	1
S:no work - consistent read ge	50253	253	-50000	1
S:table scan blocks gotten	50253	253	-50000	1
S:consistent gets	50261	258	-50003	1
S:session logical reads	50261	264	-49997	1
S:recursive calls	50994	491	-50503	1
S:sorts (rows)	52079	52079	0	100
S:table scan rows gotten	100500	50500	-50000	50
L:cache buffers chains	100522	913	-99609	1

Although in Chapter 1 we knew the pure SQL solution was simpler to code and performed better from a purely elapsed time basis (the E: row in the output above), using the RS package yields even more demonstrability. We can see that the improved performance was likely due to a reduction in logical I/O, which also yielded a reduction in cache buffer chains latching—vital for increased concurrency.

To wrap up, the RUNSTATS utility and the enhanced version we created as package RS demonstrate the ease with which PL/SQL object types can be used to represent complicated data structures, and just as importantly, they can easily be translated for use within a SQL perspective.

The Motivation for Collections in PL/SQL

The ability to reference and manipulate a complex structure as a single variable is a nice feature of object types. However, you may have noticed that in the RUN-STATS example, the process for storing the results of the query to the STATS view in the STATS_ARRAY collection was still done on a row-by-row basis. This is logically equivalent to the problems involved with fields and records, when in some instances we were forced to reference individual field items. It would be nice to retain a level of abstraction at the collection level. In other words, because collections are intended to represent a *set* of rows as a single entity, it would be nice to be able to populate a collection with a set rather than iterating through the individual elements of that set.

Our primary motivation for the use of collections is that it encourages the developer to think more in terms of sets, rather than rows. Although there is no *functional* reason that prohibits developers from processing result sets one row at a time, from an efficiency and performance perspective, it is generally bad news. Putting aside objects for a moment, consider the following simple demonstration in SQL*Plus, which shows the performance detriment by retrieving a resultset one row at a time[2]. We will compare the elapsed time when fetching a single row at a time from our large SRC table, versus that achieved when fetching in batches of 500 rows.

```
SQL> set autotrace traceonly statistics
SQL> set arraysize 1
SQL> set timing on
SQL> select * from SRC;

142304 rows selected.
```

---

2. Thanks to Jonathan Lewis for providing this demonstration.

```
Elapsed: 00:00:35.02

Statistics
----------------------------------------------------------
          0   recursive calls
          0   db block gets
      83293   consistent gets
      16551   physical reads
          0   redo size
   63311705   bytes sent via SQL*Net to client
     783040   bytes received via SQL*Net from client
      71153   SQL*Net roundtrips to/from client
          0   sorts (memory)
          0   sorts (disk)
     142304   rows processed

SQL> set arraysize 500
SQL> select * from SRC;

142304 rows selected.

Elapsed: 00:00:24.02

Statistics
----------------------------------------------------------
          0   recursive calls
          0   db block gets
      16830   consistent gets
      14758   physical reads
          0   redo size
   54736825   bytes sent via SQL*Net to client
       3623   bytes received via SQL*Net from client
        286   SQL*Net roundtrips to/from client
          0   sorts (memory)
          0   sorts (disk)
     142304   rows processed
```

Two identical queries against the same table, yet the first one took a lot longer and did more physical and logical IO. When the ARRAYSIZE is one, we are in effect telling the database to

- Register our interest in the appropriate database block

- Find the first row in that block that matches our query criteria

- Remove our interest in the block because we have filled the array of rows (in other words, one row) that the client program has requested

- Return the row data to the client program (SQL*Plus)

As soon as our SQL*Plus program wants to fetch the second row, the same process must be repeated. Of course, the likelihood of the block already being present in the buffer cache is high, but all the latching overhead of ensuring the block's presence in the buffer cache and then registering our interest in it so that it is not modified or removed from the cache during the short duration in which we retrieve the appropriate row is still present.

> **NOTE** Even when the ARRAYSIZE is explicitly set to 1, effectively the database uses an ARRAYSIZE of 2 due to the pre-fetching optimization, already discussed in Chapter 3, regarding the performance of implicit cursors.

When the ARRAYSIZE is 500, we have given the database better information as to what our requirement is (that is, "we want lots of rows"). Now we are asking the database to

1. Retrieve the appropriate database block from disk (or the buffer cache).

2. Find the first row in that block.

3. *Maintain* our interest in the block until either:

    - We have filled our array of data.

    - We have scanned every row in the block.

4. In the latter case, we move on to the next block and repeat until the array has been filled.

5. Return the array of row data to the client program (SQL*Plus).

PL/SQL applications are no different from SQL*Plus. If you want to retrieve *n* rows, you incur a performance cost if you retrieve these rows one at a time. Unfortunately, with early versions of PL/SQL this was the only option you had. Well, that is not quite accurate. Since version 7.2, it has been possible to use array processing with results in PL/SQL, but the functionality was only possible with the use of DBMS_SQL. For example, to replicate the previous SQL*Plus array processing example using DBMS_SQL, we had to produce some pretty elaborate code.

```
SQL> create or replace
  2  procedure ARRAY_PROCESS is
  3    s integer := dbms_sql.open_cursor;
  4    n1 dbms_sql.number_table;
  5    d number;
  6    c number;
  7  BEGIN
  8    dbms_sql.parse(s,'select * from SRC',
  9              DBMS_SQL.native);
 10    dbms_sql.define_array(s,1,n1,500,1);
 11    d := dbms_sql.execute(s);
 12    loop
 13        c := DBMS_SQL.FETCH_ROWS(s);
 14        DBMS_SQL.COLUMN_VALUE(s, 1, n1);
 15        exit when c < 500;
 16    end loop;
 17
 18    DBMS_SQL.CLOSE_CURSOR(s);
 19  END;
 20  /

Procedure created.
```

Compare that to the trivial amount of code required to achieve the same process, but fetching only a single row at a time.

```
SQL> create or replace
  2  procedure SINGLE_ROW_PROCESS is
  3  begin
  4    for i in ( select * from SRC ) loop
  5        null;
  6    end loop;
  7  end;
  8  /

Procedure created.
```

Historically, it's easy to see why many developers did not bother with the extra work involved in array processing. However, if you took the time to use the more complicated code for the array processing code, there were performance benefits to be had. Compare the execution times of the two procedures just created.

```
SQL> exec single_row_process;

PL/SQL procedure successfully completed.
```

Elapsed: 00:00:22.02
```
SQL> exec array_process;

PL/SQL procedure successfully completed.
```

Elapsed: 00:00:17.01

Of course, performance isn't everything. As we will discuss in Chapter 5, there are drawbacks to using dynamic SQL (loss of dependency tracking, code errors missed at compilation time, and so on). The DBMS_SQL solution is harder to code and takes more effort to maintain should the underlying table change.

In the past, PL/SQL has received a lot of criticism about its performance, but the most common cause of this was row-at-a-time processing, not anything inherent in the PL/SQL engine. This is not a PL/SQL specific issue—for example, a PREFETCH option was added to Pro*C in version 8.1 to overcome the exact same issue in that environment. This new PREFETCH option converts the runtime Pro*C code into array fetching even though the developer has coded it in a conventional row-at-a-time manner. The arrival of version 8.1 changed PL/SQL as well—it became far simpler to use array processing in PL/SQL, as we will now discuss.

Bulking Up with Collections

Collections are a vital part of the mechanism to implement array fetching in PL/SQL. In fact, the process is known as "bulk collection." In a sporting context, the term "bulking up" is often used for a competitor who has spent more preparation time in the gym (or at the counter of their local chemist) in order to deliver a stronger, faster, or more powerful result in the field of play. This terminology is similarly appropriate in the field of PL/SQL programming. Using bulk collection in PL/SQL may require slightly more preparation time (in other words, coding), but will typically deliver a faster and more powerful solution.

Sadly, the bulk facilities in PL/SQL are perhaps the most underused feature in modern PL/SQL-centric applications. Most production-deployed PL/SQL code we've come across that is running on either version 8, 9, or 10 of Oracle would successfully compile and run on a version 7.3 database. This might be a good thing if you are building programs that need to run across all these versions, but it tends to reflect more on the developer's ignorance of the available features in the newer versions than any genuine version independence requirement.

Bulk Collection

Since version 8.1, fetching rows in bulk from a database is no more difficult than fetching a single row. Here is the code required to fetch a single row from the ALL_OBJECTS table.

```
SQL> declare
  2    x number;
  3  begin
  4    select object_id
  5    into   x
  6    from   all_objects
  7    where  rownum <= 1;
  8  end;
  9  /

PL/SQL procedure successfully completed.
```

Here is the equivalent bulk collection version to get 500 rows in a single call.

```
SQL> declare
  2    type numlist is table of number;
  3    x numlist;
  4  begin
  5    select object_id
  6    bulk collect into   x
  7    from   all_objects
  8    where  rownum <= 500;
  9  end;
 10  /

PL/SQL procedure successfully completed.
```

It really is that simple. For just those few extra keywords, there are significant performance benefits to be gained. Let's return again to our REPORT_SAL_ADJUSTMENT4 procedure from Chapter 1, which we used to add records to a table. The optimal solution in that case was to code a single INSERT-SELECT statement, but what if the report must be written to a file instead of a database table? Clearly a PL/SQL solution is required that will allow us to use the UTL_FILE package.

We'll start with the standard row-at-a-time solution. First, we need to create the report directory to which our output will be directed.

```
SQL> create or replace
  2  directory REPORT_DIR as 'C:\TEMP';

Directory created.
```

> **NOTE** In Oracle 9.2, the UTL_FILE facilities no longer require the use of the
> UTL_FILE_DIR parameter— they use the directory object, originally used for
> external jobs. The UTL_FILE has undergone a number of improvements in
> version 9.2, see the "Supplied PL/SQL Packages and Types Reference" for
> more details. If you are using an earlier version of Oracle, you will need to
> add the C:\TEMP directory (or whatever directory is appropriate for your
> system) to the UTL_FILE_DIR initialization parameter.

Next, we'll convert REPORT_SAL_ADJUSTMENT4 to write the report to a file rather
than a table. We will loop around the same high performance SQL we built earlier, fetching each row in turn and outputting it to the file using UTL_FILE.

```
SQL> create or replace
  2  procedure report_sal_adjustment4 is
  3    f utl_file.file_type;
  4  begin
  5    f := utl_file.fopen('REPORT_DIR','report.dat','W');
  6    for i in (
  7      select e.empno, e.hiredate, e.sal, dept.dname,
  8        case when sal > avg_sal then 'Y'
  9        else  'N'
 10        end status
 11      from (
 12        select empno, hiredate, sal, deptno,
 13          avg(sal) over ( partition by deptno ) as avg_sal,
 14          min(sal) over ( partition by deptno ) as min_sal
 15        from emp ) e, dept
 16      where e.deptno = dept.deptno
 17      and abs(e.sal - e.avg_sal)/e.avg_sal > 0.10 ) loop
 18        utl_file.put_line(f,i.empno||
 19                            i.hiredate||
 20                            i.sal||
 21                            i.dname||
 22                            i.status);
 23    end loop;
 24    utl_file.fclose(f);
```

```
25   end;
26   /
```

Procedure created.

Now let's create a second version that uses bulk collection. You will notice that this is one of the places where there is still a requirement for explicit cursors, so we can define a collection based on the columns in the cursor. We called the cursor C_TEMPLATE because its definition forms a template for the definition of the collection, RESULTSET, into which the rows will be bulk collected.

```
SQL> create or replace
  2    procedure report_sal_adjustment4_bulk is
  3      f utl_file.file_type;
  4      cursor c_template is
  5          select e.empno, e.hiredate, e.sal, dept.dname,
  6          case when sal > avg_sal then 'Y'
  7          else   'N'
  8          end status
  9        from (
 10          select empno, hiredate, sal, deptno,
 11            avg(sal) over ( partition by deptno ) as avg_sal,
 12            min(sal) over ( partition by deptno ) as min_sal
 13          from emp ) e, dept
 14        where e.deptno = dept.deptno
 15        and abs(e.sal - e.avg_sal)/e.avg_sal > 0.10;
```

Here we have a new type definition—a collection (or an array) of rows, each of which will contain fields that map to the previous cursor definition.

```
 16      type resultset is
 17        table of c_template%rowtype;
 18      r resultset;
 19    begin
 20      f := utl_file.fopen('REPORT_DIR','report.dat','W');
 21      open c_template;
```

Here is where the difference in processing becomes apparent. Rather than looping one row at a time, we can fetch all the rows into the result set, R.

```
 22      fetch c_template
 23      bulk collect into r;
 24      close c_template;
```

Now that variable R contains the entire result set, we loop through this in-memory collection rather than repeatedly traveling back to the database for more rows from the cursor.

```
25    for i in 1 .. r.count loop
26        utl_file.put_line(f,r(i).empno||
27                              r(i).hiredate||
28                              r(i).sal||
29                              r(i).dname||
30                              r(i).status);
31    end loop;
32    utl_file.fclose(f);
33  end;
34  /
```

Procedure created.

> **NOTE** With our tests on Windows and AIX, defining a collection based on a cursor ROWTYPE failed at compile time on versions 9.2.0.1 and 9.2.0.2. A quick search on Metalink revealed that this bug was resolved in version 9.2.0.3

How much better is the bulk collection version of our procedure than the row-at-a-time version? We can use our new RUNSTATS utility, RS, to find out. We take snapshots before and after an execution of each version.

```
SQL> exec rs.snap(true);

PL/SQL procedure successfully completed.

SQL> exec report_sal_adjustment4

PL/SQL procedure successfully completed.

SQL> exec rs.snap;

PL/SQL procedure successfully completed.

SQL> exec report_sal_adjustment4_bulk

PL/SQL procedure successfully completed.
```

```
SQL> exec rs.snap;

PL/SQL procedure successfully completed.
```

Now we can use standard SQL to view where the differences (if any) are to be found.

```
SQL> select tag, run1, run2, diff2, pct2
  2  from table(rs.display)
  3  where run1 > 0
  4  and pct2 != 100
  5  order by 2
  6  /
```

TAG	RUN1	RUN2	DIFF2	PCT2
S:recursive cpu usage	151	119	-32	79
L:shared pool	152	92	-60	61
L:library cache	211	107	-104	51
S:CPU used by this session	268	208	-60	78
E:Elapsed	**326**	**270**	**-56**	**83**
L:cache buffers chains	1208	913	-295	76
S:recursive calls	15267	493	-14774	3

Use of bulk collection results in 17 percent faster execution. Notice also that there is a similar reduction in latching (the rows prefixed with L), which will increase the scalability of the solution to larger user communities.

Bulk Binding

Retrieving data in bulk from the database is, of course, only one half of the equation. PL/SQL also has bulk facilities for data traveling in the opposite direction, that is, from a PL/SQL program back to the database to insert rows into, delete from, or update existing columns in a database table. This is known as "bulk binding" and is designed to minimize a different overhead—that of *context switching* within PL/SQL. When a PL/SQL program is launched, the PL/SQL runtime engine within the database performs the code execution. When a SQL statement is encountered within the code, the PL/SQL runtime engine passes that SQL to the SQL execution engine and awaits a response. So, a typical PL/SQL block will flip back and forth between the two engines as it runs, as shown in Figure 4-1.

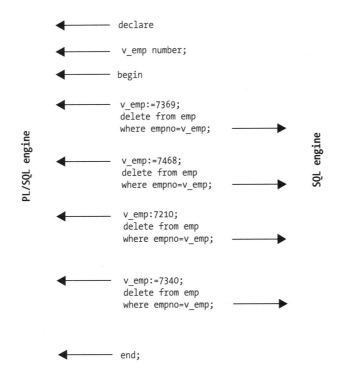

Figure 4-1. Context switching between PL/SQL and SQL engine

Some quantitative analysis on the costs of switching between the two engines is presented later in the next chapter (see the *Use PL/SQL to Expose the Data Model, Not Extend It* section in Chapter 5). With bulk binding, we batch up multiple executions of a DML statement to achieve the same processing result with fewer context switches. The same block above can be coded as shown in Figure 4-2.

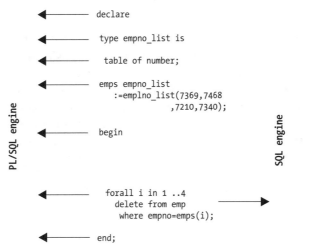

Figure 4-2. Reduced context switching

Once you get into the habit of using collections within PL/SQL, adopting bulk binding to perform DML is a simple exercise that has significant performance benefits. Bulk binding can be performed with any of the collection types: nested tables, varrays, or associative arrays. The following example shows how easy it is to convert from row-at-a-time processing to bulk binding. We will add 50,000 entries to a PL/SQL collection and then add each row in turn to a database table with a similar structure. The following table will be the target for the inserted rows:

```
SQL> create table BULK_BIND_TARGET (
  2     x number,
  3     y date,
  4     z varchar2(50) );

Table created.
```

We start with the row-at-a-time version, transferring rows from a collection to a table, using a standard FOR loop to cycle through the rows. The code is in two parts—the first section simply populates the collection with some seed data.

```
SQL> declare
  2      type numlist is table of number;
  3      type datelist is varray(50000) of date;
  4      type charlist is table of varchar2(50)
  5        index by binary_integer;
  6
  7      n numlist := numlist();
  8      d datelist := datelist();
  9      c charlist;
 10   begin
 11      for i in 1 .. 50000 loop
 12        n.extend;
 13        n(i) := i;
 14        d.extend;
 15        d(i) := sysdate+i;
 16        c(i) := rpad(i,50);
 17      end loop;
 18
```

The second section loops through each of the entries in the collection and inserts them a row at time into our target table.

```
 19      for i in 1 .. 50000 loop
 20        insert into bulk_bind_target values (n(i), d(i), c(i));
```

```
21      end loop;
22    end;
23    /
```

PL/SQL procedure successfully completed.

Elapsed: 00:00:07.03

We observe that on this system, we can achieve an insertion rate of just over 7,000 rows per second. Can we do better with bulk bind? You bet. And converting this to a bulk bind takes no more than a few keystrokes. The initial section of the code to populate the collection is unchanged.

```
SQL> declare
  2      type numlist is table of number;
  3      type datelist is varray(50000) of date;
  4      type charlist is table of varchar2(50)
  5        index by binary_integer;
  6
  7      n numlist := numlist();
  8      d datelist := datelist();
  9      c charlist;
 10    begin
 11      for i in 1 .. 50000 loop
 12        n.extend;
 13        n(i) := i;
 14        d.extend;
 15        d(i) := sysdate+i;
 16        c(i) := rpad(i,50);
 17      end loop;
 18
```

In order to use bulk binding, all we need do is convert the FOR keyword to FORALL and remove the LOOP / ENDLOOP wrapping. (No loop keywords are required because the FORALL only affects the immediately subsequent DML statement, so its scope is implicit.)

```
 19      forall i in 1 .. 50000
 20        insert into bulk_bind_target values (n(i), d(i), c(i));
 21    end;
 22    /
```

PL/SQL procedure successfully completed.

Elapsed: 00:00:01.05

Suddenly we jump up to 50,000 rows per second! You can see that this has an immediate positive impact on performance. Admittedly, the syntax seems to imply that this is still some form of row processing—in an ideal world the syntax could be something along the lines of

```
insert into bulk_bind_target values ( ALL n(i), ALL d(i), ALL c(i) )
```

But this is a minor detail. Note that in versions 8 and 9, the collections must not be sparse, that is, the index entries must be contiguous, but this restriction is lifted in Oracle 10*g*. Bulk binding is supported for inserts, updates, and deletions and should be strongly considered for any code that executes batches of DML statements.

Remember of course that one of the guidelines presented in Chapter 1 was to use SQL in preference to PL/SQL wherever possible. Using SQL instead of PL/SQL can be viewed as a special case of bulk binding, in which the collection of data is sourced from a database table.

Error Handling with Bulk Binding

There are very few drawbacks to using bulk binding other than it requiring slightly more code. One area where extra care will be required is in error handling. When a DML error occurs during conventional row-at-a-time processing, it is obvious which row caused the error—it is the row that we are currently processing! However, with bulk binding, a single operation may reference many rows within a collection, one or more of which might be the cause of the problem. For example, if we are inserting rows into a table where the column values are mandatory (that is, defined as NOT NULL), an error will result if an entry within a collection that will be bulk-bind inserted into that table is actually null.

```
SQL> create table MANDATORY_COL (
  2      x number not null );

Table created.

SQL > declare
  2      type numlist is table of number
  3          index by binary_integer;
  4      n numlist;
  5    begin
  6      for i in 1 .. 50 loop
  7        n(i) := i;
  8      end loop;
  9
```

```
10    n(37) := null;    -- will cause a problem
11
12    forall i in 1 .. 50
13       insert into MANDATORY_COL values (n(i));
14  end;
15  /
declare
*
ERROR at line 1:
ORA-01400: cannot insert NULL into ("MANDATORY_COL"."X")
ORA-06512: at line 12
```

Furthermore, the default operation for the entire bulk bind operation is to roll back so that no rows will be present in our target table.

```
SQL> select * from  MANDATORY_COL;

no rows selected
```

It's obvious that N(37) is the problem row here—after all, we explicitly set it to null—but this is only because we can see that from the code. There are no clues in the error message to indicate that this was the entry at fault, just that one (or more) of the entries must have been null.

New functionality in version 9 resolves this problem. It provides the SAVE EXCEPTIONS keywords, which allows you to direct a FORALL statement to continue past a row that causes an error, and preserve a list of where the errors occurred. We'll amend the example to demonstrate this feature.

```
SQL> set serverout on
SQL> declare
  2    type numlist is table of number
  3       index by binary_integer;
  4    n numlist;
  5  begin
  6    for i in 1 .. 50 loop
  7       n(i) := i;
  8    end loop;
  9
 10    n(37) := null;    -- will cause a problem
 11
```

This time, in the bulk bind operation, we will save any errors that occur instead of abandoning the operation completely.

```
12      forall i in 1 .. 50 save exceptions
13        insert into MANDATORY_COL values (n(i));
14
```

Now when the exception occurs, we have access to the information we need to find out what caused the error, and more importantly, the row index within our collection.

```
15   exception when others then
16     dbms_output.put_line('Errors:'||sql%bulk_exceptions.count);
17     for i in 1 .. sql%bulk_exceptions.count loop
18       dbms_output.put_line('index:'||sql%bulk_exceptions(i).error_index);
19       dbms_output.put_line('code:'||sql%bulk_exceptions(i).error_code);
20       dbms_output.put_line('message:');
21       dbms_output.put_line(sqlerrm(sql%bulk_exceptions(i).error_code));
22     end loop;
23   end;
24   /
Errors: 1
index : 37
code: 1400
message:
-1400: non-ORACLE exception

PL/SQL procedure successfully completed.
```

When the SAVE EXCEPTIONS syntax is used within a FORALL, any errors become available within a new collection, SQL%BULK_EXCEPTIONS, which contains a row for each error. Each row contains

- ERROR_INDEX: The index from the collection used in the FORALL

- ERROR_CODE: The oracle error code

Also, because the %BULK_EXCEPTIONS attribute is a collection, multiple errors can be caught and handled. Unfortunately, the example contained in the version 9.0 documentation gives the impression that because we are deferring the processing of the exceptions, an exception will not be raised. This is not true. The *text* in the documentation is actually correct—but the example code is simply missing the exception clause. We are *still* transferred to the exception handler section of the code once the FORALL statement completes.

Note that because the exception handler has dealt with the error(s) that occurred, the rows that *did* successfully get inserted are retained.

```
SQL> select * from MANDATORY_COL;

         X
----------
         1
         2
         3
         4
       ...
        36
        38
       ...
        50
```

Can I Over-Bulk?

A couple of months ago, my wife and I wanted to pave the driveway on our new house with bricks. Our local supplier very considerately dropped a pile of bricks out in our front yard pretty much as far as possible from where they would eventually be laid! I would trot back and forth between the pile and the driveway retrieving bricks for my wife, who did the bricklaying. Retrieving one brick at a time was obviously madness—the job just would never get done. I quickly got fed up with this, so I fetched the wheelbarrow from the shed and used this to transfer the bricks. I loaded up as many bricks as the wheelbarrow would hold, dumped them next to the driveway for my wife, and then headed back for the next load. This sped up the process of paving, but also revealed some issues when processing bricks in bulk.

- It takes more resources (in other words, more strength and sweat!) to push a wheelbarrow full of bricks than it did with just one brick at a time

- My wife needed to allocate space near the driveway for me to dump the bricks I fetched from the pile

- My wife sat idly by the driveway until I could get the first batch of bricks for laying, a fact which, I have to admit, didn't bother her as much as it bothered me!

- The process was certainly faster than one row at a time, but not as fast as I thought it would be—eventually as I put more and more bricks in a single wheelbarrow load, the limiting factor became how fast my wife could lay the bricks down.

Bulk processing the bricks is certainly a better option than running back and forth with only a single brick, but it took more effort, and picking up bigger and bigger batches of bricks didn't guarantee an improvement in the turnaround time.

The same arguments apply to bulk facilities in PL/SQL. When processing records in bulk, memory must be allocated for records that may be bulked up in a single operation. Hundreds or thousands of concurrent users all performing large bulk operations could easily cripple a system. In the following example, we will bulk collect *all* the rows from the ALL_OBJECTS view, which typically will contain tens of thousands of rows:

```
SQL> create or replace
  2  procedure BULK_TEST is
  3    mem_used number;
  4    t number;
  5    type recs is
  6      table of ALL_OBJECTS%rowtype;
  7    r recs;
  8    cursor c1 is select * from ALL_OBJECTS;
  9  begin
 10      t := dbms_utility.get_time;
 11    open c1;
 12    fetch c1
 13    bulk collect into r;
 14    close c1;
```

Once we have performed the bulk collection, we can query the V$MYSTATS view to determine how much memory we needed in order to hold all of this information.

```
 15      select value
 16      into mem_used
 17      from  v$mystats
 18      where name = 'session pga memory max';
 19      dbms_output.put_line('- Time: '||(dbms_utility.get_time-t));
 20      dbms_output.put_line('- Max Mem: '||mem_used);
 21  end;
 22  /
```

```
Procedure created.
```

Now we run the procedure to see the results.

```
SQL> set serverout on
SQL> exec bulk_test
- Time: 1911
- Max Mem: 98249020
```

This result will vary depending on how many rows you have in your
ALL_OBJECTS view, but here the bulk collection chewed up approximate 100
megabytes of memory! Imagine one thousand users trying to use this routine
concurrently—that's a *lot* of memory to buy for your server.

The LIMIT clause

Just like in the brick laying analogy, rather than trying to add *all* the bricks to the
wheelbarrow and making one trip, you can achieve equally good results by making multiple trips with a reasonable sized load. From version 8.1.6 onward, bulk
collection supports a LIMIT clause that will throttle back the number of rows collected in a single bulk operation. This may sound like a significant impediment
to performance, but there is a law of diminishing returns with bulk collection—a
larger bulk does not necessarily perform more quickly than another. Using the
LIMIT clause, we can determine the right balance between performance and
memory usage for bulk collections. The following LIMIT_TEST procedure will perform bulk collection from the SRC table using array fetches of 1, 4, 16, 64, 256,
1024, 4096, and 16384 rows at a time. We started a new a session to ensure that
any memory statistics we record have been reset to their initial value.

```
SQL> create or replace
  2  procedure LIMIT_TEST is
  3    mem_used number;
  4    t number;
  5    type recs is
  6      table of SRC%rowtype;
  7    r recs;
  8    cursor c1 is select * from SRC
  9  begin
 10    for i in 0 .. 7 loop
 11      t := dbms_utility.get_time;
 12      open c1;
 13      loop
 14        fetch c1
 15        bulk collect into r
 16        limit power(2,i*2);
 17        exit when c1%notfound;
 18      end loop;
 19      close c1;
```

```
20        select value
21        into mem_used
22        from  v$mystats
23        where name = 'session pga memory max';
24        dbms_output.put_line('Rows:'||power(2,i*2));
25        dbms_output.put_line('- Time: '||(dbms_utility.get_time-t));
26        dbms_output.put_line('- Max Mem: '||mem_used);
27     end loop;
28   end;
29   /
```

Procedure created.

Running the demo turns up some interesting results.

```
SQL> exec limit_test
Rows:1
- Time: 2482
- Max Mem: 566284
Rows:4
- Time: 2065
- Max Mem: 566284
Rows:16
- Time: 1915
- Max Mem: 697892
Rows:64
- Time: 1920
- Max Mem: 936532
Rows:256
- Time: 1890
- Max Mem: 2014508
Rows:1024
- Time: 1917
- Max Mem: 5288324
Rows:4096
- Time: 1921
- Max Mem: 10372420
Rows:16384
- Time: 1885
- Max Mem: 16056916

PL/SQL procedure successfully completed.
```

In this example, although the very best performance came from the largest bulk size, anything with a LIMIT setting over 16 was within one percent of an optimal result. But glance at the memory consumed when bulk collection sizes rise—collecting 16,384 rows at a time consumed 16MB per user. That is certainly a scalability inhibitor!

When you're building your applications and (hopefully) taking advantage of bulk collection, take the time to consider whether the number of collected rows will be large (or will grow from small to large as the database grows over time). If so, build in the LIMIT clause on day one—it costs nothing to do so, and protects you from unforeseen memory consumption in the future.

Be aware that when you use bulk collection with a LIMIT clause, the %NOTFOUND attribute for the cursor is set when the number of rows retrieved is less than the limiting value. Hence if you code your %NOTFOUND check immediately after the fetch statement, you will probably not process all the data you are supposed to. For example, if a table contains 20 rows, and your code is

```
loop
   fetch cursor
   bulk collect into resultset limit 50;
   exit when cursor%notfound;
   (processing)
end loop;
```

you will never enter the (*processing*) section of the code because when the twentieth and last row is retrieved, the %NOTFOUND flag is raised. The corrected version is to exit the loop after the processing phase

```
loop
   fetch cursor
   bulk collect into resultset limit 50;
   (processing)
   exit when cursor%notfound;
end loop;
```

Remember that relational databases were created out of the theory and promise of operating with *sets* of data. The bulk processing features in PL/SQL deliver that functionality. Using bulk processing, we can get close to the axiom that every set should be processed atomically. Bulk processing gives your PL/SQL applications a tighter relationship with sets of data, and more often than not, an associated performance boost for free.

Passing Variables Between PL/SQL Programs

The beauty of PL/SQL's support for larger and more complex data structures is that these structures can be easily passed to and from various parts of an application as though they were simple scalar variables. As you'll see shortly, there are some issues that you need to consider when passing large collection variables between PL/SQL programs. However, you should also be aware that there are some idiosyncrasies even when passing simple scalar or ROWTYPE variables.

> **NOTE**   This section is not intended to describe the various means through which parameters can be passed between PL/SQL subprograms; the supplied documentation is more than adequate for that purpose. To briefly paraphrase the documentation, parameters can be passed as
>
> IN—a value to be passed into a procedure
>
> OUT—a value to be received from a procedure
>
> IN OUT—equivalent to a "pass by reference" variable

Passing %TYPE and %ROWTYPE as Parameters

As noted earlier in this chapter, any variable that is linked to a database column or row should probably be anchored using a %TYPE or %ROWTYPE attribute. When it comes to defining *parameters*, the decision to use these attributes is a little less definitive. To explain why, let us consider a typical scenario in which a parameter is defined with a %TYPE anchor. First, we create a table, TEN_BYTE_COLUMN, which (predictably enough) contains a column constrained to a maximum length of 10 bytes.

```
SQL> create table TEN_BYTE_COLUMN (
  2     col varchar2(10));

Table created.
```

Next, we create a simple procedure, ADD_ROW, to add a row to that table. The procedure accepts the parameter, P_COL, which is anchored using %TYPE. (In other words, its datatype will be based on that of the COL column in our table.)

```
SQL> create or replace
  2  procedure ADD_ROW(p_col TEN_BYTE_COLUMN.COL%TYPE) is
  3  begin
  4    insert into TEN_BYTE_COLUMN
  5    values (p_col);
  6  end;
  7  /

Procedure created.
```

Inserting a literal value that is 10 bytes long works as expected.

```
SQL> exec add_row('0123456789');

PL/SQL procedure successfully completed.
```

However, if a larger value is passed a parameter

```
SQL> exec add_row('01234567890123456789');
BEGIN add_row('01234567890123456789'); END;

*
ERROR at line 1:
ORA-01401: inserted value too large for column
ORA-06512: at "ADD_ROW", line 3
ORA-06512: at line 1
```

Notice that from the line number at which the error occurred, the parameter value has been *allowed* by the procedure, and when this parameter was used in the INSERT statement (at line 3) an error did occur. Using the %TYPE attribute on a parameter checks only the datatype of the passed parameter and not any precision that is associated with the underlying database column. We can prove that the datatypes are indeed checked by building a similar test case whereby the underlying datatype on a column COL in table TEN_SIG_DIGITS is numeric, and then passing a non-numeric value.

```
SQLSQL> create or replace
  2  procedure ADD_NUM_ROW(p_col TEN_SIG_DIGITS.COL%TYPE) is
  3  begin
  4    insert into TEN_SIG_DIGITS
  5    values (p_col);
  6  end;
  7  /

Procedure created.
```

```
SQL> exec add_num_row('asd');
BEGIN add_num_row('asd'); END;

*
ERROR at line 1:
ORA-06502: PL/SQL: numeric or value error: character to number conversion error
ORA-06512: at line 1
```

Notice that the error has occurred on line 1, not line 3, as in the previous example, and that the error is a PL/SQL error, not a database error. This is only a problem with parameters—local variables anchored to a type are checked fully. Creating a very basic procedure with a local variable instead of a procedure demonstrates this.

```
SQL> create or replace
  2   procedure LOCAL_TYPE_VAR is
  3     x ten_byte_column.col%type;
  4   begin
  5     x := '01234567890123456789';
  6   end;
  7   /

Procedure created.

SQL> exec local_type_var;
BEGIN local_type_var; END;

*
ERROR at line 1:
ORA-06502: PL/SQL: numeric or value error: character string buffer too small
ORA-06512: at "LOCAL_TYPE_VAR", line 4
ORA-06512: at line 1
```

We guess that the reason for this relaxation of the rules for parameters is based on the assumption that any variable to be passed to a PL/SQL procedure would also be defined as an anchored type and thus would have already been checked for valid precision.

CAUTION We don't have any proof for this assertion so please do not take this as a statement of fact.

Similarly, as with any expression, Oracle attempts automatic datatype conversion with an anchored-type parameter so executions such as

```
SQL> exec add_row(sysdate);  -- remember, takes a varchar2 param
```

These are not deemed as errors, with the SYSDATE value implicitly converted to a VARCHAR2 before being inserted into the table.

Hence, anchoring a parameter with a %TYPE attribute achieves two results.

- Just the datatype and not its precision is checked.

- The PL/SQL subprogram is bound to the dependency tree for the underlying table.[3]

If you have already read Chapter 2, hopefully you are thinking that the second result is definitely a good thing. However, using %TYPE for parameters yields an interesting anomaly in that when used within a package, it breaks one of the great advantages of packages—the insulation from dependency issues by separating the code into specification and body. For example, if the two procedures just defined were placed into a package, the code would be

```
SQL> create or replace
  2  package PKG is
  3    procedure ADD_ROW(p_col TEN_BYTE_COLUMN.COL%TYPE);
  4    procedure ADD_NUM_ROW(p_col TEN_SIG_DIGITS.COL%TYPE);
  5  end;
  6  /

Package created.

SQL> create or replace
  2  package body PKG is
  3
  4  procedure ADD_ROW(p_col TEN_BYTE_COLUMN.COL%TYPE) is
  5  begin
  6    insert into TEN_BYTE_COLUMN
  7    values (p_col);
  8  end;
  9
 10  procedure ADD_NUM_ROW(p_col TEN_SIG_DIGITS.COL%TYPE) is
```

---

3. An interesting quirk, as pointed out to me by Tom Kyte, is that if the %TYPE attribute for a procedure parameter refers to a package specification variable, and if that package variable is defined as not null, the parameter will also preserve that constraint (whereas an equivalent %TYPE attribute referencing a not null table column does not preserve the "not null"-ness).

```
11   begin
12      insert into TEN_SIG_DIGITS
13      values (p_col);
14   end;
15
16   end;
17   /
```

Package body created.

Looking at the dependency chain, we see that the package *specifications* have also become dependent on the tables.

```
SQL> select name, type
  2  from user_dependencies
  3  where referenced_name in (
  4     'TEN_BYTE_COLUMN',
  5     'TEN_SIG_DIGITS')
  6  and name like 'PKG%'
```

NAME	TYPE
PKG	PACKAGE
PKG	PACKAGE BODY
PKG	PACKAGE
PKG	PACKAGE BODY

This is an interesting side effect, but it is of course a mandatory consequence because if we were to drop the COL column from either of the tables, the package specification would be flawed. Compare this to the results if we do not use a %TYPE anchor for the parameters.

```
SQL> create or replace
  2  package PKG is
  3     procedure ADD_ROW(p_col varchar2);
  4     procedure ADD_NUM_ROW(p_col number);
  5  end;
  6  /
```

Package created.

```
SQL> create or replace
  2  package body PKG is
  3
```

```
 4   procedure ADD_ROW(p_col varchar2) is
 5   begin
 6      insert into TEN_BYTE_COLUMN
 7      values (p_col);
 8   end;
 9
10   procedure ADD_NUM_ROW(p_col number) is
11   begin
12      insert into TEN_SIG_DIGITS
13      values (p_col);
14   end;
15
16   end;
17   /
```

Package body created.

Now when we examine the dependency tree, the package specifications have disappeared.

```
SQL> select name, type
  2   from user_dependencies
  3   where referenced_name in (
  4      'TEN_BYTE_COLUMN',
  5      'TEN_SIG_DIGITS')
  6   and name like 'PKG%';
```

NAME	TYPE
PKG	PACKAGE BODY
PKG	PACKAGE BODY

Which is best? To use a classical Oracle cliché: "it depends." We are not arguing that you should *not* use the %TYPE attribute for your parameters, but only that you should not use them indiscriminately for every parameter without considering the implications of doing so. If your project requires more dependency information between PL/SQL programs and the database tables that they are based upon so you have more complete data for analyzing the impact of change, %TYPE parameters in package specifications will be ideal. For example, consider if the ADD_ROW procedure were using dynamic instead of static SQL. One of the issues with dynamic SQL is that we typically lose the dependency information that we want. Using a %TYPE parameter ensures that it would not drop out of the dependency chain.

Conversely, be aware that if you are taking advantage of the separation of package specification and package body to limit the scope of impact when change does occur, using %TYPE parameters will affect both package body and specification, thus nullifying some of the very benefits that you are trying to achieve.

A similar situation exists for the %ROWTYPE anchor. Any reference to a ROWTYPE variable in a package specification may cause dependency chain issues. This is a harder one to resolve—whereas avoiding a dependency problem with a scalar %TYPE variable can be avoided by replacing the definition with the underlying scalar datatype, there is no such substitution that can be made for a ROWTYPE variable.

Passing Collections as Parameters

The PL/SQL documentation states that passing large collections as parameters is more costly in terms of performance than passing scalar variables, and common sense would agree with this assertion. However, some simple tests show the performance is still comparable. Let's build a definition for a collection by creating a table, REC_LIST, of records, REC.

```
SQL> create or replace
  2  type rec is object
  3    ( a number,
  4       b number,
  5       c varchar2(30));
  6  /

Type created.

SQL> create or replace
  2  type rec_list is
  3  table of rec;
  4  /

Type created.
```

Next we will create two procedures: SIMPLE_PARM, which just takes a scalar value as a parameter, and BIG_PARM, which takes the just defined collection REC_LIST.

```
SQL> create or replace
  2  procedure SIMPLE_PARM(p number) is
  3    x number;
```

```
 4  begin
 5    null;
 6  end;
 7  /
```

Procedure created.

```
SQL> create or replace
  2  procedure BIG_PARM(p rec_list) is
  3    x number;
  4  begin
  5    null;
  6  end;
  7  /
```

Procedure created.

To examine the cost of passing a collection of this size versus passing a simple scalar datatype, we will populate the collection up to 50,000 entries and then record timings for a sequence of executions to procedures SIMPLE_PARM and BIG_PARM.

```
SQL> declare
  2    x rec_list := rec_list();
  3    t1 number;
  4    t2 number;
  5  begin
  6    x.extend(50000);
  7    for i in 1 .. 50000 loop
  8      x(i) := rec(i,i,rpad(i,30));
  9    end loop;
 10    t1 := dbms_utility.get_time;
 11    for i in 1 .. 500000 loop
 12      simple_parm(i);
 13    end loop;
 14    t2 := dbms_utility.get_time;
 15    dbms_output.put_line('Simple:     '||(t2-t1));
 16    for i in 1 .. 500000 loop
 17      big_parm(x);
 18    end loop;
 19    t1 := dbms_utility.get_time;
 20    dbms_output.put_line('Collection:'||(t1-t2));
 21  end;
 22  /
```

```
Simple:      62
Collection: 50

PL/SQL procedure successfully completed.
```

A very interesting result! Repeated tests consistently show that the collection parameter was *faster* than the scalar parameter. However, it is possible that there is an optimization in effect here because no access is being made to the parameters in the called procedures. We repeat the tests with modified procedures so that we make a usage within the procedure to the passed parameters.

```
SQL> create or replace
  2  procedure SIMPLE_PARM(p number) is
  3    x number;
  4  begin
  5    x := p;
  6  end;
  7  /

Procedure created.

SQL> create or replace
  2  procedure BIG_PARM(p rec_list) is
  3    x number;
  4  begin
  5    x := p(1).a;
  6  end;
  7  /

Procedure created.
```

Let's see if there has been any change in our initial findings.

```
SQL> declare
  2    x rec_list := rec_list();
  3    t1 number;
  4    t2 number;
  5  begin
  6    for i in 1 .. 50000 loop
  7      x.extend;
  8      x(i) := rec(i,i,rpad(i,30));
  9    end loop;
 10    t1 := dbms_utility.get_time;
 11    for i in 1 .. 500000 loop
```

```
12        simple_parm(i);
13      end loop;
14      t2 := dbms_utility.get_time;
15      dbms_output.put_line('Simple:     '||(t2-t1));
16      for i in 1 .. 500000 loop
17        big_parm(x);
18      end loop;
19      t1 := dbms_utility.get_time;
20      dbms_output.put_line('Collection:'||(t1-t2));
21  end;
22  /
Simple:     97
Collection:131

PL/SQL procedure successfully completed.
```

This is probably a more expected result. However, 500,000 calls in just over a second is still very impressive. It's a very different story, however, once you start passing large parameters such as the collection used in the example with the IN OUT mode. Look what happens to the performance when the parameters are passed as IN OUT. We will revert our SIMPLE_PARM and BIG_PARM procedures to take no action on the passed parameters, but these parameters will now be defined as IN OUT.

```
SQL> create or replace
  2  procedure SIMPLE_PARM(p in out number) is
  3  begin
  4    null;
  5  end;
  6  /

Procedure created.

SQL> create or replace
  2  procedure BIG_PARM(p in out rec_list) is
  3  begin
  4    null;
  5  end;
  6  /

Procedure created.
```

Now the tests can be rerun. We had to abandon the test that was to record 500,000 executions of each procedure; it just never came back. In fact, to get the calls to BIG_PARM to finish in a reasonable time, we had to drop the number of iterations in the test all the way down to 50! We dropped the iterations for the calls to SIMPLE_PARM down to 50 as well, so we can compare the results.

```
SQL> declare
  2     x rec_list := rec_list();
  3     s number := 1;
  4     t1 number;
  5     t2 number;
  6  begin
  7     for i in 1 .. 50000 loop
  8        x.extend;
  9        x(i) := rec(i,i,rpad(i,30));
 10     end loop;
 11     t1 := dbms_utility.get_time;
 12     for i in 1 .. 50 loop
 13        simple_parm(s);
 14     end loop;
 15     t2 := dbms_utility.get_time;
 16     dbms_output.put_line('Simple:     '||(t2-t1));
 17     for i in 1 .. 50 loop
 18        big_parm(x);
 19     end loop;
 20     t1 := dbms_utility.get_time;
 21     dbms_output.put_line('Collection:'||(t1-t2));
 22  end;
 23  /
Simple:        0
Collection:1118

PL/SQL procedure successfully completed.
```

A measly 50 executions took 11 seconds! Testing with the number of entries in the REC_LIST collection varying from 1,000 to 50,000 indicates that the performance overhead is directly proportional the amount of data being passed, as shown in Figure 4-3.

Passing an IN OUT parameter to a procedure requires far more overhead because the PL/SQL engine must preserve a copy of the parameter value before the procedure is executed. This is necessary because if the procedure fails with an exception, the original parameter value must be preserved.

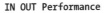

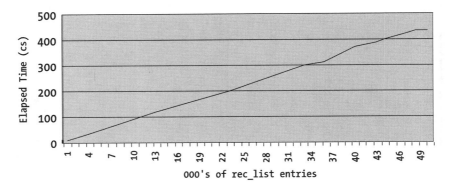

Figure 4-3. Performance for large collection parameters

Using the NOCOPY Compiler Hint

In these situations, you want to look into the NOCOPY compiler hint. The NOCOPY option instructs the compiler not to take a backup copy of the parameter that is passed. The performance improvements are remarkable. Note that in the example that follows we bumped the iterations in the test back up to 500,000 from 50. The SIMPLE_PARM procedure remains unchanged, but the BIG_PARM procedure is now compiled with the NOCOPY hint on its parameter.

```
SQL> create or replace
  2   procedure BIG_PARM(p in out nocopy rec_list) is
  3   begin
  4     null;
  5   end;
  6   /

Procedure created.

SQL> declare
  2     x rec_list := rec_list();
  3     t1 number;
  4     t2 number;
  5   begin
  6     for i in 1 .. 50000 loop
  7       x.extend;
```

```
 8        x(i) := rec(i,i,rpad(i,30));
 9      end loop;
10      t2 := dbms_utility.get_time;
11      for i in 1 .. 500000 loop
12        big_parm(x);
13      end loop;
14      t1 := dbms_utility.get_time;
15      dbms_output.put_line('Collection:'||(t1-t2));
16    end;
17    /
Collection:49
```

Performance has returned to a figure comparable to the simple scalar parameter. This does not mean that all collections should be passed with the NOCOPY hint. In particular, you need to take care with the NOCOPY hint when handling errors within your procedures. As noted, without the NOCOPY hint, an IN OUT parameter will be restored to the value it had before the procedure was called if that procedure fails. For example, we will modify the BIG_PARM procedure to remove the NOCOPY hint and deliberately raise an error after making a change to the passed parameter. We will change one of the collection elements from Z to Q, and then force a division by zero error.

```
SQL> create or replace
  2    procedure BIG_PARM(p in out rec_list) is
  3      l number;
  4    begin
  5      p(2).c := 'z';  -- change from 'q' to 'z'
  6      l := 1/0;   -- will raise error (ie division by zero)
  7    end;
  8    /

Procedure created.
```

Now we run an anonymous block to catch the BIG_PARM error, and interrogate what changes, if any, were made to the variable that we passed to BIG_PARM.

```
SQL> declare
  2      x rec_list;
  3    begin
  4      x := rec_list(
  5            rec(1,1,'p'),
  6            rec(2,2,'q'),
  7            rec(3,3,'r'));
  8      big_parm(x);
```

```
 9   exception when others then
10     for i in 1 .. 3 loop
11        dbms_output.put_line(x(i).c);
12     end loop;
13   end;
14   /
p
q   ← unchanged because BIG_PARM failed with an exception
r
```

Notice that the assignment of Z was backed out. The second element in our collection has been reverted back to Q. However, when the NOCOPY compiler hint is specified, the results are indeterminate. The values may be restored, but this is not guaranteed. Repeating the example above but adding the NOCOPY hint to BIG_PARM reveals a different result.

```
SQL> create or replace
  2   procedure BIG_PARM(p in out nocopy rec_list) is
  3     l number;
  4   begin
  5     p(2).c := 'z';
  6     l := 1/0;
  7   end;
  8   /

Procedure created.

SQL> declare
  2     x rec_list;
  3   begin
  4     x := rec_list(
  5           rec(1,1,'p'),
  6           rec(2,2,'q'),
  7           rec(3,3,'r'));
  8     big_parm(x);
  9   exception when others then
 10     for i in 1 .. 3 loop
 11        dbms_output.put_line(x(i).c);
 12     end loop;
 13   end;
 14   /
p
z   ← changed even though BIG_PARM failed!
r
```

The value of the parameter is not reset to the original value. The reason that the documentation says the results from using NOCOPY are indeterminate is that NOCOPY is a compiler *hint*. The PL/SQL compiler is under no obligation to obey the hint. Even with this issue, the NOCOPY is a vastly underused setting. Hopefully, in most applications, the proportion of successful to unsuccessful executions of procedures will be very much in favor of successful ones. If restoration of values in the event of error is mandatory, some of the benefits of the NOCOPY performance can be achieved by building your own version of NOCOPY, that is, taking your own backup copy of variable values and restoring that original value in the event of an error. This is demonstrated in the following example:

```
SQL> declare
  2     x rec_list := rec_list();
  3     orig_x rec_list;
  4     t1 number;
  5     t2 number;
  6  begin
  7     for i in 1 .. 50000 loop
  8       x.extend;
  9       x(i) := rec(i,i,rpad(i,30));
 10     end loop;
 11     t2 := dbms_utility.get_time;
 12     for i in 1 .. 50 loop
 13       orig_x := x;
 14       begin
 15         big_parm(x);
 16       exception when others then
 17         x := orig_x;
 18       end;
 19     end loop;
 20     t1 := dbms_utility.get_time;
 21     dbms_output.put_line('Collection:'||(t1-t2));
 22  end;
 23  /
Collection:553
```

Although the example shows that performance is still affected significantly by preserving a copy of the collection, if most executions of BIG_PARM succeed, it is still twice as fast as the standard IN OUT processing.

There are some restrictions on the variables that can be used and in what context they can be passed as a NOCOPY parameter. The PL/SQL reference guide provides a list of restrictions. No errors will be reported if you violate one of these restrictions; the NOCOPY hint will simply be ignored.

Transaction Processing in PL/SQL

We spent most of this chapter discussing mechanisms for retrieving data from the database and passing that data between PL/SQL programs. We can complete our discussion of data processing by looking at some of the elements of transaction processing within PL/SQL. Consider the following procedure, used to track changes to employee details. We will track the total salary of each department using a new TOT_SAL column on the DEPT table.

```
SQL> @$ORACLE_HOME\sqlplus\demo\demobld
Building demonstration tables.  Please wait.
Demonstration table build is complete.
SQL> alter table dept add tot_sal number;

Table altered.

SQL> update dept
  2   set tot_sal = ( select sum(sal)
  3                     from emp where deptno = dept.deptno );

4 rows updated.
```

We will also record the most recent change to an employee record in a table EMP_DELTAS, and keep an audit of all changes to the EMP_AUDIT table.

```
SQL> create table EMP_AUDIT (
  2     date_rec date,
  3     empno number,
  4     sal number(4));

Table created.

SQL> create table EMP_DELTAS
  2   ( empno number, change_type varchar2(10));

Table created.

SQL> insert into emp_deltas
  2   select empno, null from emp;

14 rows created.
```

Now we can code a procedure to keep all the tables in sync when we update the salary for an employee.

```
SQL> create or replace
  2  procedure UPDATE_EMP(p_empno number, p_sal number) is
  3  begin
  4     update DEPT
  5     set TOT_SAL = TOT_SAL +
  6                     ( select p_sal-sal
  7                       from    EMP
  8                       where   empno = p_empno )
  9     where deptno = ( select deptno
 10                      from    EMP
 11                      where   empno = p_empno);
 12
 13     update EMP
 14     set sal = p_sal
 15     where empno = p_empno;
 16
 17     update EMP_DELTAS
 18     set change_type = 'SAL'
 19     where empno = p_empno;
 20
 21     insert into EMP_AUDIT
 22     values (sysdate,p_empno,p_sal);
 23
 24  exception
 25     when others then
 26        rollback;
 27        raise;
 28  end;
 29  /
```

Procedure created.

Without looking closely at whether the SQL is efficient or inefficient, a problem can be immediately identified with the code. The problem lies with the lines

```
 24  exception
 25     when others then
 26        rollback;
 27        raise;
```

It's fairly clear that the desired result is that if an error occurs in any of the DML statements in the procedure, any changes that have so far been applied should be rolled back and the error re-raised to the calling environment. The code is totally redundant and could even pose a risk to data integrity, as we will see shortly. One of the great features of PL/SQL is that any block of code is always treated as a logical unit of work—it either succeeds or fails, not half of each. We'll use the example just shown to prove that this is how PL/SQL block works. We amended the code to remove the exception handler and recompiled the procedure. First, we need to ensure that the procedure works in normal operation and alters all the rows we would expect.

```
SQL> exec update_emp(7499,2000);

PL/SQL procedure successfully completed.

SQL> select empno, deptno, sal
  2  from emp
  3  where empno = 7499;

     EMPNO      DEPTNO         SAL
---------- ---------- ----------
      7499          30        2000

SQL> select *
  2  from emp_audit;

DATE_REC        EMPNO         SAL
--------- ---------- ----------
22/JUN/03        7499        2000

SQL> select *
  2  from emp_deltas;

     EMPNO CHANGE_TYP
---------- ----------
      7369
      7499 SAL
      7521
...
```

No problems there—all the tables are updated as anticipated. Now let's run the procedure to deliberately cause an error by passing in a salary value that will be too large for the EMP_AUDIT table. From our source code, note that this table is the *last* table affected by the procedure, so the change to the EMP table and the update to EMP_DELTAS will succeed before the failure on the EMP_AUDIT insert statement.

```
SQL> exec update_emp(7698,99999);
BEGIN update_emp(7698,99999); END;

*
ERROR at line 1:
ORA-01438: value larger than specified precision allows for this column
ORA-06512: at "UPDATE_EMP", line 20
ORA-06512: at line 1
```

An error occurred at line 20, but what is the state of the database? Do we need to clean up the first two DML statements issued for employee 7698? Let's take a look.

```
SQL> select empno, deptno, sal
  2  from emp
  3  where empno = 7698;

     EMPNO     DEPTNO        SAL
---------- ---------- ----------
      7698         30       2850

SQL> select *
  2  from emp_audit;

DATE_REC       EMPNO        SAL
---------  ---------- ----------
22/JUN/03       7499       2000

SQL> select *
  2  from emp_deltas;

     EMPNO CHANGE_TYP
---------- ----------
      7369
      7499 SAL
      7521
      7566
      7654
      7698
```

There have been no changes—the work done the by the entire PL/SQL block is rolled back. It is vital to understand this concept because indiscriminate use of rollback within PL/SQL blocks will typically cause undesirable side effects to the calling environment. This is where your data integrity could be compromised.

Let's put the original exception handler back into the code and see what happens to a transaction that is active *before* we execute the UPDATE_EMP procedure. Suppose we want to remove employee 7369.

```
SQL> delete from emp  -- unrelated emp change
  2  where empno = 7369;


1 row deleted.
```

We proceed to update employee 7698 with an overly large salary (which will cause an error and jump to the exception handler to rollback the changes).

```
SQL> exec update_emp(7698,99999);
BEGIN update_emp(7698,99999); END;

*
ERROR at line 1:
ORA-01438: value larger than specified precision allows for this column
ORA-06512: at " UPDATE_EMP", line 26
ORA-06512: at line 1
```

Any changes that were made in the UPDATE_EMP procedure have been rolled back, but what about the transaction that was active before the procedure was called, that is, the removal of employee 7369?

```
SQL> select * from emp
  2  where empno = 7369;


    EMPNO ENAME      JOB           MGR HIREDATE        SAL       COMM
---------- ---------- --------- --------- --------- ---------- ----------
     7369 SMITH      CLERK        7902 17/DEC/80        800
```

Employee 7369 has magically been reinstated! Not only does the PL/SQL block roll back its own changes, but any outstanding changes that preceded it as well. Things can even get worse. If we had coded the procedure to silently roll back when an error is encountered but *not* raise this error back to the calling environment, any active transactions that may have preceded the procedure's execution are also rolled back, but the calling environment will *not* be aware of this!

As we can now see, processing transactions within PL/SQL is intrinsically linked to how you code your exception handlers within your application. The implicit rollback of the work done within a PL/SQL procedure is controlled by an error not being handled by an exception handler. Even when we have the corrected code (there is no exception handler within the UPDATE_EMP), problems can still occur if exception handlers are not coded with transactions in mind. For example, consider the change in the behavior of the transaction when we wrap the call to UPDATE_EMP within an exception handler that catches (and then ignores) all errors.

```
SQL> begin
  2     update_emp(7698,99999);
  3     exception when others then null;
  4  end;
  5  /

PL/SQL procedure successfully completed.
```

Because there has been no error, no rollback of any changes has occurred. In this case, we created a very undesirable scenario by allowing a change to an employee's salary details *without* a corresponding audit record in the EMP_AUDIT table being created.

```
SQL> select * from emp
  2  where empno = 7698;

    EMPNO ENAME      JOB            MGR HIREDATE        SAL
---------- ---------- --------- ---------- ---------   -------
     7698 BLAKE      MANAGER        7839 01/MAY/81     99999

SQL> select * from emp_audit
  2  where empno = 7698;

no rows selected
```

The only place for any statements that end a transaction (commit, rollback, DDL) is in the top-level calling environment, that is, the originating application. Any program (PL/SQL or otherwise) that could be called from a higher level should never explicitly end a transaction because of the possibility of undesirable side effects. Not using COMMIT and ROLLBACK within PL/SQL code also encourages developers to build applications that commit only when necessary and not as a matter of course.

The exception to the rule is in the case of autonomous transactions, which we will cover briefly now.

Autonomous Transactions

If transaction control (COMMIT, ROLLBACK) should only be issued from the top-level calling environment, where do autonomous transactions fit in, given that an explicit COMMIT or ROLLBACK is mandatory within them? We would argue that even autonomous transactions still adhere to the guideline because a procedure that is defined as autonomous can never be part of a parent transaction, and thus we are still committing at the logical conclusion to a transaction.

This will be a very short section. With respect to autonomous transactions, we have a fairly simple maxim—they are used in far too many places. There are four typical reasons touted as being an ideal for the application of autonomous transactions, three of which are just plain wrong for autonomous transactions; only the fourth is possibly justified.

Avoiding Mutating Table Errors in Triggers

Contrary to popular belief, Oracle didn't invent the mutating table error just to cause pain for developers! Mutating table errors avoid SQL queries within a row-level trigger from seeing an inconsistent view of the data. Similarly, autonomous transactions do not see an inconsistent view of the data by simply *not seeing any* of the outstanding changes that fired the trigger in the first place. This is why autonomous transactions are not appropriate for avoiding the mutating table problem, as documented in Metalink Note:65961.1.

> *"As all database changes are part of a transaction, if a parent has modified data, but not committed it at the point the autonomous transaction begins, then those modifications are not visible to the child…It is important to remember that if a trigger is running as an autonomous transaction, although it still has access to :OLD and :NEW values as appropriate, it does not see any rows inserted into the table by the calling transaction. Thus, using an autonomous trigger to obtain a maximum value currently in the table…[in other words, a mutating table scenario]…is unlikely to work."*

Performing DDL as Part of a Transaction

A DDL statement always performs a COMMIT before and after the statement is executed, so to prevent this from affecting an existing uncommitted transaction, the logical solution appears to be to wrap the DDL within a procedure defined as autonomous. Although this appears to have overcome the immediate problem, it is no different than performing that DDL within an entirely new session—should

the initial transaction roll back, the results of DDL operation will still be apparent, demonstrated as follows. We will build a procedure that can be used to add a
column to a table, but we want to track any columns that we add in a table
LIST_OF_CHANGES.

```
SQL> create table list_of_changes
  2     ( tname varchar2(30),
  3         cname varchar2(30),
  4         changed date);

Table created.
```

So that we can run DDL statements without affecting the current transaction, we (mistakenly) create a RUN_DDL procedure to process any DDL statement
passed as a parameter within an autonomous transaction.

```
SQL> create or replace
  2  procedure RUN_DDL(m varchar2) is
  3     pragma autonomous_transaction;
  4  begin
  5     execute immediate m;
  6  end;
  7  /

Procedure created.
```

We build our ADD_COLUMN procedure that will record the column change in the
LIST_OF_CHANGES table and then use RUN_DDL to perform the change. To simulate
what would happen if this procedure were to fail, we've added a deliberate error
(division by zero) to the tail of the code.

```
SQL> create or replace
  2  procedure ADD_COLUMN(p_table varchar2,
  3     p_column varchar2) is
  4     v number;
  5  begin
  6     insert into LIST_OF_CHANGES
  7     values (p_table, p_column, sysdate);
  8     run_ddl(
  9      'alter table '||p_table||' add '||p_column);
 10     v := 1/0;  -- raises an error, rolls back insert
 11  end;
 12  /
```

```
Procedure created.
```

Now we add a column NEWCOL to the EMP table.

```
SQL> exec add_column('emp','newcol number');
BEGIN add_column('emp','newcol number'); END;

*
ERROR at line 1:
ORA-01476: divisor is equal to zero
ORA-06512: at "ADD_COLUMN", line 9
ORA-06512: at line 1
```

As we have already seen, the failure of the procedure will roll back the insertion of rows into the LIST_OF_CHANGES table.

```
SQL> select * from list_of_changes;

no rows selected
```

What about our autonomous transaction? It has still taken place!

```
SQL> desc emp
 Name                            Null?     Type
 ------------------------------- --------  ---------------
 EMPNO                           NOT NULL  NUMBER(10)
 ENAME                                     VARCHAR2(20)
 HIREDATE                                  DATE
 SAL                                       NUMBER(10,2)
 DEPTNO                                    NUMBER(6)
 NEWCOL                                    NUMBER
```

This is not to say that you cannot "transactionalize" a DDL statement, only that autonomous transactions are not the way to achieve it. Use of a database job (via DBMS_JOB) gives the desired result at the cost of a very small delay between the transaction completing and the DDL being performed. We can alter our ADD_COLUMN procedure to wrap the call to RUN_DDL within a job submission.

```
SQL> create or replace
  2  procedure ADD_COLUMN(p_table varchar2,
  3      p_column varchar2) is
  4    v number;
  5    j number;
  6  begin
```

```
 7      insert into LIST_OF_CHANGES
 8      values (p_table, p_column, sysdate);
 9      dbms_job.submit(j,
10        'run_ddl(''alter table '||p_table||' add '||p_column||''');');
11   end;
12   /
```

Procedure created.

```
SQL> exec add_column('emp','newcol2 number');
```

PL/SQL procedure successfully completed.

The DDL to add the column has not yet been executed; it has only been scheduled for execution via the job facility.

```
SQL> select what from user_jobs;

WHAT
-----------------------------------------------
run_ddl('alter table emp add newcol2 number');
```

At this point, we can choose to commit the transaction and have the job run, or issue a rollback to abandon the changes. The DDL is now part of the single transaction.

Auditing SELECT Statements

Before autonomous transactions, it was not possible to perform DML from within a SELECT statement. In all versions of Oracle, it is not possible to initiate a transaction from a SELECT statement. For example, consider the requirement to record whenever a user queries the EMP table. We will store the details within a table EMP_AUDIT.

```
SQL> drop table EMP_AUDIT;

Table dropped.

SQL> create table EMP_AUDIT (
  2      empno number(10),
  3      viewed date );

Table created.
```

We will build a function that adds a row to the EMP_AUDIT table for any employee number that is passed to it.

```
SQL> create or replace
  2  function AUDIT_ROW(p_empno number) return number is
  3  begin
  4    insert into EMP_AUDIT
  5    values (p_empno, sysdate);
  6    return 0;
  7  end;
  8  /

Function created.
```

If we want to call the AUDIT_ROW function in order to log whenever someone queries the EMP table, the following error results:

```
SQL> select AUDIT_ROW(empno)
  2  from emp;
select AUDIT_ROW(empno)
       *
ERROR at line 1:
ORA-14551: cannot perform a DML operation inside a query
ORA-06512: at "AUDIT_ROW", line 3
```

Amending the function to be an autonomous transaction is relatively straightforward, and it allows the query to take place.

```
SQL> create or replace
  2  function AUDIT_ROW(p_empno number) return number is
  3    pragma autonomous_transaction;
  4  begin
  5    insert into EMP_AUDIT
  6    values (p_empno, sysdate);
  7    commit;
  8    return 0;
  9  end;
 10  /

Function created.

SQL> select AUDIT_ROW(empno) EMPNO
  2  from emp;
```

```
      EMPNO
----------
      7369
...
```

14 rows selected.

How do we enforce that we would like to call the AUDIT_EMP function whenever we query the EMP table? By using a view of course! We can wrap the function call within a view to hide the functionality from the user.

```
SQL> create view EMP_WITH_AUDIT as
  2  select e.*, AUDIT_ROW(empno) x
  3  from emp e;

View created.

SQL> select *
  2  from emp_with_audit
  3  where rownum < 10;
```

EMPNO	ENAME	HIREDATE	SAL	DEPTNO	X
1	Name1	24/JUN/03	1000000	249	0
2	Name2	24/JUN/03	9950.33	420	0
3	Name3	24/JUN/03	8012.93	66	0
4	Name4	24/JUN/03	7688.15	200	0
5	Name5	24/JUN/03	9375.71	40	0
6	Name6	24/JUN/03	8407.97	244	0
7	Name7	25/JUN/03	7918.62	245	0
8	Name8	25/JUN/03	9061.74	122	0
9	Name9	25/JUN/03	8692.89	433	0

9 rows selected.

Having queried the view, we can now observe which rows have been viewed by querying the EMP_AUDIT table.

```
SQL> select * from emp_audit;

    EMPNO VIEWED
---------- ---------
        1 03/JUL/03
        2 03/JUL/03
```

```
              3  03/JUL/03
              4  03/JUL/03
              5  03/JUL/03
              6  03/JUL/03
              7  03/JUL/03
              8  03/JUL/03
              9  03/JUL/03

9 rows selected.
```

This all seems very impressive, but there are some problems with this approach. Let's empty our auditing table and then run several different queries against our new EMP_WITH_AUDIT view.

```
SQL> truncate table emp_audit;

Table truncated.

SQL> select count(*)
  2  from emp_with_audit;

  COUNT(*)
----------
     50000

SQL> select empno, hiredate, sal
  2  from emp_with_audit
  3  where rownum < 5;

    EMPNO HIREDATE         SAL
---------- --------- ----------
        1 24/JUN/03    1000000
        2 24/JUN/03    9950.33
        3 24/JUN/03    8012.93
        4 24/JUN/03    7688.15

SQL> select *
  2  from emp_with_audit
  3  where hiredate = to_date('27/06/03 04:44:00','DD/MM/YY HH:MI:SS');

    EMPNO ENAME                HIREDATE                   SAL     DEPTNO
---------- -------------------- -------------------- ---------- ----------
      226 Name226              27/06/03 04:44:00      8446.87         38
```

We counted all the records in the EMP table (via the EMP_WITH_AUDIT view). We also grabbed the first five rows but just for the EMPNO, HIREDATE, and SAL columns. Finally, we selected a row for a particular HIREDATE value. There should be a lot of audited rows in the EMP_AUDIT table.

```
SQL> select * from emp_audit;

    EMPNO VIEWED
---------- -----------------
       226 03/07/03 17:59:36
```

The SQL execution engine is quite smart, and it tries to avoid calling the function if at all possible. Only the very last query above actually created a row in the EMP_AUDIT table. Thus, you have not really gained a tight auditing mechanism, and for those records that are successfully audited, think of the overheads that are being introduced with such a mechanism. Every record retrieved results in a committed transaction. The only way that this will be successful will be if you have total control over every query used to retrieve data from the table. Without that level of control, probably the best auditing you can hope for would be to take advantage of the fine-grained auditing facilities available in version 9. We could add a policy to track queries to the EMP table.

```
SQL> begin
  2    DBMS_FGA.ADD_POLICY(
  3    object_schema => user,
  4    object_name   => 'EMP',
  5    policy_name   => 'AUDIT_EMP_RECORDS',
  6    audit_column  => 'salary');
  7  end;
  8  /

PL/SQL procedure successfully completed.
```

After this, queries to the EMP table can be tracked via the DBA_FGA_AUDIT_TRAIL view. A full discussion of this feature is beyond the scope of this book—refer to the *Application Developers Fundamental Guide* for a thorough coverage of this feature.

Auditing that Persists After Rollback

Perhaps the only justifiable use for autonomous transactions is "transaction-less" auditing. The most common implementation for autonomous transactions we've seen is their use for error logging within an application, in particular,

recording details about unforeseen errors within an application as part of a
generic catch-all-errors exception handler.

We cover this technique in detail in Chapter 10, "Debugging," but for the
sake of completeness here, recall the first example in this section in which the
procedure UPDATE_EMP contained a "when-others" exception handler. We can
amend this to catch details of the error before raising the error back to the calling
environment (and thus rolling back any changes the procedure made). We will
create a table, ERRS, to hold any errors that our procedure encounters.

```
SQL> create table ERRS
  2      ( module varchar2(30),
  3         errdate date,
  4         errmsg  varchar2(4000));

Table created.
```

We also create a simple procedure to add rows to the table via an
autonomous transaction.

```
SQL> create or replace
  2   procedure err_logger(p_module varchar2,
  3      p_msg varchar2) is
  4    pragma autonomous_transaction;
  5  begin
  6     insert into errs
  7     values (p_module,sysdate,substr(p_msg,1,4000));
  8     commit;
  9  end;
 10  /

Procedure created.
```

Then we adjust an UPDATE_EMP procedure to call the error logger. Notice that
the rollback has been removed, as discussed earlier in this section.

```
SQL> create or replace
  2   procedure UPDATE_EMP(p_empno number, p_sal number) is
  3  begin
  4    update DEPT
  5    set TOT_SAL = TOT_SAL +
  6                   ( select p_sal-sal
  7                      from    EMP
  8                      where   empno = p_empno )
  9    where deptno = ( select deptno
```

```
10                        from    EMP
11                        where   empno = p_empno);
12
13      update EMP
14      set sal = p_sal
15      where empno = p_empno;
16
17      update EMP_DELTAS
18      set change_type = 'SAL'
19      where empno = p_empno;
20
21      insert into EMP_AUDIT
22      values (sysdate,p_empno,p_sal);
23
24   exception
25     when others then
26       err_logger('UPDATE_EMP',sqlerrm);
27       raise;
28   end;
29   /

Procedure created.
```

Now we can call our procedure with an excessive salary value but also retain a permanent record of any errors that occur.

```
SQL> exec update_emp(7698,99999);
BEGIN update_emp(7698,99999); END;

*
ERROR at line 1:
ORA-01438: value larger than specified precision allows for this column
ORA-06512: at "UPDATE_EMP", line 26
ORA-06512: at line 1



SQL> select * from errs;

MODULE                          ERRDATE
------------------------------ ---------
ERRMSG
--------------------------------------------------------------------------
UPDATE_EMP                      03/JUL/03
ORA-01438: value larger than specified precision allows for this column
```

Summary

If there is one thing to take away from this chapter, it's that you shouldn't build a slow, unstable PL/SQL application that will still happily compile against a 7.2 database. Take advantage of the more recent features that allow a closer linkage between your PL/SQL and the underlying database structures.

After all, the ability to achieve this tight integration with the underlying data structures is perhaps the best feature of PL/SQL—no other language that accesses an Oracle database exhibits such closeness to the data. If you take the time to maximize that integration, you will build applications that are more resilient to the changes that inevitably occur in the database as your application requirements evolve over time.

As tight as that integration between PL/SQL and SQL is, there are still performance benefits to be had by minimizing the amount of transition between the two by using collections and "bulking up" your code.

PL/SQL Optimization Techniques

IF YOU'RE EMBARKING UPON your first major PL/SQL project, then the chapters in this book offer tried-and-tested techniques and advice that will ensure not only that your code works, but also that it works *well*. In keeping with our principle of demonstrability, throughout this book are many examples of how to benchmark and stress test the PL/SQL code you produce. However, no one likes to spend time benchmarking hypotheses only to find out that someone has already done the work for them.

What we present here is essentially a "tips and techniques" chapter that draws on much of what we discussed in the previous four chapters and then extends it to cover the following:

- Some specific, benchmarked solutions to commonly encountered problems within PL/SQL application development

- Some "hidden overheads" that can catch you out and ways to avoid them

- Common "gotchas" that trip people up time and again

We hope that what we document here will save you some work, and also inspire you to explore your own hypotheses and build test cases to validate them.

Minimizing Parsing and Memory Consumption

As we discussed in Chapter 1, minimizing parsing and keeping memory consumption under control are important steps toward achieving efficient PL/SQL applications. In this section, we take a look at some tips to avoid parsing issues with trigger code and invoker rights procedures, and we examine the use of pipelined functions to reduce memory consumption when transferring data between PL/SQL components.

Code Within Triggers

For many years I've been recommending to developers that, as much as possible, they limit the amount of code they put in triggers. I've suggested that they use a simple call to a procedure, passing the appropriate parameters to that procedure to do the work of the trigger. The motivation for this recommendation was based on an historical issue for trigger source code, namely that its compiled equivalent wasn't stored within the database.

In early releases of Oracle 7, the source code was stored and checked for validity when a trigger was created, but no compiled version of that source was stored. When the trigger was executed for the first time, the code was then compiled upon loading into the shared pool. If that code was aged out of the shared pool over the life of the instance, then the next time it was required, it would need to be recompiled. For procedures and packages, the compiled code *was* stored in the database and thus they didn't suffer this problem. Since Oracle 7.3, this issue has been resolved, with compiled trigger code also being stored in the database. Therefore, I gladly told developers that they were free to put as much code as they liked back into the triggers.

However, it turns out I was wrong: There are still benefits to moving all of your trigger code to stored PL/SQL units, if there are SQL statements within the trigger code. Recall from Chapter 1 that parsing is a significant performance threat in environments with a large number of concurrent users. Moving trigger code that contains SQL into PL/SQL procedures can lower the amount of parsing performed within your application, as we'll now demonstrate.

Consider the following example, in which we audit insertion of rows to a table T, using a trigger to copy some relevant details to a table T_AUDIT:

```
SQL> create table T (code number);

Table created.

SQL> create table T_AUDIT (
  2  code number,
  3  ins_date date );

Table created.

SQL> create or replace
  2      trigger TRG
  3      before insert on T
  4      for each row
  5      begin
  6          insert into T_AUDIT
  7          values (:new.code, sysdate);
```

```
8      end;
9   /
```

Trigger created.

We'll use the SQL_TRACE facility to record how much parsing activity takes place when we add some rows to table T. First, we establish our baseline by taking a "snapshot of" the parsing statistics for this session:

```
SQL> alter session set sql_trace = true;

Session altered.

SQL> set feedback off
SQL> select * from v$mystats
  2  where name like 'parse%';


NAME                           VALUE
------------------------------ ----------
parse time cpu                    16
parse time elapsed                24
parse count (total)              648
parse count (hard)                20
parse count (failures)             0
```

So, before we commence adding any rows to table T, we've performed 648 parse calls within this current session. We now insert ten rows with ten individual INSERT statements:

```
SQL> insert into T values (1);
SQL> insert into T values (1);
SQL> insert into T values (1);
SQL> insert into T values (1);
SQL> insert into T values (1);
SQL> insert into T values (1);
SQL> insert into T values (1);
SQL> insert into T values (1);
SQL> insert into T values (1);
SQL> insert into T values (1);
```

and we capture a fresh set of parsing information:

```
SQL> select * from v$mystats
  2  where name like 'parse%';
```

```
NAME                      VALUE
-----------------------   -------
parse time cpu               16
parse time elapsed           24
parse count (total)         679
parse count (hard)           20
parse count (failures)        0
```

A simple subtraction (648 from 679) tells us that we've made 31 parse calls. We'll repeat the exercise but this time, the trigger will delegate the work of inserting rows into our audit table to a procedure, T_AUDIT_PROC:

```
SQL> create or replace
  2  procedure T_AUDIT_PROC(p_code number) is
  3  begin
  4    insert into T_AUDIT
  5     values (p_code, sysdate);
  6  end;
  7  /

Procedure created.
```

We then redefine our trigger so that it simply calls this procedure:

```
SQL> create or replace
  2  trigger TRG
  3  before insert on T
  4  for each row
  6  call   t_audit_proc(:new.code)
  7  /

Trigger created.
```

We record a new baseline (the parse statistics before we perform any insertions):

```
SQL> select * from v$mystats
  2  where name like 'parse%';
```

```
NAME                        VALUE
-----------------------     ------
parse time cpu                16
parse time elapsed            24
parse count (total)          785
parse count (hard)            24
parse count (failures)        0
```

5 rows selected.

We repeat our insertion of ten rows and check the parsing statistics at the end of the exercise:

```
SQL> set feedback off
SQL> insert into T values (1);
SQL> insert into T values (1);
SQL> insert into T values (1);
SQL> insert into T values (1);
SQL> insert into T values (1);
SQL> insert into T values (1);
SQL> insert into T values (1);
SQL> insert into T values (1);
SQL> insert into T values (1);
SQL> insert into T values (1);

SQL> select * from v$mystats
  2   where name like 'parse%';
```

```
NAME                        VALUE
-----------------------     ----------
parse time cpu                16
parse time elapsed            24
parse count (total)          806
parse count (hard)            24
parse count (failures)        0
```

and then we turn off the trace collection (more on that shortly):

```
SQL> alter session set sql_trace = false;
```

The parsing count for the second test is 806 – 785 = 21! The same amount of work is being done in each case (that is, ten rows inserted into T and ten rows inserted into T_AUDIT), but by deferring the work to the procedure, we've reduced the number of parse calls from 31 to 21. To see why this is the case, we need to examine the trace file that we recorded. For the first test, we see entries in the trace file like this:

```
PARSING IN CURSOR #2
INSERT into T_AUDIT
    values (:b1, sysdate)
END OF STMT
PARSE #2:c=0,e=4843,p=0,cr=1,cu=0,mis=1,r=0,dep=1,og=0,tim=4716573269
EXEC #2:c=0,e=741,p=0,cr=1,cu=7,mis=0,r=1,dep=1,og=4,tim=4716575055

PARSING IN CURSOR #2
INSERT into T_AUDIT
    values (:b1, sysdate)
END OF STMT
PARSE #2:c=0,e=166,p=0,cr=0,cu=0,mis=0,r=0,dep=1,og=4,tim=4204155472
EXEC #2:c=0,e=266,p=0,cr=1,cu=1,mis=0,r=1,dep=1,og=4,tim=4204156643

PARSING IN CURSOR #2
INSERT into T_AUDIT
    values (:b1, sysdate)
END OF STMT
PARSE #2:c=0,e=94,p=0,cr=0,cu=0,mis=0,r=0,dep=1,og=4,tim=4204187769
EXEC #2:c=0,e=261,p=0,cr=1,cu=1,mis=0,r=1,dep=1,og=4,tim=4204189065
EXEC #1:c=0,e=2215,p=0,cr=2,cu=2,mis=0,r=1,dep=0,og=4,tim=4204189588
```

For each row added to T, we observe a parse call for the insertion into the audit table T_AUDIT. More accurately, we observe one parse call for each trigger execution. When we examine the trace file for the second case (in which we called a procedure), we see something quite different:

```
PARSING IN CURSOR #2
INSERT into T_AUDIT
    values (:b1, sysdate)
END OF STMT
```

```
PARSE #2:c=0,e=3314,p=0,cr=2,cu=0,mis=1,r=0,dep=1,og=0,tim=4960810746
EXEC #2:c=0,e=624,p=0,cr=1,cu=2,mis=0,r=1,dep=1,og=4,tim=4960812448
EXEC #2:c=0,e=179,p=0,cr=0,cu=1,mis=0,r=1,dep=1,og=4,tim=4960843780
EXEC #2:c=0,e=180,p=0,cr=0,cu=1,mis=0,r=1,dep=1,og=4,tim=4960874629
...
EXEC #2:c=0,e=182,p=0,cr=0,cu=1,mis=0,r=1,dep=1,og=4,tim=4960936653
```

We see only a single parse statement for insertion into our audit table. As long as we remain connected, any number of INSERT statements executed against table T will result in only a single parse for the auditing operation (the insert into T_AUDIT).

As you saw in Chapter 1, anything that reduces the amount of parsing will improve the overall scalability and efficiency of your systems. So, if you're looking for a simple guideline, avoid having SQL within a database trigger. If a trigger needs to run SQL, defer the work to a procedure.

Invoker Rights Procedures

We'll discuss invoker and definer rights procedures extensively in Chapter 8, but we want to discuss them here from the perspective of PL/SQL performance.

One issue that constantly confuses PL/SQL developers is the fact that, under the default definer rights mode, roles are disabled both at compilation and execution. So, for example, say a user account called CONFUSED has been granted the DBA role and thus has access to the DBA_USERS view from SQL*Plus:

```
SQL> select count(*) from dba_users;

  COUNT(*)
----------
        32
```

CONFUSED creates a procedure that uses this view:

```
SQL> conn CONFUSED/PASSWORD
Connected.
SQL> create or replace
  2  procedure GET_ROW is
  3    x number;
  4  begin
  5    execute immediate '
  6      select 1
  7      from   dba_users
```

```
8        where   rownum = 1' into x;
9   end;
10   /
```

Procedure created.

All seems well so far (although actually, this is only because our user CON-FUSED used dynamic SQL, which the database doesn't interpret at compile time). In any event, when he tries to execute the procedure, he finds that it fails:

```
SQL> exec get_row;
BEGIN get_row; END;

*

ERROR at line 1:
ORA-00942: table or view does not exist
ORA-06512: at "CONFUSED.GET_ROW", line 4
ORA-06512: at line 1
```

At this point the developer gets confused (hence the choice of username). The user in the example has the DBA privilege, but the user can't see the DBA_USERS table within his procedure. However, the user *can* see it when it's queried from SQL*Plus. This is because PL/SQL procedures run with only *directly granted* privileges, not those granted via a role (even if that role is the DBA role).

Invoker rights procedures have often been touted as the resolution to this "problem," because the standard privileges (via roles or otherwise) are retained when the procedure is executed. If CONFUSED re-creates the procedure as an invoker rights procedure, the problem is "solved":

```
SQL> create or replace
2   procedure GET_ROW authid current_user is
3     x number;
4   begin
5     execute immediate '
6        select 1
7        from    dba_users
8        where   rownum = 1' into x;
9   end;
10   /
```

Procedure created.

```
SQL> exec get_row;
```

```
PL/SQL procedure successfully completed.
```

Of course, most probably the correct solution would have been to grant select access on the DBA_USERS view to the CONFUSED account. But because of the ignorance surrounding the privileges associated with definer rights procedures, invoker rights have been viewed as a solution to a problem that doesn't exist.

Why *not* just use invoker rights for all PL/SQL programs and avoid any hassles with roles and so on? Because there is a performance overhead with invoker rights procedures. The PL/SQL guide states the following:

> *"Invoker-rights subprograms let you reuse code and centralize application logic."*

It's true that the code is reused—that is, only one copy of it is stored in the database—but in reality, the true benefit of reuse with respect to runtime performance, *sharing* of the code, doesn't occur with invoker rights procedures.

To demonstrate this, consider the following example. First, we'll create 11 user accounts, INV10 to INV20, each of which has an identical table within it called LOOKUP. We can do this with a little dynamic SQL (you need to be connected with an account with DBA privileges to run this):

```
SQL> begin
  2    for i in 10 .. 20 loop
  3      execute immediate
  4        'grant connect, resource to inv'||i||
  5        ' identified by xxx';
  6    execute immediate
  7      'create table inv'||i||'.lookup '||
  8      '( uno number primary key, '||
  9      '  data varchar2(20)) '||
 10      'organization index';
 11    execute immediate
 12      'insert into inv'||i||'.lookup '||
 13      'values ('||i||',''data'||i||''')';
 14    execute immediate
 15      'analyze table inv'||i||'.lookup estimate statistics';
 16    end loop;
 17  end;
 18  /
```

```
PL/SQL procedure successfully completed.
```

If we take a look at DBA_TABLES, we can now see the same table within each of the accounts we just created:

```
SQL> select owner, table_name
  2  from dba_tables
  3  where owner like 'INV__';

OWNER                          TABLE_NAME
------------------------------ --------------
INV10                          LOOKUP
INV11                          LOOKUP
INV12                          LOOKUP
INV13                          LOOKUP
INV14                          LOOKUP
INV15                          LOOKUP
INV16                          LOOKUP
INV17                          LOOKUP
INV18                          LOOKUP
INV19                          LOOKUP
INV20                          LOOKUP
```

Each LOOKUP table contains a single row of data that is relevant only to the owner of that table. Next, we'll create another user account called DEFINER, which contains a single table that is a consolidation of the tables owned by each of the INVnn accounts (that is, a single table with a 11 rows of data, one for each of the INVnn accounts):

```
SQL> grant connect, resource to definer identified by xxx;

Grant succeeded.

SQL> create table definer.lookup
  2  ( uno number primary key,
  3    data varchar2(20))
  4  organization index;

Table created.

SQL> insert into definer.lookup
  2  select rownum+9, 'data'||rownum
  3  from all_objects
  4  where rownum <= 11;

11 rows created.
```

We now create a procedure called GET, which is a normal definer rights procedure and will return the data for a particular user number (UNO) from the consolidated lookup table:

```
SQL> create or replace
  2  procedure definer.get(p_uno number) is
  3    d varchar2(20);
  4  begin
  5    select data
  6    into d
  7    from lookup
  8    where uno = p_uno;
  9  end;
 10  /

Procedure created.
```

Finally, we create an invoker rights procedure that will allow the INV*nn* accounts to get that same data from their own version of the LOOKUP table:

```
SQL> create or replace
  2  procedure definer.invoker_proc authid current_user is
  3    d varchar2(20);
  4  begin
  5    select data
  6    into d
  7    from lookup;
  8  end;
  9  /

Procedure created.
```

Before proceeding, let's summarize what we've created so far. We have a common table that contains 11 rows of data, one row for each of the INV*nn* accounts. Each of these INV*nn* accounts also has its own copy of the table, but it contains just the single row that is relevant to that account. There are two procedures available to the INV*nn* users to retrieve the row of data that "belongs" to them:

- **DEFINER.GET(userno number):** A *definer* rights procedure that will look up the single common table for the passed user number

- **DEFINER.INVOKER_PROC:** An *invoker* rights procedure that will query the table owned by the account that invokes this procedure

It would seem that either path would be appropriate, because each procedure involves just a single call to retrieve a single row of data. Furthermore, in terms of performance, it would seem like the invoker rights procedure should be the best option, because it only needs to process the single row of data contained in each schema's "local" table. Let's iterate through our invoker rights procedure 100,000 times and then do the same with the definer rights procedure:

```
SQL> begin
  2    for i in 1 .. 100000 loop
  3       definer.invoker_proc;   -- invokers right access to 1 row table
  4    end loop;
  5  end;
  6  /

PL/SQL procedure successfully completed.
```

Elapsed: 00:00:07.04

```
SQL> begin
  2    for i in 1 .. 100000 loop
  3       definer.get(10);   -- definers rights to 1 row from 11 row table
  4    end loop;
  5  end;
  6  /

PL/SQL procedure successfully completed.
```

Elapsed: 00:00:09.04

So, the invoker rights procedure runs a little faster. But something that isn't immediately apparent from these tests is the impact of the ability (or not) to share SQL. As we've demonstrated elsewhere, the sharing of code is an important component of scalability.

When we execute the definer rights procedure, even though we connect as 11 different schemas, they can all share the same SQL statement. Let's demonstrate this by flushing the shared pool and then running DEFINER.GET once from each of the INV*nn* accounts:

```
SQL> alter system flush shared_pool;

System altered.

SQL> conn inv10/xxx
Connected.
SQL> exec definer.get(10);
```

```
PL/SQL procedure successfully completed.

SQL> conn inv11/xxx
Connected.
SQL> exec definer.get(11);

PL/SQL procedure successfully completed.

...

...

SQL> conn inv20/xxx
Connected.
SQL> exec definer.get(20);

PL/SQL procedure successfully completed.
```

We'll now look at the shared pool for the recursive SQL from the 11 executions of this procedure:

```
SQL> select sql_text, executions
  2  from v$sql
  3  where sql_text like '%lookup%';

SQL_TEXT                                                EXECUTIONS
------------------------------------------------------- ----------
SELECT data   from lookup   where uno = :b1                     11
```

There is only one copy of the SQL in the shared pool. Any connected session that runs DEFINER.GET will share the SQL within that procedure. Compare that to what happens when we repeat the exercise with the invoker rights procedure, DEFINER.INVOKER_PROC, from each INV*nn* account:

```
SQL> alter system flush shared_pool;

System altered.

SQL> conn inv10/xxx
Connected.
SQL> exec definer.invoker_proc;

PL/SQL procedure successfully completed.
```

...

...

```
SQL> conn inv20/xxx
Connected.
SQL> exec definer.invoker_proc;

PL/SQL procedure successfully completed.
```

We once again check the shared pool and observe a startling difference:

```
SQL> select sql_text, executions
  2  from v$sql
  3  where sql_text like '%lookup%';

SQL_TEXT                                                 EXECUTIONS
-------------------------------------------------------- ----------
SELECT data    from lookup                                        1
SELECT data    from lookup                                        1
SELECT data    from lookup                                        1
SELECT data    from lookup                                        1
SELECT data    from lookup                                        1
SELECT data    from lookup                                        1
SELECT data    from lookup                                        1
SELECT data    from lookup                                        1
SELECT data    from lookup                                        1
SELECT data    from lookup                                        1
SELECT data    from lookup                                        1
```

Although the *text* of the SQL statements is the same, the fact that there are 11 copies of the SQL in the shared pool indicates that the SQL statements couldn't be shared. When sharing doesn't take place, the V$SQL_SHARED_CURSOR view can be used to determine the reason. Each column in the view describes a possible reason that sharing didn't take place:

```
SQL> desc v$sql_shared_cursor
 Name                              Null?    Type
 --------------------------------  -------  -----------
 ADDRESS                                    RAW(4)
 KGLHDPAR                                   RAW(4)
 UNBOUND_CURSOR                             VARCHAR2(1)
 SQL_TYPE_MISMATCH                          VARCHAR2(1)
 OPTIMIZER_MISMATCH                         VARCHAR2(1)
 OUTLINE_MISMATCH                           VARCHAR2(1)
```

STATS_ROW_MISMATCH	VARCHAR2(1)
LITERAL_MISMATCH	VARCHAR2(1)
SEC_DEPTH_MISMATCH	VARCHAR2(1)
EXPLAIN_PLAN_CURSOR	VARCHAR2(1)
BUFFERED_DML_MISMATCH	VARCHAR2(1)
PDML_ENV_MISMATCH	VARCHAR2(1)
INST_DRTLD_MISMATCH	VARCHAR2(1)
SLAVE_QC_MISMATCH	VARCHAR2(1)
TYPECHECK_MISMATCH	VARCHAR2(1)
AUTH_CHECK_MISMATCH	VARCHAR2(1)
BIND_MISMATCH	VARCHAR2(1)
DESCRIBE_MISMATCH	VARCHAR2(1)
LANGUAGE_MISMATCH	VARCHAR2(1)
TRANSLATION_MISMATCH	VARCHAR2(1)
ROW_LEVEL_SEC_MISMATCH	VARCHAR2(1)
INSUFF_PRIVS	VARCHAR2(1)
INSUFF_PRIVS_REM	VARCHAR2(1)
REMOTE_TRANS_MISMATCH	VARCHAR2(1)
LOGMINER_SESSION_MISMATCH	VARCHAR2(1)
INCOMP_LTRL_MISMATCH	VARCHAR2(1)
OVERLAP_TIME_MISMATCH	VARCHAR2(1)
SQL_REDIRECT_MISMATCH	VARCHAR2(1)
MV_QUERY_GEN_MISMATCH	VARCHAR2(1)
USER_BIND_PEEK_MISMATCH	VARCHAR2(1)
TYPCHK_DEP_MISMATCH	VARCHAR2(1)
NO_TRIGGER_MISMATCH	VARCHAR2(1)
FLASHBACK_CURSOR	VARCHAR2(1)

So, we can use the ADDRESS column in V$SQL for our 11 copies of the SQL statement to look into V$SQL_SHARED_CURSOR. This address is the parent address (KGLHDPAR) of the child cursors.

```
SQL> select * from v$sql_shared_cursor
  2   where KGLHDPAR =
  3   ( select address from v$sql
  4     where sql_text like 'SELECT data%'
  5     and rownum = 1 )
  6   /
```

```
ADDRESS  U S O O S L S E B P I S T A B D L T R I I R L I O S M U T N F
-------- - - - - - - - - - - - - - - - - - - - - - - - - - - - - - -
7C37C3AC N N N N N N N N N N N N N N N N N N N N N N N N N N N N N N N
7C0B8950 N N N N N N N N N N N N N Y N N N Y N N N N N N N N N N N N N
7C265E70 N N N N N N N N N N N N N Y N N N Y N N N N N N N N N N N N N
7C2A1E90 N N N N N N N N N N N N N Y N N N Y N N N N N N N N N N N N N
7C390474 N N N N N N N N N N N N N Y N N N Y N N N N N N N N N N N N N
7C3587A4 N N N N N N N N N N N N N Y N N N Y N N N N N N N N N N N N N
7C35E2C0 N N N N N N N N N N N N N Y N N N Y N N N N N N N N N N N N N
7C05C604 N N N N N N N N N N N N N Y N N N Y N N N N N N N N N N N N N
7C0604B0 N N N N N N N N N N N N N Y N N N Y N N N N N N N N N N N N N
7C3136B8 N N N N N N N N N N N N N Y N N N Y N N N N N N N N N N N N N
7C14DEE4 N N N N N N N N N N N N N Y N N N Y N N N N N N N N N N N N N
```

```
11 rows selected
```

By examining these columns, we can see that the reasons that sharing didn't occur were AUTH_CHECK_MISMATCH and TRANSLATION_MISMATCH.

The table, LOOKUP, in each SQL statement translates to a different table—that is, the local version of the LOOKUP table in each of the INVnn schemas. When you don't share SQL, you have a possible threat to scalability; thus, invoker rights procedures are such a threat. If you're building PL/SQL procedures that will be used infrequently or for small user populations, then it's unlikely that you'll encounter any dramatic problems, but be careful in other environments in which shared SQL is a key performance metric. Invoker rights procedures do have their place—for example, if you need to deploy common utilities that use dynamic SQL (because in processing the SQL you may need to observe the available privileges for the account currently executing the procedure). But they aren't a "solution" to ignorance about why definer rights procedures work the way they do.

Think Outside the Box: Using Pipelined Functions

Many PL/SQL programs are producer/consumer by nature. That is, they consume data by retrieving it from the database or, alternatively, they produce data that is then consumed by a client application or stored back into the database.

However, there is another type of use for PL/SQL programs: one that simply manipulates any data passed to it and passes the transformed result onto another process. Diagrammatically, they sit "between" a producer and a consumer process, as illustrated in Figure 5-1.

Figure 5-1. Typical procedure-consumer relationship between PL/SQL programs

> **NOTE** The terms *producer, manipulator,* and *consumer* are terms I've chosen to use here, whereas the more common industry terms used for such processes are *extract, transform, load (ETL)*. I've deliberately avoided the conventional industry terms because they tend to invoke thoughts of data warehouses, staging tables, and the like, but Oracle pipelined functions have far greater scope than that. Any procedure that receives data and performs a transformation on that data to be passed along to a further process falls under the banner of a "manipulator," and thus is worthy of consideration for pipelining, as you'll see shortly.

Figure 5-1 presents a rather simplistic view of this pipelined process and hides the cost of transferring the data between each of the three processing phases. Many producer/manipulator/consumer processes dump their results down to a database table to be read by the next phase of the process. A more realistic diagram is shown in Figure 5-2.

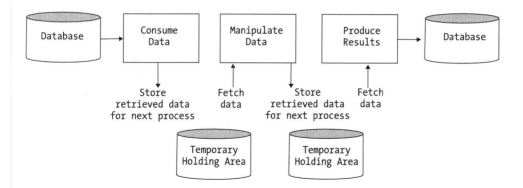

Figure 5-2. Hidden costs of producer-consumer PL/SQL programs

Often the specification for a program to handle this sort of process will detail how to retrieve the data from a temporary staging area, as well as describe another temporary staging area to store the results. However, as with many examples presented throughout this book, sometimes the key to successful PL/SQL application development involves thinking "outside the box." Rather than blindly follow the specification, it's always worth taking a little time to see if a less obvious solution might be better.

The use of temporary staging areas adds significant overhead in terms of database space usage and the redo cost of storing the additional copies of the data. With the introduction of collections in version 8, it became possible to pass complex data structures between each phase but, as you've already seen in Chapter 4, the inherent memory costs of this approach get prohibitive as the collections get large. In any event, use of a table or collection imposes a "stop/start" nature on the process. Ideally, as soon as you've retrieved the first row (or set of rows) from the database, they should be made available to the manipulation process, and then the producer process for storing back into the database. With collections or temporary tables, rather than passing data from one phase to the next as it becomes available, *all* of the data is batched up before the next phase can start.

The pipelined function facility, new to version 9, resolves this problem. Readers conversant with Unix will already be familiar with the concept of piping the output from one command to another. The Oracle concept is the same: A function can commence returning rows to a calling program *during* that function's execution, rather than having to wait until completion of that execution.

To demonstrate the potential advantages of using pipelined functions, we'll walk through an example that doesn't use pipelining, demonstrate where the drawbacks are, and then convert it to a pipelined solution to overcome those deficiencies.

For this example, we'll transform rows from the EMP table (by altering the SAL and the HIREDATE columns), and then load the modified rows into a resultant table, EMP2.

> **NOTE**   To keep the example simple, we're performing a task that could (and should) have been performed with standard SQL and not PL/SQL at all. You can assume that, although it isn't shown in the example, there exists some inherent processing layer that mandates a PL/SQL approach!

Let's take a look at the nonpipelined solution. There are three PL/SQL processes: a producer to read the rows from the EMP table, a manipulator to alter the salary and hire date, and a consumer to load the modified rows into the EMP2 table. First, we create an EMP2 table to hold the results:

```
SQL> create table EMP2 as
  2  select empno, ename, hiredate,sal, deptno
  3  from emp
  4  where rownum = 0;

Table created.
```

Next, we create a package, PKG, that will contain consumer, manipulator, and producer processes. To pass information between the processes, we define a collection, EMP_LIST, to hold employee records:

```
SQL> create or replace
  2  package PKG is
  3    type emp_list is
  4      table of emp2%rowtype;
  5
  6    function CONSUMER return sys_refcursor;
  7    function MANIPULATOR(src_rows sys_refcursor) return emp_list;
  8    procedure PRODUCER(changed_rows emp_list);
  9
 10  end;
 11  /

Package created.
```

The implementation is fairly straightforward. The CONSUMER function queries the EMP table and returns a cursor variable (a pointer) to the result set. The MANIPULATOR function takes that result set as input, queries the records, modifies the hire date and salary, and then returns a modified collection variable. The PRODUCER function cycles through the rows in the collection variable and adds those rows to the EMP2 table:

```
SQL> create or replace
  2  package body PKG is
  3
  4  function CONSUMER return sys_refcursor is
  5    src_rows sys_refcursor;
  6  begin
  7    open src_rows for
  8      select empno, ename, hiredate, sal, deptno
  9      from emp;
 10    return src_rows;
 11  end;
 12
```

```
13   function MANIPULATOR(src_rows sys_refcursor) return emp_list is
14      changed_rows emp_list;
15   begin
16      fetch src_rows
17      bulk collect into changed_rows;
18      close src_rows;
19      for i in 1 .. changed_rows.count loop
20         changed_rows(i).sal := changed_rows(i).sal+10;
21         changed_rows(i).hiredate := changed_rows(i).hiredate + 1;
22      end loop;
23      return changed_rows;
24   end;
25
26   procedure PRODUCER(changed_rows emp_list) is
27   begin
28      forall i in 1 .. changed_rows.count
29         insert into emp2 values changed_rows(i);
30      commit;
31   end;
32
33   end;
34   /
```

```
Package body created.
```

With the calls to the three routines nested within the package, the end result is a complete data transformation, whereby we fetch the EMP data, manipulate the hire date and salary, and store the modified data in the EMP2 table:

```
SQL> set timing on
SQL> exec pkg.producer(pkg.manipulator(pkg.consumer));

PL/SQL procedure successfully completed.

Elapsed: 00:00:08.02
SQL> select count(*) from emp2;

  COUNT(*)
----------
    100000
```

So far, so good. We transferred and manipulated 100,000 rows from EMP to EMP2 in 8 seconds. However, the overhead of the solution is in the amount of memory consumed, which we can gauge by examining our familiar V$MYSTATS view:

```
SQL> select * from v$mystats
  2  where name like '%pga%'
  3  /

NAME                        VALUE
-------------------------   ---------
session pga memory          55893380
session pga memory max      61660548
```

Sixty-one megabytes! The problem with this approach is obvious. In accordance with our principle of demonstrability, let's see what happens when there are 1,000,000 rows in the EMP table:

```
SQL> exec pkg.producer(pkg.manipulator(pkg.consumer));
ERROR at line 1:
ORA-04030: out of process memory when trying to allocate 16396 bytes (koh-kghu
call ,pl/sql vc2)
```

I crashed my database session (and shortly thereafter my laptop) because insufficient memory was available to hold the set of 1,000,000 employee records. The frustrating thing is that we didn't want to store the records in memory at all—we just wanted to transform them as they "flowed" from EMP to EMP2.

This is where a pipelined solution can help. We'll convert the process to use pipelined functions. Pipelined functions can't make use of PL/SQL records, only object types, so we need some object types equivalent to the EMP_LIST type in the nonpipelined solution:

```
SQL> create or replace
  2  type emp2rec is object (
  3     empno number(10),
  4     ename varchar2(20),
  5     hiredate date,
  6     sal number(10,2),
  7     deptno number(6) );
  8  /

Type created.

SQL> create or replace
  2  type emp2list as table of emp2rec;
  3  /

Type created.
```

The package specification is virtually unchanged. We simply indicate that the MANIPULATOR function is a pipelined function. Rather than batching up an entire set of records, it can pass each transformed record onto the next processing phase (in our case, the PRODUCER procedure) as soon as the transformation is complete:

```
SQL> create or replace
  2  package PKG2 is
  3     function CONSUMER return sys_refcursor;
  4     function MANIPULATOR(src_rows sys_refcursor) return emp2list pipelined;
  5     procedure PRODUCER;
  6
  7  end;
  8  /
```

```
Package created.
```

The package body is slightly different, because the emphasis here is on *not* passing data around between the various phases. But our CONSUMER function is unchanged, simply opening a REF CURSOR into the source data:

```
SQL> create or replace
  2  package body PKG2 is
  3
  4  function CONSUMER return sys_refcursor is
  5    src_rows sys_refcursor;
  6  begin
  7    open src_rows for
  8      select empno, ename, hiredate, sal, deptno
  9        from emp;
 10    return src_rows;
 11  end;
 12
```

The MANIPULATION function is also not a great deal different from the non-pipelined version, except that using the PIPE clause, modified rows are sent back to the calling environment *within* the cursor loop. As each row is changed, it is made available to the caller:

```
 13  function MANIPULATOR(src_rows sys_refcursor)
 14         return emp2list pipelined is
 15    r emp2rec;
 16    e emp2%rowtype;
 17  begin
```

```
18     loop
19       fetch src_rows into e;
20       exit when src_rows%notfound;
21       e.sal := e.sal+10;
22       e.hiredate := e.hiredate + 1;
23       pipe row (emp2rec(e.empno,e.ename,e.hiredate,e.sal,e.deptno ));
24     end loop;
25     close src_rows;
26     return;
27   end;
28
```

The PRODUCER only needs to open the cursor to the source of the data, pass that pointer (cursor variable) to the manipulator routine, and then, as the results are piped back, load them into the EMP2 table.

```
29   procedure PRODUCER is
30     rc sys_refcursor := consumer;
31   begin
32     insert into emp2
33     select * from table(cast(manipulator(rc) as emp2list ));
34   end;
35
36   end;
37   /
```

Package body created.

The end result is the same, because we haven't altered any of the desired functionality, and because we are simply passing collection elements as they become available rather than storing large collections, the memory costs are much smaller. Let's run the producer procedure and then check the memory statistics again (you need to disconnect and reconnect to clear the session-level statistics before running this second test):

```
SQL> exec pkg2.producer;

PL/SQL procedure successfully completed.

Elapsed: 00:00:22.02

SQL> select * from v$mystats
```

```
 2  where name like '%pga%'
 3  /
```

```
NAME                          VALUE
------------------------      ------
session pga memory            434676
session pga memory max        434676
```

Notice that the memory consumption is far lower, and this won't change no matter how large the number of rows processed. But the elapsed time for this result looks somewhat disappointing—recall that the nonpipelined solution took only 8 seconds. But now, we have total control over the balance between performance and memory consumption. For example, there is nothing to stop us from still using bulk facilities in the MANIPULATOR function—we can use a little more memory to get more performance. Rather then fetching and piping a single row at a time, we'll fetch 100 rows before passing them along to the consumer:

```
13  function MANIPULATOR(src_rows sys_refcursor)
14        return emp2list pipelined is
15     type elist is table of emp2%rowtype;
16     r emp2rec;
17     e elist;
18  begin
19     loop
20        fetch src_rows bulk collect into e limit 100;
21        for i in 1 .. e.count loop
22          e(i).sal := e(i).sal+10;
23          e(i).hiredate := e(i).hiredate + 1;
24          pipe row (emp2rec(
25                    e(i).empno,e(i).ename,
26                    e(i).hiredate,e(i).sal,e(i).deptno ));
27        end loop;
28        exit when src_rows%notfound;
29     end loop;
30     close src_rows;
31     return;
32  end;
33
```

```
SQL> exec pkg2.producer;

PL/SQL procedure successfully completed.
```

Elapsed: 00:00:09.08

```
SQL> select * from v$mystats
  2  where name like '%pga%'
  3  /

NAME                        VALUE
----------------------      ---------

session pga memory          1483788
session pga memory max      1549324
```

So simply by employing some controlled bulk collection, we got performance back down to that of the nonpipelined version while using only 2 percent of the memory requirements. Let's bump up the number of rows in the EMP table to 1 million and see if the memory problems we encountered before are now resolved:

```
SQL> exec pkg2.producer;

PL/SQL procedure successfully completed.

SQL> select * from v$mystats
  2  where name like '%pga%'
  3  /

NAME                            VALUE
------------------------------  -------

session pga memory              516640
session pga memory max          8643104

SQL> select count(*) from emp2;

  COUNT(*)
----------
    999999
```

This time my database session didn't crash, but there does some to be some incremental memory growth. At the time of this writing, I've been unable to determine why this growth occurs.

One other benefit is that, because the manipulator process takes a REF CURSOR as input and simply pipes rows as output, the producer and consumer routines become redundant. We can fold the manipulation process into standard SQL. The code then becomes as follows:

```
SQL> insert into emp2
  2  select *
  3  from table(
  4        cast(
  5          pkg2.manipulator(
  6            cursor( select empno, ename, hiredate,sal, deptno from emp))
  7          as emp2list ));

100000 rows created.
```

Probably the greatest challenge with pipelined functions is spotting opportunities for their use within your applications. *Any* process that requires you to stream output from a function might be improved with a pipelined function. In Chapter 1, we looked at using pipelined functions to efficiently return an arbitrary number of rows without the overhead of an underlying relational table. In Chapter 10, we'll cover how to use them to return real-time debugging information.

Data Types: Tips and Techniques

As discussed in Chapter 4, the data structures available within PL/SQL are rich and diverse. We encourage you to experiment thoroughly to examine which are the most efficient for your own applications. The results aren't always what you might anticipate.

Associative Arrays

Version 9.2 of Oracle introduced a new form of associative array, in which a string could be used as the array index. My first thought when these appeared on the scene was to wonder whether they performed as well as their index-by-binary-integer counterparts. That is, if I stored a numeric value inside a VARCHAR2 index, would it work as well as that same value stored in the conventional numeric index?

To benchmark this, we simply create two arrays, one indexed by BINARY_INTEGER and one by VARCHAR2. We then perform 100,000 assignments to each, using the familiar DBMS_UTILITY.GET_TIME to determine the elapsed time:

```
SQL> declare
  2      type varchar2_tab is table of number
```

```
 3        index by varchar2(100);
 4     vc varchar2_tab;
 5     type num_tab is table of number
 6        index by binary_integer;
 7     n num_tab;
 8     t number;
 9   begin
10     t := dbms_utility.get_time;
11     for i in 1 .. 100000 loop
12        n(i) := i;
13     end loop;
14     dbms_output.put_line('Index by Number  : '||
15         (dbms_utility.get_time-t));
16     t := dbms_utility.get_time;
17     for i in 1 .. 100000 loop
18        vc(i) := i;
19     end loop;
20     dbms_output.put_line('Index by Varchar2: '||
21         (dbms_utility.get_time-t));
22   end;
23   /
Index by Number  : 12
Index by Varchar2: 54

PL/SQL procedure successfully completed.
```

This first test appears to indicate that associative arrays aren't as efficient as the already available indexing scheme. This result is probably what you expected. After all, a numeric index for an array just "feels" more natural. But, of course, associative arrays can also be used to store data that is indexed sparsely—that is, where the indexes for the array entries aren't always contiguous. So, to be thorough, we should also benchmark this scenario.

The code is very similar. All we've done is store entries in the array with indexes 1000, 2000, 3000, and so on, instead of 1, 2, 3:

```
SQL> declare
 2     type varchar2_tab is table of number
 3        index by varchar2(100);
 4     vc varchar2_tab;
 5     type num_tab is table of number
 6        index by binary_integer;
 7     n num_tab;
 8     t number;
 9   begin
```

```
10    t := dbms_utility.get_time;
11    for i in 1 .. 100000 loop
12       n(i*1000) := i;
13    end loop;
14    dbms_output.put_line('Index by Number   : '||
15       (dbms_utility.get_time-t));
16    t := dbms_utility.get_time;
17    for i in 1 .. 100000 loop
18       vc(i*1000) := i;
19    end loop;
20    dbms_output.put_line('Index by Varchar2: '||
21       (dbms_utility.get_time-t));
22  end;
23  /
Index by Number   : 136
Index by Varchar2: 73

PL/SQL procedure successfully completed.
```

An interesting result indeed. When the indexes become sparse, having a character data type for the array index, even when that index is storing a numeric value, appears to be more efficient. Perhaps there is some special optimization in place to ensure that VARCHAR2 associative arrays are efficient when the entries are sparse. In applications in which performance is paramount, a VARCHAR2 indexed associative array may be a better alternative even if the indexes are "naturally" numeric.

Collections

Another area of exploration is to consider the handling of collections within PL/SQL, in which each entry in the collection is a %ROWTYPE or similar record variable. Given such a collection, it's possible to represent that data in two data structures:

- An array of records (create a row first, and then add it to a list)

- A record of arrays (create several lists, and then combine them to form a record)

But which structure should you use? You should consider two measures to answer this question:

- How efficiently can the structure be populated?

- How efficiently can data be retrieved from it?

The following package performs some fairly rudimentary testing to yield some initial answers. Our package, PKG, will have two procedures, REC_OF_ARRAY_TEST and ARRAY_OF_REC_TEST. Both do the same workload, but each performs the work on its namesake's data structure:

```
SQL> create or replace
  2  package pkg is
  3    procedure rec_of_array_test;
  4    procedure array_of_rec_test;
  5  end;
  6  /

Package created.
```

We need some types defined within our package to test our data structures. SREC_LIST is an array of records (SREC) in which the SREC record contains three scalar variables, and ARRAY_REC is a record in which each field within it is in itself an array (NUM_LIST):

```
SQL> create or replace
  2  package body pkg is
  3    type srec is record (a number, b number, c number, d number);
  4    type srec_list is table of srec;
  5
  6    type num_list is table of number;
  7    type array_rec is record (a num_list, b num_list,
  8                              c num_list, d num_list );
  9  procedure rec_of_array_test is
 10    s number := dbms_utility.get_time;
 11    e number;
 12    v1 srec_list;
 13    q number;
 14  begin
 15    v1 := srec_list();
 16    v1.extend(500000);
```

For each data structure we perform two (timed) tests. We make 2,000,000 assignments—that is, we iterate 500,000 times and assign a value to the four underlying record elements, A, B, C, and D:

```
 17    for i in 1 .. 500000 loop
 18      v1(i).a := i;
```

```
19        v1(i).b := i;
20        v1(i).c := i;
21        v1(i).d := i;
22      end loop;
23      e := dbms_utility.get_time;
24      dbms_output.put_line('Populate: '||(e-s));
```

Then, to test the performance of the retrieval of data, we fetch 250,000 pseudo-random entries from the structure. As usual, we record the before and after times with DBMS_UTILITY.GET_TIME:

```
25      for i in 1 .. 250000 loop
26        q := v1(i*2-1).a;
27        q := v1(i*2).b;
28        q := v1(500000-i).c;
29        q := v1(500000-2*i+1).d;
30      end loop;
31      s := dbms_utility.get_time;
32      dbms_output.put_line('Retrieve From: '||(s-e));
33    end;
34
```

We then perform the identical test for the other data structure:

```
35  procedure array_of_rec_test is
36      s number := dbms_utility.get_time;
37      e number;
38      v1 array_rec;
39      q number;
40    begin
41      v1.a := num_list();   v1.a.extend(500000);
42      v1.b := num_list();   v1.b.extend(500000);
43      v1.c := num_list();   v1.c.extend(500000);
44      v1.d := num_list();   v1.d.extend(500000);
45      for i in 1 .. 500000 loop
46        v1.a(i) := i;
47        v1.b(i) := i;
48        v1.c(i) := i;
49        v1.d(i) := i;
50      end loop;
51      e := dbms_utility.get_time;
52      dbms_output.put_line('Populate: '||(e-s));
53      for i in 1 .. 250000 loop
54        q := v1.a(i*2-1);
```

```
55      q := v1.b(i*2);
56      q := v1.c(500000-i);
57      q := v1.d(500000-2*i+1);
58    end loop;
59    s := dbms_utility.get_time;
60    dbms_output.put_line('Retrieve From: '||(s-e));
61  end;
62
63  end;
64  /
```

Package body created.

Now we're ready to run our benchmark for each of the data structures:

```
SQL> exec pkg.rec_of_array_test
Populate: 392
Retrieve From: 342

PL/SQL procedure successfully completed.

SQL> exec pkg.array_of_rec_test
Populate: 291
Retrieve From: 286

PL/SQL procedure successfully completed.
```

So, for both population and retrieval, it would appear to be more efficient to use an array of records than a record of arrays. Is it possible to explain why this is the case? Probably not—no doubt someone within the Oracle development team could tell us, but it isn't overly important to know *why*, but just that we developed a test to *prove* our assertions. In version 10g, this performance difference was still evident, but who knows what will be fastest in version 11 or 12?

Considerations When Using Record-Based DML

You saw in Chapter 4 that it's now also possible to use a ROWTYPE variable within INSERT and UPDATE statements. To recap, you can perform DML without referencing the underlying fields of a ROWTYPE variable. For example, you can code a procedure that allows an entire record to be updated without referencing any of the individual fields:

```
SQL> create or replace
  2  procedure WITH_ROWTYPE is
  3    r   T%ROWTYPE;
  4  begin
  5    select *
  6    into   r
  7    from   T
  8    where  rownum = 1;
  9
 10    update T1
 11    set row = r
 12    where rownum = 1;
 13  end;
 14  /

Procedure created.
```

Everything we've said so far about record-based DML has been positive, but there are a few issues that you need to be aware of. We'll explore these issues in the following sections.

You Can't Use the RETURNING Clause

The RETURNING clause doesn't support a record-based construct. Thus, the following code:

```
update T1
set row = r
returning * into r1;
```

will *not* compile. The individual fields are still required, thus reducing the insulation from database structure changes. This is still the case in version 10g.

Fields Are Sequenced, Not Named

When assigning the contents of a ROWTYPE variable to a database row, it's easy to visualize the fields of the record aligning with the database columns based on their names, but PL/SQL doesn't make any attempt to do this. All that matters to the PL/SQL engine is that the number of fields and the base datatypes of each field match the database columns in the order specified in the ROWTYPE definition—in other words, from left to right. The lengths and precision of numeric and character data types can differ as well. For example, we create two tables, T and T1, as follows:

```
SQL> create table T ( c1, c2) as
  2    select 1,2 from dual;

Table created.

SQL> create table T1 ( c2 number, c1 number );

Table created.
```

Notice that in creating table T1, we've reversed the order of the columns. Now we create a procedure, COPY_ROW, that simply copies a row from table T to table T1:

```
SQL> create or replace
  2   procedure COPY_ROW is
  3      r  T%ROWTYPE;
  4   begin
  5      select *
  6      into   r
  7      from   T
  8      where  rownum = 1;
  9
 10      insert into T1
 11      values r;
 12   end;
 13   /

Procedure created.
```

Now the question is, how will the column values be transferred from T to T1, as the columns in table T are sequenced as C1, C2, whereas in table T1 the sequence is C2, C1?

```
SQL> exec copy_row;

PL/SQL procedure successfully completed.

SQL> select * from t1;
```

```
       C2              C1
       ------          ------
         1               2
```

So column *names* (and hence field names within a ROWTYPE variable) make no difference—PL/SQL uses the sequencing of the columns within the database row and the fields within the record.

You May Incur Extra Redo

A fellow OakTable member, Jonathan Lewis, informed me of the little-known fact that if you update a column in a database table to the value that is already present in that column, then Oracle will still treat this as a "change," and generate undo and redo information for that change. To prove this, we'll measure how much redo information is generated for a "normal" update (in which we *change* a column value), and we'll then compare it to the case in which we update a column to its *current* value. First, we'll create a table with a 100-byte column and add some rows to it for our testing:

```
SQL> create table REDO_TEST
  2    ( col char(100));

Table created.

SQL> insert into REDO_TEST
  2    select 'x'
  3    from SRC
  4    where rownum < 100;

99 rows created.
```

Now we'll initially update the rows to a different value to establish a baseline of how much redo is required to perform a "normal" update. We'll take note of the amount of redo used so far in our session using the V$MYSTATS view that was created in Chapter 1:

```
SQL> select value
  2    from v$mystats
  3    where name = 'redo size';

    VALUE
 ----------
   2986004
```

And then we update the rows to a new value to see how much redo is generated:

```
SQL> update redo_test
  2   set col = 'y';

99 rows updated.

SQL> select value
  2   from v$mystats
  3   where name = 'redo size';

     VALUE
----------
   3028700
```

So changing a 100-byte column in 99 rows generates 3028700 – 2986004 = 42696 bytes of redo. Now the test is repeated, but the column is updated to the same value that is already there:

```
SQL> update redo_test
  2   set col = 'y';

99 rows updated.

SQL> select value
  2   from v$mystats
  3   where name = 'redo size';

     VALUE
----------
   3071192
```

We get almost the same (3071192 – 3028700 = 42492) number of bytes of redo information generated. Oracle doesn't attempt to "look under the covers" and decide if the update isn't necessary. It writes the changes (and hence the redo information) regardless.

How does this relate to record-based DML? The new record-based DML syntax is not part of some new ANSI standard; it's purely a PL/SQL convenience to insulate you from changes to the underlying data structures—in particular, reducing the areas in your code in which you need to explicitly list field-level components within a ROWTYPE variable. Enabling a trace on the execution of COPY_ROW from the earlier example reveals that the record-based DML SQL is transformed into a conventional UPDATE statement with all of the columns listed. Thus, the record-based DML for updating a row actually appears in the trace file as follows:

```
UPDATE T1
  set C1 = :b1,C2 = :b2
where rownum = 1
```

So, although there are coding and maintenance benefits to record-based DML, if a "typical" update in your application is changing only one of the columns, then converting this to a record-based update changes the operation to one in which the entire row is rewritten, with a subsequent increase in redo. Of course, if a typical update in your application involves changing most of the column values, then the amount of additional redo generated may not be an issue but, in any case, where an *unchanged* column dominates the size of an average row, converting an existing PL/SQL procedure using record-based DML might yield a nasty shock. For example, in the following REC_DML table, the Y column occupies a large percentage of the row size:

```
SQL> create table REC_DML (
  2    x number,
  3    y char(100),
  4    z number );

Table created.

SQL> insert into rec_dml
  2    select rownum, rownum, rownum
  3    from SRC
  4    where rownum < 1000;

999 rows created.
```

If conventional update code is used to update any of the fields except Y (in the following example, we'll only update the Z column), then the amount of redo will be relatively small. We've bundled up the before and after redo checks into the PL/SQL block to output the redo usage at the end of the block:

```
SQL> declare  -- conventional update code
  2    redo_amount number;
  3    p rec_dml%rowtype;
  4  begin
  5    select value
  6    into redo_amount
  7    from v$mystats
  8    where name = 'redo size';
  9    for i in ( select * from rec_dml)  loop
 10      update rec_dml
 11      set z = z + 1
```

```
12       where x = i.x;
13     end loop;
14     select value-redo_amount
15     into redo_amount
16     from v$mystats
17     where name = 'redo size';
18     dbms_output.put_line('Redo generated: '||redo_amount);
19   end;
20   /
Redo generated: 236972

PL/SQL procedure successfully completed.
```

Let's look at what happens if we blindly race out and convert this block to use record-based DML:

```
SQL> declare --new record based DML
  2     redo_amount number;
  3     p rec_dml%rowtype;
  4   begin
  5     select value
  6     into redo_amount
  7     from v$mystats
  8     where name = 'redo size';
  9     for i in ( select * from rec_dml)  loop
 10       p.x := i.x;
 11       p.y := i.y;
 12       p.z := i.z+1;
 13       update rec_dml
 14       set row = p
 15       where x = i.x;
 16     end loop;
 17     select value-redo_amount
 18     into redo_amount
 19     from v$mystats
 20     where name = 'redo size';
 21     dbms_output.put_line('Redo generated: '||redo_amount);
 22   end;
 23   /
Redo generated: 461040

PL/SQL procedure successfully completed.
```

The amount of redo generation nearly doubles from the conventional update version. Is the extra redo worth the extra insulation from code changes?

Only you can make that decision, but if you do choose to convert to record-based DML for the maintenance benefits, be sure to do some benchmarking to ensure your redo generation doesn't create problems when the code is run under production load.

You Can't Reference :OLD and :NEW Within Triggers

As with previous versions of Oracle, the :NEW and :OLD "records" that are available within row-level triggers aren't considered records, but "correlation names." Thus, you can't reference them as records and use them within record-based DML. However, as demonstrated earlier in this chapter, trigger code should defer execution of any SQL code to an underlying PL/SQL procedure. In such cases, we can use some SQL to generate trigger code that can transform the :NEW and :OLD correlation variables into ROWTYPE variables, and then pass those variables as parameters to an underlying procedure. We can then put the required functionality (including record-based DML if appropriate) in the called procedure. The following piece of SQL will create ROWTYPE variables out of the :NEW and :OLD correlation names for passing to a procedure block. The script prompts for a table name, and it outputs an appropriate CREATE TRIGGER command by querying USER_TAB_COLUMNS:

```
SQL> select
  2   case when column_id = 1 then
  3     'create or replace trigger '||table_name||
  4         '_trg'||chr(10)||
  5     'after update on '||table_name||chr(10)||
  6     'for each row'||chr(10)||
  7     'declare'||chr(10)||
  8     '  p_new '||table_name||'%rowtype;'||chr(10)||
  9     '  p_old '||table_name||'%rowtype;'||chr(10)||
 10     'begin'||chr(10)||
 11     '  p_new.'||lower(column_name)||' := :new.'||lower(column_name)||
 12           ';'||chr(10)||
 13     '  p_old.'||lower(column_name)||' := :old.'||lower(column_name)||';'
 14   else
 15     '  p_new.'||lower(column_name)||' := :new.'||lower(column_name)||
 16           ';'||chr(10)||
 17     '  p_old.'||lower(column_name)||' := :old.'||lower(column_name)||';'
 18   end trg
 19   from user_tab_columns
 20   where table_name = upper('&&table_name')
 21   union all
 22   select '  trgproc_&&table_name(p_new,p_old);' from dual
```

```
23   union all
24   select 'end;' from dual
25   /
Enter value for table_name: EMP


TRG
----------------------------------------
create or replace trigger EMP_trg
after update on EMP
for each row
declare
  p_new EMP%rowtype;
  p_old EMP%rowtype;
begin
  p_new.empno := :new.empno;
  p_old.empno := :old.empno;

  p_new.ename := :new.ename;
  p_old.ename := :old.ename;

  p_new.hiredate := :new.hiredate;
  p_old.hiredate := :old.hiredate;

  p_new.sal := :new.sal;
  p_old.sal := :old.sal;

  p_new.deptno := :new.deptno;
  p_old.deptno := :old.deptno;

  trgproc_emp(p_new,p_old);
end;
```

Adopting a script like this (or your own customized variant) can be an effective means to ensure a consistent approach to all trigger code in your application.

Calling PL/SQL

You need to take care when calling PL/SQL functions from SQL, because even if a PL/SQL function or procedure is very efficient to run, there is a cost to the actual act of *calling* such a PL/SQL module from an SQL statement. Oracle has separate engines for running PL/SQL and SQL, and there is an overhead each time you make a transition from one to the other. In this section, we'll benchmark this cost and then look at ways of reducing it. We'll also demonstrate how important it is to extend the good practices of using bind variables and minimizing parsing, as discussed in Chapter 1, to situations in which you're dynamically calling PL/SQL.

Use PL/SQL to Expose the Data Model, Not Extend It

To introduce this topic, here's a simple query of the USER_OBJECTS view from a project I'm currently working on (which is related to hospital patients):

```
SQL> select object_name
  2  from user_objects
  3  where object_type = 'FUNCTION';

OBJECT_NAME
-------------------------------------
GET_ANSWER_NAME
GET_ASSESSSMENT_NAME
GET_GENDER_NAME
GET_LEGALSTATUS_NAME
GET_PROGRAM_NAME
etc
etc
```

If you consider the underlying source code for any one of the preceding functions, a common theme is revealed:

```
SQL> select text
  2  from user_source
  3  where name = 'GET_GENDER_NAME'
  4  order by line;

TEXT
------------------------------------------------------------------
function get_gender_name(p_id sex.id%type) return sex.name%type is
  v_name sex.name%type;
begin
  select name
  into    v_name
  from    sex
  where   id = p_id;
  return v_name;
end;
```

You can see that the GET_GENDER_NAME function is part of a suite of PL/SQL functions that are designed to be used throughout the application to return the NAME (or description) from reference code tables, which are keyed with a surrogate key (ID). Incidentally, I lost the battle to get them all moved into packages!

Nevertheless, all lookups are served by these common routines, which will assist the application in both performance and future maintenance requirements. Thus, in this example, anywhere within the application where the gender name needs to be determined from a known gender ID, use of this function ensures that the SQL within the function will be shared, and that future changes to the underlying table structures need only be handled within the function, and not in myriad places within the application.

The problem is that once these PL/SQL functions are available, developers tend to think of them as "cost-free" and that *any* requirement to return a person's gender should be done through the GET_GENDER_NAME function. Thus, these functions start to appear in SQL statements. For example, to list a patient's details, including the patient's gender, the queries are written as follows:

```
SQL> select id,
  2          first_name||' '||last_name full_name,
  3          get_gender_name(sexid) gender
  4   from persons;

       ID FULL_NAME               GENDER
---------- ------------------------ ----------
    10504 John Peterson            MALE
    10507 Andrew Betent            MALE
    10514 Michelle Jones           FEMALE
    10524 Peta Lazenby             FEMALE
```

The results are correct, but one of the reasons that surrogate keys are used in the first place is that relational database are designed to join data. It's fairly obvious from the preceding query that the SEXID column in the PERSONS table is a foreign key to the SEX table. Hence, the query should simply be written as a join, and no PL/SQL should be used at all:

```
SQL> select p.id,
  2          p.first_name||' '||p.last_name full_name,
  3          sex.name
  4   from persons p,
  5          sex
  6   where sex.id = p.sexid;
```

```
       ID FULL_NAME                    NAME
---------- -----------------------    -----------------
    10504 John Peterson               MALE
    10507 Andrew Betent               MALE
    10514 Michelle Jones              FEMALE
    10524 Peta Lazenby                FEMALE
```

A further manifestation of this problem is that these utility functions start to crop up in view definitions because, more often than not, queries from views need to output a textual description for a surrogate key, not the surrogate key value itself. For example, to see the details for a PERSON record, we might define PERSON_DETAILS view as follows:

```
create or replace
view PERSON_DETAILS (
 person_id,
 first_name,
 last_name,
 gender,
 suburb,
 hospital
 ...) as
select
  person_id,
  first_name,
  last_name,
  get_gender_name(sex_id),
  get_suburb_descr(suburb_id),
  get_hospital_name(cur_hospital_id)
  ...
from  person;
```

Once these functions are defined as view columns, they also become exposed as being available for use within WHERE clause predicates. Slowly but surely, we end up rewriting the SQL join feature with a PL/SQL alternative. Think back to the motivations for the PL/SQL language: It's an *extension* to SQL (in this case, joins), not a replacement for it.

You need to take care when calling PL/SQL functions from SQL because, as we said in the introduction to this section, Oracle has separate engines for running PL/SQL and SQL, and there's an overhead each time we make a transition from one to the other. We can approximate the cost of the transition between the PL/SQL and SQL engines using the following test (thanks to Dave Ensor for providing the methodology for this experiment).

To measure the transition cost, we can compare the timing difference between a set of trigger invocations that simply do a PL/SQL assignment and an identical trigger that also performs a simple SELECT statement (and thus invokes the SQL engine). The total transition cost will be as follows:

$$Time_{transition} = Time_{trigger\_with\_select} - Time_{trigger\_without\_select} - Time_{select\_statements}$$

We can perform the test as follows. First, we trace the insertion of 20,000 rows into a table that has an underlying row-level trigger, but in which that trigger only performs a basic PL/SQL assignment:

```
SQL> create table T2 ( k number(5))

Table created.
SQL> create or replace package P is
  2    v number := 0;
  3  end;
  4  /

Package created.
```

Our trigger simply adds 1 to the package variable previously declared:

```
SQL> create or replace
  2    trigger T2_TRG
  3    before insert on T2
  4    for each row
  5    begin
  6      p.v := p.v + 1;
  7    end;
  8  /

Trigger created.
```

We enable SQL_TRACE and then add 20,000 rows to our table, thus firing the trigger 20,000 times:

```
SQL> alter session set sql_trace = true;

Session altered.

SQL> insert into T2 /* no_select_in_trigger */
```

```
  2  select rownum
  3  from all_objects
  4  where rownum <= 20000;

20000 rows created.

SQL> alter session set sql_trace = false;
```

Before analyzing the trace file, let's repeat the test, but this time within the trigger we also perform a simple SELECT statement:

```
SQL> create or replace
  2  trigger T2_TRG
  3  before insert on T2
  4  for each row
  5  declare
  6    l number;
  7  begin
  8    select 1 into l from dual;
  9    p.v := p.v + 1;
 10  end;
 11  /

Trigger created.
```

We truncate the table, and then reload it with the same 20,000 rows:

```
SQL> truncate table T2;

Table truncated.

SQL> alter session set sql_trace = true;

Session altered.

SQL> insert into T2 /* with_select_in_trigger */
  2  select rownum
  3  from all_objects
  4  where rownum <= 20000;

20000 rows created.

SQL> alter session set sql_trace = false;
```

Session altered.

When we examine the trace files, we observe the following results. First, we analyze the trace file results for the test in which the trigger performed a basic PL/SQL variable assignment:

```
insert into T2 /* no_select_in_trigger */
select rownum
from all_objects
where rownum <= 20000
```

call	count	cpu	elapsed	disk	query	current	rows
Parse	1	0.01	0.02	0	0	0	0
Execute	1	3.81	6.56	157	81540	23456	20000
Fetch	0	0.00	0.00	0	0	0	0
total	2	3.82	6.59	157	81540	23456	20000

We then compare this to the trace file results from the test in which the trigger also performed a SELECT statement:

```
insert into T2 /* with_select_in_trigger */
select rownum
from all_objects
where rownum <= 20000
```

call	count	cpu	elapsed	disk	query	current	rows
Parse	1	0.02	0.02	0	0	0	0
Execute	1	12.87	13.13	40	81541	20460	20000
Fetch	0	0.00	0.00	0	0	0	0
total	2	12.89	13.15	40	81541	20460	20000

We can see that there was an additional cost to running the trigger that executed the SELECT statement of 12.89 − 3.82 = 9.07 CPU seconds. Now, some of this will be the cost of actually running the SELECT 1 FROM DUAL statement within the trigger, which we can also get from the trace file:

```
SELECT 1
from dual
```

call	count	cpu	elapsed	disk	query	current	rows
Parse	1	0.00	0.00	0	0	0	0
Execute	20000	1.80	1.96	0	0	0	0
Fetch	20000	1.86	1.90	0	60000	0	20000
total	40001	3.66	3.86	0	60000	0	20000

This still leaves us with an additional cost in CPU time of 9.07 – 3.66 = 5.41 seconds. Because the trigger was executed 20,000 times, this gives a transition cost from SQL to PL/SQL of approximately 273 microseconds per call. Very fast, it seems, but what is important to recognize is that "very fast" isn't the same as "infinitely fast" (or zero cost).

In the preceding test, nearly 60 percent of the response time was lost in PL/SQL to SQL transition overhead. Embedding lookup functionality within PL/SQL is fine for the benefit of applications, but remember that there is a cost of calling them from SQL, and using them to avoid a join is probably robbing a database of what it's designed to do and what it does best.

If you absolutely must call a PL/SQL function repeatedly within an SQL statement, there are a number of mechanisms for handling this efficiently. Common sense dictates that the way to reduce the cost of *n* PL/SQL function calls during query execution is to do either of the following:

- Reduce *n*—that is, execute the function fewer times in the query.

- Precalculate all of the possible values of the PL/SQL function before the query is executed so that you don't need to run the PL/SQL function at all.

Let's explore each of these two approaches.

Reducing the Number of Calls

Before the number of PL/SQL function calls in a query can be reduced, obviously we need a means to count the number of times it's executed. Probably the easiest way to achieve this is with a package variable, as the following example demonstrates. The package COUNTER is just a simple set of routines to increment a package variable. We'll use this package to keep a count of the number of executions of a PL/SQL function when called from an SQL statement. We'll have three simple procedures within the package to do the following:

- Reset the counter back to zero.

- Increment the counter by 1.

- Display the current value of the counter.

The code for the COUNTER procedure is as follows:

```
SQL> create or replace
  2  package counter is
  3    procedure reset;
  4    procedure inc;
  5    procedure show;
  6  end;
  7  /

Package created.

SQL> create or replace
  2  package body counter is
  3    cnt pls_integer := 0;
  4    procedure reset is
  5    begin
  6      cnt := 0;
  7    end ;
  8    procedure inc is
  9    begin
 10      cnt := cnt + 1;
 11    end;
 12    procedure show is
 13    begin
 14        dbms_output.put_line('Execution Count: '||cnt);
 15    end;
 16  end;
 17  /

Package body created.
```

Now, if we want to record how many times a function, DO_SOMETHING, was called when run from within an SQL statement, we simply alter the function of interest to increment the package variable each time it's called:

```
SQL> create or replace
  2  function do_something(p varchar2) return varchar2 is
  3  begin
  4    counter.inc;
  5
  6    -- (whatever processing the function does)
```

```
7    return p;
8  end;
9  /
```

Function created.

Counting the executions is then just a case of executing the query and outputting the value of the counter. Before starting our test, we reset our counter to zero:

```
SQL> exec counter.reset;

PL/SQL procedure successfully completed.
```

Next, we create a table, BIG_TAB, which is a copy of the DBA_SOURCE table (you may need a DBA to set this table up for you):

```
SQL> create table big_tab
  2    as select owner, name, type, line
  3    from dba_source;

Table created.

SQL> analyze table big_tab estimate statistics;

Table analyzed.
```

Now we run a query against BIG_TAB, calling the DO_SOMETHING function for each row returned from the query:

```
SQL> select name, line, do_something(owner)
  2    from  big_tab;

NAME                       LINE  DO SOMETHING(OWNER)
-------------------------  ----  -------------------
STANDARD                      1  SYS
STANDARD                      2  SYS
STANDARD                      3  SYS
STANDARD                      4  SYS
STANDARD                      5  SYS
STANDARD                      6  SYS
STANDARD                      7  SYS
  ...
```

```
143349 rows selected.
```

The query returned 143,349 rows, and we can call our COUNTER package to find how many times the DO_SOMETHING function was called:

```
SQL> exec counter.show;
Execution Count: 143349

PL/SQL procedure successfully completed.
```

That the function was executed once for each row in the table in this example seems fair. However, more interesting results occur when more complex statements are considered. We'll reset our counter and this time run a query that references the DO_SOMETHING function three times:

```
SQL> exec counter.reset;

PL/SQL procedure successfully completed.

SQL> select name, line, do_something(owner)
  2  from   big_tab
  3  where do_something(owner) is not null
  4  order by do_something(owner) desc
  5  /

NAME                       LINE DO_SOMETHING(OWNER)
---------------------- ---------- ---------------------
STANDARD                      1 SYS
STANDARD                      2 SYS
STANDARD                      3 SYS
STANDARD                      4 SYS
STANDARD                      5 SYS
STANDARD                      6 SYS
STANDARD                      7 SYS
  ...

143349 rows selected.

SQL> exec counter.show;
Execution Count: 286698

PL/SQL procedure successfully completed.
```

The number of executions has increased by a factor of 2. This is an impressive result because it demonstrates that Oracle doesn't simply execute the function every time it appears in the SQL query. The optimizer can apply various transformations to SQL queries to improve their performance, so predicting the number of executions of a PL/SQL function within a SQL query is difficult if not impossible. However, by carefully constructing the SQL query text, a developer can "help" the optimizer to stay away from an excessive number of executions—a process we'll outline now.

In our test case, the first step in reducing the number of executions is to recognize that, although there are 143,349 rows in BIG_TAB, it's unlikely that there will be that many different values for the OWNER column. A quick check shows that there are, in fact, 15 different values for the OWNER column:

```
SQL> select count(distinct owner)
  2   from dba_source;


COUNT(DISTINCTOWNER)
--------------------
                  15
```

With this in mind, we try to code an inline view to calculate the result of DO_SOMETHING for just the distinct owner values:

```
SQL> exec counter.reset;
SQL> select name, line, function_result
  2   from big_tab a,
  3     ( select distinct owner, do_something(owner) function_result
  4       from big_tab ) f
  5       where a.owner = f.owner
  6  /
SQL> exec counter.show;
Execution Count: 143349

PL/SQL procedure successfully completed.
```

No improvement there, but the poor result of this first attempt is to be expected, because the processing to remove duplicates has to be done *after* the call to DO_SOMETHING (because each call could return any possible value). This leads to the next version of the code, in which the distinct set of owners is determined first, and the DO_SOMETHING function is applied to the results:

```
SQL> exec counter.reset;
SQL> select name, line, function_result
  2        from big_tab a,
```

```
3      ( select owner, do_something(owner) function_result
4        from ( select distinct owner
5                 from big_tab ) ) f
6      where a.owner = f.owner
7    /
SQL> exec counter.show;
```
Execution Count: 143349

```
PL/SQL procedure successfully completed.
```

Still no success. From the query text, it looks like the executions should drop, so the optimizer must be applying some sort of transformation to the inline view within the query that results in the high number of function executions. Time to head to the manuals. A quick check in the *Performance Tuning Guide* shows that "distinctness" isn't a sufficient criterion to stop the optimizer from applying transformations to inline views:

> *"The optimizer can merge a view into a referencing query block when the view has one or more base tables, provided the view does not contain any of the following:*
>
> *Set operators (UNION, UNION ALL, INTERSECT, MINUS)*
>
> *A CONNECT BY clause*
>
> *A ROWNUM pseudocolumn*
>
> *Aggregate functions (AVG, COUNT, MAX, MIN, SUM) in the select list."*

This gives a path to follow toward an appropriate solution. If we alter our inline query to reference the ROWNUM pseudo-column, then (according to the manual) the inline view won't be merged with the outer view. Let's test this hypothesis:

```
SQL> exec counter.reset;
SQL> select name, line, function_result
  2      from big_tab a,
  3      ( select owner, rownum, do_something(owner) function_result
  4        from ( select distinct owner
  5                 from big_tab ) ) f
  6      where a.owner = f.owner
  7    /

SQL> exec counter.show;
```
Execution Count: 15

```
PL/SQL procedure successfully completed.
```

Success! Another alternative to altering the query to include ROWNUM is to use the NO_MERGE hint as described within the *Performance Tuning Guide*. In either case, some careful documentation is recommended within the code, because it wouldn't be immediately apparent to a maintainer why ROWNUM or the NO_MERGE hint was required.

Precreating Values with Function-Based Indexes

Rather than try to minimize the number of times the function is to be executed, what if we could store all of the possible results of the DO_SOMETHING function so that a query wouldn't ever have to execute the function, no matter how complicated the query? Well, storing the results of the PL/SQL function is precisely a use for a function-based index, so we'll explore that option as a means of reducing the number of calls.

> **NOTE** To create and use function-based indexes requires some privileges and instance parameter settings to be appropriately set. See the "Creating a Function-Based Index" section in the *Database Administrator's Guide* for details.

Let's create a function-based index on the expression DO_SOMETHING(OWNER):

```
SQL> create index big_ix on
  2  big_tab ( do_something(owner));
create index big_ix on big_tab ( do_something(owner))
                                  *
ERROR at line 1:
ORA-30553: The function is not deterministic
```

The first thing that you'll discover is that any function to be used within a function-based index must be defined as *deterministic*; that is, you must guarantee to Oracle that, for a given input, the function will always return a consistent result. So, once the function has been redefined, it can be used within an index:

```
SQL> create or replace
  2  function do_something(p_owner varchar2)
  3    return varchar2 deterministic is
  4  begin
  5    counter.inc;
  6    return p_owner;
```

```
7   end;
8   /

Function created.

SQL> create index big_ix on
  2  big_tab ( do_something(owner));

Index created.
```

For function-based indexes to be considered by the optimizer, statistics must be present because function-based indexes are only "seen" by the cost-based optimizer:

```
SQL> analyze index big_ix estimate statistics;

Index analyzed.
```

Now all that is required is to convince the optimizer to use the index instead of executing the function. We'll start with the very first query from the first example:

```
SQL> exec counter.reset;
SQL> select name, line, do_something(owner)
  2  from  big_tab;
SQL> exec counter.show;
Execution Count: 143349
```

Examination of the execution plan revealed a full-table scan; that is, the index was not used. Moreover, delving deeper into an event 10053[1] optimizer trace showed that the index wasn't even considered. This is a correct decision by the optimizer because indexes never store null values and, of course, there's no guarantee that the DO_SOMETHING function doesn't return a null. If DO_SOMETHING did return a null for some rows, then using the function-based index would result in missing data from the result set. Unfortunately, there's no facility in Oracle to indicate to the optimizer that the result of the function used (within an index) won't be null, so the best that can be done is to tell the optimizer at query time:

```
SQL> exec counter.reset;
SQL> select name, line, do_something(owner)
```

---

1. A full discussion on the 10053 event trace is beyond the scope of this book, but a search on Google for this event will reveal many sources of information on how to use this feature and diagnose its output.

```
  2  from  big_tab
  3  where do_something(owner) is not null;
SQL> exec counter.show;
Execution Count: 286698
```

Even with this additional predicate, it appears that the optimizer won't choose the index. At least in this case, the 10053 trace indicates that the index *was* considered but was deemed to be too costly. Presumably, if the table was large enough, the index may be used by choice. In any event, the optimizer can now be forced to use the index with a hint:

```
SQL> exec counter.reset;
SQL> select /*+ INDEX(big_tab big_ix) */ name,
  2  line, do_something(owner)
  3  from  big_tab
  4  where do_something(owner) is not null
SQL> exec counter.show;
Execution Count: 0
```

Hence, for this particular example, using a function-based index to speed up PL/SQL calls from SQL is possible, but it did introduce reliance on the use of an index hint.

To wrap up, we return again to the maxim: PL/SQL is an extension to SQL, not a replacement. Don't let the benefits of PL/SQL's tight integration with the database turn into a noose around your neck in terms of performance.

Dynamically Calling PL/SQL

You've already seen in Chapter 1 the high cost of parsing within your applications. But you've also seen that one of the beauties of PL/SQL is that using bind variables and minimizing parsing all gets done automatically for you, as long as you code static SQL within your PL/SQL programs. All PL/SQL variables become bind variables, thus parsing is minimized, giving greater performance.

Although PL/SQL does all of this parsing minimization automatically, it isn't enough to adopt the good practices of static SQL and bind variables *within* the PL/SQL—you also need to take care when *executing* that PL/SQL. A commonly encountered poor coding practice is the passing of literal strings for any appropriate parameter values when *calling* the PL/SQL (typically from another environment such as Java). Just like SQL, a block of PL/SQL also needs to be parsed. For example, consider a procedure that takes a numeric parameter X:

```
SQL> create or replace
  2  procedure DO_WORK(x number) is
```

```
3    y number;
4  begin
5    y := x;
6  end;
7  /
```

Procedure created.

We can benchmark this procedure being called 10,000 times in anonymous block in which bind variables are used for the procedure parameter. Using SQL*Plus timing, we can observe that approximately 2,000 calls per seconds are possible:

```
SQL> set timing on
SQL> begin
  2    for i in 1 .. 10000 loop
  3      execute immediate 'begin do_work(:x); end;' using i;
  4    end loop;
  5  end;
  6  /
```

PL/SQL procedure successfully completed.

Elapsed: 00:00:05.05

However, PL/SQL routines are commonly called from a non-PL/SQL environment such as Java or Visual Basic, in which the anonymous block is simply built as a string, and thus literals are passed as parameters. When this is done, the performance degrades astronomically. We can simulate this with the following PL/SQL block. We'll call the DO_WORK procedure 10,000 times as before, but each time the parameter X will be passed as a literal value, not as a bind variable:

```
SQL> begin
  2    for i in 1 .. 10000 loop
  3      execute immediate 'begin do_work('||i||'); end;';
  4    end loop;
  5  end;
  6  /
```

PL/SQL procedure successfully completed.

Elapsed: 00:01:47.02

This represents a twentyfold drop in performance. There's no excuse for allowing this kind of performance problem into your database. Even if you're using a development environment in which binding is difficult or impossible, the parsing problem can still be worked around to some extent using a couple of alternatives: using a table to hold the parameter values or storing parameters in a collection, both of which we'll explore now.

Using a Table

In a bindless environment, we can take advantage of Oracle's CURSOR_SHARING[2] feature and a database table to pass the parameters. For example, we can convert the previous DO_WORK example into one that uses a table to pass the parameters. The table can be a temporary table to reduce the overhead of adding the rows.

```
SQL> create global temporary table parms
  2  ( parm_val number )
  3  on commit preserve rows;

Table created.
```

We then alter the DO_WORK procedure that we created to process all of the values in the PARMS table, rather then just a single row:

```
SQL> create or replace
  2  procedure DO_WORK is
  3  begin
  4    for i in ( select * from parms ) loop
  5      -- processing for each row
  6    end loop;
  7  end;
  8  /

Procedure created.
```

So to "pass parameters" to the procedure, we now can add values to the PARMS table. We can set the CURSOR_SHARING parameter to ensure that any SQL statements to add parameters also don't cause excessive parsing:

```
SQL> alter session set cursor_sharing = force;

Session altered.
```

---

2. "CURSOR_SHARING" was introduced in version 8*i* of Oracle. For applications that do not use bind variables, CURSOR_SHARING replaces all occurrences of literals within SQL with system-generated bind variables. This can often be used as a "Band-Aid"" solution to solving the parsing problem.

```
--
-- Simulate with PL/SQL a calling environment that cannot
-- use bind variables

SQL> begin
  2    for i in 1 .. 10000 loop
  3       execute immediate 'insert into parms values ('||i||')';
  4    end loop;
  5    execute immediate 'begin do_work; end;';
  6    execute immediate 'truncate table parms';
  7    end;
  8    /

PL/SQL procedure successfully completed.
```

Elapsed: 00:00:05.02

By using a temporary table, this solution also works in a multiuser environment, because each session can only see its own values in the PARMS table.

Using a Type

A similar alternative to avoid the repeated parse calls to a procedure is to "batch" the literal values up into a collection, and then pass that entire collection into the procedure. Continuing with the preceding example, a collection of numeric values can be passed to the procedure using a predefined type, NUM_LIST:

```
SQL> create or replace
  2    type num_list is table of number;
  3    /

Type created.

SQL> create or replace
  2    procedure DO_WORK(x num_list) is
  3    begin
  4       for i in 1 .. x.count loop
  5            null;
  6       end loop;
  7    end;
  8    /

Procedure created.
```

A little PL/SQL can be used to build the literal procedure call, so that the call to the DO_WORK procedure will be as follows:

```
do_work( num_list(1,2,3,….n));

SQL> set timing on
SQL> declare
  2     v varchar2(32767) := 'num_list(';
  3  begin
  4     for i in 1 .. 5000 loop
  5        v := v || case when i = 1 then to_char(i) else ','||i end;
  6     end loop;
  7     v := v || ')';
  8     execute immediate 'begin do_work('||v||'); end;';
  9  end;
 10  /


PL/SQL procedure successfully completed.

Elapsed: 00:00:01.08
```

So using a type or a table can avoid the parsing costs of passing literals as parameters to PL/SQL from any calling environment. Even if you're forced to use an environment that allows only pure dynamic SQL, some functionality exists to minimize the amount of parsing required. Each of these alternatives are what we refer to as "Band-Aid" solutions; that is, they're workarounds for the poor practice of not using bind variables in the first place, and each introduces some other overheads that aren't always obvious. Consider the second alternative, in which a large collection is generated and then passed to the procedure. A quick look at the session-level statistics after the call to DO_WORK shows that passing a large collection has an impact on memory consumption:

```
SQL> select * from v$mystats;

NAME                             VALUE
-------------------------------- ----------
...
session pga memory max           14910880
```

We chewed up 14MB of session memory in order to pass the large collection!

CURSOR_SHARING for "One-Off" Scripts

If you're ever presented with a large file of DML (for example, static scripts used to populate table data), the CURSOR_SHARING session-level setting can be useful. For example, if you're presented with the script of the form

```
insert into MY_TABLE values (1,2,3);
insert into MY_TABLE values (4,5,6);
insert into MY_TABLE values (7,8,9);
etc
```

then adding ALTER SESSION SET CURSOR_SHARING = FORCE to the front of the script will improve the performance of the script but, more important, it will reduce the impact on the rest of the system.

SQL Within PL/SQL

You've seen already in this chapter that there's a cost for transition between the PL/SQL and SQL engines. Unfortunately, you may be incurring the cost of that transition without even knowing it, as we'll demonstrate in this section. Of course, even with this transition cost, you can't code *all* PL/SQL programs without running any SQL—the database isn't much use if you never query it! So in this section we'll also look at ways to at least minimize the use of *dynamic* SQL, which is typically more expensive than static SQL.

SQL Functions and Recursive SQL

Oracle offers a number of functions that provide information about the current environment, such as SYSDATE, USER, and UID, and these functions can be referenced from PL/SQL. For example, we may have a table with columns CHANGE_DATE and CHANGE_BY that are used to record *who* changed an employee record and *when* that person changed it. We can use a trigger to automate the audit of these changes to the EMP table within a new table, AUDIT_EMP:

```
SQL> create table AUDIT_EMP (
  2      empno       number(10),
```

```
  3     reason      varchar2(30),
  4     change_date date,
  5     change_by   varchar2(30));

Table created.

SQL> create or replace
  2   trigger AUDIT_EMP_CHANGES
  3   before insert or update or delete
  4   on EMP
  5   for each row
  6   declare
  7     v_change date := sysdate;
  8     v_uid    number := uid;
  9     v_reason varchar2(30);
 10   begin
 11     if inserting then
 12        v_reason := 'Addition';
 13     elsif deleting then
 14        v_reason := 'Deletion';
 15     elsif updating then
 16        v_reason := 'Modification';
 17     end if;
 18     insert into audit_emp values
 19        ( :new.empno, v_reason, v_change, v_uid);
 20   end;
 21   /
```

We're using the SYSDATE and UID functions to record the current time and current user ID to add to the audit rows. However, this innocuous-looking code reveals some interesting details when we activate a trace:

```
SQL> alter session set sql_trace = true;

Session altered.
```

and then we modify 14 rows, which will fire our trigger 14 times:

```
SQL> delete from emp;

14 rows deleted.
```

After running TKPROF on the trace file, the following SQL statement appears in the trace file:

```
SELECT uid
from
 sys.dual
```

call	count	cpu	elapsed	disk	query	current	rows
Parse	1	0.00	0.00	0	0	0	0
Execute	14	0.00	0.00	0	0	0	0
Fetch	14	0.00	0.00	0	42	0	14
total	29	0.00	0.00	0	42	0	14

Our code didn't explicitly contain this statement, so where did it come from? Although various functions, such as UID and SYSDATE, are permitted in PL/SQL, some of them can only have their value assigned via the SQL engine. Thus, in order to discover the value of UID, our employee audit trigger generated a recursive SQL statement for *every* row affected by the originating DML. We saw this same behavior in Chapter 2, with the SYS_CONTEXT function. Notice that SYSDATE didn't suffer from this problem—this test was performed on version 9.2, and you may find that there are in fact recursive SQL statements for SYSDATE in your own trace files, depending on the version of Oracle you're running.

Probably the quickest way to determine if a function referenced from within PL/SQL will invoke a recursive SQL is to put together a simple test and check the trace file. For example, to check the SOUNDEX function, we enable a trace and then cycle through a number of iterations of SOUNDEX:

```
SQL> alter session set sql_trace = true;

Session altered.

SQL> declare
  2    x varchar2(80);
  3  begin
  4    for i in 1 .. 100 loop
  5       x := soundex('asdasd');
  6    end loop;
  7  end;
  8  /

PL/SQL procedure successfully completed.

SQL> alter session set sql_trace =false;
```

```
Session altered.
```

The trace file reveals that SOUNDEX is also affected:

```
SELECT soundex(:b1)
from
 sys.dual
```

call	count	cpu	elapsed	disk	query	current	rows
Parse	0	0.00	0.00	0	0	0	0
Execute	100	0.01	0.00	0	0	0	0
Fetch	100	0.01	0.00	0	300	0	100
total	200	0.02	0.00	0	300	0	100

However, with a little common sense, it's pretty easy to avoid the impact of this recursive SQL. If the functions are being used to set values that will be used in a SQL statement (such as the previous auditing trigger), then reference the function *directly* within the SQL. In the auditing example, we need not store the UID and SYSDATE in a variable. We can simply use them at the point of insertion into the auditing table. The code should be altered as follows:

```
SQL> create or replace
  2  trigger AUDIT_EMP_CHANGES
  3  before insert or update or delete
  4  on EMP
  5  for each row
  6  declare
  7    v_reason varchar2(30);
  8  begin
  9    if inserting then
 10      v_reason := 'Addition';
 11    elsif deleting then
 12      v_reason := 'Deletion';
 13    elsif updating then
 14      v_reason := 'Modification';
 15    end if;
 16    insert into audit_emp values
 17      ( :new.empno, v_reason, sysdate, uid);
 18  end;
 19  /
```

```
Trigger created.
```

If the functions are *not* going to be used within SQL (for example, you might be auditing to a file instead of an audit table), then you should aim to eliminate any redundant calls to the functions. For example, the value of the USER and UID functions aren't going to change throughout the duration of a session, so these could be assigned to package variables and then referenced where required. We could create a variable within the package specification that is initialized upon the first reference to the user ID:

```
SQL> create or replace
  2  package U is
  3     id number := uid;
  4  end;
  5  /
```

```
Package created.
```

Here's a version of the auditing trigger that writes the details to a file and avoids excessive reference to the UID function by accessing the package variable instead:

```
SQL> create or replace
  2  trigger AUDIT_EMP_TO_FILE
  3  before insert or update or delete
  4  on EMP
  5  for each row
  6  declare
  7     f utl_file.file_type;
  8     v_reason varchar2(30);
  9  begin
 10     f := utl_file.fopen('/tmp','audit.dat','A');
 11     if inserting then
 12        v_reason := 'Addition';
 13     elsif deleting then
 14        v_reason := 'Deletion';
 15     elsif updating then
 16        v_reason := 'Modification';
 17     end if;
 18     utl_file.put_line(f,'EMPNO '||:new.empno);
 19     utl_file.put_line(f,'REASON '||v_reason);
 20     utl_file.put_line(f,'DATE '||sysdate);
 21     utl_file.put_line(f,'UID '||u.id);
```

```
22      utl_file.fclose(f);
23   end;
24   /
```

Trigger created.

Tracing the entire session through several different DML changes to the EMP table shows that we only incurred a single recursive SQL statement:

```
SELECT uid
from
 sys.dual
```

call	count	cpu	elapsed	disk	query	current	rows
Parse	1	0.00	0.00	0	0	0	0
Execute	1	0.00	0.00	0	0	0	0
Fetch	1	0.00	0.00	0	3	0	1
total	3	0.00	0.00	0	3	0	1

Readers curious to get a definitive list of which functions will generate recursive SQL can find out probing the PL/SQL baseline package body, STANDARD. The source for this module is stored in $ORACLE_HOME/rdbms/admin/stdbody.sql. A search through this file reveals which functions are populated with a "select from dual." For example, the SOUNDEX function is defined as follows:

```
function SOUNDEX(ch VARCHAR2 CHARACTER SET ANY_CS)
        return VARCHAR2 CHARACTER SET ch%CHARSET is
    c VARCHAR2(2000) CHARACTER SET ch%CHARSET;
  begin
    select soundex(ch) into c from sys.dual;
    return c;
  end SOUNDEX;
```

At the time of this writing, the list of functions in version 9.2 that may generate recursive SQL is as follows:

```
NLS_CHARSET_NAME
NLS_CHARSET_ID
NLS_CHARSET_DECL_LEN
USERENV
SYS_CONTEXT
```

```
SYS_GUID
SOUNDEX
UID
USER
SYSTIMESTAMP
DBTIMEZONE
```

If you're using any sort of code generation tool, be sure to have a quick scan over the code. In my experience, generated code (for example, the table APIs in Designer) is often overgenerous with its references to the USER function in particular.

Effective Dynamic SQL

As discussed in Chapter 1, every new SQL statement presented to the database must be parsed to ensure that it's valid before it can be executed, so the fewer new SQL statements presented to the system, the better the system will scale.

This doesn't mean that dynamic SQL has no place in PL/SQL—if it was never required, Oracle wouldn't have developed the DBMS_SQL package and certainly wouldn't have extended this to the "execute immediate" facilities that arrived with version 8*i*. However, it does mean that you have to be judicious in your use of it.

Curiously enough, the most common textbook example I see for use of dynamic SQL is the "unknown" table example. The following code accepts the name of a table as a parameter and returns the count of rows for that table:

```
SQL> create or replace
  2   procedure GET_ROW_COUNT(p_table varchar2) is
  3     c number;
  4   begin
  5     execute immediate
  6     'select count(*) from '||p_table
  7     into c;
  8    dbms_output.put_line(c||' rows');
  9   end;
 10   /

Procedure created.

SQL> set serverout on
SQL> exec get_row_count('emp');
17 rows
```

```
PL/SQL procedure successfully completed.

SQL> exec get_row_count('dept');
4 rows

PL/SQL procedure successfully completed.
```

But seriously, think about the number of times in a project in which code is built and there is no knowledge in advance of what the table name might be for a particular query. There may be some very quirky niche applications out there that have this behavior, but I would contend that these are extremely rare. Within a production environment, I see only two main uses for dynamic SQL in PL/SQL.

Processing DDL

With the advent of global temporary tables, there are very few reasons for developers to be creating, altering, or dropping objects in a production database. However, for administrators, the ability to wrap DDL within a PL/SQL procedure is a very useful feature. For example, you might want a manager to be able to reset the password only for users in the manager's department. Clearly, an administrator doesn't want to give the ALTER USER privilege to the manager, because the manager could then alter any user (and not just the user's password), so wrapping the DDL within a procedure makes the process controlled and secure. The following RESET_PASSWORD procedure checks to ensure that a manager can only reset passwords for those users who are members of the manager's department. An administrator would then grant execute privileges on this procedure to the manager:

```
SQL> create or replace
  2    procedure reset_password(p_empno varchar2) is
  3      v_username varchar2(30);
  4    begin
  5      select ename
  6      into   v_username
  7      from   emp
  8      where  empno = p_empno
  9      and    mgr = ( select empno from emp where ename = user );
 10      execute immediate
 11        'alter user "'||v_username||'" '||
 12        ' identified by '||v_username;
 13    exception
 14      when no_data_found then
 15        raise_application_error(-20000,
```

```
16          'You are not authorised to alter employee '||p_empno);
17   end;
18   /
```

Procedure created.

Consider what happens when the manager, BLAKE, logs on and tries to reset the password for an employee who isn't in his department:

```
SQL> conn blake/blake
Connected.
SQL> exec admin.reset_password(7788);
BEGIN admin.reset_password(7788); END;

*
ERROR at line 1:
ORA-20000: You are not authorised to alter employee 7788
ORA-06512: at "ADMIN.RESET_PASSWORD", line 14
ORA-06512: at line 1
```

However, when ADAMS logs on, he's allowed to reset this password:

```
SQL> conn adams/adams
Connected.
SQL> exec admin.reset_password(7788);

PL/SQL procedure successfully completed.
```

Using PL/SQL, we can extend the processing of DDL so that we can also include it within an open transaction. Unlike some other relational databases in the marketplace, whenever Oracle processes a DDL statement, it ends the current transaction (with a commit) before running the DDL statement within its own transaction. This can be problematic when DDL is being run within your own applications. Considering the preceding example, what if we wish to audit password changes by logging them to an audit table? We have two options here:

- We add a record to the audit table first, and then process the DDL to reset the password.

- We reset the password first, and then add a record to the audit table.

Both options have data integrity problems. If we add an audit record first, but then the password reset DDL fails for some reason, then we've audited an event that didn't occur. If we reset the password first, but the audit record fails to insert, then we lose the audit information. We need both steps to either succeed or fail.

The solution here is to wrap the DDL processing within the DBMS_JOB facility. First, we create a table to hold the audit records, and then recode the RESET_PASS-WORD procedure to use DBMS_JOB:

```
SQL> create table PASSWORD_AUDIT (
  2    empno number,
  3    date_change date );

Table created.

SQL> create or replace
  2  procedure admin.reset_password(p_empno varchar2) is
  3    v_username varchar2(30);
  4    v_job number;
  5  begin
  6    select ename
  7    into    v_username
  8    from    emp
  9    where   empno = p_empno
 10    and     mgr = ( select empno from emp where ename = user );
 11    insert into password_audit values (
 12      p_empno, user, sysdate);
 13    dbms_job.submit(v_job,
 14      'begin execute immediate ' ||
 15      '''alter user "'||v_username||'" ' ||
 16      ' identified by '||v_username||'''; end;');
 17  exception
 18    when no_data_found then
 19      raise_application_error(-20000,
 20        'You are not authorised to alter employee '||p_empno);
 21  end;
 22  /

Procedure created.
```

Now we run our procedure to reset the password for CLARK, whose employee number is 7782:

```
SQL> exec admin.reset_password(7782);

PL/SQL procedure successfully completed.
```

Note that at this point, we have an open transaction. The password reset hasn't yet taken place. We've added a row to the PASSWORD_AUDIT table for CLARK:

```
SQL> select * from password_audit;

    EMPNO DATE_CHAN
---------- ---------
     7782 31/OCT/03
```

and we've submitted a database job to reset the password for CLARK:

```
SQL> select what from user_jobs;

WHAT
------------------------------------------------------------------------
begin execute immediate 'alter user "CLARK"  identified by CLARK'; end;
```

Because job submission is transactional, at this point we can either roll back the change, which will abandon both the password audit and the job to reset the password, or we can commit the change, at which point both the audit and the job will take place.

Dealing with Variable WHERE Clauses

Any system that allows any form of ad-hoc query facility may benefit from dynamic SQL in order to build a WHERE clause that isn't known until runtime. In fact, one of the very first examples of dynamic SQL provided in the *PL/SQL Reference* is precisely this:

```
CREATE PROCEDURE delete_rows (
   table_name IN VARCHAR2,
   condition IN VARCHAR2 DEFAULT NULL) AS
   where_clause VARCHAR2(100) := ' WHERE ' || condition;
BEGIN
   IF condition IS NULL THEN
    where_clause := NULL;
   END IF;
   EXECUTE IMMEDIATE
     'DELETE FROM ' || table_name || where_clause;
END;
```

Does an unknown WHERE clause justify the overheads of dynamic SQL? It's
hard to say—as always, it's a balancing act. Using dynamic SQL is easy, but as
you've seen, it may introduce increased parsing overheads. Alternatively, if there
are a manageable number of anticipated permutations, then using static SQL to
cater for each of those permutations may be a better option. For example, consider a procedure to allow variable WHERE clause predicates on the standard DEPT
table:

```
SQL> desc dept
 Name                          Null?     Type
 ----------------------------- --------- --------------
 DEPTNO                                  NUMBER(2)
 DNAME                                   VARCHAR2(14)
 LOC                                     VARCHAR2(13)
```

Assuming that any predicates to this table will be of the form COLUMN = VALUE
and the logical operations between predicates will only be AND and OR, then this
gives rise to 15 possible queries:

1. deptno = …

2. dname = …

3. loc = …

4. deptno = … and dname = …

5. deptno = … or dname = …

6. deptno = … and loc = …

7. deptno = … or loc = …

8. loc = … and dname = …

9. loc = … or dname = …

10. deptno = … and dname = … and loc = …

11. deptno = … and (dname = … or loc = …)

12. (deptno = … and dname =) … or loc = …

13. (deptno = … or dname =) … and loc = …

14. deptno = … or (dname = … and loc = …)

15. deptno = … or dname = … or loc = …

However, given that DEPTNO is a primary key for this table, some of the preceding permutations can probably be discarded as redundant. In this case, permutations 4, 5, 6, 10, 11, and 12 are unlikely to provide any great benefit, leaving nine possible SQL queries that will be run against the DEPT table. This is possibly a small enough set to simply statically code each of the queries within a procedure, in which the parameter P_OPTION is indicative of the particular permutation that the user is interested in. Purely to assist with cataloging each of the possible static SQL statement, we've used an explicit cursor so that the SQL statements are grouped together at the top of the procedure. A static SQL solution would look like this:

```
SQL> create or replace
  2  procedure STATIC_ADHOC (
  3      p_deptno number,
  4      p_dname varchar2,
  5      p_loc   number,
  6      p_option number ) is
  7      cursor c1 is
  8        select * from dept
  9        where deptno = p_deptno;
 10      cursor c2 is
 11        select * from dept
 12        where dname = p_dname;
 13      cursor c3 is
 14        select * from dept
 15        where loc = p_loc;
 16      cursor c7 is
 17        select * from dept
 18        where deptno = p_deptno or loc = p_loc;
 19      cursor c8 is
 20        select * from dept
 21        where loc = p_loc and dname = p_dname;
 22      cursor c9 is
 23        select * from dept
 24        where loc = p_loc or dname = p_dname;
 25      cursor c13 is
 26        select * from dept
 27        where ( deptno = p_deptno or dname = p_dname)  and loc = p_loc;
 28      cursor c14 is
 29        select * from dept
```

```
30       where deptno = p_deptno or ( dname = p_dname and loc = p_loc);
31    cursor c15 is
32       select * from dept
33       where deptno = p_deptno or dname = p_dname or loc = p_loc;
34    r dept%rowtype;
35  begin
36    if p_option = 1 then
37       open  c1; fetch c1 into r; close c1;
38    elsif p_option = 2 then
39       open  c2; fetch c2 into r; close c2;
40    elsif p_option = 3 then
41       open  c3; fetch c3 into r; close c3;
42    elsif p_option = 7 then
43       open  c7; fetch c7 into r; close c7;
44    elsif p_option = 8 then
45       open  c8; fetch c8 into r; close c8;
46    elsif p_option = 9 then
47       open  c9; fetch c9 into r; close c9;
48    elsif p_option = 13 then
49       open  c13; fetch c13 into r; close c13;
50    elsif p_option = 14 then
51       open  c14; fetch c14 into r; close c14;
52    elsif p_option = 15 then
53       open  c15; fetch c15 into r; close c15;
54    end if;
55  end;
56  /


Procedure created.
```

It is, of course, trivial to build a purely dynamic equivalent in which the caller is entirely responsible for the WHERE clause. We can simply use a REF CURSOR (see Chapter 3) to create a cursor based on any passed WHERE clause:

```
SQL> create or replace
  2  procedure DYN_ADHOC(p_where varchar2) is
  3    type rc is ref cursor;
  4    c rc;
  5    r dept%rowtype;
  6  begin
  7    open c for 'select * from dept where '||p_where;
  8    fetch c into r;
  9    close c;
 10  end;
 11  /
```

```
Procedure created.
```

But this will be at the expense of not using bind variables for each query. As demonstrated in Chapter 1, for a high concurrency system, this could be a critical performance bottleneck. Let's test the two versions previously presented. We'll create a copy of the DEPT table that will be used to drive a number of queries. In this example, the table has 5,000 rows (from the data generated with the REPTEST.SQL script used in Chapter 1):

```
SQL> create table DEPT_COPY as select * from DEPT;

Table created.
```

Then we'll truncate the original DEPT table so that the performance of each of the possible permutation queries will be identical (that is, none of them will find any rows):

```
SQL> truncate table DEPT;

Table truncated.
```

And now to test the performance, each procedure will be exercised with some of the variants of WHERE clause predicates that are anticipated. By cycling through the copy of the DEPT table taken earlier, the ROWNUM pseudo-column can be used to generate some "random" choices of the allowable predicates:

```
SQL> set timing on
SQL> begin
  2    for i in (
  3      select dc.*,
  4             rownum r,
```

We modulo the row number to yield one of nine different WHERE clauses:

```
  5             decode(mod(rownum,9)+1,
  6             1,'(deptno= '||deptno||' or dname='''||dname||''')  and loc='||loc,
  7             2,'deptno='||deptno||' or ( dname='''||dname||''' and loc='||loc||')',
  8             3,'deptno = '||deptno||' or dname = '''||dname||''' or loc = '||loc,
  9             4,'deptno = '||deptno||' or loc = '||loc,
 10             5,'deptno = '||deptno,
```

```
11          6,'dname = '''||dname||'''',
12          7,'loc = '||loc||' and dname = '''||dname||'''',
13          8,'loc = '||loc||' or dname = '''||dname||'''',
14          9,'loc = '||loc)  where_clause
15   from dept_copy dc ) loop
```

We then pass the WHERE clause to the dynamic SQL version that takes the entire clause, including any literals as a parameter:

```
16      DYN_ADHOC(i.where_clause);
17   end loop;
18   end;
19   /
```

```
PL/SQL procedure successfully completed.
Elapsed: 00:01:57.00
```

Now we'll do the same for the static version, in which we've precoded all of the possible WHERE clauses within the STATIC_ADHOC, so all we need to do is pass a numeric option ranging from 1 to 9:

```
SQL> declare
  2     options num_list := num_list(1,2,3,7,8,9,13,14,15);
  3     v_where varchar2(500);
  4   begin
  5    for i in ( select dc.*, rownum r from dept_copy dc ) loop
  6      STATIC_ADHOC(i.deptno, i.dname, i.loc, options(mod(i.r,9)+1));
  7    end loop;
  8   end;
  9   /
```

```
PL/SQL procedure successfully completed.
Elapsed: 00:00:43.01
```

So although more code was required in the procedure STATIC_ADHOC in which static SQL was used, there was a large gain in performance. The static SQL procedure does have some other limitations—if a new WHERE clause variant is introduced, then the code will need alteration, whereas DYN_ADHOC would not. As with most things in Oracle, you'll need to find the right balance for your application requirements. If parsing concerns are paramount, then taking the extra time to build procedures that canvas the various static SQL permutations may alleviate stress on parsing at the cost of a more restrictive solution than a truly dynamic one.

Unless you definitely know in advance that the cost of parsing can be afforded (for example, in a DSS system or similar system in which SQL execution counts will be small), ensuring that parsing is minimized is an admirable goal, even in the dynamic SQL case. To do this, dynamic SQL should still use bind variables. Because in the previous example, the number of bound variables isn't known at compile time, there are three coding options available:

- Use DBMS_SQL instead of EXECUTE IMMEDIATE.

- In a similar way to how the number of query permutations was treated in the STATIC_ADHOC procedure, you can have three dynamic cursors: one that handles just a single bind variable being passed, one for two bind variables, and one for three bind variables. This is more difficult than it first appears, because a mapping between each bind variable and the column to which it is bound to is then required.

- Use application context and SYS_CONTEXT function instead of bind variables.

The first two options are fairly straightforward to implement, but some more explanation on the last alternative is warranted. As you've already seen, you must create a context that can be accessed with the SYS_CONTEXT function:

```
SQL> create or replace context DEPT_WHERE
  2   using RUN_TEST;

Context created.
```

where RUN_TEST is the name of the procedure that will use the context to "pass" values to the dynamic SQL procedure DYN_ADHOC. The RUN_TEST procedure is similar to the PL/SQL block we used to test DYN_ADHOC previously, but rather than passing literals in the WHERE clause, we'll set a context value and then pass the appropriate SYS_CONTEXT function within the WHERE clause literal:

```
SQL> create or replace
  2   procedure RUN_TEST is
  3     w_deptno varchar2(80) := 'SYS_CONTEXT(''DEPT_WHERE'',''DEPTNO'')';
  4     w_dname varchar2(80) := 'SYS_CONTEXT(''DEPT_WHERE'',''DNAME'')';
  5     w_loc varchar2(80) := 'SYS_CONTEXT(''DEPT_WHERE'',''LOC'')';
  6   begin
  7     for i in (
  8       select dc.*,
  9             rownum r,
 10             decode(mod(rownum,9)+1,
```

```
11          1,'(deptno='||w_deptno||' or dname='||w_dname||')  and loc='||w_loc,
12          2,'deptno='||w_deptno||' or ( dname='||w_dname||' and loc='||w_loc||')',
13          3,'deptno = '||w_deptno||' or dname = '||w_dname||' or loc = '||w_loc,
14          4,'deptno = '||w_deptno||' or loc = '||w_loc,
15          5,'deptno = '||w_deptno,
16          6,'dname = '||w_dname,
17          7,'loc = '||w_loc||' and dname = '||w_dname,
18          8,'loc = '||w_loc||' or dname = '||w_dname,
19          9,'loc = '||w_loc)  where_clause
20     from dept_copy dc ) loop
21       dbms_session.set_context('DEPT_WHERE','DEPTNO',i.deptno);
22       dbms_session.set_context('DEPT_WHERE','DNAME',i.dname);
23       dbms_session.set_context('DEPT_WHERE','LOC',i.loc);
24       DYN_ADHOC(i.where_clause);
25     end loop;
26   end;
27   /
```

```
SQL> exec run_test;

PL/SQL procedure successfully completed.
```

It isn't immediately apparent what has been done here, but the advantage of using a context can be seen by dumping a few rows from the view V$SQL:

```
SQL> select sql_text from v$sql
  2  where sql_text like '%SYS_CONTEXT%'
  3  /

SQL_TEXT
------------------------------------------------------------------------
select * from dept where deptno = SYS_CONTEXT('DEPT_WHERE','DEPTNO')
select * from dept where loc = SYS_CONTEXT('DEPT_WHERE','LOC')
select * from dept where dname = SYS_CONTEXT('DEPT_WHERE','DNAME')
...
```

By setting the context values as opposed to using literals, parsing is reduced due to the reduced number of distinct SQL statements. The SYS_CONTEXT call is as effective as a bind variable for SQL sharing purposes.

Like static SQL, dynamic SQL also gets benefits from bulk binding and bulk collection, as discussed in Chapter 4.

Other Issues with Dynamic SQL

Besides the performance and concurrency impacts we dwelled upon earlier, there are two other serious considerations when using dynamic SQL.

No Compilation Errors

Consider the following PL/SQL procedure that builds an SQL statement that can't possibly be correct (as indicated by the comments within the code):

```
SQL> create or replace
  2    procedure SILLY_PROC is
  3      c sys_refcursor;
  4    begin
  5      open c for
  6      'select no_such_column,,, '||  -- too many commas
  7      '          avg() '||            -- missing expression
  8      'from '||                       -- no table!
  9      'where colx = 1 4 5';           -- literals wrong
 10    end;
 11    /

Procedure created.
```

Yet the procedure compiles without error. We can code anything we like in dynamic SQL and the compiler will quite happily accept it. We get no feedback on the quality (in this case, lousy) of the code until runtime:

```
SQL> exec silly_proc;
BEGIN silly_proc; END;

*
ERROR at line 1:
ORA-00936: missing expression
ORA-06512: at "SILLY_PROC", line 4
ORA-06512: at line 1
```

No Dependency Checking

Any object referenced within dynamic SQL doesn't take part in the sophisticated dependency checking within the data dictionary. This makes impact analysis more difficult when objects are changed and, in effect, takes you back to the issue we just covered: Problems aren't detected until runtime.

Summary

All developers have their own "horror stories" of problematic code they've seen and also "success stories" of the solutions they've found to those problems. This chapter represents some of the common pitfalls that we've observed over the years in PL/SQL applications, as well as the solutions and workarounds to those pitfalls.

We hope that you too will share your own experiences within your organization and in the wider Oracle community. Nothing is more frustrating for developers than spending their time on problems, only to discover that these problems have already been encountered and solved in the past by others. Collectively, we can reduce the amount of duplicated effort by sharing our experiences. We recommend strongly that you take the time to read and contribute to such forums as USENET, ORACLE-L, and OTN, and that you also become active within your local Oracle user group.

CHAPTER 6

Triggers

AN ACTIVE DATABASE EXECUTES procedures when specific events occur and when specified conditions are satisfied. These automatically executed procedures are called *triggered procedures* or *triggers* for short

Triggers are usually classified by triggering event. DML (data manipulation) triggers fire (are executed) when rows are added, modified, or deleted. Instead-of triggers fire when views are updated. DDL (data definition language) triggers fire when objects are created, modified, or dropped. Database event triggers are fired when, for example, the database starts or shuts down, when users log on and log out, or when errors are raised. Sometimes triggers are divided into just two groups; user-event triggers and system-event triggers. User-event triggers encompass DML, DDL, logon, and logout triggers. System-event triggers include database startup, database shutdown, and the triggers on other system-wide events.

Active databases also respond to temporal events by executing procedures at specified points in time or at certain intervals. Oracle provides this function-ality by means of the PL/SQL job queue and DBMS_JOB supplied package.

Two other Oracle9*i* features are also relevant to this discussion. Oracle Streams permits the database server to capture DML and DDL changes directly from the redo log and provides a means of sharing these changes with other processes. Table versioning permits a table to contain multiple versions of its data.

NOTE Versions of the Oracle database differ in features and sometimes even in the implementation of these features. The examples in this chapter have been tested against Oracle enterprise edition version 9.2.0.3 running on Microsoft Windows 2000. All the examples (except for those based on Oracle Streams) will work on the standard Oracle edition as well.

Trigger Concepts

A trigger is a database object that specifies an event and the procedural code that should be executed when the event occurs. The event is called the trigger condition, and the procedural code is called the trigger body.

In the following example, the event is a specific user logon. The procedure or trigger body consists of a few lines of code (the conditional statement between the BEGIN and END keywords) that define what Oracle will do when the user logs on.

```
-- Logon trigger for Alex
create or replace trigger save_the_database_from_alex
after logon on alex.schema
begin
    if to_char(current_timestamp,'hh24') between 08 and 18 and
        to_char(current_timestamp,'d') between 2 and 5 then
            raise_application_error(-20000,
                'Do you realize that this is a production database?');
    end if;
end;
```

After the trigger is created, if Alex (the developer named in the code) attempts to connect to the database, the following occurs:

```
SQL> connect alex/xxxxx

ERROR:
ORA-00604: error occurred at recursive SQL level 1
ORA-20000: Do you realize that this is a production database?
ORA-06512: at line 4
Warning: You are no longer connected to ORACLE.
```

A logon event fired a trigger, and the trigger code associated with the logon event disallowed the logon because it took place during normal business hours.

Trigger Types

Let's look more closely at the different kinds of triggers: DML triggers, instead-of triggers, DDL triggers, and database event triggers.

DML triggers are associated with either a statement or a row in a database table. A statement trigger executes once per command and isn't affected by the number of rows in the result set. A row trigger may fire many times per command depending on the number of rows in the result set. (An example will follow).

Instead-of triggers are specific to database views. You can't create a DML trigger on a view, (although you can create DML triggers on the base tables that underlie a view). An instead-of trigger overrides the way the view is updated or allows updates to views where they would usually be prohibited by the database.

DDL triggers and data-event triggers can be created at the database level or at the schema level. The logon trigger shown in the previous section is an example of a database-event trigger created at the schema level.

Event Attributes

Each triggering event makes certain attributes about itself available to the trigger body. For example, the ORA_LOGIN_USER attribute identifies the logon user name. The ORA_SYSEVENT attribute identifies the event that fired the trigger. The SQL text of the triggering statement (ORA_SQL_TXT) is also available within the triggering event. Some of these event attributes are common to all types of triggers whereas others apply only to specific types of triggers. You'll find a complete list in the Oracle documentation (currently in the *Oracle9i Application Developer's Guide—Fundamentals*).

DML row triggers have access to the column values being modified by the triggering statement. A delete trigger is able to see the column values in the deleted row. An insert trigger can see the column values of the newly inserted row, and an update trigger can see both the original and the updated values. These values are called the :OLD and :NEW column values. Old and new are the correlation names. They are used as a prefix to the column name; for example, :OLD.AMOUNT refers to the original value of the amount field in the context of the current row.

Trigger Timing

Triggers can execute before or after their triggering statement. Logon, startup, and server error triggers can't fire before the database startup or before the database error has occurred. Logoff and shutdown triggers can't execute after the user has logged off or after the database has been shut down. But DML statements, row triggers, and most other types of triggers can fire before or after their initiating event. The following code creates two triggers on the DEPT table to capture all possible DML triggering conditions:

```
SQL> -- create full set of triggers on dept table
SQL> -- Create a Before Statement trigger
SQL> create or replace trigger deptbs
  2  before insert or update or delete
  3  on dept
  4  begin
  5     dbms_output.put_line('before statement (dept)');
  6  end;
  7  /
```

```
Trigger created.

SQL> -- Create a Before Row Trigger
SQL> create or replace trigger dept_br
  2  before insert or update or delete
  3  on dept
  4  for each row
  5  begin
  6     dbms_output.put_line('...before row (dept)');
  7  end;
  8  /

Trigger created.

SQL> -- Create an After Row Trigger
SQL> create or replace trigger dept_ar
  2  after insert or update or delete
  3  on dept
  4  for each row
  5  begin
  6     dbms_output.put_line('...after row (dept)');
  7  end;
  8  /

Trigger created.

SQL> -- Create an After Statement Trigger
SQL> create or replace trigger deptas
  2  after insert or update or delete
  3  on dept
  4  begin
  5     dbms_output.put_line('after statement (dept)');
  6  end;
  7  /

Trigger created.
```

We've also created the same triggers on the EMP table. We'll now delete a couple of rows by issuing a standard SQL delete command.

```
SQL> -- Delete 3 rows from emp
SQL> delete from
  2  emp
```

```
    3   where   deptno = 10;
before statement (emp)
...before row (emp)
...after row (emp)
...before row (emp)
...after row (emp)
...before row (emp)
...after row (emp)
after statement (emp)
```

```
3 rows deleted.
```

The before-statement trigger fires first. For each row processed by the DML statement, the before-row trigger is executed, the row is changed, and the after-row trigger fires. Finally, when all the rows have been processed, the AFTER-statement trigger fires.

When two tables are related by a foreign key constraint action, the triggers on both tables fire in concert. Here we've declared a DELETE CASCADE rule such that deleting one row from the DEPT table also deletes three rows from the EMP table. It's interesting that the first before-statement trigger executed is the one on the EMP table, but the last after-statement trigger fired is the one on the DEPT table.

```
SQL> delete from dept
  2   where deptno = 10;
before statement (emp)
before statement (dept)
...before row (dept)
...before row (emp)
...after row (emp)
...before row (emp)
...after row (emp)
...before row (emp)
...after row (emp)
...after row (dept)
after statement (emp)
after statement (dept)
```

```
1 row deleted.
```

Multiple Similar Triggers

It's possible to define many triggers for the same event. You can define many before-statement DML triggers on the same table, or many DDL triggers for the same event on the same schema. When this is the case, the firing order of the similar triggers is undefined. That is, it's indeterminate, so the same-type triggers may or may not fire in any specified order. If interdependencies exist between multiple triggers, the best resolution is to move the code from each trigger into a stored procedure, and call that procedure from a single trigger.

Performance of Before and After DML Row Triggers

Assuming that you can code the same logic in either a before-row or an after-row trigger, which is the better choice? We'll perform an experiment using a trigger that implements a transition constraint, that is, a rule that governs how a value in a column is allowed to change. The following trigger is common to preventive maintenance systems; the equipment is run for some time and then the total runtime is updated while a trigger enforces the rule.

```
 1   -- Check that the new value for number of hours flown is reasonable
 2   -- this column which is called flying_hrs is defined not null
 3   create or replace trigger check_flying_hrs
 4   after update of flying_hrs on aircraft
 5   for each row
 6   begin
 7       if :new.flying_hrs < :old.flying_hrs then
 8         raise_application_error(-20001,
 9             'The number of flying hours doesn't look right.');
10       end if;
11*  end;
SQL> /

Trigger created.
```

The experiment uses two identical tables. The triggers on each table are identical except the first table has a before-row trigger and the second table has an after-row trigger. Each table will have enough rows so that any differences in processing will be measurable. Here's the baseline.

```
SQL> select trigger_name,table_name,trigger_type
  2  from    user_triggers
  3  where   table_name like 'AIR%';
```

TRIGGER_NAME	TABLE_NAME	TRIGGER_TYPE
CHECK_FLYING_HRS1	AIRCRAFT1	BEFORE EACH ROW
CHECK_FLYING_HRS2	AIRCRAFT2	AFTER EACH ROW

The before-row trigger should be less efficient because it must re-read the affected data. Let's check this out by benchmarking the relative cost of before-row and after-row triggers using the RUNSTATS package.

```
SQL> exec runStats_pkg.rs_start;

PL/SQL procedure successfully completed.

SQL> update aircraft1
  2   set flying_hrs = flying_hrs + 3.15;

2048 rows updated.

SQL> exec runStats_pkg.rs_middle;

PL/SQL procedure successfully completed.

SQL> update aircraft2
  2   set flying_hrs = flying_hrs + 3.15;

2048 rows updated.

SQL> exec runStats_pkg.rs_stop(1000);
Run1 ran in 77 hsecs
Run2 ran in 136 hsecs
run 1 ran in 56.62% of the time
```

Name	Run1	Run2	Diff
STAT...redo entries	4,595	2,547	-2,048
LATCH.redo allocation	4,606	2,551	-2,055
STAT...session logical reads	4,755	2,676	-2,079
STAT...db block gets	4,718	2,637	-2,081
STAT...db block changes	9,231	5,120	-4,111
LATCH.cache buffers chains	25,422	13,263	-12,159
STAT...redo size	933,000	546,660	-386,340

```
Run1 latches total versus runs -- difference and pct
Run1     Run2     Diff      Pct
31,091   16,816   -14,275 184.89%
```

The after-row trigger performed about half as many logical reads and used about half as many resources as the before-row trigger.

Privileges

There aren't any execution privileges associated with a trigger. If you have the privilege to run the triggering statement, the trigger will be fired implicitly. Triggers operate under the privilege domain of the trigger's owner and they run with roles disabled. For a trigger to access a database object, the owner of the trigger must either own the database object or have been granted privileges on the object directly.

You'll need the CREATE TRIGGER privilege to create a trigger in your own schema, and the CREATE ANY TRIGGER privilege to create a trigger in any schema. There's also an ADMINISTER DATABASE TRIGGER privilege for creating a trigger on the database.

Triggers and the Data Dictionary

The CREATE TRIGGER statement stores information about the trigger in the data dictionary. Unlike PL/SQL procedures (which are stored as text lines), trigger bodies are stored in the database in long columns. This makes it difficult to relate an error message line number with the corresponding line of the trigger body. For example

```
SQL> alter trigger reorder compile;

Warning: Trigger altered with compilation errors.

SQL> show error
Errors for TRIGGER REORDER:

LINE/COL ERROR
-------- ----------------------------------------------------------------
10/23    PLS-00103: Encountered the symbol "=" when expecting one of the
            following:
         := . ( @ % ; indicator

12/4     PLS-00103: Encountered the symbol "END"
```

The Oracle server reports an error at line number 10, but which line is number 10? We can count the lines in the trigger body ourselves, but it's preferable to automate the task. Following is a database function that examines trigger code by line number and can be shared among developers.

```
-- Create an array
create or replace type outputLines as table of varchar2(4000);
/

-- Function to display trigger text by line number
-- Counts the chr(10) linefeed character
create or replace function
TriggerText (p_owner in varchar2, p_trigger in varchar2) return outputLines
authid current_user
pipelined
as
    body long;
    j number; -- position of linefeed character
    begin
        select trigger_body
        into    body
        from    all_triggers
        where   trigger_name = p_trigger and
                owner = p_owner;

        body := body || chr(10);
        while ( body is not null ) loop
            j := instr( body, chr(10) );
            pipe row ( substr( body, 1, j-1 ) );
            body := substr( body, j+1 );
        end loop;
    return;
  end;
```

We use the function this way:

```
SQL> select rownum,column_value
  2  from    table (triggertext('SCOTT','REORDER'));

  ROWNUM COLUMN_VALUE
-------- --------------------------------------------------------
       1 begin
       2     if :new.qty_on_hand - :new.qty_allocated +
       3          :new.qty_on_order < :new.reorder_level then
       4
       5          insert into Pending_orders
```

```
 6                 (item_no,qty,ord_date)
 7          values (:new.item_no, :new.reorder_level,
 8                    sysdate);
 9
10          :new.qty_on_order = :new.qty_on_order + :new.reorder_level;
11
12      end if;
13  end;
```

We can also zoom in to the lines identified by the error message.

```
SQL> select *
  2  from
  3  (select  rownum line, column_value
  4   from     table (system.triggertext(user,'REORDER')) )
  5  where line between 8 and 12;

    LINE COLUMN_VALUE
---------- ------------------------------------------------------------------
       8                    sysdate);
       9
      10          :new.qty_on_order = :new.qty_on_order + :new.reorder_level;
      11
end if;
```

Trigger Dependencies

We can select from USER_TRIGGER_COLS to see the :NEW and :OLD columns that a trigger uses.

```
SQL> -- Query the reorder trigger column usage
SQL> select column_name,column_usage
  2  from   user_trigger_cols
  3  where  trigger_name = 'REORDER';
```

COLUMN_NAME	COLUMN_USAGE
ITEM_NO	NEW IN
QTY_ON_HAND	NEW IN
QTY_ON_ORDER	NEW IN OUT
QTY_ALLOCATED	NEW IN
REORDER_LEVEL	NEW IN

The results (for the trigger shown earlier) indicate that the QTY_ON_ORDER column is updated in the trigger, and the other columns are read.

We can query USER_DEPENDENCIES to track tables or procedures that a trigger references.

```
SQL> select referenced_name,referenced_type
  2  from    user_dependencies
  3  where   name='REORDER';


REFERENCED_NAME          REFERENCED_TYPE
----------------         -----------------
STANDARD                 PACKAGE
PENDING_ORDERS           TABLE
INVENTORY                TABLE
```

Trigger Status

A trigger can exist in one of two possible states: enabled or disabled. Usually, a trigger is enabled and functional, but there are occasions, for example, when you are performing table maintenance, you don't want the trigger code to be operational so you disable the trigger (alter trigger TRIGGER_NAME disable). A disabled trigger is never fired. When the maintenance work is done, you enable the trigger again. The following SQL gets the enabled/disabled status of a trigger from the USER_TRIGGERS view:

```
SQL> select status
  2  from    user_triggers
  3  where   trigger_name = 'REORDER';

STATUS
--------
ENABLED
```

Like many other database objects, a trigger can be invalid. This means that there is something in the trigger code that prevents the trigger from successfully compiling. The problem may be caused by a syntax error or by a reference to an object that the trigger owner cannot access. An invalid trigger is not operational. The following SQL statement extracts the valid/invalid trigger status information from the USER_OBJECTS view:

```
SQL> select status
  2  from    user_objects
```

```
    3  where object_name = 'REORDER';
```

```
STATUS
------
VALID
```

Trigger Failures

If a trigger raises an error (an unhandled exception), all actions performed by the trigger and all actions performed by the triggering statement are rolled back. The triggering action won't succeed if the trigger fails.

One exception to this rule occurs when the user executing the trigger has DBA privileges, and the trigger is a database event trigger like a database startup, shutdown, or logon. Then the action succeeds even if the trigger fails.

Trigger Limitations

When you create a trigger, you're not creating an entire program, you're adding some code to a much larger invisible body of event-processing logic. This means that triggers are subject to many restrictions. These restrictions relate to the events that fire triggers and the type of statements that triggers are allowed to execute.

Some of these restrictions are listed here. This list isn't exhaustive and isn't in any particular order. In some cases, there are workarounds, which we'll see later on.

- DML triggers are tied to a specific table or view. You can't create a database-wide or schema-wide DML trigger. Conversely, DDL triggers are related either to a schema or to the database as a whole, but not to a specific object.

- DML row triggers have access to :NEW and :OLD column values but you can write :NEW values only in before-insert or before-update triggers. You can't write :NEW values in AFTER triggers, and you can never modify :OLD values.

- DML row triggers can't read from mutating tables. We discuss mutating tables later in this chapter.

- There are no triggers associated with data control statements like COMMIT or ROLLBACK. DML triggers are fired at the time of the INSERT, UPDATE, or DELETE statement, whether or not the transaction is committed.

- Data control statements like COMMIT, ROLLBACK, and SAVEPOINT are not allowed inside DML triggers. If the trigger calls a procedure, the procedure also can't perform any data control statements.

- DDL commands are not allowed in DML triggers because they perform an implicit COMMIT, and hence violate the previous restriction. Only a limited number of DDL statements are allowed in DDL triggers.

- You cannot create a trigger on a SELECT statement. You cannot create a trigger that will fire whenever you access a sequence generator. Fine-grained auditing (the DBMS_FGA package) allows you to monitor SELECT statements.

- You can't create DML triggers on tables owned by SYS.

If you're unaware of these restrictions, you'll run into a problem when you try to create the trigger or when the trigger tries to execute. The following example shows an error that is encountered, not when you created the trigger but at runtime:

```
update emp
       *
ERROR at line 1:
ORA-04092: cannot COMMIT in a trigger
ORA-06512: at "SCOTT.ZEMPBS", line 3
ORA-04088: error during execution of trigger 'SCOTT.ZEMPBS'
```

DML Triggers

We'll now turn our attention to DML triggers specifically and look at a few simple examples.

Storing Audit Information

The following trigger will save the Oracle username of the user who performed the last change and the date on which the last change was made. It's a before trigger because we can't write :NEW values in an after trigger.

```
1    CREATE OR REPLACE TRIGGER deptBR
2    before update or insert
3    ON dept
4    FOR EACH ROW
```

```
5   DECLARE
6   begin
7       :new.last_update := sysdate;
8       :new.last_user := user;
9*  end;
```

The triggering event is an INSERT or UPDATE. It would not make sense to set column values in a delete trigger because the row is about to be erased anyway. Note that this is a row trigger. If an UPDATE statement affects many rows, the trigger will fire for each row. Here you can see the trigger at work.

```
SQL> select *
  2  from dept
  3  where deptno = 10;

    DEPTNO  DNAME           LOC          LAST_UPDA LAST_USER
---------- -------------- ------------ --------- -------------
        10  ACCOUNTING      NEW YORK

SQL> update dept
  2  set    loc = 'ULAN BATOR'
  3  where  deptno = 10;

1 row updated.

SQL> select *
  2  from dept
  3  where deptno = 10;

    DEPTNO  DNAME           LOC          LAST_UPDA  LAST_USER
---------- -------------- ------------ --------- -------------
        10  ACCOUNTING      ULAN BATOR   01-SEP-03  ALEX
```

Implementing a Transition Constraint

We've seen one example of a trigger that implements a transition constraint. Now we'll take a look at one that implements an ordered update. The following TBUR_SCOUT trigger enforces the order in which ranks are assigned to our SCOUT table:

```
SQL> create table scout
  2  (id number,
```

```
  3    rank varchar2(30) not null
  4    constraint check_rank
  5    check (rank in
  6    ('Scout','Tenderfoot','Star Scout','Life Scout','Eagle Scout'))
  8* );
```

Table created.

```
SQL> create or replace trigger tbur_scout before update on scout
  2    for each row
  3    when (new.rank <> old.rank)
  4    declare
  5    type ranklist is varray(10) of varchar2(30);
  6    ranks ranklist := ranklist('Scout','Tenderfoot','Star Scout',
  7    'Life Scout','Eagle Scout');
  8    function diff (p_new in varchar2,p_old in varchar2)
  9    return number is
 10    newRank number;
 11    oldRank number;
 12    begin
 13    for i in 1..ranks.last loop
 14       if p_new = ranks(i) then
 15          newRank := i;
 16       elsif
 17          p_old = ranks(i) then
 18          oldRank := i;
 19       end if;
 20    end loop;
 21    return newRank - oldRank;
 22    end;
 23
 24    begin
 25
 26    if  diff(:new.rank,:old.rank) != 1 then
 27          raise_application_error(-20001,'Rank is out of sequence');
 28    end if;
 29
 30    end;
 31    /
```

Trigger created.

```
SQL> select *
  2    from scout;
```

```
          ID RANK
---------- --------------
          1 Star Scout

SQL> update scout
  2   set rank = 'Eagle Scout';
update scout
*
ERROR at line 1:
ORA-20001: Rank is out of sequence
ORA-06512: at "SCOTT.TBUR_SCOUT", line 26
ORA-04088: error during execution of trigger 'SCOTT.TBUR_SCOUT'
```

Generating a Surrogate Key

From a programmer's point of view there are just two ways to create record identifiers in a database: either the user inputs a value or the application generates a
value. In the latter case, database triggers are often used to retrieve a number
from a sequence generator and then to add that number into the newly created
database row. The following code demonstrates this. The before-INSERT trigger on
the WORK_ORDERS table uses a sequence generator to populate the WO_ID primary
key column.

```
SQL> create table work_orders
  2   (wo_id number);

Table created.


create or replace trigger trg_wo_id
before insert
on work_orders
for each row
when (new.wo_id is null)
begin
    select wo_seq.nextval
    into    :new.wo_id
    from dual;
end;
```

This is useful when we don't have control over the text of the INSERT statement. But it's more efficient to generate the sequence number as part of the INSERT statement itself, if possible, as the following RUNSTATS session demonstrates.

The following code benchmarks the relative performance of sequence population via trigger and via direct SQL. In this interaction, run1 (the WORK_ORDERS1 table) has the before-insert trigger (shown earlier). Run2 (WORK_ORDERS2 table) performs the same amount of work by means of the INSERT SQL statement without a trigger:

```
SQL> exec runStats_pkg.rs_start;

PL/SQL procedure successfully completed.

SQL> insert into
  2   work_orders1
  3   select null
  4   from   all_objects
  5   where  rownum < 1000;

999 rows created.

SQL> exec runStats_pkg.rs_middle;

PL/SQL procedure successfully completed.

SQL> insert into
  2   work_orders2
  3   select wo_seq.nextval
  4   from   all_objects
  5   where  rownum < 1000;

999 rows created.

SQL> exec runStats_pkg.rs_stop(1500);
Run1 ran in 188 hsecs
Run2 ran in 103 hsecs
run 1 ran in 182.52% of the time
```

Name	Run1	Run2	Diff
STAT...db block changes	3,203	1,212	-1,991
STAT...calls to get snapshot s	3,156	159	-2,997
STAT...consistent gets	7,317	4,320	-2,997
LATCH.shared pool	4,398	1,391	-3,007

```
LATCH.library cache pin alloca      4,256        258     -3,998
STAT...session logical reads        9,012      5,005     -4,007
LATCH.library cache pin             8,485      2,495     -5,990
LATCH.cache buffers chains         22,769     11,772    -10,997
LATCH.library cache                17,906      3,873    -14,033
STAT...redo size                  326,312    112,612   -213,700


Run1 latches total versus runs -- difference and pct
Run1      Run2      Diff     Pct
70,659    30,979   -39,680 228.09%
```

Instead-of Triggers

Instead-of triggers fire when you perform an update on a database view. As you
know, a database view can be thought of as a derived table. When you query a
view, you're actually querying one or more underlying tables. When you update a
view, you are actually updating the underlying tables. However, not all views lend
themselves easily to updates, and in some cases, the Oracle server, not knowing
how to proceed with an update, raises an error to the effect that the view you're
working with is not updateable. An instead-of trigger replaces the triggering
statement with your own procedural code. Here is an example.

```
-- Create a view that displays average salary by department
  1  create view dept_sal
  2  as
  3  select dname,round(avg(sal),2) avgSalary
  4  from    emp,dept
  5  where   emp.deptno = dept.deptno
  6* group by dname
SQL> /

View created.

SQL> select *
  2  from dept_sal;

DNAME           AVGSALARY
--------------  ----------
ACCOUNTING        2916.67
RESEARCH          2175.00
SALES             1566.67
```

Suppose we want to reduce the average salary of the accounting department by two percent (this is obviously a hypothetical example).

```
SQL> update dept_sal
  2  set     avgsalary = avgsalary * .98
  3  where   dname = 'ACCOUNTING'
  4  /
update dept_sal
       *
ERROR at line 1:
ORA-01732: data manipulation operation not legal on this view
```

This view is not updateable. The Oracle server can't figure out which employee (or employees) should be adjusted in order to change the department's average salary. An instead-of trigger can provide the necessary logic. For example, we can distribute the salary adjustment evenly across all the employees of the department.

```
-- Instead of trigger to update emp and dept table
-- when updating the dept_sal view
    create or replace trigger dept_sal_trg
    instead of update on dept_sal
    begin
    if (nvl(:new.avgsalary,-1) <> nvl(:old.avgsalary,-1)) then
        update emp
        set     sal = (:new.avgsalary/:old.avgsalary) * sal
        where deptno = (select deptno
                        from    dept
                        where   dname = :old.dname);
    end if;
        update dept
        set     dname = :new.dname
        where   dname = :old.dname;
    end;
```

> **CAUTION**   The DNAME column is used to access the dept row. To avoid problems, the DNAME column should be declared unique.

```
-- Rows have unique department names
SQL> update dept
  2   set dname='ACCOUNTING';
update dept
*
ERROR at line 1:
ORA-00001: unique constraint (SCOTT.DNAME_UK) violated)
```

The instead-of trigger is like a DML row trigger in that it acts on each row and has access to :OLD and :NEW values.

```
SQL> update dept_sal
  2   set     avgsalary = avgsalary * .98
  3   where   dname = 'ACCOUNTING';

1 row updated.

SQL> select *
  2   from    dept_sal;

DNAME            AVGSALARY
--------------   ----------
ACCOUNTING         2858.33
RESEARCH           2175.00
SALES              1566.67
```

Because we created an update trigger rather than an INSERT or a DELETE trigger, we won't be able to perform inserts or deletes on this view.

```
  1   insert into dept_sal
  2*  values ('HR',6000)
SQL> /
insert into dept_sal
            *
ERROR at line 1:
ORA-01732: data manipulation operation not legal on this view
```

We'll return to instead-of triggers again when we discuss version-enabled tables.

Mutating Tables

A row-level DML trigger acts on a table while the triggering statement is executing. During that time, the table is called a mutating table. Mutating tables are subject to certain restrictions, as we'll describe now in the context of a reservation system.

A passenger train is composed of a variable number of passenger cars (coaches). When you make a reservation on a train, the agent, using a computerized-booking program, checks the seat availability. If there are not enough available seats, the agent adds another coach to the train and thus makes more seats available. The problem is that in order to add the coach, the agent must walk to a different computer terminal and use a different computer program. You, the potential traveler, are left hanging on the phone until the additional seats are made available.

We will automate this process. More precisely, instead of modifying a number of booking programs, we're going to create a database centralized DML trigger that checks the seat availability whenever a reservation is made. The trigger will count the number of free seats on the train and if the total is too low, the program will add a coach. The agents will never have to manually add a coach again.

> **NOTE** In the manual system, it's possible that two reservation agents will add two new coaches to the same train at more or less the same time, even though only one new coach is needed. That isn't a problem and we're not trying to correct it. The engine can easily pull an extra coach.

A table called TRAIN_RIDES contains a row for every seat on the train. All the columns are pre-filled except for the reservation number.

```
SQL> describe train_rides
Name                 Null?     Type
-----------------    --------  ----------
 TRAIN_NO                      NUMBER
 TRAVEL_DATE                   DATE
 COACH_NO                      NUMBER
 SEAT_NO                       NUMBER
 RESERVATION_NO                NUMBER
```

The RESERVATION_NO column is updated when a seat is sold.

```
SQL> -- sell any available seats
SQL> update train_rides
  2  set      reservation_no = :r
  3  where    train_no     = :a
  4  and      travel_date = :b
```

```
  5  and     reservation_no is null
  6  and     and rownum <= least (:nbr_of_seats_being_sold,:nbr_of_seats_avail-
able);
```

The new application is based on this trigger. It adds a new coach to the train when there are less then 50 available seats.

```
-- Trigger to automatically add a coach when we are running low on seats
create or replace trigger check_free_space_on_train
before update of reservation_no
on train_rides
for each row
declare
free_seats number;

begin
      select  count(*)
      into    free_seats
      from    train_rides
      where   reservation_no is null and
              train_no = :new.train_no and
              travel_date = :new.travel_date;
      if free_seats < 50
         then add_a_coach(:new.train_no,:new.travel_date);
      end if;
end;
```

Now it's time to see what happens when the trigger fires.

```
update train_rides
       *
ERROR at line 1:
ORA-04091: table RR.TRAIN_RIDES is mutating, trigger/function may not see it
ORA-06512: at "RR.CHECK_FREE_SPACE_ON_TRAIN", line 5
ORA-04088: error during execution of trigger 'RR.CHECK_FREE_SPACE_ON_TRAIN'
```

A runtime error is generated because a row trigger is not allowed to read from the table that it's based on. Intuitively, the trigger is trying to read the table while some rows have been modified and some haven't. This isn't allowed. Tables are mutating only in the context of DML triggers. During normal database operations, concurrent database users each work with a consistent view of the data and don't see other users' uncommitted changes in progress. A trigger, however, would see its own previous modifications.

Because the mutating table restriction applies only to row-level triggers, the way to avoid it is to save information in a row trigger and perform the actual work in an after-statement trigger. The solution requires a third trigger as well—a before-statement trigger to initialize our variables and wipe out any residue from an aborted execution. We'll call this solution the delayed or deferred processing solution.

Another frequently suggested approach for avoiding a mutating-table-related error is to use an autonomous transaction in the trigger. The autonomous transaction doesn't see a mutating table—it sees the table as it existed before the triggering statement started, so it doesn't raise an error. But the fact that the autonomous transaction doesn't see the work in progress usually means that it can't implement the logic we're trying to accomplish. We will come back to this notion soon.

The Delayed Processing Solution

The delayed processing solution works by moving the table-read from the row trigger to the after-statement trigger. The row trigger saves the identifier of each affected row into an array. The after-statement trigger retrieves each saved row identifier and uses that identifier to access the table, which, by this time, is no longer mutating.

The following code shows the specific solution for the problem we've described. The SET_INITIAL_STATE procedure is called by a before-statement trigger. The SAVE_TRAIN_NO procedure is called by a row trigger. The CHECK FREE SPACE_ON_TRAIN procedure, which does the actual work, is called by the after-statement trigger.

```
-- Package to work around mutating table error
 create or replace package train_ride_package is
    procedure set_initial_state;
    procedure save_train_no (trainid number,dateid date);
    procedure check_free_space_on_train;
end;
/
create or replace package body train_ride_package
is
-- This package body creates the procedures that the
-- triggers will execute
    type train_table is table of date index by pls_integer;
        position train_table;
    empty     train_table;

-- initialize the associative array
```

```
procedure set_initial_state is
begin
    position := empty;
end;

-- save the trainId and travelDate
procedure save_train_no (trainid number, dateid date) is
begin
    position(trainid) := dateid;
end;

-- retrieve the trainId and travelDate
-- check the seat availability
-- conditionally, add a coach
procedure check_free_space_on_train
is
trainid_in number;
free_seats number;

begin
    trainid_in := position.FIRST;
    while trainid_in is not null loop
        select  count(*)
        into    free_seats
        from    train_rides
        where   reservation_no is null and
                    train_no  =  trainid_in and
                    travel_date = position(trainid_in);
        if free_seats < 50
            then add_a_coach(trainid_in,position(trainid_in));
        end if;
        position.delete(trainid_in);
        trainid_in := position.next(trainid_in);
    end loop;
end;
end;
```

These are the triggers we'll need to implement the deferred processing work-around.

```
-- Before Statement Trigger
--   Initialize the package array
create or replace trigger trg_tr_bs
before update
```

```
on train_rides
begin
    train_ride_package.set_initial_state;
end;

-- Row Trigger
-- save the row information in the pakage array
CREATE OR REPLACE TRIGGER trg_tr_AR
after update
on train_rides
FOR EACH ROW
begin
    train_ride_package.save_train_no
        (:new.train_no,:new.travel_date);
end;

-- Statement After Trigger
-- Perform the work by reading from the pacakge array
CREATE OR REPLACE TRIGGER trg_tr_AS
After update
on train_rides
begin
    train_ride_package.check_free_space_on_train;
end;
```

Before we can test this, we'll need to create a procedure called ADD_A_COACH. Following is such a procedure, obviously not the real one, but it will allow us to continue.

```
-- Add an additional train car
create or replace
procedure add_a_coach(id in number, dt in date)
as
begin
    insert into train_rides
    (train_no,travel_date,coach_no,seat_no)
     select train_no,travel_date,coach_no + 1,rownum
     from     train_rides
     where    rownum < 101
     and      train_no = 1;
end;
```

To test it, we'll reserve all of the available seats.

```
SQL>-- count the seats
SQL> select count(*)
  2   from   train_rides
  3   where  reservation_no is null;

 COUNT(*)
----------
      100

SQL>  update train_rides
  2    set    reservation_no = 1;

100 rows updated.

SQL> select count(*)
  2   from   train_rides;

 COUNT(*)
----------
      200

SQL> select count(*)
  2   from   train_rides
  3   where  reservation_no is null;

 COUNT(*)
----------
      100
```

There is a concurrency safety issue here, which we've ignored until now. The problem is that two agents might simultaneously reserve all the train's seats without either agent/transaction adding the coach. This problem isn't related to mutating tables as such, it's a byproduct of Oracle's multi-version consistency model—each agent/trigger reads data from the committed state of the database. Each agent/transaction sees available seats and operates under the assumption that the data isn't changing.

The general solution to this type of problem is to design the application so that it can guarantee serializability, which means that the application has to allow only one update at a time. We can accomplish this by postulating that all the seats are allocated with the following SQL statement:

```
-- Enforce serialization
update train_rides
set    reservation_no = :b1
```

```
where   reservation_no is null and
        rownum <= :b2;
```

Mutating Tables and Autonomous Transactions

We'll now try to use an autonomous transaction to work around the same mutating table error. Instead of the package and the triggers we just illustrated, we'll try to accomplish the same goal with one autonomous transaction trigger. Notice that we are using the same trigger that failed with the ORA-4091 error, but now it has been converted to run autonomously.

> **NOTE** We've mentioned earlier that data control statements are prohibited in triggers. The COMMIT in the autonomous transaction isn't an exception. It doesn't affect the triggering statement or the transaction that the triggering statement belongs to. It only terminates the autonomous transaction itself.

```
-- After Row Autonomous Trigger
-- Reads from the triggered table
create or replace trigger check_free_space_on_train
after update of reservation_no
on train_rides
for each row
declare
free_seats number;
PRAGMA AUTONOMOUS_TRANSACTION;
begin
      select count(*)
      into    free_seats
      from    train_rides
      where   reservation_no is null and
              train_no = :new.train_no and
              travel_date = :new.travel_date;

      if free_seats < 50
          then add_a_coach(:new.train_no,:new.travel_date);
      end if;

      commit;
```

```
end;
```

The trigger still doesn't work, so we'll try the test again. First let's count the number of available seats and then allocate those seats.

```
SQL> select count(*)
  2   from    train_rides
  3   where   reservation_no is null;

  COUNT(*)
----------
       100
SQL> update train_rides
  2   set reservation_no = 1;

100 rows updated.
```

According to the requirements, the database should have noticed that the train has less than the minimum number of available seats and added a new car, but that didn't happen. After the update, the train has no free seats at all.

```
SQL> select count(*)
  2   from    train_rides
  3   where   reservation_no is null;

  COUNT(*)
----------
         0

SQL> select count(*)
  2   from    train_rides;

  COUNT(*)
----------
       100
```

The explanation for the trigger failure is that although the autonomous trigger may have run as each row was updated (100 times), it never saw any of the changes that were being made. From its perspective, every time it looked there were still 100 free seats on the train. Contrast this with the deferred processing approach shown earlier. The deferred processing occurs after the statement has executed and the statement changes are visible to the trigger.

More on Mutating Table Errors

There are other, less common situations that might raise the mutating table error. One scenario involves constraint actions like ON DELETE CASCADE. When a constraint action is defined, a trigger on the parent table may not query the child table.

```
alter table emp
add constraint fk_deptno
foreign key (deptno) references dept
on delete set null;

CREATE OR REPLACE TRIGGER deptAR after delete
 ON dept
 FOR EACH ROW
 DECLARE
 v_ename varchar2(30);
 begin
     select ename
     into    v_ename
     from    emp
     where   deptno = :old.deptno
     and rownum=1;

-- do some stuff

 exception
 when no_data_found then
     null;
 end;
SQL> delete from dept
  2   where deptno=10;
delete from dept
            *
ERROR at line 1:
ORA-04091: table ALEX.EMP is mutating, trigger/function may not see it
ORA-06512: at "ALEX.DEPTAR", line 4
ORA-04088: error during execution of trigger 'ALEX.DEPTAR'
```

A mutating table error may also be related to a simple design (or coding) error. Suppose table A has a trigger defined on it and that trigger updates table B. But table B also has a trigger on it, and that trigger updates table C. Finally, table C has a trigger on it that turns around and updates table A.

```
update A
       *
ERROR at line 1:
ORA-04091: table SAMPLE.A is mutating, trigger/function may not see it
ORA-06512: at "SAMPLE.T_C", line 2
ORA-04088: error during execution of trigger 'SAMPLE.T_C'
ORA-06512: at "SAMPLE.T_B", line 2
ORA-04088: error during execution of trigger 'SAMPLE.T_B'
ORA-06512: at "SAMPLE.T_A", line 2
ORA-04088: error during execution of trigger 'SAMPLE.T_A'
```

It's useful to have a query that can identify circular trigger references.

```
SQL> select name as "Trigger",
  2          table_name as "Base Table",
  3          referenced_name as "References TableName"
  4  from    user_dependencies,user_triggers
  5  where   type='TRIGGER' and
  6          referenced_type = 'TABLE' and
  7          table_name != referenced_name and
  8          name = trigger_name
  9  order by 1;
```

Trigger	Base Table	References TableName
T_A	A	B
T_B	B	C
T_C	C	A

Data Auditing

A common application, data-value auditing, is concerned with saving the changes made to application data. The record of changes (the audit trail) comprises the :OLD and :NEW values of each INSERT, UPDATE, or DELETE. Oracle has an auditing feature implemented by the AUDIT command, but that command doesn't track the :OLD and :NEW column values.

Triggers can be used to implement data auditing by creating a shadow table.A shadow table is a clone of the table we're auditing but with a few extra columns to identify the last time the row was changed and identify the user who made that change. Here is the code to create our shadow table:

```
create table dept$audit
(      deptno number(2,0),
       dname varchar2(14),
       loc varchar2(13),
       change_type varchar2(1),
       changed_by varchar2(30),
       changed_date date
);
```

For updates, it's possible to create two rows in the audit trail or keep only the :NEW values or only the :OLD values. We can query the audit table, sorting by date and unique key to reconstruct the complete change history of the data.

```
-- Audit trail creation trigger
CREATE OR REPLACE TRIGGER auditdeptar
after INSERT or UPDATE or DELETE on dept
for each row
declare
my DEPT$audit%ROWTYPE;
begin

    if inserting then
        my.change_type := 'I';
    elsif updating then
        my.change_type :='U';
    else
        my.change_type := 'D';
    end if;

    my.changed_by := user;
    my.changed_time := sysdate;

    case my.change_type
        when 'I' then
            my.DEPTNO := :new.DEPTNO;
            my.DNAME := :new.DNAME;
            my.LOC := :new.LOC;
        else
            my.DEPTNO := :old.DEPTNO;
            my.DNAME := :old.DNAME;
            my.LOC := :old.LOC;
    end case;
```

```
      insert into DEPT$audit values my;


   end;
```

Generating Data Auditing Triggers

It's tedious to create triggers like these manually. A procedure can do the work for
us. The following procedure will create the trigger just shown. Note that it doesn't
create the shadow table.

```
-- Accepts a table name and creates a simple auditing trigger
-- A shadow table (called <tname>$audit) has to exist already
Procedure generateTrigger(p_tableName in varchar2)
authid current_user
as
b varchar2(4000);
cursor c1 is
select column_name
from   user_tab_columns
where  table_name = p_tableName
order by column_id;

procedure appendx (destination in out varchar2,
                   string_in varchar2)
is
begin
destination := destination||string_in||chr(10);
end;

begin
-- build the create trigger command
   appendx(b,'create or replace trigger '||p_tableName||'ar');
   appendx(b,'after update or insert or delete on '||p_tableName||' ');
   appendx(b,'for each row');
   appendx(b,'declare');
   appendx(b,'my '||p_tableName||'$audit%ROWTYPE;');
   appendx(b,'begin ');
   appendx(b,'if inserting then my.change_type := ''I'';');
   appendx(b,'elsif updating then my.change_type :=''U'';');
   appendx(b,'else my.change_type := ''D'';');
   appendx(b,'end if;');
   appendx(b,'my.changed_by := user;');
```

```
   appendx(b,'my.changed_time := sysdate;');
   appendx(b,'case my.change_type');
   appendx(b,'when ''I'' then');

   for x in c1 loop
      appendx(b,'my.'||x.column_name||' := :new.'||x.column_name||';');
   end loop;
   appendx(b,'else');

   for x in c1 loop
      appendx(b,'my.'||x.column_name||' := :old.'||x.column_name||';');
   end loop;
   appendx(b,'end case;');

   appendx(b,'insert into '||p_tableName||'$audit values my;');
   appendx(b,'end;');

-- create the trigger
   execute immediate b;

end;
```

Many developers are understandably uncomfortable with the work involved in creating numerous shadow tables and unique triggers in order to perform data auditing as we've just described—even if the code can be generated. Oracle9*i* provides supplied packages that can audit data changes without the developer having to write very much code at all. There are two techniques; the first uses Oracle Workspace Manager's table versioning feature, and the second uses the "single database capture and apply" capability of Oracle Streams.

Table Versioning

A version-enabled table is a table that stores the previous incarnations of its data in addition to its current data. When you update a row in a version-enabled table, the update is translated into an insert. The original row is left unchanged and a new row is added. When you delete a row from the table, the row is logically deleted but no data is removed.

Because a version-enabled table contains current and historical data, it's easy to audit all the changes that were ever performed on that table. When you use the following simple procedure call to start up this feature, all changes to the EMP table will be kept:

```
SQL> begin
  2   dbms_wm.enableversioning('EMP','VIEW_WO_OVERWRITE');
  3   end;
  4   /

PL/SQL procedure successfully completed.
```

Now we'll try a few updates.

```
SQL> update emp
  2   set job = 'ARTIST'
  3   where job = 'CLERK'
  4   and   ename = 'MILLER';

1 row updated.

SQL> delete from emp
  2   where ename = 'MILLER';

1 row deleted.
```

Every version-enabled table has a corresponding history view that contains the columns in the table, the name of the user that performed the change, the type of change, and the time when the row was created, updated, or deleted. We can now take a look at the history of changes for the employee.

```
SQL> select user_name,job,type_of_change,createtime,retiretime
  2   from    emp_hist
  3   where   ename='MILLER'
  4   order by createtime;

USER_NAME   JOB       T CREATETIME       RETIRETIME
----------  --------- - ---------------  ---------------
SCOTT       CLERK     I 25-AUG-03 20:52 25-AUG-03 20:57
SCOTT       ARTIST    U 25-AUG-03 20:57 25-AUG-03 20:58
SCOTT       ARTIST    D 25-AUG-03 20:58
```

When a table is version-enabled, a number of things happen in the background.

1. The table is renamed: table X becomes table X LT. Oracle does not publish the meaning of the LT suffix, but it may possibly stand for LOCKED_TABLE. The locked table has all the columns of the original table,

but it has six additional columns as well. Its primary key is composed of the original primary key plus a version number and a status code.

2. A view is created with the same name as the original table. The view provides the end users with the version of the row they're interested in (usually the latest version).

3. A number of instead-of triggers are created on the view in order to implement the logic necessary for versioning. Any modifications done to the view are translated into inserts in the locked table. The locked table stores every change as a new and different row in the locked table.

4. Other views are created as well, including the history view that we referred to before.

Here's something interesting that you can do with version-enabled tables. We've already deleted the row identified by ENAME = MILLER; we can set the time to before the delete and view the table as it was then.

```
SQL>  select *
  2    from emp
where ename='MILLER';

no rows selected

SQL> begin
  2  dbms_wm.gotodate(to_date('25-AUG-03 20:57:02','dd-mon-yy hh24:mi:ss'));
  3  end;

SQL> select empno,ename,job
  2  from    emp
  3  where   ename = 'MILLER';

    EMPNO ENAME        JOB
---------- ---------- ---------
     7934 MILLER      ARTIST
```

It's easy to undo table versioning.

```
execute dbms_wm.DisableVersioning('EMP')
```

Once a table is version-enabled, you have to treat it carefully. For instance, if you version enabled the EMP table, you wouldn't be able to export it by itself. EMP is a view and you can't export views. You also would have to transfer any triggers from EMP to the EMP_LT table, taking into account that there are no deletes on the EMP_LT table.

> **NOTE** You can find out more about version-enabled tables in the *Oracle9i Application Developer's Guide—Workspace Manager Release 2.*

Oracle Streams

For those who want to centralize the data auditing function to create a generic audit procedure, Oracle Streams might be the answer. We want a single data audit table that acts as the repository for all changes made to the database. This single database-wide audit table will then be a single insert point for multiple processes, which raises some other performance issues that are outside the scope of this book, but those issues can be mitigating by adjusting the object's freelists storage parameters.

The centralized data audit trail will consist of a master and detail table, which we'll call AUDIT_TRAIL_1 and AUDIT_TRAIL_2. AUDIT_TRAIL_1 is simply as follows:

```
create audit_trail_1
(change_id number,
 command_type varchar2(1),
 table_name varchar2(30),
 user_name  varchar2(30),
 change_date date);
```

Audit_trail_2 is

```
create table data_audit_trail
(change_id       number,
 column_name     varchar2(30),
 actual_data_new sys.anydata,
 actual_data_old sys.anydata);
```

Streams use the SYS.ANYDATA type to store column values. (An ANYDATA type column contains an instance of some data and a description of that type of data.) We'll use the same data type in our audit table.

A simple Streams configuration consists of two processes: A capture process retrieves the DML changes from the redo logs and writes them to a database queue. The apply process de-queues the changes and passes them to a DML handler procedure that we'll write ourselves. The DML handler procedure will write the DML changes to the data audit trail.

Before using Streams, a number of prerequisites must be met. We need to use the Enterprise edition of Oracle and the database must be running in Archive Log mode. A number of initialization parameters must be set, and a Streams administrator account must be created and configured. Showing each of these steps will take us too far off our topic, but we'll cover enough detail so you will get a feeling for the way that auditing with Streams works.

Streams are configured through PL/SQL procedure calls:

```
begin
dbms_streams_adm.set_up_queue(
queue_table => 'streams.queue_table',
queue_name  => 'streams_queue',
queue_user  => 'streams');
end;
```

Configure the capture and apply processes for the DML of a specific table. This is the equivalent, in an approximate way, to turning auditing on.

```
begin
    DBMS_STREAMS_ADM.ADD_TABLE_RULES(
        table_name => 'SCOTT.EMP',
        streams_type => 'capture');

    DBMS_STREAMS_ADM.ADD_TABLE_RULES(
        table_name => 'SCOTT.EMP',
        streams_type => 'apply');
end;
```

We add extra information to the redo logs so that each change in the stream will include the row's primary key.

```
alter table emp
add supplemental log group log_group_emp_pk
(empno) always;
```

We associate a user procedure with the apply process. This will be done for INSERT and DELETE operations as well.

```
begin
   DBMS_APPLY_ADM.SET_DML_HANDLER(
         object_name            => 'scott.emp',
         object_type            => 'TABLE',
         operation_name         => 'UPDATE',
         error_handler          => false,
         user_procedure         => 'streams.dml_handler',
         apply_database_link => NULL);
end;
```

The DML_HANDLER is a program we'll write to insert data into the AUDIT_TRAIL
tables. It's a generic program that can be used for any table.

The streams capture process reads changes from the redo logs. These
changes don't include the name of the user who performed the change or the
date on which the change was made, but we need this information for our audit
trail. We can make it available to the DML_HANDLER this way.

```
CREATE OR REPLACE TRIGGER empar
after delete or update or insert
ON emp
FOR EACH ROW
DECLARE
   old_scn number;
begin
   old_scn := dbms_flashback.get_system_change_number;
   insert into streams.audit_temp
   values (old_scn,sysdate,user);
end;
```

This trigger retrieves the SCN number of our transaction, associates it with the
username and a time stamp, and saves these three values in a table. (We'll have
to delete this table from time to time.) The Streams apply process now has the
information it needs to build a complete audit trail. It will retrieve the username
and the date that were saved using the transaction's SCN and add that information
to the audit trail. Here is the DML_HANDLER.

```
-- Generic code to save any table changes
-- and write the data audit trail
PROCEDURE dml_handler(in_any IN SYS.ANYDATA) IS
   lcr          SYS.LCR$_ROW_RECORD;
   rc           PLS_INTEGER;
   oldlist      SYS.LCR$_ROW_LIST;
   newlist      SYS.LCR$_ROW_LIST;
   command      varchar2(32);
```

```
    tname          varchar2(30);
    v_scn          number;
    v_user         varchar2(30);
    v_date         date;
    v_change_id    number;
    newdata        sys.AnyData;

BEGIN

    -- Access the LCR
    rc       := in_any.GETOBJECT(lcr);
    command := lcr.GET_COMMAND_TYPE();
    tname    := lcr.GET_OBJECT_NAME;
    v_scn    := lcr.GET_SCN;
    oldlist := lcr.GET_VALUES('old');
    newlist := lcr.get_values('new');

-- lookup the info that we associated with this scn
-- and insert into audit_trail_1
    insert into audit_trail_1
    (change_id, command_type, table_name, user_name,change_date)
    select data_audit_seq.nextval,substr(command,1,1),
           tname,scn_user,scn_date
    from    audit_temp
    where   scn = v_scn;


-- write audit_trail_2
    IF command = 'DELETE' then
        FOR i IN 1..oldlist.COUNT LOOP
            insert into audit_trail_2
            (change_id, column_name,actual_data_old)
            values (data_audit_seq.currval,
                    oldlist(i).column_name,oldlist(i).data);
        END LOOP;
    ELSIF command = 'INSERT' then
        FOR i IN 1..newlist.COUNT LOOP
            insert  into audit_trail_2
            (change_id, column_name,actual_data_new)
          values (data_audit_seq.currval,
                    newlist(i).column_name,newlist(i).data);
        END LOOP;
    ELSIF command = 'UPDATE' then
        FOR i IN 1..oldlist.COUNT LOOP
            newdata := lcr.get_value('new',oldlist(i).column_name);
```

```
        if newdata is null then
                newdata := oldlist(i).data;
        end if;
        insert into audit_trail_2
            (change_id, column_name,actual_data_new,actual_data_old)
            values (data_audit_seq.currval,
                    oldlist(i).column_name,newdata,oldlist(i).data);
    END LOOP;
END IF;

END;
```

Here is an example of the auditing being captured with streams.

```
SQL> update scott.emp
  2   set     job = 'ENGINEER',
  3           deptno = 10
  4   where   ename='JONES';

1 row updated.

SQL> commit;

Commit complete.

SQL> select *
  2   from audit_trail_1;

 CHANGE_ID C TABLE_NAME USER_NAME  CHANGE_DA
---------- - ---------- ---------- ---------
        24 U EMP        SCOTT      28-Aug-03


SQL> select change_id,column_name, disp_any(actual_data_old) as old,
  2          disp_any(actual_data_new) as new
  3   from    audit_trail_2
  4   where change_id = 24;

 CHANGE_ID COLUMN_NAM OLD          NEW
---------- ---------- ------------ ------------
        24 EMPNO      7566         7566
        24 JOB        ARTIST       ENGINEER
        24 DEPTNO     20           10
```

GoodsOnline
GoodsOnline, 1341 W Spencer St
Appleton, WI, 54914
UNITED STATES
goods_online@gwicc.org

To: Dipesh Shrestha
3556 SQUIRECREEK CIR

SAN JOSE, CALIFORNIA 95121-1847
UNITED STATES

Marketplace:	Amazon US
Order Number:	1516948
Ship Method:	Standard
Customer Name:	Dipesh Shrestha
Order Date:	9/25/2013
Marketplace Order #:	107-0475253-0221828
Marketplace Ship Method:	MarketStandard

Qty	Item	Locator	Condition	Price
1	Mastering Oracle PL/SQL: Practical Solutions David C. Knox, Joel R. Kallman, Christopher Beck, Chaim Katz, Connor McDonald SKU: mon000348756 ISBN: 1590592174 - Books	L01-1-C -007-001-1812	Very Good	$5.14

Subtotal:	$5.14
Shipping:	$3.99
Total:	$9.13

Thanks for your order! If you have any questions or concerns regarding this order, please contact us at goods_online@gwicc.org

Note that in the audit trail we see the actual changes and the primary key but not all the columns of the table. Here is an example of a DELETE.

```
SQL> delete from emp
  2  where empno = 7566;

1 row deleted.

SQL> commit;

Commit complete.
```

If we'd like to see the column data in the usual order, we can join the audit trail to the TAB_COLUMNS view.

```
SQL> select change_id,a.column_name, disp_any(actual_data_old) as old,
  2         disp_any(actual_data_new) as new
  3  from   audit_trail_2 a,all_tab_columns u
  4  where  change_id = 25
  5  and    a.column_name = u.column_name
  6  and    u.table_name = 'EMP'
  7  and    u.owner='SCOTT'
  8  order by column_id;

CHANGE_ID COLUMN_NAM OLD          NEW
--------- ---------- ------------ ------------
       25 EMPNO      7566
       25 ENAME      JONES
       25 JOB        ENGINEER
       25 MGR        7839
       25 HIREDATE   02-APR-81
       25 SAL        2975
       25 COMM
       25 DEPTNO     10

SQL> select *
  2  from   audit_trail_1
  3  where  change_id=25;

CHANGE_ID C TABLE_NAME USER_NAME  CHANGE_DA
--------- - ---------- ---------- ---------
       25 D EMP        STREAMS    28-Aug-03
```

You may be wondering about the DISP_ANY function that's used to display SYS.ANYDATA data types. Here are the values stored in a SYS.ANYDATA column.

```
-- Display values stored in a sys.anydata column

function disp_any(data IN SYS.AnyData)
return varchar2 IS
    str VARCHAR2(4000);
    return_value varchar2(4000);
    chr CHAR(255);
    num NUMBER;
    dat DATE;
    res number;
begin
    if data is null then
        return_value := null;
    else
        case data.gettypename
            when 'SYS.VARCHAR2' then
                res := data.GETVARCHAR2(str);
                return_value := str;
            when 'SYS.CHAR' then
                res := data.GETCHAR(chr);
                return_value := chr;
            when 'SYS.NUMBER' THEN
                res := data.GETNUMBER(num);
                return_value := num;
            when 'SYS.DATE' THEN
                res := data.GETDATE(dat);
                return_value := dat;
            else
                return_value := data.gettypename()||' ????';
        end case;
    end if;
    return return_value;
end;
```

Streams processes can automatically execute programs based (loosely) on an event. The event is the Streams capture process, which can act on all DDL and DML changes recorded in the database redo log. It doesn't take very much programming to build an impressive Streams application.

Job Queue (Temporal Event Triggers)

The DBMS_JOB supplied package allows you to execute a procedure at a specific time or at a specific interval (for example, every hour or every day). It's used to schedule "batch" jobs; that is, jobs that run without any user interaction. For instance, if you need to exchange data with another system regularly by uploading or creating flat files and you want the job to run tonight at midnight and then exactly seven days later, you can submit the job this way.

```
declare
jobno number;
begin
    dbms_job.submit(job = > jobno,
                    what => 'AnotherDataLoad;',
                    next_date => trunc(sysdate) + 1,
                    interval => 'trunc (sysdate) + 7');
    commit;
end;
```

The JOB parameter is an IN OUT parameter, which will be assigned a unique job sequence number used to identify the job. The WHAT parameter is the source of the anonymous PL/SQL block or the name of the PL/SQL procedure that will be executed, and NEXT_DATE and INTERVAL are parameters that control the job schedule.

To submit a job, you need only the privilege of executing procedures in the DBMS_JOB package.

Using the DBMS_JOB packaged procedures, you can add jobs to the job queue, modify jobs, and remove jobs. You can also mark a job as broken so that it won't execute. (The database initialization parameter JOB_QUEUE_PROCESSES must be greater than zero for jobs to run.)

You can inspect your own jobs in the queue to see, among other things, when a job will run next and the last time the job ran.

```
SQL> select job,what,last_date,last_sec,
  2         next_date,next_sec
  3  from    user_jobs
  4* order   by job


JOB WHAT                   LAST_DATE LAST_SEC NEXT_DATE NEXT_SEC
---- -------------------- --------- -------- --------- --------
   5 dataload;             03-Aug-03 04:00:00 03-Aug-04 04:00:00
```

Job Scheduling

The schedule is controlled by the NEXT_DATE and INTERVAL parameters. NEXT_DATE is an in parameter of type date. If NEXT_DATE isn't supplied or if the supplied date has already past, the job will run immediately. The parameter, INTERVAL, is of type VARCHAR2. It doesn't represent the duration between two times as you might expect. Instead it consists of a date expression that becomes the new time for the job to run (NEXT_DATE). It must evaluate to a time in the future or be set to null. If the INTERVAL is set to null (or is not provided), the job will run only once.

For example, to run a job at the top of every hour, you could specify an interval like this.

```
interval => 'trunc(sysdate,'hh24') + 1/24'
```

To run a job every Friday evening at 6PM

```
interval => 'next_day(trunc(sysdate), ''friday'') + 18/24'
```

To execute on job on the third day of the month at 4AM

```
interval => 'trunc(last_day(sysdate)+3) + 4/24'
```

These intervals specify the next execution in an absolute way; the computation isn't based on the current time. The reason for avoiding the current time is that jobs often run a bit later than the specified NEXT_DATE, depending on when the job queue process wakes up and how busy the job queue process is. If the NEXT_DATE depends on the current time, the interval will start to slide.

The following example shows a job scheduled to run every five minutes, based on an interval of SYSDATE + .003742.

```
-- job set to run .003472 of a day or 5 minutes from current time
begin
    dbms_job.submit(
    :job,'anotherJob;', sysdate,
    'sysdate + .003472');
commit;
end;
```

The following shows the times that the job actually ran compared to the ideal calculations. The ideal time is exactly five minutes from the preceeding ideal time, but the acutal times drift from there.

```
Job Schedule Slide
Actual      Ideal
Time        Time
----------  --------
16:42:57    16:42:57
16:48:02    16:47:57
16:53:06    16:52:57
16:58:11    16:57:57
17:03:15    17:02:57
17:08:19    17:07:57
```

Jobs and DML Triggers

In addition to its use for batch jobs, the job queue can also be used to enhance the functionality of other triggers. Suppose your application needs to send an email whenever a new row is inserted into a table. You can create a trigger to satisfy the email requirement, but whenever the user inserts a row, the trigger has to wait for the email process to finish, so the user has to wait for the trigger to finish. To make matters worse, the user can roll back the transaction, but the email message gets sent anyway. There is no two-phase commit mechanism that keeps the database and the email server consistent.

Both these issues can be resolved if the trigger hands over the email portion of the work to the job queue. In this scenario, the email is sent only if the triggering statement (the original insert) is committed. Only then is the request added to the job queue. If a rollback occurs, the entry to the job queue is also rolled back. In addition, the user doesn't have to wait for the email portion to be completed because the email is sent asynchronously.

```
-- Trigger that submits a PL/SQL job
create or replace trigger
worknotification after insert
on work_orders for each row
declare
jobno number;
begin
   dbms_job.submit(
   job => jobno,
   what => 'email('''||:new.recipient||''');'
   );
end;
```

Jobs and the Shared Pool

Although this trigger works, it is inefficient. The problem is that each job issues a distinct command. When we submit jobs like `email('Isabelle@server1.com')`, `email('Theodoros@server2.com')`, and `email('Jean@server4.com')`, we are asking the job process to execute three individual commands. The server stores every unique command in the shared pool as shown here:

```
SQL> select sql_text
  2   from v$sqlarea
  3   where sql_text like '%server%';

SQL_TEXT
---------------------------------------
DECLARE job BINARY_INTEGER := :job;
next_date DATE := :mydate;  broken
BOOLEAN := FALSE; BEGIN
email('jean@server4.com'); :mydate :=
next_date; IF broken THEN :b := 1; ELSE
:b := 0; END IF; END;

DECLARE job BINARY_INTEGER := :job;
next_date DATE := :mydate;  broken
BOOLEAN := FALSE; BEGIN
email('isabelle@server1.com'); :mydate
:= next_date; IF broken THEN :b := 1;
ELSE :b := 0; END IF; END;

DECLARE job BINARY_INTEGER := :job;
next_date DATE := :mydate;  broken
BOOLEAN := FALSE; BEGIN
email('theodoros@server2.com'); :mydate
:= next_date; IF broken THEN :b := 1;
ELSE :b := 0; END IF; END;
```

If there are many unique recipients in our table, there will be many unique statements in our shared pool, and this will negatively affect the performance of our entire system. The solution is as follows.

Remember that we're talking about a row trigger; a trigger that's fired when inserting a row into a table. We know that one of the table's columns is the email address of the recipient. Another one of the columns in the table will be used to store the number of the job. The before row trigger, in addition to firing off the email job will populate this job number field:

```
create or replace trigger
worknotbr before insert
on work_orders for each row
declare
jobno number;
begin
    dbms_job.submit(job  => jobno, what => 'email( job );');
    :new.email_jobNo:= jobno;
end;
```

One of the special parameters that the job system recognizes is JOB, which is an IN parameter and identifies the number of the current job. The email procedure will use this job number to retrieve the recipient's email address.

```
procedure email (job in number)
is
lv_recipient work_orders.recipient%type;
begin
        select recipient
        into   lv_recipient
        from   work_orders
    where  email_jobNo = job;

  send_email(lv_recipient);
end;
```

We've avoided clogging up the shared pool by submitting a single command that can be shared by any number of distinct recipients.

Job Errors

If a job fails because of an unhandled exception, the server writes a trace file in the background dump directory and a message to the database alert log. The job queue process will attempt to rerun the failed job. The first attempt is made a minute later, the second try is made two minutes later, another four minutes later, another eight minutes later, and so on. The time between executions grows but cannot exceed the job's initial interval parameter. If the original interval is set to five minutes, the retries will occur after one minute, two minutes, four minutes five minutes, five minutes, five minutes, and so on. After 16 tries, the job is marked as broken and isn't run anymore. If, like the email script in the previous example, it is a "one off" job, there is no interval ceiling and the interval between tries grows very rapidly. The tenth attempt is made 1,024 minutes (about 17 hours) later.

We can modify this behavior and have the failing job resubmit itself every 10 minutes or so even though the original job was submitted without an interval parameter. Perhaps (using again the previous example) the email server is temporarily down, so we'd like to try sending email about 16 times over about three hours (instead of 16 times spread over the next couple of months).

The NEXT_DATE parameter can help us solve this problem because it can be used to set the time of the next run. However, an adjustment to the NEXT_DATE is made only if the job finishes successfully. If the job fails, the NEXT_DATE parameter is ignored.

Compare the following two procedures, both of which were submitted without specifying an interval. The first one will be subject to the normal scheduling calculations and will be marked broken after 16 times. The second will run every five minutes but will never be marked as broken. It will stay in the queue until it's manually removed.

```
-- Job which will always fail
-- adjustment to next date will be ignored
procedure fail_a_job_1 (next_date in out date)
as
begin
    next_date := sysdate + .00347;
    raise_application_error(-20000,'fail this job');
end;

-- Job will not fail. There is an exception handler
-- next date will be set
-- job will run "forever" until it is removed from queue
procedure fail_a_job_2 (next_date in out date)
as
begin
    raise_application_error(-20000,'fail this job');
exception
when others then
  next_date := sysdate + .00347 -- 5 minuts;
end;
```

So, the job queue allows programs to execute automatically at a specified time or interval. The job schedule can be considered the clock event that triggers the job. One off jobs are useful for sharing workload among processes; if the job fails, a different execution job schedule takes over. Use the DBMS_JOB package to schedule jobs.

DDL Triggers

DDL (data definition language) statements make up a small portion of application program code, but they are used quite often by the database administrators for setting up or modifying the environment. Suppose you're the DBA responsible for running a script that creates new tables. In addition, you have to perform an object grant on each new table. Wouldn't it be nice if you could automate the grant creation? The following trigger attempts to add a newly created table to the SELECT privilege domain of the BI_ROLE:

```
-- This trigger will not work
create or replace
trigger SystemGrantSelect
after create on database
begin
if ora_dict_obj_type='TABLE' then
    execute immediate('grant select'||' on '||
            ora_dict_obj_owner||'.'||
            ora_dict_obj_name||' to bi_role');
 end if;
end;
```

Unfortunately, this trigger doesn't work.

```
create table customized_items (
*
ERROR at line 1:
ORA-00604: error occurred at recursive SQL level 1
ORA-30511: invalid DDL operation in system triggers
ORA-06512: at line 3
```

Let's try something else. Suppose that an application creates Oracle user accounts but doesn't specify their default tablespace. We'd like to ALTER the Oracle user account in this way.

```
create or replace
trigger SystemAlterUser
after create on database
begin
if ora_dict_obj_type = 'USER' then
   execute immediate ( 'alter user ' ||ora_dict_obj_name||
' default tablespace users');
end if;
end;
```

But again:

```
create user milton identified by xxxx;
*
ERROR at line 1:
ORA-00604: error occurred at recursive SQL level 1
ORA-30511: invalid DDL operation in system triggers
ORA-06512: at line 5
```

Most DDL commands don't work in DDL triggers. The only supported DDL operations are table operations (like CREATE TABLE or DROP TABLE) and ALTER COMPILE operations. We can work around this limitation by having the DDL trigger submit a job to the PL/SQL job queue, similar to what we showed in the "Jobs and DML Triggers" section, earlier in this chapter.

First we create a procedure that accepts a username and alters the user's default tablespace,

```
procedure AlterUser (usernameIn in varchar2) is
begin
    execute immediate ( 'alter user ' ||usernameIn||
' default tablespace users');
end;
```

Then we rewrite the trigger to submit a job that executes this procedure.

```
create or replace
trigger SystemAlterUser
 after create on database
 declare
 jobno number;
 begin
 if ora_dict_obj_type = 'USER' then
     dbms_job.submit(job => jobno, what =>
'alteruser('''||ora_dict_obj_name||''');');
 end if;
 end;
```

DDL Integrity Trigger

An Oracle user automatically has privileges on schema objects created in their own schema, including the privilege to drop any of those objects. There are times when you might like users to be a little less powerful. How can you prevent users from dropping any of their own objects?

```
create or replace trigger prevent_drop
before drop on alex.schema
begin
    raise_application_error(-20000,'Invalid command: DROP ');
end;

SQL> drop table b;
drop table b
*
ERROR at line 1:
ORA-00604: error occurred at recursive SQL level 1
ORA-20000: Invalid command: DROP
ORA-06512: at line 2
```

DDL triggers can be created for a schema or for the database. Here, we created the trigger for a schema called ALEX.

DDL Audit Trail

Tom Kyte at http://asktom.oracle.com suggested the following DDL audit trail application after someone asked him this question:

> *If a developer overwrites a function, is there a way to see how the function looked at first, i.e., to see how that function looked before it was changed? In other words, is there a way to keep an audit trail of changes to functions?*

His solution (modified slightly here) uses two audit trail tables and the following DDL trigger:

```
-- Save the code before any changes are made to it
create or replace trigger save_old_code
before create on database
begin
    if ora_dict_obj_type in
        ( 'PACKAGE','PACKAGE BODY','PROCEDURE','FUNCTION' )  then

            insert  into old_source_header
                    (username,change_id,change_date)
            values  (ora_login_user,source_seq.nextval,sysdate);
```

```
            insert into old_source_detail
            select source_seq.currval,dba_source.*
            from   dba_source
            where  owner = ora_dict_obj_owner and
                   name = ora_dict_obj_name and
                   type = ora_dict_obj_type;
    end if;
end;
```

The two audit trail tables save the text of the stored procedure because it existed before the change was made.

```
SQL> desc old_source_header
    Name                 Null?      Type
    ------------------   --------   --------------
    USERNAME                        VARCHAR2(30)
    CHANGE_ID                       NUMBER
    CHANGE_DATE                     DATE

SQL> desc old_source_detail
    Name                 Null?      Type
    ------------------   --------   --------------
    CHANGE_ID                       NUMBER
    OWNER                           VARCHAR2(30)
    NAME                            VARCHAR2(30)
    TYPE                            VARCHAR2(12)
    LINE                            NUMBER
    TEXT                            VARCHAR2(4000)

SQL>  select *
   2    from   old_source_header;

USERNAME      CHANGE_ID  CHANGE_DATE
-----------   ----------  ------------------
ALEX                 10   28-Aug-03 10:20:44

SQL> select text as "Here is how it looked before"
   2  from   old_source_detail
   3  where  change_id=10
   4  order by line;

Here is how it looked before
------------------------------------------------
procedure monitor_db_size
```

```
as
begin
    insert into dbresults
    (runtime,instance,parameter_id,result)
    select sysdate,instance_name,'3',
        round(sum(bytes)/(1024*1024),2)
    from    dba_segments,v$instance;
end;
```

To give you an idea of what it was that motivated this application in the first place, here is the procedure, as it exists today.

```
SQL> select text
  2  from    dba_source
  3  where   name = 'MONITOR_DB_SIZE';


TEXT
----------------------------------
procedure monitor_db_size
as
begin
    null;
end;
```

Database Event Triggers

Database event triggers are fired by a few different events. We'll look at some of them now.

Logon Triggers

We saw one logon trigger at the beginning of this chapter. Although database event triggers are very useful, here is one that is quite useless:

```
Create or replace trigger loginCheckTrg after logon on database
declare
    m_count number;
begin
    select count(*)
    into    m_count
    from    v$session
```

```
    where   audsid=sys_context('userenv','sessionid')
    and     program like '%MSQRY32.EXE%';
    if m_count > 0 then
       raise_application_error(-20000,'Please try again later');
    end if;
end;
```

The trigger checks the program you're running and if it's MSQRY32, the trigger raises an error and prevents you from logging on. (We're trying to prevent users from employing desktop tools to access the database.) The problem with this type of trigger is that many users are often in complete control over the program names on their own machine. It's easy enough to copy an executable, rename it, run it, and circumvent the purpose of this logon trigger.

Logon triggers can be used to initialize database sessions in various ways; for example, to write a SQL_TRACE file or to save some session statistics or to change the current schema. The reason for changing the current schema relates to the design of many database environments in which a centralized application schema is shared by many application user schemas. Typically, users access the centralized application tables through public or private synonyms, or by prefixing every table reference with the application schema name.

Each of these setups is associated with a problem. Public synonyms hurt performance. Private synonyms are difficult to maintain, and hard-coding schema names makes the application much less flexible. A much better approach is to modify the user's session so that it points to the application schema. A logon trigger can accomplish this:

```
CREATE OR REPLACE TRIGGER change_schema
AFTER logon ON DATABASE
begin
 execute immediate('alter session set current_schema=app_master');
end;
```

Server Error Trigger

The server error trigger provides a centralized method of trapping database errors, including those user errors that aren't recorded in the database's alert log. Suppose a user is running a query, and that query runs out of temporary storage space. You can trap the error, including the SQL code that the user was running, and then determine the cause of the problem.

```
-- Save information about all errors
create or replace trigger log_errors
```

```
     after servererror on database
declare
   sql_text ora_name_list_t;
   msg varchar2(2000) := null;
   stmt varchar2(2000):= null;
begin
   for i in 1 .. ora_server_error_depth loop
      msg := msg||ora_server_error_msg(i);
   end loop;
   for i in 1..ora_sql_txt(sql_text) loop
      stmt := stmt||sql_text(i);
   end loop;
   insert into user_errors
   (error_date,username,error_msg,error_sql)
   values (sysdate,ora_login_user,msg,stmt);
end;


SQL> desc user_errors
 Name                        Null?    Type
 ----------------------- -------- --------------
 ERROR_DATE                          DATE
 USERNAME                            VARCHAR2(30)
 ERROR_MSG                           VARCHAR2(2000)
 ERROR_SQL                           VARCHAR2(2000)


SQL> select *
  2  from   user_errors;


ERROR_DAT USERNAME
--------- -----------------
ERROR_MSG
---------------------------
ERROR_SQL
---------------------------
20-MAY-03 SAMPLE
ORA-01652: unable to extend temp segment by 64 in tablespace TEMP_1
ORA-27059: skgfrsz: could not reduce file size
OSD-04005: SetFilePointer() failure, unable to read from file
O/S-Error: (OS 112) There is not enough space on the disk.
select nunavut.userlisting, nunavut.phone_number, woodbury.phone_number
from   nunavut_phone_book nunavut, woodbury_phone_book woodbury
```

In this example, the user omitted the WHERE clause, so it's no wonder the query ran out of space. You can also use the suspend event trigger to help correct space shortages without aborting the query, as we describe next.

Suspend Event Trigger

The suspend event trigger is used to investigate insufficient space situations. Usually, when a SQL statement encounters a runtime error caused by a lack of space or a mismatch between an object's storage parameters and its storage requirements, the SQL statement fails and its changes are rolled back. However, if the session is *resumable*, the SQL statement suspends itself and waits for a specified length of time. If the problem is corrected, the statement will continue to execute. Otherwise, the suspended SQL statement will time out and raise the original space-related error message. Using the suspend event trigger, when a session is suspended, you can capture the SQL statement (much as we did in the previous server error trigger example) or do any other type of relevant processing.

The developer, Alex, ran the following SQL hoping to trap the unsuspecting nighttime DBA into giving him more space for his objects (more quota).

```
alter session enable resumable
    name 'Help, I really need more space';
```

The DBA has however anticipated the problem with the following suspend trigger:

```
create or replace trigger respond_to_resumable_session after suspend
on database
declare
jobno number;
begin
    if ora_login_user = 'ALEX' then
        raise_application_error(-20000,'Alex, I told you, you shouldn''t '||
            'be doing this. There''s no way you''re getting more space.');
    else
      dbms_job.submit(
                job   => jobno,
                what  => 'space_shortage_notification;'
                );
    end;
```

This is what Alex sees the following morning.

```
insert into
*
ERROR at line 147:
ORA-00604: error occurred at recursive SQL level 1
ORA-20000: Alex, I told you, you shouldn't be doing this. There's no way you're
getting more space.
ORA-06512: at line 164
ORA-01653: unable to extend table ALEX.EMP_HOURS_BACKUP
```

If any other user's job runs out of space, the DBA is notified and can respond immediately by making more space available or adjusting the space allocation parameters. The user statement will then resume and complete successfully.

Errors and Database Event Triggers

When working with database event triggers, it's necessary to grant the "administer database trigger" privilege directly to whichever account owns the trigger. Otherwise you might encounter an error.

```
(table char)
 *
ERROR at line 2:
ORA-04045: errors during recompilation/revalidation of SYSTEM.LOG_ERRORS
ORA-01031: insufficient privileges
ORA-00904: invalid identifier
```

Here's some background about the error message: A user was creating a table and attempted to use the word table (an invalid identifier) as a column name. A system-wide server error event trigger was in place, but at that moment, the trigger happened to be invalid. The Oracle server attempted to recompile the trigger but the compilation failed because the trigger owner had the administer database trigger privilege granted through a role.

Errors in database event triggers have a significant impact. If there's an error in a logon trigger, it most probably will prevent unprivileged users from logging on. If a server error event trigger is logging all errors into an error table and that table fills up (or hits another error condition), any session that raises an error will freeze.

Don't Re-Invent the Wheel

There will be times when it will be difficult to decide if you need to create triggers or not. Many requirements that can be solved with triggers can also be solved with built-in Oracle functionality. It's wise to examine the requirements carefully before rushing into a custom crafted trigger application. Here's a small example.

Database Usage Report

We want a monthly summary report for each database user. The raw data looks like this.

```
USERID AUDSID LOG_ON          LOG_OFF          CPU_USED
------ ------ --------------  --------------   -----------
SCOTT     439 03/11/03 11:10  03/11/03 11:41        231
TEST      440 03/11/03 11:43  03/11/03 11:44         30
TEST      441 03/11/03 11:44  03/11/03 11:47        108
```

The data will be summarized by month, and it will help us determine how much CPU each department consumes. It takes only one table and two triggers to build this application.

```
-- table to store information on sessions
create table usage_log
(user_id  varchar2(30),
 audsid   varchar2(30),
 log_on   date,
 log_off  date,
 cpu_used number);

-- database login trigger
create or replace trigger usage_start
after logon on database
begin
  insert into system.usage_log
  (user_id,audid,log_on,log_off,cpu_used)
   values (sys_context('userenv','session_user'),
           sys_context('userenv','sessionid'),
           sysdate, null, null);
end;

-- database logoff trigger
create or replace trigger usage_stop
before logoff on database
begin
  update system.usage_log
```

```
set     log_off = sysdate,
        cpu_used = (select value
                        from   v$mystat s,v$statname n
                        where  s.statistic# = n.statistic# and
                               n.name like 'CPU used by this session')
    where   sys_context('USERENV', 'SESSIONID') = audid and
            sys_context('userenv','session_user') = user_id and
            log_off is null;
end;
```

There isn't anything wrong with this design or with these two database event triggers except that by turning on auditing (AUDIT SESSION), you'll produce the same reports and they will be stored in the database's default audit trail. Here is the default audit report.

```
SQL> select username, sessionid,
  2          to_char(timestamp,'mm/dd/yy hh24:mi') timestamp,
  3          to_char(logoff_time,'mm/dd/yy hh24:mi') logoff_time,
  4          session_cpu
  5 from    dba_audit_trail;
```

USERNAME	SESSIONID	TIMESTAMP	LOGOFF_TIME	SESSION_CPU
SCOTT	439	03/11/03 11:10	03/11/03 11:41	232
TEST	440	03/11/03 11:43	03/11/03 11:44	31
TEST	441	03/11/03 11:44	03/11/03 11:47	109

A difference between the trigger version and the audit command version emerges when the database is shut down in a way that requires recovery on startup (SHUTDOWN ABORT) or when a user process is killed (ALTER SESSION). In either scenario, the logoff trigger isn't fired at all. Therefore, the trigger application will contain rows with logon times, but without matching log off times. In contrast, the database's audit trail will contain the log off times and will even contain a matching comment saying that the logoff was performed by cleanup.

On the other hand, the system's audit trail record has a fixed number of fields. It keeps track of only a limited set of statistics (logical reads and writes, physical reads, CPU used, number of deadlocks). If your requirements are different, you'll most likely need to write triggers.

Trigger applications that you should avoid include triggers that implement referential integrity and triggers that enforce check constraints. The declarative constraints provided by the database server are always preferred.

Summary

Triggers are programs that the server executes every time certain events occur. DML and instead-of triggers are associated with data update events, DDL triggers are associated with creating and deleting database objects, and database event triggers fire when certain database events occur.

In this chapter, we discussed examples of DDL and database event triggers. You saw a technique for avoiding errors related to mutating tables and some DML trigger examples. We introduced you to table versioning and Oracle Streams, either of which might be used to satisfy data auditing requirements.

We covered the PL/SQL job queue and explained how these jobs can execute at certain times or on certain intervals. The jobs can be utilized in combination with triggers to accomplish work that would take too long if performed by the trigger itself, or to accomplish work that the trigger is restricted from performing.

Finally, we discussed trigger applications to avoid in situations when your expectations can be met by the database's supplied functionality.

The chapter covered many ideas and used much new terminology. Check your comprehension by defining each of these terms: trigger, trigger status, object status, DML trigger, mutating table error, statement and row triggers, data audit trails, table versioning, Oracle streams, jobs and the job queue, interval and next date, DDL trigger, schema and database triggers, database event trigger, server error trigger, and suspend event trigger.

CHAPTER 7

DBA Packages

IF YOU'RE RESPONSIBLE FOR maintaining an Oracle database, you'll already know that your job is split between two types of tasks.

- Ad hoc tasks, which include creating users or other database objects, granting privileges, altering storage properties, and so on.

- Recurring activities that are performed as part of ongoing system maintenance, such as performance diagnosis and troubleshooting, backup and recovery, monitoring the database for faults, and tracking whether these faults have already occurred or are about to.

Both aspects of your job can benefit from the use of PL/SQL. For the first type of task, we saw in Chapter 5 that we can deploy utilities, such as password resetting, with a more granular level of control than is provided by the standard Oracle ALTER USER privilege. Similarly, once such tools are wrapped within PL/SQL, you can deploy those processes to a Web-enabled environment via the OWA Web toolkit, as discussed in Chapter 9. You are limited only by your imagination in the administrative tasks you can gain additional control and flexibility over using PL/SQL.

In this chapter, we will focus on the second group—the recurring activities required to maintain an Oracle database. Of course, certain aspects of the recurring activities ought to be automated because automation helps standardize these tasks, simplifying your work and making you more efficient.

We will discuss using PL/SQL to create automated, standardized database-monitoring solutions. We'll describe how to keep an eye on the available free space in the database and the archive log destination directory. We'll check that the backups have completed successfully. We'll also gather information about database growth and database usage. We'll demonstrate how to scan the Oracle alert file for error messages and how to send notifications when new error messages are encountered.

There are four packages that we'll present in this chapter.

- An alert file package for monitoring and managing the Oracle alert file

- A notification package that handles emails

- A monitoring package for procedures that checks the status of the backups and monitors free space, allowing you to react in a proactive way to potential problems

- An historical data package containing procedures that compute the size of the database, count the number of database sessions, and measure key resource limits within the database

You'll find the complete code in the download section of the Apress Web site (http://www.apress.com).

Alert File Package

During database operation, the Oracle server writes messages to an alert file (often called the **alert log**). Usually, the alert file resides in the ORACLE_BASE/ADMIN/DB_NAME/BDUMP directory, but it can be stored anywhere. Its location is specified by the BACKGROUND_DUMP_DEST parameter in the initialization file, so you can locate it by issuing

```
SQL> show parameter background_dump_dest

NAME                     TYPE     VALUE
--------------------     ------   ------------------------------
background_dump_dest     string   C:\oracle\admin\oratest\bdump
```

Since Oracle9*i*, the name of the alert file, ALERT_*SID*.LOG, has been standardized across Windows and Unix platforms. If an error message appears in the file, the DBA is expected to respond quickly. In particular, entries in the alert file can indicate the slow onset of a problem that may lead to something more traumatic, such as a database crash. Timely monitoring of the alert file not only allows for problem detection, but problem avoidance. Generally, these errors describe problems that affect the entire database. Such errors include, for example, errors generated by background processes, internal ORA-600 errors, space related errors, block corruption errors, and so on. This is what an extract of the alert file might look like.

```
Fri Jun 27 11:49:53 2003
Thread 1 advanced to log sequence 16386
  Current log# 2 seq# 16386 mem# 0: C:\ORACLE\ORADATA\REP9\REDO02.LOG
Fri Jun 27 11:49:53 2003
ARC1: Evaluating archive   log 1 thread 1 sequence 16385
ARC1: Beginning to archive log 1 thread 1 sequence 16385
Creating archive destination LOG_ARCHIVE_DEST_1:
```

```
'C:\ORACLE\ORAARCHIVES\A16385.ARC'
ARC1: Completed archiving  log 1 thread 1 sequence 16385
Fri Jun 27 12:04:02 2003
Errors in file c:\oracle\admin\rep9\udump\rep9_j000_640.trc:
ORA-12012: error on auto execute of job 147
ORA-00376: file 8 cannot be read at this time
ORA-01110: data file 8: 'C:\ORACLE\ORADATA\REP9\TOOLS01.DBF'
ORA-06512: at "SCOTT.ROUTINEJOB", line 5
ORA-06512: at line 1
```

Package Structure

Our alert file package will monitor the alert file, count the number of new Oracle error messages in the file, and send a notification email that includes the contents of the error message to interested parties. The package specification is as follows:

```
SQL> CREATE OR REPLACE  PACKAGE ALERT_FILE  is
  2  /**
  3  * =======================================================================
  4  * Project:       Alert file
  5  * Description:   Monitor and manage the alert file
  6  * DB impact:     reads exernal table
  7  * Commit inside:  no
  8  * Rollback inside: no
  9  * -----------------------------------------------------------  ----
 10  */
 11        procedure monitor_alert_file;
 12  end;
 13  /

Package created.
```

As you can see, it has one entry point, a procedure called MONITOR_ALERT_FILE. This public procedure calls a number of private procedures in the package body.

- **READ_ALERT_FILE**: This procedure processes our alert file

- **UPDATE_SKIP_COUNT**: This procedure ensures that we do not re-read old messages in the alert file

- **RENAME_ALERT_FILE**: This procedure renames the alert file on a daily basis

- **REVIEW_ALERT_FILE**: This procedure sends a copy of the daily alert file to the appropriate recipients via email

The code for the whole package is freely available for download from the http://www.apress.com Web site. In the following sections, we'll explain the code that constitutes each of these procedures, but first we need to take a look at the structure of the alert file that we'll be working with.

Structure of the Alert File

Taking a closer look at our example alert file extract, we can see a line beginning with ORA-12012, indicating that there was an error executing a PL/SQL job. Where does the error message start and where does it finish? This question isn't relevant if we always inspect the file manually, but it is important if we automate the inspection and error notification process. Clearly the message starts at the line preceding the ORA-12012. Similarly, we can ask how many error messages the extract contains. Obviously only one, although the phrase ORA-XXXX repeats a number of times.

An alert message in the alert file is always at least two lines long. It begins with one line containing a date and time stamp, for example, FRI JUN 27 12:01:04 2003. The message continues for one or more lines and ends before the next date/time stamp, or at the end of the file. In fact, the alert file is composed of a sequence of such messages. This can be expressed in Backus-Naur form (BNF) as follows:

```
alert file ::= {date line {message line}}
```

Our MONITOR_ALERT_FILE procedure must respect the structure of the alert file. It must recognize multi-line messages so that it can send an accurate notification. It would be wrong for the monitor program to send five notification messages (corresponding to the five lines beginning with ORA- in the extract). It would also be wrong for the notification to omit the date of the error message and the trace file information that also belongs to the error message. In summary, the alert file extract contains three messages. There is a message concerning a log switch.

```
Fri Jun 27 11:49:53 2003
Thread 1 advanced to log sequence 16386
  Current log# 2 seq# 16386 mem# 0: C:\ORACLE\ORADATA\REP9\RED002.LOG
```

There is a message about the status of archiving an inactive redo log file.

```
Fri Jun 27 11:49:53 2003
ARC1: Evaluating archive    log 1 thread 1 sequence 16385
ARC1: Beginning to archive log 1 thread 1 sequence 16385
Creating archive destination LOG_ARCHIVE_DEST_1:
'C:\ORACLE\ORAARCHIVES\A16385.ARC'
ARC1: Completed archiving  log 1 thread 1 sequence 16385
```

And finally, there is a message indicating that a database job failed because a file was offline.

```
Fri Jun 27 12:04:02 2003
Errors in file c:\oracle\admin\rep9\udump\rep9_j000_640.trc:
ORA-12012: error on auto execute of job 147
ORA-00376: file 8 cannot be read at this time
ORA-01110: data file 8: 'C:\ORACLE\ORADATA\REP9\TOOLS01.DBF'
ORA-06512: at "SCOTT.ROUTINEJOB", line 5
ORA-06512: at line 1
```

We should note that Oracle doesn't publish the specification of the alert file. We have no guarantee that Oracle agrees with our description of the file. All we can say is that our description of the alert file seems to fit, although the structure of the file might change in the future.

> **NOTE** We deal with a few cases where an error message does not conform to the structure given above, or will simply not be written to the alert file, in the *Caveats* section, a little later.

Alert File as an External Table

An easy way for PL/SQL to read the alert file is to associate it with an external table—a table whose data lives outside the database. External tables allow us to query data from flat files.

> **NOTE** External tables are a new feature to Oracle 9*i*.

External tables rely on a DIRECTORY object to specify the location of the file to which we will write, so the first thing we need to do is create this object. As we saw earlier, this is the directory indicated by the BACKGROUND_DUMP_DEST parameter.

```
SQL> Create or replace directory alert_dir
  2   as 'c:\oracle\admin\rep9\bdump';

Directory created.
```

Once we've created the directory (or any database object for that matter), we can extract its definition from the data dictionary using the DBMS_METADATA package.

```
SQL> select dbms_metadata.get_ddl
  2   ('DIRECTORY','ALERT_DIR')
  3   from dual;

DBMS_METADATA.GET_DDL('DIRECTORY','ALERT_DIR')
--------------------------------------------------------------------------
   CREATE OR REPLACE DIRECTORY "ALERT_DIR" AS 'c:\oracle\admin\rep9\bdump'
```

A complete description of the syntax[1] to create an external table is beyond the scope of this book, but we can see that it resembles a blend of the standard CREATE TABLE command and a SQL Loader control file.

```
  CREATE TABLE "ALERT_FILE_EXT"
  (    "MSG_LINE" VARCHAR2(1000)
  )
  ORGANIZATION EXTERNAL
   ( TYPE ORACLE_LOADER
     DEFAULT DIRECTORY "ALERT_DIR"
     ACCESS PARAMETERS
     ( RECORDS DELIMITED BY NEWLINE CHARACTERSET US7ASCII
   nobadfile nologfile nodiscardfile
   skip 0
   READSIZE 1048576
   FIELDS LDRTRIM
   REJECT ROWS WITH ALL NULL FIELDS
   (
     MSG_LINE (1:1000) CHAR(1000)
   )
    )
```

---

1. See the SQL Reference in the Oracle 9.2 documentation for the complete syntax for the creation of external tables.

```
   LOCATION
     ( 'alert_rep9.log'
     )
   )
 REJECT LIMIT UNLIMITED
/
```

We've created an external table, ALERT_FILE_EXT, which displays data from the ALERT_REP9.LOG operating system file, which resides in the c:\oracle\admin\rep9\bdump directory (this database server machine is running Microsoft Windows), as specified by our ALERT_DIR directory object. Again, if you need to retrieve the definition of your external table, you can use the DBMS_METADATA package.

Each external record ends with a new line character; the maximum field size for an external table is 1,000 characters. If the alert file contains a line longer than 1,000 characters, it will not appear when we query the external table (the longest alert line I've ever seen was about 140 characters long). The external table can now be queried as per any conventional table. For example, to see the first nine lines from the alert file, we can query

```
SQL> select *
  2  from alert_file_ext
  3  where rownum < 10;

MSG_LINE
-------------------------------------------------------------------------------
Fri Jun 27 11:49:53 2003
Thread 1 advanced to log sequence 16386
  Current log# 2 seq# 16386 mem# 0: C:\ORACLE\ORADATA\REP9\RED002.LOG
Fri Jun 27 11:49:53 2003
ARC1: Evaluating archive   log 1 thread 1 sequence 16385
ARC1: Beginning to archive log 1 thread 1 sequence 16385
Creating archive destination LOG_ARCHIVE_DEST_1:
'C:\ORACLE\ORAARCHIVES\A16385.ARC'
ARC1: Completed archiving  log 1 thread 1 sequence 16385
Fri Jun 27 12:01:04 2003

9 rows selected.
```

Our basic assumption is that querying the external table without an ORDER BY clause retrieves the rows from the alert file sequentially although this is not guaranteed to be the case. On Oracle's technet forum, I found the following description (attributed to an anonymous member of Oracle's kernel group):

> *"Whenever you access an external table SERIALLY, you're getting the records (that are selected and not rejected) in the same order that they are in the flat file, I don't see the business benefit of such behavior (yet). Unlike SQL*Loader, where the process is to INSERT data in a well defined way, external tables only provide ACCESS to the external data, but have no control over the subsequent usage. The subsequent usage is SQL, and it's a fact that any ordered output in SQL is only guaranteed by issuing an ORDER BY clause...*
>
> *For serial access we currently maintain order. For parallel access we do not maintain order."*

In other words, querying an external table serially, today, will return the rows in the sequential order of the flat file, but this may change. If Oracle does in fact make some underlying change in future releases, we can still create a solution that ensures the rows are returned sequentially using a pipelined function to read the alert file.

As we've seen in earlier chapters, a pipeline function must return a collection, so we'll create one to hold each line from our alert log.

```
SQL> create or replace type varchar2_list
  2  as table of varchar2(1000);
  3  /

Type created.
```

Now we'll create a function to read each line from the alert file. A "line" is defined as the content between subsequent carriage returns, that is, the character represented by ASCII code 10. Thus, we simply open the alert file as a BFILE and search through the file for carriage returns, piping out rows as we go.

```
SQL> create or replace
  2    function alert_log return varchar2_list pipelined is
  3      v_alert_log    bfile := bfilename('ALERT_DIR','alert_rep9.log');
  4      v_prev_chr10   number := 1;
  5      v_this_chr10   number;
  6      chr10          raw(4) := utl_raw.cast_to_raw(chr(10));
  7    begin
  8      dbms_lob.fileopen( v_alert_log );
  9      loop
 10       v_this_chr10 := dbms_lob.instr( v_alert_log, chr10, v_prev_chr10, 1 );
 11         exit when (nvl(v_this_chr10,0) = 0);
```

```
12              pipe row ( utl_raw.cast_to_varchar2(
13                        dbms_lob.substr( v_alert_log,
14                        v_this_chr10-
15                        v_prev_chr10+1,
16                      v_prev_chr10 ) ) ) ;
17          v_prev_chr10 := v_this_chr10+1;
18      end loop;
19      dbms_lob.fileclose(v_alert_log);
20      return;
21    end;
22  /
```

Function created.

We can then query our function using the familiar TABLE construct to see the content of the alert log. Because the file is being read sequentially by our function, the rows will be in order.

```
SQL> select * from table(alert_log);

MSG_LINE
------------------------------------------------------------------------
Fri Jun 27 11:49:53 2003
Thread 1 advanced to log sequence 16386
  Current log# 2 seq# 16386 mem# 0: C:\ORACLE\ORADATA\REP9\REDO02.LOG
Fri Jun 27 11:49:53 2003
ARC1: Evaluating archive   log 1 thread 1 sequence 16385
ARC1: Beginning to archive log 1 thread 1 sequence 16385
Creating archive destination LOG_ARCHIVE_DEST_1:
'C:\ORACLE\ORAARCHIVES\A16385.ARC'
ARC1: Completed archiving   log 1 thread 1 sequence 16385
Fri Jun 27 12:01:04 2003
```

Thus, whether we implement an external table or read directly from the alert file by referencing it as an external LOB, we will be able to query it via SQL, which leads onto our next section—processing the results of that query.

Processing the Alert File

The following is the procedure in the ALERT_FILE package that processes the alert file. It finds a date line and then assembles each alert file message until it finds another date line, or until it finds no more rows. Once we've assembled a message, it's a simple matter to search through it for a match with ORA-, in order to classify it as an error message.

```
procedure read_alert_file (error_msg_arry out monitor.msgs,
                                 linecount out integer)
as
-- reads the alert file
-- Save any error messages in an associative array
cursor c1 is
       select msg_line
       from   alert_file_ext;

l_buffer     varchar2(1000);
l_msg_text   varchar2(32767);
error_count binary_integer :=0;
begin
-- open the cursor
   open c1;

-- read ahead
   fetch c1 into l_buffer;

   while c1%FOUND loop
--       save the date line
         l_msg_text := l_buffer;

--       read the first msg body line
         fetch c1 into l_buffer;
         while (l_buffer not like '___ __ __ __:__:__ ____'  and c1%FOUND) loop
               l_msg_text := l_msg_text||chr(10)||l_buffer;
               fetch c1 into l_buffer;
               end loop;

--       check for error
         if (instr(l_msg_text,'ORA-') > 0) then
               error_count := error_count + 1;
               error_msg_arry(error_count) := l_msg_text;
         end if;

         end loop;
   linecount := c1%ROWCOUNT;
   close c1;
end;
```

At the completion of the procedure, our collection variable ERROR_MSG_ARRY contains the list of date-stamped alert log messages. If we modify the code to print out the entries in the collection, we see the following output:

```
Sat Sep 20 23:44:00 2003
alter tablespace example offline
---------------------
Sat Sep 20 23:44:01 2003
Completed: alter tablespace example offline
---------------------
Sat Sep 20 23:50:39 2003
Errors in file c:\oracle\admin\rep9\udump\rep9_j000_1772.trc:
ORA-12012: error on auto execute
of job 244
ORA-20000: Testing...
ORA-06512: at "SCOTT.TEST", line 4
ORA-06512: at line 1
---------------------
Sat Sep 20 23:50:39 2003
ARC1: Evaluating archive   log 1 thread 1 sequence 17474
ARC1: Beginning to archive log 1
thread 1 sequence 17474
Creating archive destination LOG_ARCHIVE_DEST_1:
 'C:\ORACLE\ORAARCHIVES\ARCH_17474.ARC'
ARC1:
Completed archiving  l
---------------------
```

We have built a solution with PL/SQL. But as we saw in Chapter 1, we should be asking ourselves if vanilla SQL might also be up to this task. Although there is no simple SQL predicate we can construct that would allow us to identify an individual alert message, a little creative use of some analytic functions allows us to construct a view whose rows equate to the entries in the ERROR_MSG_ARRY collection just shown.

```
-- View that displays the alert file's error messages
create or replace view alert_log_errors
as
select *
  from (
select *
  from (
select lineno,
       msg_line,
```

```
            thedate,
            max( case when ora_error like 'ORA-%'
                      then rtrim(substr(ora_error,1,instr(ora_error,' ')-1),':')
                      else null
                  end ) over (partition by thedate) ora_error
      from (
    select lineno,
           msg_line,
           max(thedate) over (order by lineno) thedate,
           lead(msg_line) over (order by lineno) ora_error
      from (
    select rownum lineno,
           substr( msg_line, 1, 132 ) msg_line,
           case when msg_line like '___ ___ __ __:__:__ ____'
                then to_date( msg_line, 'Dy Mon DD hh24:mi:ss yyyy' )
                else null
           end thedate
      from alert_file_ext
           )
           )
           )
           )
    where ora_error is not null
    order by thedate
```

Rows in the view correspond to error messages in the alert file, although we've also added an RTRIM function around the Oracle error code because for some errors (ORA-4031, for example), the entries in the alert log are suffixed with a colon (:). If the view returns no rows, there are currently no errors in the alert file. The view allows us to search the alert file in a number of ways. We can query by error code.

```
SQL>  select ora_error, msg_line
  2    from    alert_log_errors
  3    where ora_error = 'ORA-1652';


ORA_ERROR   MSG_LINE
----------  -------------------------------------------------------------------
ORA-1652:   Tue Sep 23 12:54:54 2003
ORA-1652:   ORA-1652: unable to extend temp segment by 8 in tablespace TOOLS
```

We can also query the view based on the contents of the MSG_LINE field or by the THEDATE field.

```
SQL> select thedate,msg_line
  2  from    alert_log_errors
  3  where   thedate between to_date('21-Sep-03 11:15','dd-mon-yy hh24:mi') and
  4                          to_date('21-Sep-03 11:30','dd-mon-yy hh24:mi')
  5  /

THEDATE    MSG_LINE
---------  --------------------------------------------------------------------------
21-SEP-03  Sun Sep 21 11:15:06 2003
21-SEP-03  ORA-000060: Deadlock detected. More info in file c:\oracle\admin\dev92
21-SEP-03
```

There is one little quirk to be aware of when using this view. If two messages in the alert file have the same date and time, the view will amalgamate both messages, even if only one of them is an error message.

```
SQL> select ora_error,msg_line
from alert_log_errors;

ORA_ERROR   MSG_LINE
----------  -----------------------------------------------------------------
ORA-20000:  Sat Sep 20 23:50:39 2003
ORA-20000:  Errors in file c:\oracle\admin\rep9\udump\rep9_j000_1772.trc:
ORA-20000:  ORA-12012: error on auto execute of job 244
ORA-20000:  ORA-20000: Testing...
ORA-20000:  ORA-06512: at "SCOTT.TEST", line 4
ORA-20000:  ORA-06512: at line 1
ORA-20000:  Sat Sep 20 23:50:39 2003
ORA-20000:  ARC1: Evaluating archive    log 1 thread 1 sequence 17474
ORA-20000:  ARC1: Beginning to archive log 1 thread 1 sequence 17474
ORA-20000:  Creating archive destination LOG_ARCHIVE_DEST_1:
                'C:\ORACLE\ORAARCHIVES\ARCH_17474.ARC'
ORA-20000:  ARC1: Completed archiving   log 1 thread 1 sequence 17474
```

As we discussed in Chapter 1, if we were querying a large alert log, this view may give superior performance over the PL/SQL solution. However, if your alert file is getting very large, you probably have more pressing concerns than the performance of the view...like what all those errors are doing in there in the first place! For the rest of this section, we will stick with the PL/SQL solution—after all, it's a PL/SQL book, and we can easily extend the code to suit any needs we have. For example, if at some point we want to monitor messages other than ORA- (such as CHECKPOINT NOT COMPLETE errors), it is very simple to add this functionality to the procedural PL/SQL program.

Nevertheless, we wanted to demonstrate once again how SQL code can perform quite sophisticated logic in a rather elegant fashion.

Exceptions

Both the procedural program and the view are subject to errors. If the alert file isn't where you think it is, you will see something like the following error:

```
SQL> select *
  2  from    alert_file_ext;
select *
*
ERROR at line 1:
ORA-29913: error in executing ODCIEXTTABLEOPEN callout
ORA-29400: data cartridge error
KUP-04040: file alert_rep9.log in ALERT_DIR not found
ORA-06512: at "SYS.ORACLE_LOADER", line 14
ORA-06512: at line 1
```

The file isn't found in the directory that we specified. The correct response to this error depends on the situation. In a stable environment where the alert file is frequently rolled-over (the alert file is renamed, effectively deleting it—more on this in a moment), there may be a short time when there is no alert file. The bottom line is that it may be perfectly acceptable for the alert file to be missing temporarily.

On the other hand, on a large multi-DBA site, or a site with an absent minded DBA, it's possible that someone will move the alert file, in which case our program will be looking in the "wrong" directory. That certainly is a problem, and our alert file-monitoring program should raise an error.

We can distinguish between these cases by comparing the value of the background dump destination (the actual location of the alert file) with the location (the directory path) of the DIRECTORY object that we created to identify the location of our external table.

```
-- check location of alert file
select count(*)
from    v$parameter
where   name = 'background_dump_dest'
and     value = (select directory_path
                 from    dba_directories
                 where   directory_name = 'ALERT_DIR')
```

If the destination described by the background dump destination initialization parameter doesn't match that described by the ALERT_DIR directory, the query will return a count of zero. Someone moved the alert file, so we should raise an error. On the other hand, if the directories match, we know we're looking for the file in its proper place.

In the MONITOR_ALERT_FILE procedure that we'll show at the end of this discussion (and that is available in the code download file), you'll see that we've combined this query with one that retrieves the name of the instance. Instead of using the count, we rely on the NO_DATA_FOUND exception to decide if the alert directory object is pointing to the wrong directory.

```
-- check location of alert file
    select instance_name
    into   l_instance_name
    from   v$parameter,v$instance,dba_directories
    where  directory_name = 'ALERT_DIR' and
           name='background_dump_dest' and
           value = directory_path;
-- more code comes here
exception
    when no_data_found then
raise_application_error(-20000,'ALERT_DIR is not current');
```

On Windows, you could potentially create a background dump destination named "D:\oracle…" and an object directory named, "d:\oracle…." You'll have a problem matching these two names because of the upper and lower case letters. The best way to avoid this situation is to be consistent with the directory names. However, you might consider recasting the query to ignore case issues.

```
select count(*)
  from   v$parameter
  where  name = 'background_dump_dest'
  and    upper(value) = (select upper(directory_path)
                         from   dba_directories
                         where  directory_name = 'ALERT_DIR')
```

The procedure is sensitive to another problem as well—it assembles messages by appending subsequent lines of text into a buffer defined as

```
l_msg_text varchar2(32767);
```

If the size of the assembled message is larger that this, the concatenation will raise an error.

```
ORA-20000: ORA-06502: PL/SQL: numeric or value error
ORA-06512: at "DBMON.ALERT_FILE", line 174
ORA-06512: at line 2
```

But this is highly unlikely. Almost all messages in the alert file are one or two lines long. Error messages can consist of a number of lines but are still only a few hundred characters in length. The longest message I've ever seen is the message written when the database starts. Then, the server writes all the non-default system parameters as one long message and that is also much fewer than 32,767 characters.

If you encounter this problem, the solution is to truncate the oversized message. We haven't included this test in our code.

```
-- set an upper limit to the length of a message
if length(l_msg_text)+length(l_buffer) < 32765 then
    l_msg_text := l_msg_text||chr(10)||l_buffer;
  else
    l_msg_text := substr(l_msg_text,1,length(l_msg_text))
        ||chr(10)||'** Message truncated';
end if;
```

Notification Life Cycle

As it currently stands, the procedural code reads all the lines in the external table. Most of these lines are informational messages unrelated to errors. Error messages have the string ORA- embedded in them.

```
if instr(l_msg_text,'ORA-') > 0 then
        error_count_out := error_count_out + 1;
end if;
```

Once we discover an error message in the alert file, we will notify the DBA. However, after that notification has taken place, we would not want to send the *same* error time and time again—we should send only errors that have occurred since the last time we checked the alert file. Thus the requirement becomes to notify the DBA only when there's been some change to the alert file; that is, if a new error message was written to the file since the program last ran. We can accomplish this goal by modifying the definition of the external table. If the alert file was, for example, 1,000 lines long the last time it was checked, the next time we check, we want to start at line 1,001. We can achieve this by manipulating the SKIP value for the external table.

```
SQL> select access_parameters
  2  from    user_external_tables
  3  where   table_name = 'ALERT_FILE_EXT';

ACCESS_PARAMETERS
----------------------------------------------------
RECORDS DELIMITED BY NEWLINE CHARACTERSET US7ASCII
    nobadfile nologfile nodiscardfile
    skip 0
    READSIZE 1048576
    FIELDS LDRTRIM
    REJECT ROWS WITH ALL NULL FIELDS
    (
      MSG_LINE (1:1000) CHAR(1000)
    )
```

The ACCESS_PARAMETERS of the external table specify that we skip zero records before reading the alert file. This is how we created the external table initially. But after we read the external file, (and we'll be reading the file every ten minutes or so), we'd like to modify the number of records to skip so that we always start reading from the point where we finished last time.

```
procedure update_skip_count(p_count in number default 0,
                    reset boolean default false)
as
-- update access parameters of external table
i number;
j number;
adj number := p_count;
begin
    for x in (select replace(access_parameters,chr(10)) param
              from    user_external_tables
              where   table_name = 'ALERT_FILE_EXT') loop

        i := owa_pattern.amatch(x.param,1,'.*skip',i);
        j := owa_pattern.amatch(x.param,1,'.*skip \d*');

--  to reset the count (to zero)
        if reset then
        adj := -1 * to_number(substr(x.param,i,j-i));
        end if;

        execute immediate 'alter table alert_file_ext access parameters ('||
    substr(x.param,1,i)||
```

```
        (to_number(substr(x.param,i,j-i))+ adj)||
        substr(x.param,j)||')';

    end loop;
end;
```

We're using the PL/SQL pattern-matching package, OWA_PATTERN, instead of trying to accomplish the task with a combination of INSTR and SUBSTR. The AMATCH function returns the position in the input where the match ends. The two consecutive AMATCH function calls give us the beginning and ending positions of the SKIP *nn* parameter. We update the number of lines to skip and then alter the external table's definition. It's interesting that altering the external table in this way doesn't invalidate any dependent objects.

Rolling Over the Alert File

A number of years ago, I was working with Oracle support on a problem when they asked me to check the alert file. I tried to open the file while Oracle support waited on the phone. I don't know exactly how big the alert file was, but it was over a few hundred megabytes. I don't remember exactly what editor I was using (or what O/S I was working on), but I do remember waiting while the editor slowly loaded the contents of the alert file into its buffer, and after about 15 minutes, either the editor crashed or Oracle support had me move on to something else.

The Oracle server continuously appends information to the alert file. If we leave the file alone, it will grow and grow. A very large file takes up disk space that could be used for other purposes. A very large file probably responds more slowly to write requests and is almost impossible to open with some editors. It's definitely a bad idea to have an alert file that's too big to open.

To avoid super large alert files, you can delete the file every now and then. But it's better to take a more structured approach to the problem and let a PL/SQL procedure rename the alert file. Here is a listing of a background dump directory that is managed by a PL/SQL job.

```
06/26/2003   05:45p              32,345 alert_rep9Wed.log
06/27/2003   05:27a               6,673 alert_rep9Thu.log
06/28/2003   05:13a               5,207 alert_rep9Fri.log
06/29/2003   05:59a              10,787 alert_rep9Sat.log
06/30/2003   05:05a               5,551 alert_rep9Sun.log
07/01/2003   05:16a               5,551 alert_rep9Mon.log
07/02/2003   05:15a              20,910 alert_rep9Tue.log
07/02/2003   09:56a               1,281 alert_rep9.log
```

You're looking at a week's worth of alert files. Tomorrow morning, the PL/SQL job will rename the current ALERT_REP9.LOG to ALERT_REP9WED.LOG and overwrite the older file of the same name.

We use the FRENAME (file rename) procedure in the UTL_FILE supplied PL/SQL package to roll over the alert file. The FRENAME procedure accepts a source directory name, a source file name, a destination directory name, and a destination file name. We rename the alert file to ALERT_SID<YESTERDAY>.LOG, where the value of yesterday is computed using SYSDATE - 1. We indicate the location of the file with the directory object we've already created.

```
Procedure rename_alert_file (l_instance_name in varchar2)
as
-- Assume that the alert log is named alert_<INSTANCE>.log
-- Rename it to alert_<INSTANCE>Day.log
alert_file_does_not_exist EXCEPTION;
PRAGMA exception_init(alert_file_does_not_exist, -29283);
begin
-- rename the alert file
   utl_file.frename (
       src_location  => 'ALERT_DIR',
       src_filename  => 'alert_'||l_instance_name||'.log',
       dest_location => 'ALERT_DIR',
       dest_filename => 'alert_'||l_instance_name||
                             to_char(sysdate - 1,'Dy')||'.log',
       overwrite     =>  true);

exception
       when alert_file_does_not_exist then
           null;
end;
```

When we roll over the alert file in this way, we have to remember to reset the external table access parameters (the number of rows to skip). There's another reason for rolling over the alert files daily: Many DBAs have a practice of checking the entire alert file (not just the errors in the file—the entire file) on a regular basis. This task is much easier to schedule and accomplish if the alert file is not too large. We'll cover this later in this chapter when we discuss the REVIEW_ALERT_FILE procedure.

Of course, not every site wants to roll over the alert file every day. Some may want to perform a weekly or monthly cycle. Similarly, just because we rename the file, for example, every day, we may want to format the renamed file in a manner different than the renaming frequency. Does this mean we can't use the PL/SQL solution? Certainly not. With just a little enhancement, we can achieve a more generic alert file maintenance procedure as follows:

```
create or replace
procedure rename_alert_file (l_instance_name in varchar2,
                   p_format_mask varchar2 default 'DD',
                   p_filename_mask varchar2 default 'Dy') as
   alert_file_does_not_exist EXCEPTION;
   PRAGMA exception_init(alert_file_does_not_exist, -29283);
   v_prev_date date := trunc(sysdate,p_format_mask);
begin
   utl_file.frename (
      src_location => 'ALERT_DIR',
      src_filename => 'alert_'||l_instance_name||'.log',
      dest_location => 'ALERT_DIR',
      dest_filename => 'alert_'||l_instance_name||
                          to_char(v_prev_date - 1,p_filename_mask)||'.log',
      overwrite    =>   true);
exception
      when alert_file_does_not_exist then
         null;
end;
```

If this procedure is called with just the instance name, per its previous version, the alert file will be renamed to ALERT_SID<YESTERDAY>.LOG as before. However, the two new parameters P_FORMAT_MASK and P_FILENAME_MASK can be used to achieve far greater flexibility as Table 7-1 shows. Using the format mask, you can schedule the job to rename your alert file to correspond with your file recycling requirements. For example, if you want to keep a week's worth of alert log information, use the IW format mask and run the process weekly.

Table 7-1. Alert File History Naming Options

P_FORMAT_MASK	P_FILENAME_MASK	DESIRED EFFECT ON AN ALERT FILE BEING WRITTEN TO ON (SAY) AUGUST 4TH
DD	DY	Alert file cycled on a daily basis today's file would be ALERT_SID_MON.LOG tomorrow's file would be ALERT_SID_TUE.LOG Files hence would be recycled after seven days
DD	MMDD	Alert file cycled on a daily basis today's file would be ALERT_SID_0804.LOG tomorrow's file would be ALERT_SID_0805.LOG Files hence would be recycled after 365 days

Table 7-1. Alert File History Naming Options (Continued)

MM	MM	Alert file cycled on a monthly basis
		today's file would be `ALERT_SID_08.LOG`
		next month's file would be `ALERT_SID_09.LOG`
		Files hence would be recycled after
		12 months
IW	YYYYMMDD	Alert file cycled on a weekly basis
		today's file would be `ALERT_SID_20030804.LOG`
		next week's file would be
		`alert_SID_20030811.LOG`
		Files hence would be never recycled

It is worth noting, before we move on, that if on your particular system you do things differently and work with a large alert log, then using the bulk collect facilities described in Chapter 4 will give a performance boost.

Scheduling and Concurrency

The MONITOR_ALERT_FILE procedure (the "monitor job") runs in the PL/SQL job queue at 10- or 15-minute intervals. The RENAME_ALERT_FILE procedure (the "rollover job") runs once a day. We have to be careful that these two schedules don't conflict. Consider this scenario: At 5:55AM, the server background process writes an error message to the alert file. At 6:00AM, the rollover job runs and moves the alert file to ALERT<YESTERDAY>.LOG. At 6:01AM the monitor job runs but it doesn't see the error message. It probably doesn't find an alert file. If there is a new alert file, it doesn't contain the message that was written at 5:55.

We could use a table to record when each of the routines was running, or was last run, to control their execution, or we could use DBMS_LOCK to ensure serialized access to the alert file. However, a simpler way to minimize the problem is to integrate the rollover program into the alert file monitor procedure instead of scheduling the rollover program separately. As soon as we've checked for any new errors in the alert file, we perform the following test:

```
-- If it is between 6 and 6:20 in the morning then rename the alert file
if to_char(sysdate,'hh24')= '06' and
 to_char(sydate,'mi') < '20' then
        rename_alert_file;
   end if;
```

To be certain that we don't roll over the alert file twice in the same day, we also check for a minimum file size before we call the rename procedure. Of course, if you choose to schedule the alert file monitoring routine using DBMS_JOB, you could just as easily ensure only a single execution per day by querying USER_JOBS to determine the last time the process ran.

Here are the contents of the MONITOR_ALERT_FILE procedure. This should tie together everything we've discussed so far. (Note that the code uses a notification procedure that we haven't covered yet but will shortly.)

```
procedure monitor_alert_file
as
error_msg_arry monitor.msgs;
lcount integer;
l_instance_name varchar2(16);
exists_p boolean;
flength number;
bsize number;
alert_file_does_not_exist exception;
PRAGMA EXCEPTION_INIT(alert_file_does_not_exist, -29913);

begin
-- Check location of alert file
    select instance_name
    into   l_instance_name
    from   v$parameter,v$instance,dba_directories
    where  directory_name = 'ALERT_DIR' and
           name='background_dump_dest' and
           value = directory_path;

--  Monitor the alert file and save errors
    read_alert_file(error_msg_arry,lcount);

--  update the external tables's access parameters
    update_skip_count(lcount);

--  send any any error messages
    if error_msg_arry.last > 0 then
          monitor.notify(l_instance_name, error_msg_arry,
              'Alert file error messages');
    end if;

--  Is it time to rename the alert file?
    if to_char(sysdate,'hh24')= '06' and
          to_char(sysdate,'mi') < '19' then
--        Check the size of the alert file
          utl_file.fgetattr (
```

```
                 location => 'ALERT_DIR',
                 filename => 'alert_'||l_instance_name||'.log',
                 fexists  => exists_p,
                 file_length => flength,
                 block_size  => bsize);

    --       Rename the alert file
             if flength > 3000 then
                 update_skip_count(reset=>true);
                 review_alert_file(l_instance_name);
                 rename_alert_file(l_instance_name);
             end if;
      end if;
exception
   when alert_file_does_not_exist then
        null;
   when no_data_found then
raise_application_error(-20000,'ALERT_DIR is not current');
end;
```

Caveats for Using the Alert file

We are now very close to having a complete Oracle alert log monitoring system—
certainly it's one that would cater to the vast majority of alert file issues you are
likely to encounter. Unfortunately, there are a few cases when the structure in
which the error message is written causes us difficulties, or when errors are not
written to the alert file at all.

ORA-01555 Errors

With the advent of 9*i*, Oracle now writes ORA-01555 ("snapshot too old") error
messages to the alert file, as the following extract illustrates:

```
Mon Sep 29 13:18:32 2003
ORA-01555 caused by SQL statement below (Query Duration=0 sec, SCN:
0x0000.0083568e):
Mon Sep 29 13:18:32 2003
select empno,ename,sal
from    emp
as of  timestamp (SYSTIMESTAMP - INTERVAL '1' HOUR)
```

According to our definition of a message, this extract contains two messages: the first message describes an error condition, ORA-01555, and the second lists a SQL statement. But on examination we see that the second message is dependent on the first and ideally should be part of it. The problem is that our error-monitoring program will capture the first message but will ignore the second one. The result is that the program alerts the DBA to the ORA-01555 error but doesn't include the SQL statement information in the notification.

It takes just a little PL/SQL to modify the MONITOR_ALERT_FILE procedure to allow for these types of piggyback messages. When we encounter an ORA-01555 error, we simply set a flag to indicate that the next occurrence of a date string should be ignored. The fact that Oracle is a little "loose" in terms of the structure of the alert log means that, unfortunately, our code becomes a little less elegant. However, it does the trick and the recast solution looks as follows (with the changes in bold):

```
procedure read_alert_file (error_msg_arry out monitor.msgs,
                              linecount out integer)
as
-- reads the alert file
-- Save any error messages in an associative array
cursor c1 is
      select msg_line
      from   alert_file_ext;

  l_buffer      varchar2(1000);
  l_msg_text    varchar2(32767);
  error_count binary_integer :=0;
  date_to_be_skipped boolean := false;
begin
-- open the cursor
   open c1;

-- read ahead
   fetch c1 into l_buffer;

   while c1%FOUND loop
--    save the date line
      l_msg_text := l_buffer;

--    read the first msg body line
      fetch c1 into l_buffer;
      loop
         exit when ( ( l_buffer like '___ __ __ __:__:__ ___'
```

```
                    and not date_to_be_skipped )
              or c1%NOTFOUND );

       l_msg_text := l_msg_text||chr(10)||l_buffer;
       fetch c1 into l_buffer;

       date_to_be_skipped := ( instr(l_msg_text,'ORA-01555') > 0 )
               and not ( date_to_be_skipped and
               l_buffer like '__ __ _ __:__:__ ___' ) ;
     end loop;

-- check for error
    if (instr(l_msg_text,'ORA-') > 0) then
       error_count := error_count + 1;
       error_msg_arry(error_count) := l_msg_text;
    end if;

   end loop;
   linecount := c1%ROWCOUNT;
   close c1;
end;
```

Unreported Errors

There are a few cases in which an error or problem is simply not reported to the alert file. Here is one example from a queue monitor process trace file (QMN0).

```
*** 2003-09-21 00:10:04.000
*** SESSION ID:(22.13) 2003-09-21 00:10:04.000
kwqicaclcur: Error 376
                Cursor Session Number : 21
                Cursor Session Serial : 63
                Cursor Pin     Number : 10
Error 376 in Queue Table QS.QS_ORDERS_SQTAB
kwqitmmsgs: error 604
error 604 detected in background process
OPIRIP: Uncaught error 447. Error stack:
ORA-00447: fatal error in background process
```

```
ORA-00604: error occurred at recursive SQL level 1
ORA-00376: file 5 cannot be read at this time
ORA-01110: data file 5: 'C:\ORACLE\ORADATA\DEV92\EXAMPLE01.DBF'
Dump file c:\oracle\admin\dev92\bdump\dev92_qmn0_1116.trc
```

The problem here—a contrived example—is that an optional background process for Oracle Advanced Queuing failed. The error (ORA-00376) indicates that most likely a tablespace is offline. But this error stack doesn't occur in the alert file; it shows up only in the trace file associated with the advanced queue time manager.

> **NOTE**   Trace files (like the alert file) are written to the background dump destination. They can be named in various ways depending on which Oracle process writes the trace. Often, the Oracle background or server process that writes a trace file also writes an error message to the alert file, but as this example shows, there are some exceptions.

There are other situations that are not considered errors, although we know that they are problems that could be corrected. For example, consider this alert file message.

```
Fri Sep 26 14:39:22 2003
Thread 1 cannot allocate new log, sequence 17746
Checkpoint not complete
  Current log# 2 seq# 17745 mem# 0: C:\ORACLE\ORADATA\REP9\REDO02.LOG
```

The CHECKPOINT NOT COMPLETE message isn't considered an error. There is no ORA- line associated with it. Our error monitor program as it currently stands won't notice it, although it is simple to alter the check within the code from

```
if (instr(l_msg_text, 'ORA-') > 0)  then
    error_count := error_count + 1;
    error_msg_arry(error_count) := l_msg_text;
end if;
```

To this

```
if (instr(l_msg_text, 'ORA-') > 0)  or

   (instr(l_msg_text, 'Checkpoint not complete') > 0)  then
    error_count := error_count + 1;
```

```
        error_msg_arry(error_count) := l_msg_text;
    end if;
```

Finally, there are errors that Oracle doesn't consider serious enough to be included either in the alert file or in a trace file. (The ORA-1555: SNAPSHOT TOO OLD error was one of these in previous versions of Oracle. It is now logged, as we discussed earlier.) An unusable index, for example, raises only a session error.

```
SQL> select *
  2  from emp_history
  3  where empno = 7934;
select *
*
ERROR at line 1:
ORA-01502: index 'SCOTT.EMPHIX' or partition of such index is in unusable state
```

We don't want to drift too far away from our topic of alert file monitoring, but even these types of errors could be trapped using a system event server error trigger.

Reviewing the Alert File's Contents

In addition to being informed about errors explicitly occurring in the alert log, many database administrators inspect the entire contents of the alert files every morning. Maybe there will be something in the alert file that will stand out, something of interest that requires attention or a trend that may warn of a pending problem. Our automated monitoring solution already assists in this process because we rename the alert file on a daily basis, but we can also do more.

We can automate the reviewing process somewhat by sending a copy of the daily alert file via email, or by generating a daily report and placing the output in an accessible location. The code to review the alert file by email is very simple (and also relies on the notification package of the next section).

```
-- Send the contents of the alert file as an email
procedure review_alert_file ( p_instance_name_in in varchar2)
is
alert_msg_arry notification.msgs;
begin
    select msg_line
    bulk collect
    into alert_msg_arry
    from alert_file_ext;
    notification.notify(instance_name_in => p_instance_name_in,
```

```
                              msgs_in => alert_msg_arry,
                              subject_in => 'Review Alert File',
                              email_p => true,
                              db_p => false);
end;
```

Alert File Wrap-Up

The Oracle alert file is the focus of much of our attention. We monitor the file for Oracle server errors and to get an overview of the database's condition. From time to time, we'll delete or rename the file to save disk space.

In this section, we've seen how a PL/SQL package can automate these tasks. The alert file package allows you to monitor the alert file for errors. The package sends email messages when it discovers new error messages and emails the entire contents of the alert file (or the first part of it, if it is too large) to you every morning so that you can easily review the file's contents.

Database administrators increasingly need to standardize database procedures and to simplify database administration. Managing the alert file is an important step in that direction.

Notification Package

The notification package we use contains two procedures: one that sends email and another that saves information into a database table. Without the notification package, we wouldn't have a monitoring system. We wouldn't be able to inform the DBA about a new error in the alert file or any other conditions that we'll test for. Our email client is, in a sense, our centralized console—it's here that we'll receive messages from any of our monitoring scripts.

The mail routine is placed in its own distinct package, rather than including it with the alert file package we've already discussed. This is a more normalized approach. The logic that deals with the alert file and the logic that deals with emailing messages aren't dependent on each other.

There is information about the system that we want to gather and keep for a long time. The notification package has a procedure, SAVE_IN_DB, which makes this possible. This is what the notification package header looks like.

```
SQL> create or replace
  2  package notification is
  3
  4      type msgs is table of varchar2(4000) index by binary_integer;
  5      type recipients is table of varchar2(255);
  6
  7      procedure notify (instance_name_in in varchar2, msgs_in in msgs,
  8                              subject_in in varchar2 default null,
  9                              result_in in number default null,
 10                              email_p in boolean, db_p in boolean,
 11                              recip recipients default null);
 12
 13  end;
 14  /

Package created.
```

The list of email recipients is passed with a collection type, RECIPIENTS, and the content of the email is built from an array of strings passed as a collection type, MSGS. The two Boolean input parameters in the public procedure, NOTIFY, are used to determine if an email is sent and/or if the message is saved in the database.

```
procedure notify (instance_name_in in varchar2, msgs_in in msgs,
                        subject_in in varchar2 default null,
                        result_in in number default null,
                        email_p in boolean, db_p in boolean,
                        recip recipients default null); is
begin
if email_p = true then
    send_email (instance_name_in, msgs_in,
                subject_in, recip);
end if;

if db_p = true then
    save_in_db ( instance_name_in, msgs_in,
                subject_in, result_in);
end if;
end;
```

The SEND_EMAIL Procedure

The UTL_SMTP supplied package is designed for sending email over Simple Mail Transfer Protocol. We supply the body of the email in an array. We also pass the instance name and the email subject as inputs to the email procedure. Using HTML to format the messages allows the contents of the email to be displayed more neatly.

There is a maximum length to the text written by UTL_SMTP.WRITE_DATA of about 1,000 characters, so our message sizes need to conform to this (or we need to break them down into smaller pieces).

We simply specify a list of recipients (the first recipient is the sender). Here is the SEND_EMAIL procedure.

```
-- Send SMTP mail
procedure send_email (instance_name_in varchar2,
                      msgs_in msgs,
                      subject_in varchar2,
                      recip recipients) is

   sender        constant varchar2(60)  := 'dba1@foo.com';

   smtp_server constant varchar2(255)   := 'SERVER100';
   local_domain constant varchar2(255) := 'foo.com';
   -- format the email date
   lvDate varchar2(30) := to_char(sysdate,'mm/dd/yyyy hh24:mi');
   lvBody varchar2(32000);
   c utl_smtp.connection;

   recipient_list varchar2(1000) := sender;

   -- local procedure to reduce redundancy
   procedure write_header (name in varchar2, header in varchar2)  is
   begin
        utl_smtp.write_data(c, name || ': ' || header || utl_tcp.CRLF);
   end;
begin

   for i in 1 .. recip.count loop
     recipient_list := ','||recip(i);
   end loop;

    -- Open SMTP connection
    c := utl_smtp.open_connection(smtp_server);
    -- Perform initial handshaking with the SMTP server after connecting
    utl_smtp.helo(c, local_domain );
```

```
   -- Initiate a mail transaction
   utl_smtp.mail(c, sender);
--Specify the recipients
   utl_smtp.rcpt(c, sender);
   for i in 1 .. recip.count loop
       utl_smtp.rcpt(c, recip(i));
   end loop;
   -- Send the data command to the smtp server
   utl_smtp.open_data(c);
   -- Write the header part of the email body
   write_header('Date',lvDate);
   write_header('From',sender);
   write_header('Subject',instance_name_in||' '||subject_in);
   write_header('To',recipient_list);
   write_header('Content-Type', 'text/html;');

   -- format the message body in html
   lvbody := '<html><head><style type="text/css">
               BODY, P, li, {font-family: courier-new,courier; font-size : 8pt;}
                </style></head><body>';

   -- the body of the email consists of the input message array
     for i in 1.. msgs_in.last loop
    lvbody := lvbody||'<br>'||
             replace(msgs_in(i),chr(10),'<br>');
       end loop;
   lvbody := lvbody||'</body></html>';

-- write out the email body
-- write less than 1000 characters at a time
   for x in 1 .. (length(lvbody)/800 + 1) loop
       utl_smtp.write_data(c, utl_tcp.CRLF ||
             substr(lvBody,(x-1)*800 +1,800));
    end loop;

   -- end the email message
   utl_smtp.close_data(c);
   -- disconnect from the SMTP server
   utl_smtp.quit(c);

exception
  when others then
      utl_smtp.quit(c);
      raise;
end;
```

Saving Alert Messages in the Database

The notification package also includes a procedure to save messages in the database. As we discussed, our alert file package allows alert files to be kept for about a week before the files are overwritten. However, for reporting purposes, there may be certain data that we would like to keep longer. (Perhaps we'll be asked to provide a report on the number of server errors there have been per month because the senior DBA was laid off.) This will only be possible if we save the error messages. We'll create a table with this code.

```
CREATE TABLE ALERTS
(    EVENT_DATE DATE,
     EVENT_TYPE VARCHAR2(16) NOT NULL ENABLE,
     RESULT NUMBER,
     RESULT_TEXT VARCHAR2(4000),
     INSTANCE_NAME VARCHAR2(16),
      CONSTRAINT EVENT_TYPE_IN CHECK (event_type in ('ALERT FILE',
         'BACKUPS','STORAGE','ARCHIVE','GROWTH','SESSIONS',
         'RESOURCE LIMIT')) ENABLE
);
```

The SAVE_IN_DB procedure assumes that each message begins with a string that evaluates to a date and that the date is in a specific format. This is a convention that we copied from the messages in the alert file, and it is a useful standard to which to adhere. We're also allowing each message to be categorized by a subject field in the table called EVENT_TYPE. Here is the procedure text. Because we may be creating multiple entries in the table, we've used the bulk-bind facilities as described in Chapter 4 to ensure performance is optimal.

```
-- Save notification messages in database
procedure save_in_db(instance_in varchar2, msgs_in msgs,
                       subject_in varchar2, result_in number) is
begin
   forall i in 1.. msgs_in.last
      insert into alerts (event_date, instance_name,
            event_type, result, result_text)
      values (to_date(substr(msgs_in(i),1,24),
               'Dy Mon dd hh24:mi:ssyyyy'),
         instance_in,subject_in,
         result_in,msgs_in(i));

end;
```

Here is a sample that we've saved. This message isn't an ORA- type error message from the alert file. It's a message generated by a proactive space monitoring procedure (called CHECK_FREE_SPACE) that we'll show in the next section.

```
SQL> select instance_name,event_date,result_text
  2  from    alerts
  3  where event_type = 'STORAGE';

INSTANCE EVENT_DATE RESULT_TEXT
-------- ---------- ------------------------------------
TOTO     04-JUL-03  Fri Jul 04 13:40:35 2003
                    Tablespace TOOLS is 80.4% full.
```

Notification Wrap-Up

We described a notification package that has two procedures in it: one that sends an email and one that saves information in the database. These two procedures correspond to two types of notifications: one that requires a quicker response and another that doesn't require any response. The saved data can be used as a basis for management type reports.

In the email procedure, we had to hard-code a number of values—the mail server name and so on. If you intend to deploy this solution across your enterprise, you may want to either store these values in a database table or allow them to be passed as parameters.

Proactive Monitoring Package

In this section, we'll discuss a package used to identify potential problems. Unlike the alert file package that monitored errors after they had already occurred, the proactive package looks for potential problems before they occur. This is possible because of the trend in recent Oracle versions to include much additional system-wide information in the data dictionary, for example: information regarding the status of database backups and information regarding the status of the archive destination directory.

Based on this type of information, Oracle 10*g* introduces a lot of automatic health monitoring functionality, such as the Automatic Database Diagnostic Monitor (ADDM). We suggest that you check this out when you move over to this version. In the meantime, there are many things we can check in a proactive monitoring package, and it should give you useful insight into how these automatic features work. We'll focus on three checks.

- The backup ran successfully

- The archive destination directory isn't nearly full

- The database has adequate free space

The following is the specification for the PROACTIVE package:

```
package proactive
is
/**
* ========================================================================
* Project:        Database monitoring
* Description:    This is the package for procedures the proactivly
*                  monitor the database. If there is a problem then we can
*                  email a notification and or save message in database
* DB impact:      minimal
* Commit inside:  no
* Rollback inside: no
* ------------------------------------------------------------------------
*/
procedure checkStatusOfLastBackup (p_instance_name_in in varchar2);
procedure checkArchiveDestination (p_instance_name_in in varchar2);
procedure checkFreeSpace (p_instance_name_in in varchar2);
end;
```

Backups

A DBA needs to monitor that database backups are running correctly. More specifically, the DBA should check that the last backup ran successfully. If the last backup failed (and even more important, if previous backups have been failing), the DBA is heading for a problem. Hot backups and RMAN (recovery manager) backups both use the data dictionary to store backup information and status.

RMAN information is generally stored in a set of V$ views. These views display information from the control file. The view we'll look at, V$BACKUP_SET, contains a record for every complete RMAN backup. If you're using the RMAN with a recovery catalog, the information will be stored in the RC views.

Say we're performing a full database RMAN online backup every night (without a recovery catalog).

```
RMAN> backup database;
```

There are only two columns in the V$BACKUP_SET row that are relevant to us: the COMPLETION_TIME identifies the time that the backup finished, and the BACKUP_TYPE identifies whether this backup was a full or incremental backup. Full backups have a BACKUP_TYPE of D (probably for "Database backup"). As an alternate to the BACKUP_TYPE field, we could use the INCREMENTAL_LEVEL field. Full backups have an increment level of 0.

As we mentioned earlier, we're performing a full database backup each night, so we check the last time that the full backup was run, or more accurately, we check the age of the most recent full backup. If the most recent backup is more than a day old, we can infer that the most recent backup didn't complete successfully.

```
Procedure checkStatusOfLastBackup (p_instance_name_in in varchar2)
is
-- Check that there was an RMAN full database online backup
-- sometime within the last day (threshold = 1)
notes notification.msgs;
THRESHOLD number(4,2) := 1;
Begin
    -- build a message containing the date of the last full RMAN backup
    select    to_char(sysdate,'Dy Mon dd hh24:mi:ss yyyy')||chr(10)||
              'Most recent full backup was '||
              extract(day from (systimestamp - completion_time))|| ' Days and '||
              extract(hour from (systimestamp - completion_time))|| ' hours ago.'
bulk collect into notes
from        v$backup_set a
where       completion_time=
               (select max(completion_time)
                 from v$backup_set
                 where nvl(incremental_level,10) =
                        nvl(a.incremental_level,10) and
                        backup_type = a.backup_type) and
             backup_type='D' and
             incremental_level is null and
             sysdate - completion_time > THRESHOLD;

-- If there is a message to send, then send it.
if notes.last > 0 then
    notification.notify(instance_name_in => p_instance_name_in,
                        msgs_in => notes,
                        subject_in => 'BACKUPS',
                        email_p => false,
                        db_p => true);
end if;
end;
```

If the query in this procedure returns no rows, it means there was a full backup within the last 24 hours (or there were never any backups!). If the query returns a row, it means that last night's backup didn't run or didn't run successfully and we'll see a message such as the following:

```
SQL> select event_date,result_text
  2  from   alerts
  3  where  event_type = 'BACKUPS';


EVENT_DATE RESULT_TEXT
---------- -------------------------------------------------------
  03-OCT-03  Fri Oct 03 10:10:10 2003
             Most recent full backup was 2 days and 10 hours ago.
```

Free Space in the Archive Log Destination

One of the more important proactive monitoring tasks you can do is to keep an eye on the amount of free space in the archive destination directory (assuming that the database is running in ARCHIVELOG mode). If the archive directory fills up, the database will hang. More accurately, if the server can't overwrite a redo log file because the redo log hasn't been archived yet, and it can't archive the redo log because the archive destination is full, new connections will be refused and no more work will take place. The alert file monitor may not be of any help either at that time because by then, the PL/SQL job queue probably won't be able to start any jobs.

There is no PL/SQL supplied package that allows you to retrieve a disk's available free space, but for Oracle9i Enterprise Edition users, there's an attribute of the LOG_ARCHIVE_DEST_N initialization parameter called QUOTA_SIZE, which will definitely help. By specifying a quota size for LOG_ARCHIVE_DEST_N, you're indicating the maximum amount of physical storage that may be used by the archive processes. From then on, the Oracle server will dynamically keep track of the space in the archive destination. The information is available by querying the V$ARCHIVE_DEST view.

```
SQL> select destination,quota_size,quota_used
  2  from   v$archive_dest
  3* where  destination is not null;


DESTINATION                     QUOTA_SIZE QUOTA_USED
------------------------------- ---------- ----------
c:\oracle\OraArchives                18192       5509
```

The following procedure checks the available free space in the archive destination directory by comparing the quota used to the quota size. If the percentage of quota used is greater than a specified threshold, the procedure will fire off an email and save a notification message in an Oracle table.

```
-- Check free space in archive destination
procedure checkArchiveDestination (p_instance_name_in in varchar2)
is
-- check the space used in the archive1 destination
-- (threshold 80%)
THRESHOLD number(4,2):= 80.0;
notes notification.msgs;
begin
-- build a message identifying the destination(s) that is atleast 80% full
select    to_char(sysdate,'Dy Mon dd hh24:mi:ss yyyy')||chr(10)||
          'Archive: '||dest_name||' '||destination||
          ' is '||
          to_char(round(1 - (quota_size-quota_used)/(quota_size),4)*100 )||
          '% full.'
bulk collect into notes
from      v$archive_dest
where     round(1 - (quota_size-quota_used)/(quota_size),4)*100 > THRESHOLD
          and schedule = 'ACTIVE';

-- if the previous query found any rows, the messages will be contained
-- in the notes array. If the array is not empty send an email
if notes.last > 0 then
    notification.notify(instance_name_in => p_instance_name_in,
                        msgs_in => notes,
                        subject_in => 'ARCHIVE',
                        email_p => true,
                        db_p => true);
end if;
end;
```

If the procedure discovers a problem, it will generate a message similar to the following:

```
SQL> select event_date,result_text
  2  from alerts
  3  where event_type = 'ARCHIVE';
```

```
EVENT_DATE RESULT_TEXT
---------- ---------------------------------------------------------------
03-OCT-03  Fri Oct 03 10:31:48 2003
           Archive: LOG_ARCHIVE_DEST_1 c:\oracle\OraArchives is
           81.4% full.
```

Monitoring Free Space in the Database

One of the most common DBA practices is to monitor the availability of free space in the database. Some would argue that the free space test is obsolete because you can always create (or alter) a data file so that it automatically increases in size whenever necessary (AUTOEXTEND ON). Thus, in theory, tablespaces should never run out of space but of course, every DBA should be aware of any growth that objects within their databases are undergoing.

On the other hand, raw devices can't autoextend, and in any event, practically speaking the amount of available free space doesn't depend on the data file's attributes but on the hardware reality. Why specify a maximum size of 50GB when creating a 2GB data file if the disk has no free space left or if the database already contains 24 2GB-sized data files? If you are using automatic data file extension, it makes more sense to set the maximum size of the file to something reasonable—something you know can be accommodated, and to reserve some space free for emergencies. In other words, enabling auto-extend reduces the amount of maintenance you may have to do, but it doesn't solve real space shortage issues. And if there is a space shortage, you better monitor it closely.

The following procedure monitors the free space in all tablespaces. In its calculations, it includes the current size of the file as well as the size the file can grow to based on its auto extensible parameters. By comparing the file's size with the amount of free space in the tablespace, it can determine if the percent of space used is greater than a preset threshold.

```
procedure checkFreeSpace (p_instance_name_in in varchar2)
is
-- Check spaced used by tablespaces
THRESHOLD number(4,2):= 80.0;
notes notification.msgs;
begin
-- build a message after checking the free space and the used
-- space if the used space is greater than the threshold
    select  to_char(sysdate,'Dy Mon dd hh24:mi:ss yyyy')||chr(10)||
        'Tablespace '||a.tablespace_name||
        ' is '||
        to_char(round(1 - (free+potential)/(allocated+potential),4)*100)||
        '% full.'
bulk collect into notes
```

```
from
   (select     tablespace_name,sum(bytes) free
    from       dba_free_space
    group by tablespace_name) f,
   (select     tablespace_name,sum(bytes) allocated,
               sum(maxbytes) potential
    from       dba_data_files
    group by tablespace_name) a
where a.tablespace_name = f.tablespace_name (+) and
      round(1 - (free+potential)/(allocated+potential),4)*100
      > THRESHOLD;

-- If there are any rows retrieved by the above query then
-- send a notification
if notes.last > 0 then
   notification.notify(instance_name_in => p_instance_name_in,
                       msgs_in => notes,
                       subject_in => 'STORAGE',
                       email_p => false,
                       db_p => true);
end if;
end;
```

If this procedure discovers any tablespaces that are more full than the percentage threshold allows, it will raise a message similar to the following:

```
SQL> select event_date,result_text
  2  from    alerts
  3  where event_type = 'STORAGE';

EVENT_DATE RESULT_TEXT
--------- ----------------------------------------
03-OCT-03  Fri Oct 03 11:46:42 2003
           Tablespace TOOLS is 84.75% full.
```

Proactive Monitoring Wrap-Up

We described a proactive monitoring package with three packaged procedures: a procedure to monitor the status of the backups, a procedure to monitor the free space outside the database in the archive destination directory, and a procedure to check the free space inside the database. In each procedure, we specify a threshold value. When the value is exceeded, the procedure records the information in the `ALERTS` table via the `NOTIFICATION` package.

Historical Data Package

In addition to looking for problems, the DBA is also supposed to be the repository for all types of knowledge pertaining to the database. Is the database growing or shrinking? If it's growing, how fast? How long until we run out of disk space? On average, how many sessions does the database support? Is the database being used more since we brought that new application on line?

Questions like these can sometimes be answered by querying the data dictionary, but the data dictionary doesn't store a lot of history. To accomplish this goal properly, you will usually collect your own historical data. The historical data package stores information by instance and by date (although it doesn't perform any analysis on that information). We'll discuss three procedures.

- Compute the database size

- Count the number of sessions

- Store a set of database resource limit metrics

The following is the specification for the `HISTORY` package.

```
package history
is
/**
*  ========================================================================<
*  Project:        Database monitoring
*  Description:    Contains procedures that collect history of the database
*  DB impact:      minimal
*  Commit inside:  no
*  Rollback inside: no
*  ----------------------------------------------------------------------
*/
procedure databaseSize (p_instance_name_in in varchar2);
procedure databaseSessions (p_instance_name_in in varchar2);
procedure resourceLimit (p_instance_name_in in varchar2);
end;
```

The history package is different from the previous two packages in that it doesn't send email notifications. The reason for this is that the history package doesn't identify problems, it collects data that can later be used to identify trends and to analyze history. The historical data may be used to discover potential problems, but the problems aren't known when the history is collected.

Another unique aspect about the history package is that it passes a numeric value to the notification procedure in addition to passing a message text. The numeric value (the result parameter) is stored in the ALERTS table and provides the data for the historical reports and queries.

Database Size

Some databases are in a steady state vis-à-vis the amount of space they occupy—their size fluctuates between known values based on data input and data purges either on a monthly or yearly cycle. But other databases are forever expanding. In either case, but especially if the database is growing, it's a good idea to save readings of the database size. This is true even if there is plenty of free space in the database and no danger of running out of space any time soon.

The main reason for collecting database size readings is that this historical data allows you to interpret space related events. Suppose someone notices that a few hundred megabytes have been added to a tablespace (maybe one of the underlying tablespace files has autoextended). The only way you'll know if that change is a cause for concern is by comparing the current growth spurt with the general growth rate of the tablespace or database. If the database has never grown this way before, you'll probably want to investigate further.

The other reason for collecting and saving information about the size of the database over time is to be in a position to predict if and when the database will run short on space. If the database is growing by a certain amount each month, you can extrapolate the growth statistics to determine when there will be a shortage of space.

The following DATABASESIZE procedure computes the total size of the database by querying the number of bytes in DBA segments. It can be run once a month or once a week.

```
-- Get the size of the database by summing the size of all the db objects
procedure databaseSize (p_instance_name_in in varchar2)
is
notes notification.msgs;
begin
-- Get the size of the database (Mb) text message
select to_char(sysdate,'Dy Mon dd hh24:mi:ss yyyy')||chr(10)||
       'DB Size(Mb) '||
       to_char(round(sum(bytes)/(1024*1024),2))
bulk   collect into notes
from   dba_segments;
```

```
-- Extract the size from the above message and save it as the result_in
notification.notify(instance_name_in => p_instance_name_in,
                           msgs_in => notes,
                           subject_in => 'GROWTH',
                           result_in => substr(notes(1),37),
                           email_p => false,
                           db_p => true);
end;
```

This SQL query selects the database size from the historical data. The result column has been renamed to SIZE(MB).

```
SQL> col result heading  "Size(Mb)"
SQL> select event_date,result,result_text
  2  from    alerts
  3   where  event_type='GROWTH' and
  4   event_date > '01-OCT-03';

EVENT_DATE    Size(Mb) RESULT_TEXT
---------- ---------- -------------------------
03-OCT-03      281.38 Fri Oct 03 13:37:00 2003
                      DB Size(Mb) 281.38
```

The number we're measuring here (database size) is useful as a simple measurement. It doesn't describe exactly how much user data the database contains. As long as the database objects aren't grossly over-sized, though, the number we're calculating can be used to answer some interesting questions like the ones we posed at the beginning of this section. Suppose we have collected the following measurements:

```
SQL> select trunc(event_date,'mm') EVENT_DATE,
  2   round(max(result),0)  result
  3   from   alerts
  4   where event_type = 'GROWTH'
  5   group by trunc(event_date,'mm')
  6   order by 1;

EVENT_DATE  Size (Mb)
---------- ----------
01-JAN-03      31,714
01-FEB-03      32,545
01-MAR-03      33,257
01-APR-03      34,040
```

01-MAY-03	36,204
01-JUN-03	36,808
01-JUL-03	37,494
01-AUG-03	39,019
01-SEP-03	39,406
01-OCT-03	40,046

We can calculate the monthly growth of this database (using analytical functions) as follows:

```
SQL> select trunc(event_date,'mm') event_date,
  2          max(result) result,
  3          max(result) - lag(max(result),1) over
  4          (order by trunc(event_date,'mm')) as growth
  5  from alerts
  6  group by trunc(event_date,'mm');
```

EVENT_DATE	Result(Mb)	Growth(Mb)
01-JAN-03	31,714	
01-FEB-03	32,545	831
01-MAR-03	33,257	712
01-APR-03	34,040	783
01-MAY-03	36,204	2164
01-JUN-03	36,808	604
01-JUL-03	37,494	686
01-AUG-03	39,019	1525
01-SEP-03	39,406	387
01-OCT-03	40,046	640

This database is growing about 1000MB per month (on average). Once we have enough data, we can calculate the growth per year as well.

Database Sessions

Another measurement that's worth keeping track of is the number of sessions logged in to the database at a particular time every day. This can help you determine how much the database instance is being used, and it may have implications regarding your Oracle or application licenses, depending on how the database users log in.

Assuming that each user creates a separate database session, it's a simple task to count the number of sessions by querying the V$SESSION view.

```
-- Get the number of user sessions logged in right now
procedure databaseSessions (p_instance_name_in in varchar2)
is
notes notification.msgs;
begin
-- Get the number of sessions
select to_char(sysdate,'Dy Mon dd hh24:mi:ss yyyy')||chr(10)||
        'Sessions '||count(*)
bulk   collect into notes
from   v$session
where  type = 'USER';

-- extract the number of sessions from the above text and save as result_in
notification.notify(instance_name_in => p_instance_name_in,
                          msgs_in => notes,
                          subject_in => 'SESSIONS',
                          result_in => substr(notes(1),34),
                          email_p => false,
                          db_p => true);

end;
```

The resulting entry in the history table looks like the following:

```
SQL> col result heading "Sessions"
SQL> select event_date,result,result_text
  2  from    alerts
    3  where   event_type = 'SESSIONS' and
    4  event_date > '01-OCT-03';

EVENT_DATE  SESSIONS  RESULT_TEXT
----------  --------  -----------------------------
03-OCT-03        134  Fri Oct 03 15:12:51 2003
                      Sessions 134
```

Here's a query that calculates the average number of "sessions" per month. The measurements that make up the average were taken at the same time each day. To be valid, the data should exclude weekends and holidays.

```
SQL> select trunc(event_date,'MON') event_date,
  2              round(avg(result),0) avgSessions
  3  from    alerts
  4  where   event_type = 'SESSIONS'
  5  group by trunc(event_date,'MON');
```

```
EVENT_DATE      AVGSESSIONS
----------      -----------
01-DEC-02       192
01-JAN-03       208
01-FEB-03       227
01-MAR-03       217
01-APR-03       207
01-MAY-03       203
01-JUN-03       207
```

Resource Limits

Recording the number of connected sessions that exist at any given instant, as described earlier, is a useful trending tool for monitoring user activity within your database. However, it is also very important to know how "close to the wire" the database is with respect to the various resources within it. We can observe this data via the V$RESOURCE_LIMIT view as the following query demonstrates:

```
SQL> select resource_name, max_utilization, limit_value
  2  from v$resource_limit;
```

RESOURCE_NAME	MAX_UTILIZATION	LIMIT_VALUE
processes	11	150
sessions	10	170
enqueue_locks	18	2230
enqueue_resources	11	UNLIMITED
ges_procs	0	0
ges_ress	0	UNLIMITED
ges_locks	0	UNLIMITED
ges_cache_ress	0	UNLIMITED
ges_reg_msgs	0	UNLIMITED
ges_big_msgs	0	UNLIMITED
ges_rsv_msgs	0	0
gcs_resources	0	2500
gcs_shadows	0	2500
dml_locks	29	UNLIMITED
temporary_table_locks	1	UNLIMITED
transactions	4	UNLIMITED
branches	0	UNLIMITED
cmtcallbk	1	UNLIMITED

sort_segment_locks	1	UNLIMITED
max_rollback_segments	11	38
max_shared_servers	0	20
parallel_max_servers	0	6

22 rows selected.

For many of the resources, the allowable limit is UNLIMITED, which in practical terms means that your hardware is the only constraint. However, for the other resources, it makes sense to record their maximum utilization over time to ensure that you are not close to encountering a resource shortfall. The procedure RESOURCELIMIT achieves this.

```
-- Measure the elapsed time for a fixed amount of work
procedure resourceLimit (p_instance_name_in in varchar2)
is
notes notification.msgs;

begin
select to_char(sysdate,'Dy Mon dd hh24:mi:ss yyyy')||chr(10)||
        rpad(resource_name,30)||' Max: '||lpad(max_utilization,10)
bulk collect into notes
from v$resource_limit
where trim(limit_value) != 'UNLIMITED';

-- save the elapsed time as result_in
notification.notify(instance_name_in => p_instance_name_in,
                        msgs_in => notes,
                        subject_in => 'RESOURCE LIMIT',
    result_in => -1,
                        email_p => false,
                        db_p => true);
end;
```

Historical Data Wrap-Up

We described a historical data package. It contains a procedure that computes the size of the database, a procedure that counts the number of database sessions, and a procedure that measures key resource limits within the database. Each procedure appends the result of its calculation to a database table. These accumulated results provide the basis for queries and reports that help identify trends in the database.

Summary

More scripts could still be written. We could perform a health check by looking for database triggers that have been disabled or database objects that are invalid. We could check for over-privileged users, that is, users who have administrator privileges or other powerful privileges they don't need. We could check for objects that shouldn't be inside the SYSTEM tablespace, and we could measure the amount of redo generated. We've shown examples that we find useful.

The procedures we've shown are tied to a notification package that uses a PL/SQL supplied package for sending emails. Scheduling the procedures is taken care of by the PL/SQL job queue, which is also implemented by an Oracle supplied package. The combination (scheduling and email) allows you to create an automated monitoring system.

One can choose how to monitor an Oracle database. One can monitor the database interactively in an ad hoc manner, though it's obvious that such an approach isn't very organized or scaleable. One can purchase a monitoring tool. One can create monitoring scripts and run them automatically using a scheduler program. In this last procedure, the monitoring script and scheduling tool can either be external to the database, or they can run internally, as PL/SQL does.

We demonstrated how to use PL/SQL packages to monitor an Oracle database. In terms of the outside world, PL/SQL can read and write operating system files and can send emails. Inside the database, PL/SQL can easily access all the information that the Oracle server stores; this includes information about backups, free space, and blocking locks.

A PL/SQL monitoring solution is fairly easy to create and manage. You don't need to purchase anything. You don't need to learn a new language, follow complicated installation and initialization procedures, set up users passwords and privileges, or create another database repository.

Due to the nature of PL/SQL and the way that it runs in the database, there are some monitoring tasks that it cannot accomplish. A PL/SQL script can't detect if the database is down or if it's not accepting connections. (It may be possible for PL/SQL in one instance to monitor another instance's database using database links, but it's really too convoluted to recommend.) In a sense, this is a problem that exists with every monitoring solution because there is always a risk that the monitoring software is unavailable to do the work we ask of it. On the other hand, with a PL/SQL solution, if we bring the database down for some reason, we don't have to worry about a monitoring application reporting useless warnings and alerts.

The PL/SQL monitoring solution can be extended as you learn more about the database and more about what you would like to monitor. A PL/SQL solution will also work on any Oracle platform (NT, Unix, or anything in between). PL/SQL code can be wrapped, so you can build a protected suite of monitoring tools that can be deployed to external customers. In summary, a PL/SQL solution based on packages easily allows you to standardize and simplify the way you monitor your database.

CHAPTER 8

Security Packages

WHY IS SECURITY IMPORTANT? The question in itself seems ridiculous, but the reality is that most people don't think about security when creating database applications. Although many people gauge the success of an application on its performance, ability to scale, or ease of use, the ultimate success or failure may in fact rely on whether the application and subsequently the database can be or is compromised. If you know what's available and how to use it properly, designing and building secure applications with PL/SQL is not only possible, but also relatively easy.

This chapter explores several areas of security in regards to PL/SQL programming in an Oracle database.

- **Design issues**: understanding how to construct programs in a way that maximizes security.

- **Database triggers**: implementing different aspects of security.

- **Protecting the source**: exploring the available options.

Design Considerations

The decisions you make about the design of your PL/SQL are critical to the overall performance and security of any PL/SQL program or application. Because PL/SQL procedures can do many things—from enforcing business rules to ensuring data integrity—there is no single solution to any one problem. Therefore, getting the design right is essential. The areas you need to consider include the rights models, the organization of your code, and the relationships between schemas, objects, users, and privileges.

Review of Definer and Invoker Rights

When designing and creating PL/SQL applications, a thorough understanding of the rights models used in the Oracle database is vital for an effective security design. The mode that is right for your needs will depend upon the specific application and its associated requirements. Later, we'll explore a few best practices, but for now, let's get an overview of what the modes are and how they work. The Oracle database provides two modes of operation for executing stored procedures, summarized in Table 8-1.

- The **definer rights** mode: This is the default mode of operation, whereby Oracle uses the security privileges and object resolution from the creator and thus "definer" of the procedure. This has been the traditional model for application development over the years.

- The **invoker rights** mode: Introduced in Oracle 8.1.5, this mode works the same as definer rights during program compilation. However, at execution time, the database uses the privileges and object resolution of the **invoker** of the procedure.

Table 8-1. Oracle Modes for Executing Stored Procedures

	DEFINER RIGHTS		**INVOKER RIGHTS**	
	Compilation	*Execution*	*Compilation*	*Execution*
Object Resolution	Definer	Definer	Definer	**Invoker**
Privileges	Definer	Definer	Definer	**Invoker**
Roles	Disabled	Disabled	Disabled	**Enabled**

Using definer rights, at both compilation and execution, the database will use the privilege set of, and the objects belonging to, the definer of the procedure. An important point to note is that database roles are disabled. When using invoker rights, at execution, the database uses the privilege set and objects belonging to the invoker of the procedure (the schema whose privileges are currently in effect during a particular session). Unlike definer rights, roles are enabled at execution time.

This point about roles is important. Failing to understand what is happening often causes frustration and unwarranted support calls. A quick example will demonstrate what we mean.

One of the most common problems experienced by PL/SQL developers is illustrated in the following example. We want to create a function that returns the module name (or program) for the current users' session. The module name is obtained from joining the V$SESSION and V$PROCESS views. To ensure access to these objects, we will build the function as the SYSTEM user (this is not a recommended approach, but it is common for people to do this). SYSTEM has been granted the DBA role that allows access to the V$ views. The first thing we'll do is to create an anonymous block to test our logic. An anonymous block, unlike a definer rights program, runs with roles enabled.

```
system@KNOX10g> set serveroutput on
system@KNOX10g> declare
  2   l_module varchar2(48);
  3   begin
  4     select b.module into l_module
  5       from v$process a, v$session b
  6       where a.addr = b.paddr
  7       and b.audsid = sys_context('userenv','sessionid');
  8     dbms_output.put_line('Current Program is ' || l_module);
  9   end;
 10   /
Current Program is SQL*Plus

PL/SQL procedure successfully completed.
```

The anonymous block works perfectly. Now, through the power of cut and paste, we'll place the same logic into a function so that we can easily call this program any time we desire this information.

```
system@KNOX10g> create or replace function get_my_program
  2   return varchar2
  3   as
  4   l_module varchar2(48);
  5   begin
  6     select b.module into l_module
  7       from v$process a, v$session b
  8       where a.addr = b.paddr
  9       and b.audsid = sys_context('userenv','sessionid');
 10     return l_module;
 11   end;
 12   /

Warning: Function created with compilation errors.

system@KNOX10g> sho errors
Errors for FUNCTION GET_MY_PROGRAM:

LINE/COL ERROR
-------- -------------------------------------------------
6/3      PL/SQL: SQL Statement ignored
7/23     PL/SQL: ORA-00942: table or view does not exist
```

This is not a bug. The function fails to compile because the DBA role is disabled. As such, the V$ views are not accessible inside the (named) PL/SQL program. We could alter the code to embed the query in dynamic SQL. That would allow the procedure to compile, but at execution time, the procedure would again fail with the same error.

Under definer rights, named PL/SQL programs compile and run with *directly granted* privileges only. Any privileges granted to roles for either the invoker of the procedure or the definer of the procedure are not available. We can verify this by echoing the enabled roles inside a named program. First we'll show all the default roles available, and then we'll run the program and compare the results.

```
system@KNOX10g> -- show roles
system@KNOX10g> select * from session_roles;

ROLE
------------------------------
DBA
SELECT_CATALOG_ROLE
HS_ADMIN_ROLE
EXECUTE_CATALOG_ROLE
DELETE_CATALOG_ROLE
EXP_FULL_DATABASE
IMP_FULL_DATABASE
GATHER_SYSTEM_STATISTICS
SCHEDULER_ADMIN
WM_ADMIN_ROLE
JAVA_ADMIN
JAVA_DEPLOY
XDBADMIN
OLAP_DBA
AQ_ADMINISTRATOR_ROLE
MGMT_USER

16 rows selected.

system@KNOX10g> -- show roles in a procedure
system@KNOX10g> create or replace procedure show_privs
  2  as
  3  begin
  4    dbms_output.put_line('ROLES:');
  5    for rec in (select * from session_roles)
  6    loop
  7      dbms_output.put_line(rec.role);
  8    end loop;
  9  end;
 10  /
```

```
Procedure created.

system@KNOX10g> set serveroutput on
system@KNOX10g> exec show_privs
ROLES:

PL/SQL procedure successfully completed.
```

The output clearly shows that inside the SHOW_PRIVS procedure, all roles are disabled. Consequently, all privileges granted to all roles for the user are disabled inside the procedure too. Don't be confused. Don't file a bug or an enhancement request. This is how it is supposed to work.

Knowing that roles are enabled for invoker rights programs, one might immediately resort to this mode as the solution for the GET_MY_PROGRAM function. Beware, invoker rights is not always the easy solution to the problem of roles being disabled in definer rights mode. If we re-create the GET_MY_PROGRAM function using invoker rights (we will come back to this in detail shortly) and dynamic SQL, the problem appears to be "solved."

```
system@KNOX10g> create or replace function get_my_program
  2      return varchar2
  3      authid current_user
  4    as
  5    l_module varchar2(48);
  6    l_query  varchar2(500);
  7    begin
  8      l_query := 'select b.module ' ||
  9        'from v$process a, v$session b ' ||
 10        'where a.addr = b.paddr '||
 11        'and b.audsid = sys_context(''userenv'',''sessionid'')';
 12      execute immediate l_query into l_module;
 13      return l_module;
 14    end;
 15    /

Function created.

system@KNOX10g> select get_my_program from dual;

GET_MY_PROGRAM
----------------

SQL*Plus
```

Unfortunately, the problem is only solved for the SYSTEM user. Anyone without the DBA role or privileges to query the V$ tables will be unable to execute this function. The real solution to this problem is to grant the privileges to query V$SESSION and V$PROCESS directly to the schema that owns the GET_MY_PROGRAM function (in reality, it is probably not the SYSTEM schema). The function would then be compiled using definer rights.

The definer rights mode provides a very effective and secure mode of operation and is, in fact, the mode that you will most commonly want to use. In this mode, your PL/SQL programs are owned by the schema against which they run, and execution privileges are granted as appropriate. This provides a natural and effective encapsulation of the access and change methods to the underlying tables in a schema.

Of course, that is not to say that invoker rights have no use (as we will see shortly). As we have said many times, if this were the case, Oracle would not have invented them. It's just that they should not be seen as a way around the roles problem.

Using Definer Rights

If you have written PL/SQL programs in the past, you're probably very familiar with the definer rights mode. Hopefully, you haven't been stymied by a situation similar to the one just described. Let's summarize our previous knowledge and expand upon it a little more.

- Definer rights is the default mode used when creating named procedures in the database. If you don't specify a mode when you create a program, the database will default to the definer rights mode.

- Roles are disabled.

- The procedure owner's rights are used when compiling and executing the procedures.

- The procedure owner's object resolution is used.

The third point says that Oracle uses the security privileges from the owner (the creator and thus definer) of the procedure, both while the PL/SQL is being compiled and when it is being executed. For example, say we have a user, SCOTT, who creates a procedure, UPDATE_SAL, which updates the EMP table. This procedure will always execute with the base privileges of SCOTT, even if another user is executing it. In order to create and successfully compile the procedure, SCOTT will need update privileges on EMP that have been granted *directly* to him (more about this in a moment). Any invoker of the procedure does not need update privileges on the table, just privileges to execute the procedure. Note the privilege to execute the procedure can be obtained indirectly through a database role.

The last point says unqualified objects are resolved to the definer's schema. If our UPDATE_SAL procedure contains the following statement:

```
Update EMP set sal = 5000;
```

The database will resolve the statement to the following:

```
Update SCOTT.EMP set sal = 5000;
```

The same resolution properties hold true for other objects such as procedures and synonyms.

Definer Rights Example

Let's continue with our UPDATE_SAL procedure. The procedure will leverage the definer rights model. This is a good illustration of a sound security design. Users don't have direct access to the data objects. Rather, they only have access to them indirectly via stored procedures.

The procedures can perform business integrity checks, data integrity checks, and security checks prior to data manipulation to ensure that everything is as it should be. If access to data should be restricted, for example, when you don't trust the users or want to audit their actions, using the definer rights model is a good first choice. Additionally, consider a requirement that data manipulation should only happen between 9AM and 5PM Monday through Friday. The procedure could validate that the current time fell within those operating hours and only then allow the operation(s) to succeed. Otherwise the procedure would reject the attempted operation(s). This represents an excellent security model because it allows the developer or DBA to further control access to the data.

We start with a table owned by SCOTT. SCOTT wants BLAKE to be able to update the SAL column in EMP. However, SCOTT doesn't want BLAKE to issue direct updates so SCOTT creates a procedure called UPDATE_SAL that will perform the updates.

```
scott@KNOX10g> CREATE PROCEDURE update_sal (p_empno in number,
  2                                          p_sal in number)
  3  AS
  4  BEGIN
  5    /*
  6     * Could have done data and/or security checking:
  7     * Examples:
  8     *   p_sal > sal;
```

```
 9      *    updating during "normal" operating hours;
10      *    user executing procedure is updating just
11      *        their salary;
12      */
13      update EMP set sal = p_sal where empno = p_empno;
14   END;
15   /
```

Procedure created.

The comments include additional ways to maintain security and integrity of the data. SCOTT then allows BLAKE to execute the UPDATE_SAL procedure and select from the table.

```
scott@KNOX10> grant execute on update_sal to blake;
```

Grant succeeded.

```
scott@KNOX10> -- let user see the data
scott@KNOX10> grant select on EMP to blake;
```

Grant succeeded.

Now BLAKE, who still cannot directly update the table, can update the salaries by executing the procedure UPDATE_SAL. In fact, anyone who has EXECUTE privileges on UPDATE_SAL can update SCOTT's EMP table. This process is illustrated in Figure 8-1.

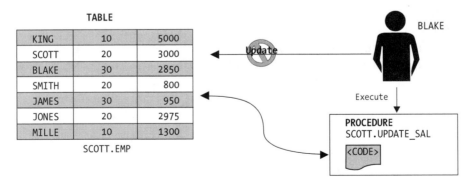

Figure 8-1. SCOTT's *table is protected from direct updates via the UPDATE_SAL procedure.*

When BLAKE executes the procedure, the database treats it as though SCOTT is performing the action. From an auditing perspective, BLAKE's identity is not lost; it is still BLAKE making the changes, but SCOTT's privileges and objects are used. Because SCOTT can update the table, the procedure executes successfully. If the procedure used BLAKE's privileges, it would fail because BLAKE does not have the ability to update the table.

Next we connect as BLAKE to test. First, we show BLAKE has read-only access. Then the procedure performs the update on BLAKE's behalf.

```
scott@KNOX10> -- test as blake (recreated for this example)
scott@KNOX10> connect blake/blake
Connected.
blake@KNOX10> -- show data
blake@KNOX10> select ename, empno, sal from SCOTT.EMP where ename = USER;

ENAME            EMPNO        SAL
-----------------------------------
BLAKE            7698        2850


blake@KNOX10> -- show direct updates don't work
blake@KNOX10> update SCOTT.emp set sal = sal * 1.1;
update SCOTT.emp set sal = sal * 1.1
              *
ERROR at line 1:
ORA-01031: insufficient privileges

blake@KNOX10> -- show procedure invocation works
blake@KNOX10> execute SCOTT.update_sal(p_empno => 7698, p_sal => 3000)

PL/SQL procedure successfully completed.

blake@KNOX10> -- show data
blake@KNOX10> select ename, empno, sal from SCOTT.EMP where ename = USER;

ENAME            EMPNO        SAL
-------------------------------------
BLAKE            7698        3000
```

This example illustrates how effective definer rights can be in ensuring a secure environment. Also, note the object resolution. The procedure referenced the unqualified table name EMP and not the fully qualified name SCOTT.EMP. This worked because definer rights resolve unqualified objects to the definer of the PL/SQL. The direct query issued from BLAKE had to reference the fully qualified object or the database will throw an error, as illustrated in the following example, which issues two queries. The first uses the unqualified object reference.

```
blake@KNOX10> select ename from emp where ename like 'B%';
select ename from emp
                    *
ERROR at line 1:
ORA-00942: table or view does not exist

blake@KNOX10> select ename from SCOTT.EMP where ename like 'B%';

ENAME
----------
BLAKE
```

Definer Rights Uses

Certain use cases dictate definer rights modes. One of the real benefits of definer rights is in performance. Definer rights SQL can be cached as shared SQL and yield stellar performance, as we proved in Chapter 5, "PL/SQL Optimization Techniques." Therefore, people pick definer rights to maximize the shared SQL.

From a security perspective, we often see definer rights as an optimal solution in obtaining the **principle of least privileges**. This principle says that a user should have only the privileges he needs to do his job or perform a function, and nothing more.

For example, say we want to create a procedure that allows a user to kill her session (a session owned by that user). This presents a challenge because the ALTER SYSTEM privilege, which is required to perform the task, will allow a user to kill *anyone's* session, and can do many other things as well. The solution is to create the procedure using definer rights in a schema with the ALTER SYSTEM privilege. When a request is received to kill a session, the procedure can check that the session in question is owned by the person invoking the procedure.

Here are some instances when definer rights is the mode of choice.

- You want to prevent users from directly querying or manipulating the data tables.

- Users share a database account, so privileges can be granted directly to that schema.

- Many users will be connected and you want to maximize the shared SQL. Shared SQL is important to ensuring high performance because the work done by the database parsing and optimization routines can be shared.

This is because the work done by one session to parse and optimize a query can be reused by another session.[1]

- You want to maximize performance of your PL/SQL because all privileges and object resolution is done at compile time.

- Any time you don't need to rely on roles for the user's privileges (note that execute privileges for definer rights procedures can be granted via roles).

Because it has been around longer, definer rights is much more popular and used far more often than invoker rights.

Why Are Roles Disabled?

Two questions naturally arise with regard to definer rights.

- Why are roles disabled?

- Isn't this a severe limitation of definer rights mode?

The answer to the first question is best answered by reconstructing what the database has to do during program compilation and execution. From a security perspective, all data access has to be validated. Consider, for example, a procedure that updates a table. The database has to ensure the user has the privilege to issue the update on that table. As you know, privileges can be granted to roles. Roles can be granted to other roles in an almost endless number of ways. Finally, a role, or roles, is granted to the user.

On program compilation, the database has to check privileges and maintain a dependency mapping. The mapping is done to ensure integrity from an access perspective. If the privilege to update the table is revoked, the procedure must be invalidated. With roles enabled, any privilege revocations on any of the roles would almost certainly invalidate all the programs from which the objects are called. The database would spend a significant part of its time recompiling and revalidating programs and this, of course, would have a detrimental performance impact. The bottom line is that definer rights works the way it does to maintain high performance and security for PL/SQL.

The answer to the second question is simply "No, this is not a limitation of definer rights mode." Definer rights can be used to meet a lot of real business and security requirements. However, if we don't understand or remember what occurs with roles in definer rights programs, confusion and wasted time filing technical assistance requests may delay an implementation. As described in the final solution to the GET_MY_PROGRAM function, roles being disabled is not a show

---

1. See Tom Kyte's book, *Expert One-on-One Oracle* (Apress, 2003), for more information.

stopper. However, it may influence the design, or at least, the manner in which privileges are granted.

Using Invoker Rights

In invoker rights mode, at execution time, the PL/SQL procedure operates in the opposite manner of definer rights. In other words, the database uses the privileges and object resolution of the invoker of the procedure. Compile time privileges and resolution happen the same way as in definer rights mode. That is, roles are disabled during compilation and object resolution happens for the definer (of the invoker rights procedure).

Overall invoker rights allows for some very useful designs. To make something run in invoker rights mode, you simply add AUTHID CURRENT_USER after the definition and before the AS/IS. Let's re-create our previous SHOW_PRIVS procedure in invoker rights mode.

```
scott@KNOX10> create or replace procedure show_privs
  2    authid current_user
  3    as
  4    begin
  5      dbms_output.put_line('ROLES:');
  6      for rec in (select * from session_roles)
  7      loop
  8        dbms_output.put_line(rec.role);
  9      end loop;
 10    end;
 11  /

Procedure created.

scott@KNOX10> execute show_privs
ROLES:
CONNECT
RESOURCE

PL/SQL procedure successfully completed.
```

Not only can we see the roles, but all the privileges for all the roles would also be available.

Invoker Rights Example

When working in invoker rights mode, compile time privileges and object resolution are checked as in definer rights. You cannot just lift code that was not compiling under definer rights, add AUTHID CURRENT_USER, and hope it will recompile.

```
blake@KNOX10> CREATE PROCEDURE update_sal (p_empno in number, p_sal in number)
  2     authid current_user
  3     AS
  4     BEGIN
  5       update SCOTT.EMP set sal = p_sal where empno = p_empno;
  6     END;
  7     /

Warning: Procedure created with compilation errors.

blake@KNOX10> show errors
Errors for PROCEDURE UPDATE_SAL:

LINE/COL ERROR
-----------------------------------------------------
5/5        PL/SQL: SQL Statement ignored
5/18       PL/SQL: ORA-01031: insufficient privileges
```

There are several solutions to this challenge. The first is to give the procedure definer access to the objects. If you cannot do that, you might use dynamic SQL:

```
blake@KNOX10> CREATE OR REPLACE procedure update_sal
  2   (
  3   p_empno in number,
  4   p_sal in number
  5   )
  6     authid current_user
  7     as
  8     begin
  9       execute immediate 'update SCOTT.EMP set ' ||
 10                         'sal = :x ' ||
 11                         'where empno = :y' using p_sal, p_empno;
 12     end;
 13   /
Procedure created.

blake@KNOX10> exec update_sal (7698,5000);

PL/SQL procedure successfully completed.

blake@KNOX10> select ename, empno, sal from SCOTT.EMP where ename = USER;
```

ENAME	EMPNO	SAL
BLAKE	7698	5000

Another solution is to create a template object. A template object is an object that looks like the real object (the column names and column types match), but its only purpose is to allow the database to match SQL and PL/SQL data types. That is, if we had a procedure that updated the EMP table, we would create a template EMP table with the same profile.

```
blake@KNOX10> -- create template EMP table
blake@KNOX10> create table EMP as select * from SCOTT.EMP where 1=2;

Table created.

blahe@KNOX10> CREATE OR REPLACE PROCEDURE update_sal
  2  (
  3  p_empno in number,
  4  p_sal in number
  5  )
  6      authid current_user
  7      AS
  8      BEGIN
  9         update EMP set sal = p_sal where empno = p_empno;
 10      END;
 11  /
Procedure created.
```

The template does not need indexes or data, just something for the database to validate against. This will allow the procedures to compile successfully. The procedure would also compile as a definer rights procedure; the major difference is that at execution time the invoker rights procedure will use a different set of objects. Note that in the example just shown, the table is not fully qualified. EMP will be resolved at runtime for each and every invoker. This could be a different EMP object for every invoker or the same EMP for every invoker.

Consequently, the invoker rights model could be applicable for a hosting environment. Each company could have its own set of tables (structures would be identical across schemas), with their own data, and only one code base to manage. You could write the code once using invoker rights, and due to the object resolution and privileges, you would be ensured that Company A's data went in the Company A's tables and Company B's data went into Company B's tables. Furthermore, the companies could insert only into their tables, not another company's tables. Additionally, you could use database roles to maintain all user privileges.

Invoker Rights Uses

Invoker rights procedures, just like definer rights procedures, can do all the auxiliary checking you desire—business rules, data integrity, security—so the procedures can still act as gate keepers for the data.

What else can you get with invoker rights? Most have concluded that the only valid use of invoker rights is for utilities. This is not to diminish the value of invoker rights—utilities can be very valuable. Many of the DBMS_* PL/SQL packages are compiled using invoker rights. As an example of a useful utility that would work well within invoker rights, consider a program that takes random SQL and returns a report formatted in a specific way. This utility could be developed by one person and then made available to many users. With invoker rights, you write the procedure once and then let the database resolve the privileges and objects for you at runtime. A classic example of a generic invoker rights utility is the PRINT_TABLE procedure, written by Tom Kyte (see *Expert One-on-One Oracle*, Apress, ISBN 1590592433, for full details). We create the procedure in a low-privilege account called UTILS.

```
utils@ORA817> create or replace
  2    procedure print_table( p_query in varchar2 )
  3    AUTHID CURRENT_USER
  4    is
  5        l_theCursor      integer default dbms_sql.open_cursor;
  6        l_columnValue    varchar2(4000);
  7        l_status         integer;
  8        l_descTbl        dbms_sql.desc_tab;
  9        l_colCnt         number;
 10    begin
 11        dbms_sql.parse( l_theCursor, p_query, dbms_sql.native );
 12        dbms_sql.describe_columns( l_theCursor, l_colCnt, l_descTbl);
 13
 14        for i in 1 .. l_colCnt loop
 15            dbms_sql.define_column(l_theCursor, i, l_columnValue, 4000)
 16        end loop;
 17
 18        l_status := dbms_sql.execute(l_theCursor);
 19
 20        while ( dbms_sql.fetch_rows(l_theCursor) > 0 ) loop
 21            for i in 1 .. l_colCnt loop
 22                dbms_sql.column_value( l_theCursor, i, l_columnValue );
 23                dbms_output.put_line( rpad( l_descTbl(i).col_name, 30 )
```

```
24                                            || ': ' ||
25                                         l_columnValue );
26            end loop;
27            dbms_output.put_line( '-----------------' );
28         end loop;
29    exception
30       when others then
31            dbms_sql.close_cursor( l_theCursor );
32            RAISE;
33    end;
34  /
```

Procedure created.

```
utils@ORA817>
utils@ORA817> grant execute on print_table to public;
```

Grant succeeded.

We can even go so far as to effectively "lock" the UTILS account by revoking the CREATE SESSION procedure.

```
utils @ORA817> connect tkyte/tkyte

utils @ORA817> revoke create session, create procedure
  2  from utils_acct;
```

Revoke succeeded.

However, we can then log on to the SCOTT schemas and make free use of PRINT_TABLE to get nicely formatted output.

```
scott@ORA817> exec utils.print_table('select * from scott.dept');
DEPTNO                         : 10
DNAME                          : ACCOUNTING
LOC                            : NEW YORK
-----------------
DEPTNO                         : 20
DNAME                          : RESEARCH
LOC                            : DALLAS
-----------------
```

Here are other cases when invoker rights may be preferred.

- You want to manage one code base for multiple schemas. This is described in the hosting example.

- You already deployed database roles. The difficulty arises when many users run ad hoc query tools *and* access a Web application into the same database. The ad hoc query allows direct queries via roles, and the Web application connects as the end-user and calls PL/SQL procedures to perform DML (most often seen with the mod PL/SQL Web interface). Use of bind variables and fully qualified objects would be needed to ensure the best performance. This may seem somewhat contrived, but we have come across this requirement many times.

Invoker Rights Limitations

There are also a few instances when invoker rights is not the best choice.

- You are writing a trigger or a view. Sorry, you can only use definer rights on views and triggers.

- Performance is at a premium. At execution time, the database will have to resolve all ambiguous object references and check privileges for the user. Also, it will be more difficult to use shared SQL with invoker rights because the objects being referenced could be different.

- You need guaranteed dependability. There are good reasons for checking things at compile time. However, with invoker rights, there is no sure way to ensure it will run successfully for all users. It might run for Alice but not for Bob.

Beware of Mixing Modes

Be careful about mixing modes. It may seem desirable, but it can be confusing. Object resolution in particular can be confusing. Definer rights calling an invoker rights procedure forces the invoker rights to act as the definer of the invoking procedure. Confused? Good—so be careful how you design. We find it best to pick a homogeneous design mode and stick with it. Any deviations are carefully thought through and documented so that the next (unfortunate) person looking at the code has some clue why you did what you did.

It's also a good idea to include the specifics on the mode you are using. With invoker rights, you have to specify the AUTHID; with definer rights you don't. If you intend to use both, include AUTHID DEFINER for definer rights too. In this manner, you are showing that you made a conscious decision to use one mode or the other.

Package Construction

The next important element of design is how your packages are constructed. As we discussed in Chapter 2, "Package It All Up," packages are composed of two parts: the package specification and the package body. In addition to the two parts, there are two access abilities: public and private. It is very important to remember that a user with EXECUTE privileges on a package also has EXECUTE privileges on all public procedures and functions within the package. It also gives read/write access to any variables defined in the specification. Consider carefully when constructing packages to ensure that everyone with EXECUTE privileges should also have EXECUTE privilege on all the public procedures and functions.

The package specification defines what is publicly available when users execute or describe the PL/SQL package. Anything not listed in the specification is considered private. A DESCRIBE on a package yields only the procedures and functions in the package specification.

```
scott@KNOX10> CREATE OR REPLACE package sample_package
  2  as
  3    pv_this_is_public varchar2(6) := 'Hello';
  4    function a_function return varchar2;
  5    procedure a_procedure;
  6  end;
  7  /

Package created.

scott@KNOX10>
scott@KNOX10> describe sample_package
FUNCTION A_FUNCTION RETURNS VARCHAR2
PROCEDURE A_PROCEDURE
```

Note that no package variables declared in the package specification are seen in the output of the describe statement. They can, however, be viewed when looking at the source.[2]

```
scott@KNOX10> select text from user_source
  2    where name = 'SAMPLE_PACKAGE' order by line;
```

2. See "Protecting the Source," later in this chapter, for more information.

```
TEXT
--------------------------------------------------------
package sample_package
as
  pv_this_is_public varchar2(6) := 'Hello';
  function a_function return varchar2;
  procedure a_procedure;
end;
```

6 rows selected.

As a general rule, variables should be private. If they are to be manipulated, it is often advantageous to have corresponding "getter" and "setter" functions for manipulating their values. Any procedure that will not be called directly should not be declared in the package header. This allows you to hide implementation details and security functionality from the users. They will not be able to see or even know about your helper functions unless, of course, they query the data dictionary, but fortunately, they would have to own the package or have the EXECUTE ANY PROCEDURE system privilege to do this.

Overall, from a security perspective, we always try to obtain our **least-privilege** environment: a user only has enough privileges to do their job and no more. However, in many cases, other factors such as performance and manageability compete with our security objectives. We are motivated from a performance and manageability perspective to try and put most of our related processing in a package. The challenge with packages is that once a user has EXECUTE privileges on the package, the user has EXECUTE on all procedures within. Consequently, you have to ensure that all procedures and functions within a package specification are necessary for all users with EXECUTE privileges. Otherwise, you have violated the least-privilege model.

An example of an extreme violation of this principle will help to clarify the point. One could easily create a package that contained some useful utilities such as returning the user's application name or converting the current time to a standard representation. These are useful and more importantly harmless activities. We could also combine a procedure in that same package that allowed the invoker to kill database sessions. Killing database sessions, as we discussed earlier, has different restrictions in as much as you don't want users arbitrarily killing another user's session.

This is obviously contrived, but often there is one group of users that require one set of procedures and a different set of users that require some of the first set of procedures as well as a few new procedures. It is bad practice to create a single package with all procedures and then grant EXECUTE privileges on that package to both communities of users.

The design consideration comes down to the granularity of the packages. Breaking up packages and assigning privileges can often be effectively done several different ways. In the following example, one package is needed by a group of users, Alpha. A separate group of users, Beta, needs access to some of the procedures that the Alpha users need as well as some different procedures.

```
system@KNOX10> create user alpha identified by a;

User created.

system@KNOX10> create user beta identified by b;

User created.

system@KNOX10>
system@KNOX10> conn scott/tiger
Connected.
scott@KNOX10> create or replace package alpha_package
  2   as
  3      PROCEDURE P1;
  4      PROCEDURE P2;
  5      PROCEDURE P3;
  6      FUNCTION F1 return number;
  7      FUNCTION F2 return number;
  8   end;
  9   /

Package created.

scott@KNOX10> grant execute on alpha_package to alpha;

Grant succeeded.

scott@KNOX10>
scott@KNOX10> create or replace package beta_package
  2   as
  3      PROCEDURE P3;
  4      PROCEDURE P4;
  5      PROCEDURE P5;
  6      FUNCTION F1 return number;
  7      FUNCTION F3 return number;
  8   end;
  9   /

Package created.
```

```
scott@KNOX10> grant execute on beta_package to beta;

Grant succeeded.
```

The implementation body of the BETA_PACKAGE can simply delegate its calls to the ALPHA_PACKAGE.

```
scott@KNOX10> create or replace package body beta_package
  2   as
  3      PROCEDURE P3
  4      as
  5        begin
  6          ALPHA_PACKAGE.P3;
  7        end;
  8
  9      FUNCTION F1 return number
 10      as
 11        begin
 12          return ALPHA_PACKAGE.F1;
 13        end;
 14
 15      PROCEDURE P4
 16      as
 17        begin
 18          null;
 19        end;
 20
 21      PROCEDURE P5
 22      as
 23        begin
 24          null;
 25        end;
 26
 27      FUNCTION F3 return number
 28      as
 29        begin
 30          return 1;
 31        end;
 32   end;
 33   /

Package body created.
```

This design is illustrated in Figure 8-2.

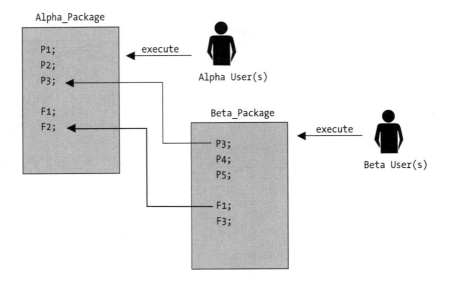

Figure 8-2. Implementation of Alpha *and* Beta *packages*

Alpha users execute ALPHA_PACKAGE and Beta users execute BETA_PACKAGE which delegates common calls P3 and F1 to the implementation in the ALPHA_PACKAGE. Separation of packages ensures the least-privilege principle is upheld. Updates to P3 and/or F1 can be done once in the ALPHA_PACKAGE thereby easing the maintenance burden.

Another nice element of this design is that the separation of packages allows for different levels of security for the respective packages. For example, we might want to audit executes on the BETA_PACKAGE but not the ALPHA_PACKAGE. We may choose to do this when we have a high-risk user group such as Web-based users (not that the users themselves are nefarious, but that Web applications can be higher-risk applications). The Beta users are the high-risk group in this example.

```
system@KNOX10> audit execute on scott.beta_package by access;

Audit succeeded.
```

Above all, the implementation just shown should abide by the following:

- Do not duplicate code in both packages. If you do, any updates to P2 and F1 will have to be done to both packages. This is bad programming style.

- Do not grant privileges on both packages to either or both users. This violates the least-privilege principle.

- Do not create a single package with all the procedures from both packages. This also violates the least-privilege principle.

Note that nesting calls may negatively impact performance, so don't get too carried away without testing your design first!

Schemas, Schemas Everywhere

One of your biggest decisions will be what objects to put in which schema. You will need to make decisions about where to place

- Data objects

- Procedures

- Users

These decisions are critical to a successful (from the security context) implementation.

It is poor practice, for example, to lump everything together into one schema. In other words, don't put the data tables and the procedures that manipulate them in the schema to which the user(s) connect. If you do, you run the risk of users inadvertently, or maliciously, doing things to the data or procedures that they're not supposed to. We find that this bad practice occurs quite frequently in Web-based applications.

A related and very important point, and one that is constantly violated, is that users should not be logging in or connected as any of the *SYS* accounts— SYS, SYSTEM, CTXSYS, MDSYS, OLAPSYS, WKSYS, and so on. These are *not* user accounts; the privileges are much too high.

This concept extends to other privileged application accounts. An application may need to do many things. As such, it is not uncommon for people to grant the application (which in this case is represented by a schema) the DBA role. Then, in a stroke of insecurity, the application designers allow users to connect to this privileged application schema. The designer may think the application will control the security so there is no risk, but this is wrong and is very bad practice. There is a lot of risk involved in this from the database security perspective. Every user running that application is running with DBA privileges. The simple question to ask is "how are the users connecting to the database?" If they are connecting as themselves to individual schemas, great, if not, you may need to dig a little deeper to ensure that someone has not made the mistake of allowing users to connect to an over-privileged database account.

Remember that you are striving for a least-privileges environment. This is often lost in translations to applications. Here are some suggestions for how to do it.

Three-Tiered Approach

One approach is to put the data objects in one schema, the users in another, and the procedures to manipulate the data into a third, as shown in Figure 8-3. This is a very conservative approach and requires the most maintenance (it requires the most schemas), but also gives you the most flexibility.

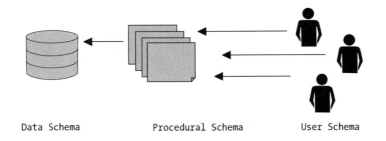

Data Schema   Procedural Schema   User Schema

Figure 8-3. A three-tiered approach to schema design

Data Schema

In this schema, the data schema owns all the data tables and no procedures. Users should not connect to this schema because the owner of the tables has implicit rights on the tables. Therefore, you should remove the create session privilege and/or the CONNECT role from the data schema account. Alternatively, or additionally (layers of defense are good), you can lock the account. Why? In prior releases, the account would have to be accessed to allow permissions (grants and revokes) and DDL to occur on objects contained in the data schema. As of Oracle 9*i* Database 9.2, the GRANT ANY OBJECT PRIVILEGE (GAOP) privilege allows the grantee to create objects and control privileges in schemas other than the one to which they are connected. Therefore, no one, not even administrators, needs to log on to the data schema.

PL/SQL Schema

The next schema is for the PL/SQL. Separating the data and the applications allows flexibility in several ways. First, data can be exported or replicated at a schema level without either specifying every table individually or dragging along all the procedures. Another common situation occurs when multiple applications are accessing the same data. Separating the data and the applications into distinct schemas has the advantage of managing the applications at the schema level (auditing, backups, privileges on the data, and so on).

Separating the user schemas from the procedure schemas helps to ensure that nobody inadvertently or maliciously changes the code. This is critical, especially if you have specialized integrity and security checks. The only effective way for your PL/SQL to act as your trusted agents is if it cannot be tampered with. This account should also be locked.

Version control is also done more readily with this design because you can simply create a new schema and load the new procedures. From a security perspective, procedural schemas allow for either a definer rights or invoker rights model. Typically, the definer rights model represents the most secure approach. It is much easier to grant privileges on the data schema to the procedural schema than it is to grant privileges on the data schema to every one of the user schemas.

User Schema

User schemas should be created independently of the other schemas. These schemas could be for exclusive use or shared amongst a group of users. Oracle supports both designs very well. If the data schema or procedural schema is compromised, very bad things could happen (data could be corrupted or deleted, and procedures could be altered or dropped, etc.). Compromises to the individual accounts help mitigate potential damage by restricting access to just the things that the account can do. This is known as *compartmentalization* in the security world, and it is a fundamental tenet to security best practices. If you adhere to least-privileges and implement your architecture as suggested here, you would comply with security best practices too.

Code Distribution

Security requirements are generally based on what you are trying to protect. If you are trying to protect data, the sensitivity of the data determines the level of security required to protect it. For example, insensitive or commonly known data, such as the current weather, does not require a lot of security because it is easily obtainable and uninteresting. On the opposite end, privacy data, proprietary data, and so on, obviously requires much stronger security.

The same argument applies to PL/SQL. If you have a function that returns the current time, no security is required (thus the SYSDATE function is executable to PUBLIC.) If the PL/SQL is used to alter the state of something significant, there should be definite restrictions on who can access that code. This concept should be maintained as you design your PL/SQL packages and decide on schema designs and access.

Also consider the consequences of not only the permissions to execute the code, but also the privileges to change what the code does. For example, a user with inappropriate access to a PL/SQL schema could easily modify a critical procedure and comment out auditing code. He could change a procedure that updates records into one that deletes records, and trap an unwitting user into performing the action.

How could this happen? The user could guess a password and log into the account that owns the PL/SQL, guess the SYSTEM password, or acquire one of many system privileges that we discussed earlier. This last scenario can happen when a Web application, connected to an over-privileged user, is hacked and tricked into granting another user, or worse yet PUBLIC, system privileges or roles (DBA).

Consider the management aspect of your design as well as how you plan to grant and revoke privileges to the users. Your decision drives how you might organize the schemas, packages, and rights modes.

Triggers for Security

We discussed Triggers in detail in Chapter 6 and here we'll extend that discussion to cover the use of triggers as an auxiliary security tool. They can be used for auditing and for other covert activities, such as alerting administrators to certain actions. Data integrity can be checked and additional security measures taken. Autonomous triggers allow you to embed a transaction inside a transaction so that even a failed attempt will be "audited." This is consistent with the way the database performs auditing. That is, failed attempts are audited.

Performance is sometimes an issue with triggers, so the following recommendations should be used as suggestions and adapted to meet the performance requirements of your production systems.

A final warning: triggers can easily be disabled and re-enabled without much notice. Consider auditing trigger manipulation if you are depending on triggers for a vital security functionality. Also, bear in mind that certain operations (such as direct path loads) do not fire triggers at all.

Security Checks

The nice thing about triggers is that they can be slipped into existing applications transparently. This transparency is attractive from a security perspective. For example, if we want to prevent a user from performing an update, we can use a simple DML trigger to perform security checks and allow the operation to succeed only if our security measures are not violated. If a user is trying to do something malicious, we can fail the operation.

To underline the importance of this section, it is useful to consider Web application security. Web applications are particularly vulnerable to several types of attack, many of which are simple to implement. There are several papers and a few good books detailing how this can and does occur. We'll use a simple but common example as the prime motivator for this section—you will see that not only can you not *rely* on a Web application to provide complete security; you should *assume* that it will not.

Picture a simple Web application that acts as an employee lookup directory. It allows users to search by entering names or phone numbers. The searches are executed against an internal Oracle database table. Some of the information in the database is sensitive, and consequently, security is very important.

The application allows users to update their records in a self-service mode. This helps ease the administration required to populate and update records as well as ensure that the data is up-to-date and accurate.

The following snippet is from the user update HTML form the application presents to an authenticated user who wants to change his or her photo. The photo is optionally displayed in the results of queries for which their record is returned. Names and actual code have been changed to protect the innocent.[3]

```
<HTML>
  <BODY>
    <FORM action="http://someserver.com/appPkg.proc" method="post" enctype="mul-
tipart/form-data">
      <input type="hidden" name="p_empno" value="7788">
      <input type="file" name="p_userImage" size="30" >
      <input type="SUBMIT" value="Upload Photo">
    </FORM>
  </BODY>
</HTML>
```

The hack comes when a user downloads the HTML and modifies it. The Web application accepts this form and updates the image in the record for the person with an employee number equal to the one in the P_EMPNO field. This is a hidden field and thus not displayed on the screen. In this hack, SCOTT will change the value from 7788 (SCOTT's employee number) to 7698 (BLAKE's number). By saving the file locally, changing the value, and then submitting the file from his local machine, SCOTT can update BLAKE's picture! If you think this is fiction, it's not. This happens all the time!

This example also reinforces a very important security best practice: by implementing security in the database, we have defense in-depth. Defense in-depth means that there is more than one security mechanism active. Assuming

---

3. Any resemblance to any characters living or dead is purely coincidental.

the application is already applying security, if the application is hijacked as it is in the example just given, the database security would provide an extra protection barrier.

In the following example, we have a simple table that relates a user with his associated picture. The application displays this image when displaying a detailed user information page.

```
create table user_info
(
username varchar2(30) constraint user_info_pk primary key,
image_url varchar2(2000)
);
/

insert into user_info values
('SCOTT','http://imageserver.company.com/img/scott.gif');
insert into user_info values
 ('BLAKE','http://imageserver.company.com/img/blake.gif');
commit;
```

Next, we want to create an update trigger to ensure that only the user associated with a particular record can update that record.

```
CREATE OR REPLACE TRIGGER user_img_update_check
    BEFORE UPDATE OF image_url
    ON user_info
    FOR EACH ROW
DECLARE
BEGIN
    IF (sys_context('USERENV','SESSION_USER') != :new.username)
    then
      raise_application_error(-20001,'Unauthorized update!');
    END IF;
END;
/
```

Now let's run a simple update as SCOTT. Here we see a successful update of SCOTT'S record when SCOTT issues the update (the SQL shown here would have been issued by the application procedure that accepted the input from the previous HTML form).

```
scott@KNOX10> update user_info
    2      set image_url = 'http://funnypictures.com/img/tomCrusie.jpg'
    3   where username = 'SCOTT';
    1 row updated.
```

When SCOTT attempts his hack and tries to update BLAKE's picture, the trigger catches the incongruity and raises the exception.

```
scott@KNOX10> -- trigger raises errors for session user SCOTT
scott@KNOX10> update user_info
   2    set image_url = 'http://funnypictures.com/img/chewbacca.lg.jpg'
   3  where username = 'BLAKE';
update user_info
       *
ERROR at line 1:
ORA-20001: Unauthorized update!
ORA-06512: at "SCOTT.USER_IMG_UPDATE_CHECK", line 5
ORA-04088: error during execution of trigger 'SCOTT.USER_IMG_UPDATE_CHECK'
```

It would be quite easy to amend the trigger just shown so that when this sort of hack was attempted, the relevant person was sent an email notification. We could have our trigger call a notification package, such as that described in Chapter 7. Our trigger might look something like this.

```
CREATE OR REPLACE TRIGGER user_img_update_check
    BEFORE UPDATE OF image_url
    ON user_info
    FOR EACH ROW
DECLARE
v_notification_msg varchar2(1000);
BEGIN
    IF (sys_context('USERENV','SESSION_USER') != :new.username)
    then
      v_notification_msg := 'Unauthorized update to image URL from ' ||
        sys_context('USERENV','SESSION_USER') ||
        ' on ' || :new.username;
      send_mail(p_to=>'securityAdmin.yourCompany.com',
                         p_message=>v_notification_msg);
      raise_application_error(-20001,'Unauthorized update!');
    END IF;
END;
/
```

Now, when we run the update again, a SEND_MAIL procedure is called and an email is sent with a message that says, Unauthorized update to image URL from SCOTT on BLAKE.

Auditing

Many applications require auditing capabilities to track data changes and monitor user activities. The database has many standard and advanced auditing capabilities, but those are sometimes inappropriate for the task at hand. The best example of this is when auditing is only desired after hours. Many hacks happen after hours because there is less chance the hacker will be caught in the act. Standard database auditing is either on or off. You cannot configure the database to only audit after 5PM Monday through Friday, and then all day Saturday and Sunday.

However, we can create time-sensitive, context-sensitive, or data-sensitive auditing ourselves by employing triggers. Additionally, we can audit by either inserting into an AUDIT table or by writing to a file on the file system. Don't forget that triggers can be disabled and re-enabled[4] so this technique, although effective, is not 100 percent guaranteed.

You may want to consider creating the trigger as an autonomous transaction. An autonomous transaction allows a transaction inside a transaction. Typically, the insert done in a trigger would be rolled back with the transaction that it resides in. Exploiting this, sneaky people can still get the information they need. For example, a user without SELECT privileges on a table could indirectly determine information without issuing a SELECT. The following UPDATE statement indicates that there are four people with salaries higher than BLAKE. The rollback would act to cover his trail as the audit information done by the trigger would also be rolled back.

```
blake@KNOX10g> update emp set sal = 0
  2     where sal >
  3        (select sal from emp
  4          where ename = 'BLAKE');

4 rows updated.

blake@KNOX10g> -- cover trail
blake@KNOX10g> rollback;

Rollback complete.
```

In the following example, we write audit information to a table via an update trigger. Let's first create our auditing table.

```
scott@KNOX10> create table aud_emp_tab (
  2     username varchar2(30),
```

---

4. Triggers can only be disabled by authorized users.

```
 3     action      varchar2(6),
 4     column_name varchar2(255),
 5     empno       number(4),
 6     old_value   number,
 7     new_value   number,
 8     action_date date
 9     )
10   /
```

Table created.

Next we create a trigger to audit updates on the salaries. We'll create this trigger using the autonomous transactions. The autonomous transaction capability will separate our audit functionality in the trigger from the rest of the transaction that caused the trigger to fire.

```
scott@KNOX10> CREATE OR REPLACE TRIGGER aud_emp
 2     BEFORE UPDATE OF SAL
 3     ON EMP
 4     FOR EACH ROW
 5
 6   DECLARE
 7   PRAGMA AUTONOMOUS_TRANSACTION;
 8
 9   BEGIN
10     INSERT into aud_emp_tab
11       values (sys_context('USERENV','SESSION_USER'),
12               'UPDATE',
13               'SAL',
14               :old.empno,
15               :old.sal,
16               :new.sal,
17               SYSDATE );
18     COMMIT;
19   END;
20   /
```

Trigger created.

Returning to our Web application-only security model, we assume that the application allows an HR person to update salaries and that BLAKE works in HR. Therefore, we have to allow BLAKE to update salaries.

```
scott@KNOX10> grant update(sal) on emp to blake;

Grant succeeded.
```

However, BLAKE is not supposed to update his own salary. Unfortunately for
BLAKE, the application enforces this security. However, if BLAKE successfully
hijacks the Web application (code not shown here), the following SQL would be
issued.

```
blake@KNOX10> update SCOTT.EMP set sal = 5000 where empno=7698;

1 row updated.
```

The autonomous transaction ensures that the audit record will remain, even
if the transaction rolled back. This would be a valuable way to detect situations
in which someone was trying to do something but either failed or got scared. We
continue our example by rolling back and checking the audit table.

```
blake@KNOX10> -- cover trail
blake@KNOX10> rollback;

Rollback complete.

blake@KNOX10> @conn scott/tiger
scott@KNOX10> col username format a8
scott@KNOX10> col column_name format a12
scott@KNOX10> select username, empno, old_value, new_value,
  2    to_char(action_date, 'Mon-DD-YYYY HH24:MI:SS') Time
  3    from aud_emp_tab;

USERNAME    EMPNO OLD_VALUE  NEW_VALUE        TIME
--------------------------------------------------------------
BLAKE        7698 2850            5000 Oct-03-2003  18:23:34

1 row selected.
```

The implementation works best if the trigger code calls previously defined
procedures. This makes it easier to test and debug because you don't have to
mess with the table to get the code to fire. Additionally, as pointed out earlier,
the code is more scalable because the SQL code in the procedure is cached and
the trigger code is not.

Also note that triggers (and views) only fire in definer rights mode, so any
privileges required inside the trigger need to be granted directly to the user and
not inherited through roles. You might also consider writing the records to the

OS to help protect them from (privileged) database users. The UTL_FILE package facilitates this task but this only works when the users from whom you are trying to protect the records do not have access to the OS directory specified by the UTL_FILE_DIR parameter.

Finally, a word on TRUNCATE statements: they do not fire table triggers. Therefore, it's easy for someone to erase the data without being caught by a delete trigger. However, you can audit from the database on TRUNCATE operations.

Fine-Grained Auditing

Although there may be a few instances when standard or fine-grained auditing (FGA) is inappropriate, there are countless more when it is the correct tool to use (instead of triggers). Using FGA, which was introduced in Oracle9*i*, we simply use the DBMS_FGA package to set an audit condition on our table view. We can set the condition on a specific column in the table, enabling us to audit very specific queries. When a query is submitted that matches the condition, it is audited. For example, if we want to audit the updates to the salary column on the EMP table, we could simply invoke FGA to do the job for us. Additionally, FGA allows us to call an event handler when the audit event occurs.

In the following example, we enable FGA for any INSERT or UPDATE on the SAL column (this example will only work in 10g since FGA was only supported for SELECT in 9*i*).

```
system@KNOX10> begin
   2     DBMS_FGA.ADD_POLICY(object_schema => 'SCOTT',
   3                         object_name=>'EMP',
   4                         policy_name => 'EMP_INS_UPD',
   5                         audit_condition => '1=1',
   6                         audit_column =>'SAL',
   7                         handler_schema => NULL,
   8                         handler_module => NULL,
   9                         enable => TRUE,
  10                         statement_types=> 'INSERT,UPDATE');
  11  end;
  12  /

PL/SQL procedure successfully completed.
```

BLAKE issues the same update as before, including the rollback statement.

```
blake@KNOX10> update SCOTT.EMP set sal = 5000 where empno=7698;

1 row updated.
```

```
blake@KNOX10> -- cover trail
blake@KNOX10> rollback;

Rollback complete.
```

Querying the audit trail, we see quite a bit of information relevant to auditing.

```
system@KNOX10> select db_user, statement_type action,
  2      object_schema schema, object_name object,
  3      to_char(timestamp, 'Mon-DD-YYYY HH24:MI:SS') Time,
  4      SQL_TEXT
  5      FROM sys.dba_fga_audit_trail;

DB_USE ACTION  SCHEMA OBJE TIME                  SQL_TEXT
-------------------------------------------------------------------
BLAKE  UPDATE  SCOTT  EMP  Oct-03-2003 18:58:36 update SCOTT.EMP
set sal = 5000 where empno=7698
```

Note that, just as in an autonomous transaction example, the auditing captured the action even though the user issued a rollback. The only thing our trigger captured that this audit did not was the new and old values. If auditing captured new and old values, the audit logs would probably fill up in a matter of minutes. In order to get this information from auditing, the audit records would have to be combined with the REDO LOGS that captured the new and old values.

There are many benefits to built-in auditing. First, no coding is required. Second, this mode of auditing is less error-prone (using our equivalent trigger example, someone may, for example, disable the trigger for debugging and then forget to re-enable it). Finally, although not implemented in this example, FGA allows an event handler to be called, which means that, as with our earlier triggers example, we could raise an alert and send an email on the occurrence of any suspicious activity.

Logon Triggers: The First Line of Defense

We briefly introduced logon triggers in Chapter 6, and we'll revisit them here in more detail because they are one of the most interesting types of trigger from a security perspective. One of the greatest virtues of login triggers is, again, that they can be created or removed transparently to any application that is accessing the database. It has many uses in the area of security and we will explore some of the most popular.

Facilitating Security

Login triggers are commonly used as a convenient means of initializing or setting some values in the database. From a security perspective, login triggers gained much of their popularity by allowing developers the opportunity to set an Application Context that could be used elsewhere. The Oracle database allows users to create application contexts. These user-defined application contexts are name-value pairs, held in memory that can be set for individual database sessions. The application context can only be manipulated by a single PL/SQL program that is specified when you create the application context. We can have different users accessing an application context, each with values distinct to their session. We can then use this information in audit trails (or to impose specific access control for each session). Typically, at login, a database login trigger executes and sets the application context for the user by calling the DBMS_SESSION.SET_CONTEXT procedure. This procedure allows us to set various bits of information about the user, including his or her name, the application name, and so on.

Oracle also provides a default application context. It has the namespace of USERENV. Most attribute values are automatically set by the database. We'll use one that is not. In our example, we'll use this default Application Context, which has an attribute called the CLIENT_IDENTIFIER. On logon, we will set some environmental information into the CLIENT_IDENTIFIER via the DBMS_SESSION.SET_IDENTIFIER procedure.

```
DBMS_SESSION.SET_IDENTIFIER ( client_id VARCHAR2);
```

The procedure takes a VARCHAR2 string and has no default value. It can be accessed at anytime using the SYS_CONTEXT function.

```
SYS_CONTEXT('userenv', 'client_identifier')
```

The CLIENT_IDENTIFIER is logged in the audit trails so, in this way, we can augment the auditing capabilities of the database. In this example, our login trigger will add the IP address and the client's program to the CLIENT_IDENTIFIER:

```
sys@NH101> create or replace trigger set_client_id
  2  after logon on database
  3  DECLARE
  4  l_module v$session.module%type;
  5  BEGIN
  6    select upper(module) into l_module
  7      from v$process a, v$session b
  8    where a.addr = b.paddr
  9      and b.audsid = userenv('sessionid');
```

```
10      dbms_session.set_identifier(sys_context('userenv','ip_address')
11                                  ||':' ||
12                                  nvl(l_module,'No Module Specified'));
13  END;
14  /
```

```
Trigger created.
```

The trigger is created by SYS because it queries protected views that are available to SYS or to the DBA role. Because the trigger is created with definer rights, the DBA role is disabled, so SYSTEM could not create this trigger unless SYS has granted the SELECT privileges to SYSTEM directly.

> **CAUTION**   Both the IP Address and client program can be spoofed by a professional hacker. This does not mean this technique is invalid, only that it could be subverted by a determined and skilled attacker (as can practically everything else).

Next, we add a FGA policy to capture activity on the EMP table. FGA is being used because we will look at the SQL_TEXT column in the audit trail, which is not available in standard auditing in Oracle 9*i*. Auditing is generally performed by a privileged account, so the following example is done via the SYSTEM user.

```
system@NH101> begin
  2      DBMS_FGA.ADD_POLICY(object_schema => 'SCOTT',
  3                          object_name=>'EMP',
  4                          policy_name => 'EMP_TRIG_AUD',
  5                          audit_condition => '1=1',
  6                          audit_column => NULL,
  7                          handler_schema => NULL,
  8                          handler_module => NULL,
  9                          enable => TRUE,
 10                          statement_types=> 'SELECT,INSERT,UPDATE,DELETE');
 11  end;
 12  /
```

```
PL/SQL procedure successfully completed.
```

The EMP table was then queried three times through three different programs from three different machines, after which we query the audit trail. We'll use Tom

Kyte's PRINT_TABLE utility function, which runs with invokers rights, to format our output.

```
system@NITEHAWK> declare
  2    l_aud_str varchar2(256);
  3    begin
  4      l_aud_str := 'select db_user, client_id, ' ||
  5        'userhost, substr(sql_text,1,50) SQL, '||
  6        'timestamp day, to_char(timestamp,''HH24:MI:SS'') time ' ||
  7        'from sys.dba_fga_audit_trail ' ||
  8        'where object_schema = ''SCOTT'' and ' ||
  9        'object_name = ''EMP''';
 10      print_table(l_aud_str);
 11    end;
 12    /
DB_USER                          : SCOTT
CLIENT_ID                        : 141.144.98.80:EXCEL.EXE
USERHOST                         : US-ORACLE\DKNOX-PC
SQL                              : SELECT EMP.EMPNO, EMP.ENAME, EMP.JOB, EMP.MGR,
EMP
DAY                              : 09-NOV-03
TIME                             : 14:57:52
-----------------
DB_USER                          : SCOTT
CLIENT_ID                        : 127.0.0.1:SQLPLUS@NIGHTHAWK (TNS V1-V3)
USERHOST                         : nighthawk
SQL                              : select ename from emp order by sal desc
DAY                              : 09-NOV-03
TIME                             : 14:57:31
-----------------
DB_USER                          : SCOTT
CLIENT_ID                        : 141.144.98.80:TOAD.EXE
USERHOST                         : US-ORACLE\DKNOX-PC
SQL                              : SELECT rowid, "SCOTT"."EMP".* FROM
"SCOTT"."EMP"

DAY                              : 09-NOV-03
TIME                             : 14:57:44
-----------------

PL/SQL procedure successfully completed.
```

The query results tell us not only who executed the query, but also when, how, and from where. Note that the ability to audit on INSERT, UPDATE, and DELETE from within FGA is new to Oracle Database 10*g*. The audit trail might help in determining if an "incident" was due to an application blunder, a user blunder, or a conscious and intentional hack.

Bear in mind that because the DBMS_SESSION package is granted to PUBLIC, there is a risk that a user could reset the Client Identifier. You can guard against this possibility by adhering to the least-privilege principle and wrapping your source code, as we will discuss shortly.

Failing Logins

If you have ever written a logon trigger, you may already be painfully aware of this first point: *If the logon trigger fails, the user cannot log in.* This is consistent with the action of table triggers which, upon failure, roll back the current transaction. The exception to this rule is that users with the DBA role, or SYSDBA, will not be kicked out. Normal, non-DBA users however, will be disconnected.

Although the failure is often due to bad programming or a result of an unexpected condition such as the code calling a procedure that has been dropped, this simple concept can help implement a security capability.

Here is a simple example. We want to ensure that users are not connecting to the database from Excel. We have to check not only for EXCEL.EXE, but also the MSQRY32 program because it assists Excel in setting up the ODBC connection. If a user logs in using Excel, we fail the login trigger, thus kicking them out. The following trigger will not compile unless created by a user with direct privilege grants (that is, not granted via a role) on V$PROCESS, and V$SESSION. For simplicity, this example is run as the SYS user.

```
sys@NH101> create or replace trigger user_logon_module_check
  2  after logon on database
  3  DECLARE
  4  l_module v$session.module%type;
  5  BEGIN
  6    select upper(module) into l_module from v$process a, v$session b
  7      where a.addr = b.paddr
  8      and b.audsid = userenv('sessionid');
  9    IF ( l_module = 'EXCEL.EXE' OR
 10         l_module = 'MSQRY32.EXE') THEN
 11      raise_application_error(-20001,'Unauthorized Application');
 12    END IF;
 13  END;
 14  /

Trigger created.
```

An attempted login with Excel produces an error. The user can, however, connect through other applications such as SQL*Plus. Due to the transparency of logon triggers, they become the natural method for initializing the Client Identifer and user-defined Application Contexts.

Protecting the Source

When you compile PL/SQL in the database, the database stores both the source code and the compiled code or object code. The stored source code can be used in two ways:

- To recompile your code should it become invalidated

- To extract the source code to see what the execution code is doing

The second point can be advantageous in fixing the code as well as verifying the code. However, there are many reasons why you would not want someone to see your source code. Intellectual property rights and proprietary information are among the most important. Having your code fall into the hands of a competitor could be devastating. It could also neutralize your value to an organization when they realize how your business or security algorithms are implemented!

Other times, you may simply want to prevent people from manipulating your code. Although their intentions may be good, they can (and often do) break the code and then call for support claiming, "It just broke."

Of course, this issue becomes critical if the PL/SQL performs some security-specific tasks. Most would agree that access to the source code would help someone figure out what your code is doing, thus allowing them better ways to subvert or bypass it.

There are several ways to protect the PL/SQL code. First and foremost, the database prevents users from viewing source code that they don't have permission to execute. The problem is that if a user is given EXECUTE privileges, he or she can query the ALL_SOURCE view to get the source code for procedures, and function. Given this, let's now discuss how to obfuscate the PL/SQL code to prevent this from happening.

Viewing the Source of Procedures and Functions

The first area of concern is procedures and functions. If a user has EXECUTE privileges on a procedure or function, he or she can look at the *entire* source code for that procedure or function. This is different than packages because EXECUTE privileges for packages allow the user only to see the package specification.

The following example highlights the risks. A simple procedure is created in one schema and EXECUTE privileges are granted to another user.

```
scott@KNOX10> create or replace procedure MY_PROC
  2     as
  3     v_local_var varchar2(30) := 'This is a secret string';
  4     begin
  5             -- here is the source code.  it is
  6             -- beneficial if users can't see the source code.
  7      null;  -- this is the sensitive part
  8     end;
  9  /

Procedure created.

scott@KNOX10> grant execute on my_proc to blake;

Grant succeeded.
```

Connecting as BLAKE, we see that not only can he successfully execute the procedure, he can query the source of the procedure from the data dictionary.

```
blake@KNOX10> exec scott.my_proc

PL/SQL procedure successfully completed.

blake@KNOX10> col text format a65
blake@KNOX10> select text from all_source where name='MY_PROC' order by line;

TEXT
-----------------------------------------------------------------
procedure MY_PROC
  as
  v_local_var varchar2(30) := 'This is a secret string';
  begin
          -- here is the source code.  it is
          -- beneficial if users can't see the source code.
   null;  -- this is the sensitive part
  end;

8 rows selected.
```

As you can see, careful attention must be paid to what information is available within the procedures and functions. Keep in mind also that comments in your code, although helpful and generally encouraged, may give away too much information if it is handling sensitive data.

Wrapping the Code

One simple solution to the problem is to wrap the call to the procedure that does the secret work with another procedure to which the user has access. In this example, the contents of MY_SECRET_PROC are to be protected. The code is secured, or wrapped, by the MY_PROC procedure. MY_PROC simply delegates its call to MY_SECRET_PROC.

```
scott@KNOX10> create or replace procedure MY_SECRET_PROC
  2     as
  3     v_local_var varchar2(30) := 'This is a secret string';
  4     begin
  5             -- here is the source code.  it is
  6             -- beneficial if users can't see the source code.
  7      null;  -- this is the sensitive part
  8     end;
  9  /

Procedure created.

scott@KNOX10>
scott@KNOX10> create or replace procedure MY_PROC
  2     as
  3     begin
  4      MY_SECRET_PROC;  -- call the real code
  5     end;
  6  /

Procedure created.
```

The procedure MY_PROC is created using the definer rights mode in order to prevent the executing user from seeing the source of the code that we're trying to hide. BLAKE executes the secret procedure via MY_PRO.

```
blake@KNOX10> exec scott.my_proc

PL/SQL procedure successfully completed.
```

Because he can execute, he can also view the source.

```
blake@KNOX10> col text format a65
blake@KNOX10> select text from all_source where name='MY_PROC' order by line;

TEXT
-----------------------------------------------------------------
procedure MY_PROC
  as
  begin
   MY_SECRET_PROC;   -- call the real code
  end;

5 rows selected.
```

However, he is no longer able to see sensitive information and the source of MY_SECRET_PROC is protected.

```
blake@KNOX10> select text from all_source where name='MY_SECRET_PROC' order by
line;

no rows selected
```

An alternative to this wrapping technique would be to create the procedure as part of a package. In this technique, users with EXECUTE privileges on the package would not be able to view the implementation. With respect to wrapping, there are two important things to note.

- It does not hide the code from everyone. If you are concerned about intellectual or proprietary rights, then this will not solve your issues.

- There is a performance overhead in having procedures call procedures. It takes up more memory and more CPU.

Package Source

As discussed earlier, packages are composed of two parts: the package specification and the package body. The package specification, or package header as it's sometimes called, defines what is publicly available for people when they execute or describe the PL/SQL package. Anything not listed in the header is considered private. Private procedures, functions, and variables cannot be executed or referenced.

Users with execute privileges on the packages can query the data dictionary for the package source. The big difference here is that you do not get source for the package body. This is critical and helps to maintain a secure environment. The one exception is for users with the EXECUTE ANY PROCEDURE privilege.

An often-used technique that helps ensure security is obfuscating the names of procedures, packages, functions, parameters, and variables. Although this technique is less effective than other practices, it may still be desirable in scenarios where you know that people will have access to the source code and you are concerned that if they can examine the set of APIs, the inner-workings will be divulged. I have even known of cases where the names and comments were intentionally incorrect and misleading so as to push people in the wrong direction.

This method should only be considered after employing all other good security practices such as least privilege, good modeling, and so on. The problem with this technique is that code maintenance becomes difficult for anyone other than the original developer.

PL/SQL Wrap Utility

Oracle recognized the challenge of securing the source a long time ago and provided a utility function called WRAP. The function quite simply obfuscates (not wraps) your code by converting it into (what appears to be) garbage. However, the database can still read this obfuscated code, and it will be able to compile and execute it. Upon viewing the source from the data dictionary, your users will probably not be able to discover what the code actually does.

The Oracle documentation, PL/SQL User's Guide and Reference 9.2, lists the following limitations:

> *"String literals, number literals, and names of variables, tables, and columns remain in plain text within the wrapped file. Wrapping a procedure helps to hide the algorithm and prevent reverse-engineering, but it is not a way to hide passwords or table names that you want to be secret."*

This means that certain tasks may still prove challenging. Even though the code is obfuscated (not to be confused with the obfuscation toolkit which really does encryption), string literals are quite common. For example, let's look at the MY_PROC code. Originally, the code will be loaded from a plain text SQL file.

```
scott@KNOX10> @my_proc_wrap_demo.sql

Procedure created.
```

Viewing the source as the privileged owner shows us everything.

```
scott@KNOX10> select text from user_source where name='MY_PROC' order by line;

TEXT
-----------------------------------------------------------------

procedure MY_PROC
  as
  v_local_var varchar2(30) := 'This is a secret string';
  begin
          -- here is the source code.  it is
          -- beneficial if users can't see the source code.
    null;  -- this is the sensitive part
  end;

8 rows selected.
```

To hide this, we use the aforementioned command-line tool from Oracle, WRAP. It takes the input file we used and creates an obfuscated output file. We will do this twice; first with Oracle 9*i*, and then with Oracle 10*g*.

```
C:> wrap iname=my_proc_wrap_demo.sql

PL/SQL Wrapper: Release 9.2.0.4.0- Production on Mon Oct 06 19:00:51 2003

Copyright (c) Oracle Corporation 1993, 2001.  All Rights Reserved.

Processing my_proc_wrap_demo.sql to my_proc_wrap_demo.plb
```

The output file is created automatically. You can specify an output filename by using ONAME=<OUTPUT FILENAME>. Next, we'll load the code and view it again to see how well this procedure hid our code.

```
scott@KNOX10> @my_proc_wrap_demo.plb

Procedure created.

scott@KNOX10> select text from user_source where name='MY_PROC' order by line;

TEXT
------------------------------------------

procedure MY_PROC wrapped
0
abcd
```

```
abcd
abcd
abcd
abcd
abcd
abcd
abcd
abcd
abcd
abcd
abcd
abcd
abcd
abcd
3
7
9200000
1
4
0
5
2 :e:
1MY_PROC:
1V_LOCAL_VAR:
1VARCHAR2:
130:
1This is a secret string:
0

0
0
17
2
0 9a b4 55 6a a3 a0 51
a5 1c 6e 81 b0 4f b7 a4
b1 11 68 4f 1d 17 b5
17
2
0 3 17 18 1c 3e 24 28
2b 2c 34 39 23 20 45 47
4b 4d 59 5d 5f 60 69
17
2
0 b 0 :2 1 3 f 18 17
```

```
f  1f  f  3  4  :2  3  :7  1
17
4
0  1  0  :2  1
:8  3  7  :2  4  :7  1

6b
4
:3  0  1  :a  0  12
1  :8  0  2  :2  0
12  1  3  :3  0
e  0  5  3
:3  0  4  :2  0  3
6  8  :6  0  5
:4  0  c  9  a
10  0  2  :6  0
7  11  :3  0  11
9  11  10  e
f  :6  0  12  :2  0
1  3  11  15
:3  0  14  12  16
:8  0
b
4
:3  0  1  7  1
5  1  d  1
b
1
4
0
15
0
1
14
1
2
0  0  0  0  0  0  0
0  0  0  0  0  0  0
0  0  0  0
5  1  0
1  0  1
0
```

```
1 row selected.
```

Interesting that there is only one row returned. You can in fact see the VAR-CHAR2 string. This can be bad, not only for variables, but also when you are using dynamic SQL. As the documentation states, you can also see the names of other procedures, and functions, and tables. This is fixed in Oracle Database 10g, as shown in the following example.

```
C:>wrap iname=my_proc_wrap_demo.sql

PL/SQL Wrapper: Release 10.1.0.1.0- Beta on Mon Oct 06 19:05:00 2003

Copyright (c) 1993, 2003, Oracle.  All rights reserved.

Processing my_proc_wrap_demo.sql to my_proc_wrap_demo.plb
```

Loading and querying the source table shows the following:

```
scott@KNOX10> @my_proc_wrap_demo.plb

Procedure created.

scott@KNOX10> select text from user_source where name='MY_PROC' order by line;

TEXT
-----------------------------

procedure MY_PROC wrapped
a000000
b2
abcd
abcd
abcd
abcd
abcd
abcd
abcd
abcd
abcd
abcd
abcd
abcd
abcd
abcd
abcd
```

```
abcd
7
80 aa
RcGafTHY40C+bHa3WU170KbmIFMwg5nnm7+fMr2ywFyl8F8opsBTjo521jeiVDTQnQOMrs91
C8jhL9oSVzmI3gT9EcVUMcVNB5GRb9WmzFHmUifAzCfO5lKhzMmHRUUqaYy3CpiwLMhA+yHo
DO3QOCp1KfzB4Nempi4EHPM=
```

```
1 row selected.
```

The string is now hidden! The PL/SQL wrap is a great utility because it hides the code from the prying eyes of nefarious users. You should note that if you need to modify the source, you have to do it with the original source, rewrap it, and then reload the wrapped version into the database.

Summary

The ultimate success or failure of an application may well reside in whether it is compromised. It does not matter how quick the application performs, how easy it is to use, or how much value it provides to key decision makers. If it provides all these capabilities to a hacker, the application may be considered a failure.

Security begins with the design. It includes understanding the relationship among users, PL/SQL, and database objects. Adhering to certain basic security tenets such as practicing the least privilege principle also helps to ensure a sound security environment. Guarding access to PL/SQL has two facets. First is the privilege to execute. Second, and just as important, is guarding the code.

Combining security with the other parts of this book will enable you to build successful PL/SQL regardless of the evaluating criteria.

CHAPTER 9

Web Packages

DEVELOPERS CAN CHOOSE BETWEEN Java, Active Server Pages, PHP, Perl, and many other technologies to create HTML applications. More often than not, these HTML applications present dynamic content retrieved from a database. And what better way to present dynamic content from a database than from directly within a database? This is precisely what Oracle provides via the PL/SQL Web Toolkit. The PL/SQL Web Toolkit is a set of sophisticated PL/SQL packages that can be used to render HTML pages in real-time.

In this chapter, we will cover the following topics:

- Concise history and architecture of the PL/SQL Web Toolkit

- Basic functionality of the PL/SQL Web Toolkit

- Exploiting cookies in a Web application

- Uploading files from a browser and retrieving them in an application

- Managing a table through a Web application

- Initiating HTTP requests from the database

PL/SQL Web Toolkit Basics

The PL/SQL Web Toolkit began in the early 1990s when an Oracle consultant created a way to generate dynamic Web pages directly from an Oracle database. Oracle took this early work and released it as a product called the Oracle Web Agent. Through subsequent product iterations, including Oracle Web Server 2.x, Web Application Server 3.x, Oracle Application Server 4.x, Oracle9*i* Application Server, and the Oracle Application Server 10*g*, the goals and architecture of the PL/SQL Web Toolkit have remained consistent.

In practical terms, the fundamental purpose of the PL/SQL Web Toolkit is to easily generate dynamic content from an Oracle database. It is used in conjunction with the Oracle HTTP Server and an HTTP Server component, called MOD_PLSQL, which invokes stored procedures in an Oracle database and streams the results back to the requesting client. Whereas scripting technologies like

Active Server Pages, PHP, and Perl will retrieve data from an Oracle database and perform the page composition in a separate engine, the PL/SQL Web Toolkit is unique in that you can perform data access and page composition entirely within the Oracle database.

The Oracle HTTP Server is bundled with the Oracle 9*i* Database and Oracle Database 10*g*, and also with Oracle 9*i* Application Server and Oracle Application Server 10*g*.

Architecture

The architecture associated with the creation of Web pages via the PL/SQL Web Toolkit is refreshingly simple, as shown in Figure 9-1.

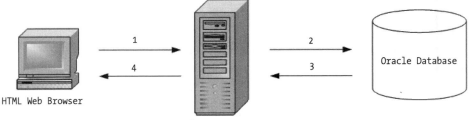

Figure 9-1. Architecture associated with the PL/SQL Web Toolkit

The process of producing Web pages via the PL/SQL Web Toolkit can be described as follows:

1. A client makes a request to the Oracle HTTP Server from its Web browser

2. The Oracle HTTP Server invokes a stored procedure in an Oracle database on behalf of the client

3. The stored procedure(s) populate an internal buffer with HTML and other data

4. The Oracle HTTP Server streams the results of the internal buffer back to the client, whereby the client's Web browser will render the page

How does the Oracle HTTP Server know a request is for a specific stored procedure and which Oracle database contains it? Oracle HTTP Server and Oracle Application Server, which both use the Apache HTTP Server as their foundation, employ an Apache module called **MOD_PLSQL** to perform the processing between the HTTP Server and an Oracle database.

> **NOTE** In previous versions of the Toolkit, when it was part of the Oracle Web Server product, a dedicated module was bound to the HTTP Server and was called a Web agent or a Web "cartridge."

The `MOD_PLSQL` module can determine which database to connect to and how to connect to it via a Database Authentication Descriptor (DAD). The DAD is used to maintain configuration information, including the database username and password to connect as, the database TNS connect string, the type of authentication to perform (Basic Database, Single Signon, and so on), PL/SQL session state management, settings for a document upload/download table, and more.

Once a request is made from the `MOD_PLSQL` module to a database, an in-memory buffer is initialized, execution of the procedure populates the buffer with data, and at the end of the request, the `MOD_PLSQL` module reads the contents of the buffer and streams it back to the requesting client.

An important implication of this architecture is that data *does not* begin streaming back to the client until the request is complete. Thus, if you invoke a stored procedure that takes two wall-clock minutes to execute and returns 4MB of data, the stream of data from `MOD_PLSQL` back to the requesting client will not even commence until the in-memory buffer is filled with all 4MB of data and the server request is completed. This isn't necessarily bad, but it is clearly inefficient. Hopefully, this is something that will be addressed in future versions of `MOD_PLSQL`.

Configuring DADs

Configuration of a DAD can be handled via a browser interface to the Oracle HTTP Server in the Oracle Database and Oracle Application Server, or it can be performed manually by editing the Oracle HTTP Server configuration files for `MOD_PLSQL`. The names, locations, and syntax of these files are different between the Oracle HTTP Server bundled with the Oracle Application Server and the one bundled with the Oracle database. Complete instructions can be found in the *Oracle HTTP Server Administration Guide*.

The syntax for a typical request using mod_plsql is

```
http://<host>:<port>/pls/<DAD>/[<schema>.]<PL/SQL_procedure>
```

The `PLS` component of the request signals the Oracle HTTP Server that the request should be handled by the `MOD_PLSQL` module. The information corresponding to the named DAD will then be read and a connection will be established to the database using the specified database username and password. The PL/SQL procedure will then be executed, the results will be streamed back to the requesting client, and the HTTP connection with the client will be terminated.

Summary of Packages

The PL/SQL Web Toolkit is comprised of the following PL/SQL packages:

- **HTP:** Hypertext procedures: write data and HTML tags to the output buffer

- **HTF:** Hypertext functions: same specification as the htp procedures, but instead of writing to the output buffer, it returns the value as the result of the function

- **OWA_COOKIE:** HTTP cookie utilities: easily send and retrieve cookies from the requesting client

- **OWA_IMAGE:** HTML imagemap management: facilitates creation and use of an HTML imagemap

- **OWA_OPT_LOCK:** Optimistic locking utilities: enables lost update detection and prevention in a Web application

- **OWA_PATTERN:** String pattern utilities: provides support for regular expressions and other string matching functions

- **OWA_SEC:** Security facilities: enables customized authentication

- **OWA_TEXT:** Various string utilities: especially useful when submitting an arbitrary number of elements in an HTML form

- **OWA_UTIL:** General utilities: includes functions to retrieve values from the CGI environment as well as send values in the HTTP header

Of these packages, in this chapter we will explore HTP, HTF, OWA_COOKIE, and OWA_UTIL.

If you installed the PL/SQL Web Toolkit as part of the Oracle HTTP Server installation of the Oracle9*i* database, the source package specifications and bodies can be found in the directory: $ORACLE_HOME/APACHE/MODPLSQL/OWA. When the PL/SQL Web Toolkit is installed, it is typically created in the SYS schema. Additionally, EXECUTE privilege is granted to PUBLIC, and public synonyms are created for each one of the packages in the PL/SQL Web Toolkit.

It is very important that no more than one instance of the PL/SQL Web Toolkit package exists in any given database instance. Due to the implementation and architecture of the Toolkit, incorrect results can occur with more than one set of the Toolkit packages in an instance.

With the Toolkit installed, any database user who has the privilege to create procedures and packages can perform all the examples in this chapter. The demonstration database user, SCOTT, typically included in most Oracle database installations, is more than sufficient to perform all of the examples.

*Testing the Toolkit from SQL*Plus*

Before we begin exploring some of the basic functionality of the PL/SQL Web Toolkit, you need to be aware of a couple of procedures that will be used extensively throughout the examples in this chapter. The first procedure is OWA_UTIL.SHOWPAGE. Remember that MOD_PLSQL typically operates through the Oracle HTTP Server listener and directly streams data back to the requesting client. Fortunately, OWA_UTIL.SHOWPAGE is invaluable in both demonstrating and debugging functionality of the Web Toolkit because it permits us to dump the in-memory buffer utilized by the Web Toolkit and display the contents via SQL*Plus. This procedure displays the buffer contents via DBMS_OUTPUT and thus, you must first specify SET SERVEROUTPUT ON in order to display the output. The OWA_UTIL.SHOWPAGE procedure takes no arguments.

One other PL/SQL package you need to be aware of is OWA. The OWA PL/SQL package is used to maintain the internal memory buffer from which MOD_PLSQL reads. However, prior to use, we must first initialize the Common Gateway Interface (CGI) environment variables for the package. The Oracle HTTP Server and MOD_PLSQL automatically initialize the CGI environment for every request, so as an end developer, you will almost never invoke the methods of this package directly. However, when invoking the PL/SQL Web packages manually from SQL*Plus, we must perform this initialization ourselves. The following OWAINIT procedure will do the trick (and the examples in this chapter rely on this procedure being created in the database):

```
create or replace procedure owainit
as
    l_cgivar_name owa.vc_arr;
    l_cgivar_val  owa.vc_arr;
begin
    htp.init;
    l_cgivar_name(1) := 'REQUEST_PROTOCOL';
    l_cgivar_val(1)  := 'HTTP';
    owa.init_cgi_env(
        num_params => 1,
        param_name => l_cgivar_name,
        param_val  => l_cgivar_val );
end;
```

Additionally, this procedure initializes the environment to set the client request protocol to HTTP. We'll see some interesting behavior from that shortly.

If for some reason you fail to initialize the CGI environment for the OWA PL/SQL package, you may get an error similar to

```
SQL> exec htp.p('Oracle');
BEGIN htp.p('Oracle'); END;

*
ERROR at line 1:
ORA-06502: PL/SQL: numeric or value error
ORA-06512: at "SYS.OWA_UTIL", line 323
ORA-06512: at "SYS.HTP", line 860
ORA-06512: at "SYS.HTP", line 975
ORA-06512: at "SYS.HTP", line 993
ORA-06512: at line 1
```

The HTP and HTF Packages

The primary purpose of the HTP procedures and HTF functions contained in these packages is to directly write data to the Web Toolkit's buffer. The following HTP.P procedure is used to write the value of the first argument to the internal buffer and terminate the value with a newline character, \N.

```
SQL> set serveroutput on
SQL> exec owainit;

PL/SQL procedure successfully completed.

SQL> begin
  2       htp.p('Ohio State');
  3       htp.p('Buckeyes');
  4   end;
  5   /
PL/SQL procedure successfully completed.

SQL> exec owa_util.showpage;
Content-type: text/html
Content-length: 20
```

```
Ohio State
Buckeyes

PL/SQL procedure successfully completed.
```

After initializing our environment, we made two calls to HTP.P to print the contents of the argument into the output buffer. We then viewed the results as a Web browser would, but via SQL*Plus, using the OWA_UTIL.SHOWPAGE procedure. The first line of the output is simply the output MIME type. Because we didn't specify a MIME type, the default, TEXT/HTML, was generated. The next line contains the HTTP content-length of the output, followed by the strings we printed.

> **NOTE** In versions of the Web Server prior to release of the Oracle HTTP Server, the Content-type and Content-length lines are generated and delivered by the Web server itself and not from within the PL/SQL Web Toolkit. Thus, you would not see these lines when executing these examples from SQL*Plus.

The HTP and HTF PL/SQL packages contain a large variety of different methods to generate HTML markup as part of the output. Methods are provided for HTML table creation and manipulation, text formatting, frame generation, lists, forms, image references, anchors, and much more.

For the most part, there are higher-level procedures in the HTP and HTF packages for each type of HTML tag. For example, the following listing shows three anonymous PL/SQL blocks that generate the equivalent HTML output (remember that white space is irrelevant in HTML).

```
-- Example 1
begin
    htp.tableOpen;
    htp.tableRowOpen;
    htp.tableHeader( cvalue => 'TheHeader', calign => 'left' );
    htp.tableRowClose;
    htp.tableRowOpen;
    htp.tableData( cvalue => 'DataVal' );
    htp.tableRowClose;
    htp.tableClose;
end;
/
exec owa_util.showpage;
```

```
-- Example 2
declare
    l_str varchar2(32000);
begin
    l_str := '<TABLE>';
    l_str := l_str || '<TR>';
    l_str := l_str || '<TH ALIGN="left">TheHeader</TH>';
    l_str := l_str || '</TR>';
    l_str := l_str || '<TR>';
    l_str := l_str || '<TD>DataVal</TD>';
    l_str := l_str || '</TR>';
    l_str := l_str || '</TABLE>';
    htp.p( l_str );
end;
/
exec owa_util.showpage;

-- Example 3
begin
    htp.p('<TABLE><TR><TH ALIGN="left">TheHeader</TH></TR>');
    htp.p('<TR><TD>DataVal</TD></TR></TABLE>');
end;
/
exec owa_util.showpage;
```

You may be wondering why you would want to use the methods of the HTP and HTF packages to generate HTML. Isn't it more efficient to invoke one PL/SQL procedure rather than multiple procedures to generate the same result? Yes. But the differences in execution time between the two are nominal, even when invoked thousands of times for a single MOD_PLSQL request. The major benefit of using the HTP and HTF methods is one of readability, and implicitly, maintainability. If we wanted to change the data value for the table data entry in the examples just shown, it would be quite straightforward to modify the first example, and rather difficult to modify the third example. This point is often overlooked but it far outweighs the negligible performance differences.

Using Environment Variables

In a Web application, it is often useful to employ environment variables. Historically, these variables are classified as CGI environment variables and are used to pass information from a Web server to a server-side CGI script.

Using the PL/SQL Web Toolkit and MOD_PLSQL, the standard CGI 1.1 environment variables are directly accessible from within a PL/SQL program unit (with the exception of QUERY_STRING). The function to fetch a specific CGI environment variable is

```
owa_util.get_cgi_env( param_name in varchar2 ) return varchar2
```

The function to print a listing of all CGI environment variables is

```
owa_util.print_cgi_env return varchar2
```

Therefore, a simple PRINTENV procedure, which displays all CGI environment variables, would look as follows:

```
SQL> create or replace procedure printenv
  2  as
  3  begin
  4      owa_util.print_cgi_env;
  5  end;
  6  /

Procedure created.
```

The normal CGI environment variables are not initialized when invoking the packages directly from SQL*Plus. Therefore, the PRINTENV procedure will display two very different results when invoked from SQL*Plus versus a Web browser. Here, we call the procedure directly from SQL*Plus.

```
SQL> exec owainit;

PL/SQL procedure successfully completed.

SQL> exec printenv;

PL/SQL procedure successfully completed.

SQL> exec owa_util.showpage;
REQUEST_PROTOCOL = HTTP<BR>

PL/SQL procedure successfully completed.
```

This presents only the REQUEST_PROTOCOL CGI environment variable. Not coincidentally, this is the same environment variable that is manually set in the call to the procedure OWAINIT, which was defined earlier.

Invoking this same procedure through a Web browser and connecting via a DAD as database user SCOTT produces a dramatically different result.

```
REMOTE_USER = scott
WEB_AUTHENT_PREFIX =
DAD_NAME = scott_dad
DOC_ACCESS_PATH =
DOCUMENT_TABLE =
PATH_INFO = /printenv
SCRIPT_NAME = /pls/scott_dad
PATH_ALIAS =
REQUEST_CHARSET = WE8MSWIN1252
REQUEST_IANA_CHARSET = WINDOWS-1252
SCRIPT_PREFIX = /pls
PLSQL_GATEWAY = WebDb
GATEWAY_IVERSION = 2
SERVER_SOFTWARE = Oracle HTTP Server Powered by Apache/1.3.22 (Win32) PHP/4.2.3
mod_plsql/3.0.9.8.3b mod_ssl/2.8.5 OpenSSL/0.9.6b mod_fastcgi/2.2.12
mod_oprocmgr/1.0 mod_perl/1.25
GATEWAY_INTERFACE = CGI/1.1
SERVER_PORT = 80
SERVER_NAME = jkallman-home
REQUEST_METHOD = GET
REMOTE_ADDR = 127.0.0.1
SERVER_PROTOCOL = HTTP/1.1
REQUEST_PROTOCOL = HTTP
HTTP_USER_AGENT = Mozilla/4.0 (compatible; MSIE 6.0; Windows NT 5.1; YComp
5.0.0.0)
HTTP_HOST = 127.0.0.1
HTTP_ACCEPT = image/gif, image/x-xbitmap, image/jpeg, image/pjpeg, */*
HTTP_ACCEPT_ENCODING = gzip, deflate
HTTP_ACCEPT_LANGUAGE = en-us,de;q=0.8,ko;q=0.6,zh;q=0.4,ja;q=0.2
```

Here we can see that the full CGI environment is initialized for every request through MOD_PLSQL. Some of the more interesting environment variables include

- **REMOTE_USER**: The username by which the session is authenticated. In the example just shown, the DAD was configured to always connect as database user SCOTT.

- **REQUEST_METHOD**: The name of the method for the current request, typically either GET or POST.

- **HTTP_USER_AGENT**: Details about the browser client for the current request.

Beyond the normal CGI/1.1 environment variables, there are also a handful of environment variables specific to MOD_PLSQL and the Web Toolkit. They include

- **DAD_NAME**: The name of the DAD being used for the current request.

- **WEB_AUTHENT_PREFIX**: The prefix to append to the current session's username prior to authentication. This would be used if you wanted to configure a class of database users exclusively for Web authentication. If a user authenticated as LELLISON and the Web authentication prefix was set to WEB$, authentication would be attempted against database user WEB$LELLISON.

- **DOCUMENT_TABLE**: The name of the database table where files will be uploaded directly via MOD_PLSQL. Files POSTed via the HTML form element type <INPUT TYPE. = "FILE"> will be stored in a BLOB column in this table. Note that there is the option to also store uploaded documents in a column of type LONG, but it is not recommended to use this deprecated datatype.

- **REQUEST_CHARSET**: The Oracle database character set of the client. In the case of requests through MOD_PLSQL, the database character set is ultimately determined by the configuration of the DAD.

- **REQUEST_IANA_CHARSET**: The formal IANA character set name, as determined from the requesting browser client.

- **REMOTE_ADDR**: The IP address of the client making the current request.

- **HTTP_REFERER**: The Web address from which the current request was obtained. If the user clicks a link from one Web page to a second page, the value of HTTP_REFERER would be the URI of the first page.

The ability to access the CGI environment variables within a PL/SQL procedure can be useful in many situations. We could easily create a basic usage-logging package by accessing and saving the values from the REMOTE_ADDR, REMOTE_USER, and HTTP_USER_AGENT. A user modifying or tampering with the URL could be detected by inspecting the HTTP_REFERER environment variable. All CGI environment variables, including a few Oracle-specific ones, are all easily accessible via the OWA_UTIL.GET_CGI_ENV procedure.

For example, to create a simple logging procedure that can be used anywhere within a PL/SQL program, you first need to create a table to store certain pieces of information, as shown in the following listing:

```
SQL> create table web_log(
  2      log_date     date,
  3      ip_address   varchar2(255),
  4      user_agent   varchar2(4000),
  5      script_name  varchar2(4000),
  6      path_info    varchar2(4000),
  7      http_referer varchar2(4000))
  /
Table created.
```

All that's left to do is create another procedure, LOG_IT, which derives all values from the CGI environment variables and inserts them into the WEB_LOG table as follows:

```
SQL> create or replace procedure log_it
  2   as
  3   begin
  4       insert into web_log(
  5           log_date,
  6           ip_address,
  7           user_agent,
  8           script_name,
  9           path_info,
 10           http_referer )
 11       values(
 12           sysdate,
 13           owa_util.get_cgi_env( 'REMOTE_ADDR' ),
 14           owa_util.get_cgi_env( 'HTTP_USER_AGENT' ),
 15           owa_util.get_cgi_env( 'SCRIPT_NAME' ),
 16           owa_util.get_cgi_env( 'PATH_INFO' ),
 17           owa_util.get_cgi_env( 'HTTP_REFERER' ) );
 18   end;
  /
Procedure created.
```

Remember that the procedure, OWAINIT, initializes the CGI environment but it does not set up any of these environment variables. We can prove this by running the following procedure directly from SQL*Plus:

```
scott@COMM.US.ORACLE.COM> exec owainit;
PL/SQL procedure successfully completed.

scott@COMM.US.ORACLE.COM> exec log_it;
PL/SQL procedure successfully completed.
```

```
SQL>column ip_address    format a15
SQL>column user_agent    format a10 word_wrapped
SQL>column script_name   format a10 word_wrapped
SQL>column path_info     format a10 word_wrapped
SQL>column http_referer format a10 word_wrapped
SQL>set linesize 120
SQL>select * from web_log;


LOG_DATE  IP_ADDRESS       USER_AGENT SCRIPT_NAM PATH_INFO  HTTP_REFER
--------- ---------------- ---------- ---------- ---------- ----------
02-AUG-03
```

Only the date value, determined by SYSDATE, is populated in our logging table. All the other CGI environment variables returned null values when invoked. However, if we invoke the LOG_IT procedure through the Oracle HTTP Server, we'll see much more interesting results. Let's rewrite the PRINTENV procedure so that it calls our LOG_IT procedure as follows:

```
SQL>create or replace procedure printenv as
  2  begin
  3      owa_util.print_cgi_env;
  4      log_it;
  5  end;
  6  /

Procedure created.
```

We then delete all previous rows from the WEB_LOG table, invoke the PRINTENV procedure from a Web browser, and then query the table again as follows:

```
SQL>delete from web_log;
1 row deleted.

SQL>commit;
Commit complete.

--Invoke through Oracle HTTP Server, then query
SQL>select * from web_log;

LOG_DATE  IP_ADDRESS       USER_AGENT SCRIPT_NAM PATH_INFO  HTTP_REFER
--------- ---------------- ---------- ---------- ---------- ----------
02-OCT-03 127.0.0.1        Mozilla/4. /pls/comm  /printenv
                             0
```

```
(compatibl
e; MSIE
6.0;
Windows NT
5.0)
```

Cookies

Most moderately experienced Web application developers understand that cookies are a piece of data read and written during a standard HTTP request and response. They can be used for a variety of purposes, including tracking recent usage by a visitor over an extended period of time, maintaining a unique identifier on a user-by-user basis for the maintenance of session data persistence across multiple HTTP requests, and even to ensure that a user has authority to access a particular Web application or resource. The primary attributes of a cookie are as follows:

- NAME: The name of the cookie.

- VALUE: The value of the cookie.

- EXPIRES: The date of expiration of the cookie. Cookies can be valid for an extended period of time (for example, years). If you want to expire a cookie on demand, this attribute can be set to a date in the past.

- PATH: The path for which the cookie is valid, with a default of the path of the calling document.

- DOMAIN: The domain for which the cookie is valid, with a default value of the domain of the calling document.

- SECURE: The Boolean value that specifies if the transmission of the cookie must be done securely.

Cookie manipulation in the PL/SQL Web Toolkit is performed via the OWA_COOKIE package. There are only two primary methods in this package that you need to become familiar with, namely OWA_COOKIE.GET:

```
owa_cookie.get( name in varchar2 ) return owa_cookie.cookie
```

And OWA_COOKIE.SEND

```
owa_cookie.send(
        name in varchar2,
        value in varchar2,
        expires in date default NULL,
        path in varchar2 default NULL,
        domain in varchar2 default NULL,
     secure in varchar2 default NULL )
```

A cookie can be used to store a scalar value on the requesting client's computer. If you want to store multiple values on a client's computer, you can send multiple cookies or simply encode many values into a single string and use that as your single cookie value.

A cookie can be used for a variety of purposes, from tracking usage of an application to maintaining a session cookie that indicates the current user is authenticated against your application. The following is a simple example:

```
exec owainit;
begin
    owa_util.mime_header('text/html', FALSE);
    owa_cookie.send('NAME','Brutus.Buckeye',sysdate+1);
    owa_util.http_header_close;
    htp.p('Hello world');
end;
```

Executing this example will produce the following output:

```
SQL> exec owa_util.showpage;
Content-type: text/html
Set-Cookie: NAME=Brutus.Buckeye; expires=Sunday, 29-Jun-2003 04:11:52 GMT;
Content-length: 12
Hello world
```

If you created this as a procedure and executed it through MOD_PLSQL via a Web browser, the end user would see only the string HELLO WORLD. However, part of the HTTP header in the request would have been the SET-COOKIE directive. As long as the user is able to accept cookies via a Web browser, a cookie with the name of NAME and the value BRUTUS.BUCKEYE for the default domain and path would have been written to the client's list of cookies.

Note that the MIME header was explicitly overridden in this example and then subsequently closed after the cookie procedure was invoked. As determined by the HTTP protocol, in the PL/SQL Web toolkit all invocations of OWA_COOKIE.GET and OWA_COOKIE.SEND must be made in the context of an HTTP

header. Additionally, the HTTP header should be closed via
OWA_UTIL.HTTP_HEADER_CLOSE before a call to any of the HTP methods.

It is important to note that cookies set in an HTTP request will not be accessible via an immediate GET of the same cookie in the same request. The OWA_COOKIE.GET method can access cookies that are already established on the client, but not within the same request in which they are being set. The values of cookies set via OWA_COOKIE.SEND in the first request would not be accessible with OWA_COOKIE.GET until a second request was made.

Managing Files

Even in the utopian world of HTML Web applications, present-day users still employ a variety of applications in files—from documents created in office productivity applications to source code control. Because of this, many applications must be able to store and manage these files. This is most often accomplished via sharing operating system file systems across a network, but it would be nice to provide this functionality via a simple and lightweight HTML Web application. Fortunately, MOD_PLSQL and the PL/SQL Web Toolkit include easy-to-use facilities to create applications for uploading and downloading files while storing the files directly in an Oracle database.

When configuring DAD settings for MOD_PLSQL, you can specify certain document table settings that will enable you to exploit these upload/download capabilities. The attributes related to document access for MOD_PLSQL are as follows:

- **Document Table:** The name of the table where documents will be uploaded. This table must be accessible to the Oracle database user that MOD_PLSQL will use to connect to the Oracle database. If necessary, this table name can be fully qualified with the schema containing the table.

- **Document Access Path**: A virtual path to be used in combination with the DAD and document name when downloading a file (for example, DOCS).

- **Document Access Procedure**: The PL/SQL procedure to be invoked by MOD_PLSQL when a request is made to download a file using the specific DAD.

- **Extensions to be uploaded as LONG RAW**: The list of file extensions (for example pdf, txt, hqx) that will be stored and retrieved in a column of datatype LONG RAW in the document table. You should never use the deprecated LONG RAW datatype for new applications. The BLOB datatype is a more efficient and feature-rich replacement for LONG RAW.

The document table cannot be just any ordinary table containing a column of type BLOB. The document table *must* contain certain columns of a specific name and of a specific datatype. Additional columns not associated with file upload/download can be added to the document table, but at a minimum, the following columns must exist and have the specified datatype and minimum length:

- **NAME**: varchar2(256) unique not null

- **MIME_TYPE**: mime_type varchar2(128)

- **DOC_SIZE**: number

- **DAD_CHARSET**: varchar2(128)

- **LAST_UPDATED**: date

- **CONTENT_TYPE**: varchar2(128)

- **BLOB_CONTENT**: blob

One of the limitations of the document table architecture in MOD_PLSQL and the PL/SQL Web Toolkit is that one and only one document table can be specified per DAD. Therefore, if your Oracle database contains multiple applications that use the same DAD, you would be forced to use a single document table if you wanted to upload files through MOD_PLSQL. To get around this limitation, you would have to either use a different DAD for each application that requires its own document table (which is an administrative hassle), or provide functionality that would copy the BLOB contents from the DAD's document table to the specific application table.

First, create a document table, MYDOCS, using the DDL.

```
create table mydocs(
    id            number primary key,
    name          varchar2(256) not null,
    mime_type     varchar2(128),
    doc_size      number,
    dad_charset   varchar2(128),
    last_updated  date,
    content_type  varchar2(128),
    blob_content  blob
)
/

create sequence mydocs_seq
```

```
/

create or replace trigger biu_mydocs
    before insert or update on mydocs
    for each row
begin
    if :new.id is null then
        select mydocs_seq.nextval into :new.id from dual;
    end if;
end;
/
```

Next, configure a DAD with MYDOCS as the document table. Then you can easily create a simple Web-based interface to upload documents by using the following two listings.

```
create or replace procedure my_doc_listing( p_name in varchar2 default null )
as
begin
    htp.htmlOpen;
    htp.bodyOpen;
    if p_name is not null then
        htp.bold('Document ' || p_name || ' successfully uploaded!');
    end if;
    htp.tableOpen;
    htp.tableRowOpen;
    htp.tableHeader('Name');
    htp.tableHeader('Size');
    htp.tableRowClose;
    --
    for c1 in (select id, name, doc_size
                  from mydocs
               order by name) loop
        htp.tableRowOpen;
        htp.tableData( c1.name );
        htp.tableData( c1.doc_size );
        htp.tableRowClose;
    end loop;
    --
    htp.tableClose;
    htp.anchor('upload_doc','Upload a new document');
    htp.bodyClose;
    htp.htmlClose;
end;
/
```

Here is the second listing.

```
create or replace procedure upload_doc
as
begin
    htp.htmlOpen;
    htp.bodyOpen;
    htp.formOpen(curl      => 'my_doc_listing',
                 cmethod => 'POST',
                 cenctype => 'multipart/form-data');
    -- No procedure provided in toolkit for file
    htp.p('<input type="file" name="p_name">');         htp.formSubmit;
    htp.formClose;
    htp.anchor('my_doc_listing','Document listing');
    htp.bodyClose;
    htp.htmlClose;
end;
/
```

The procedure MY_DOC_LISTING will generate an HTML table containing the stored name and document size of all documents uploaded to the MYDOCS document table. The procedure UPLOAD_DOC is a simple HTML form to upload a file. On this page, users can select a file from their local file system and upload it directly into the database by clicking the Submit button. Note that the target of the form is the MY_DOC_LISTING procedure, as shown in Figure 9-2.

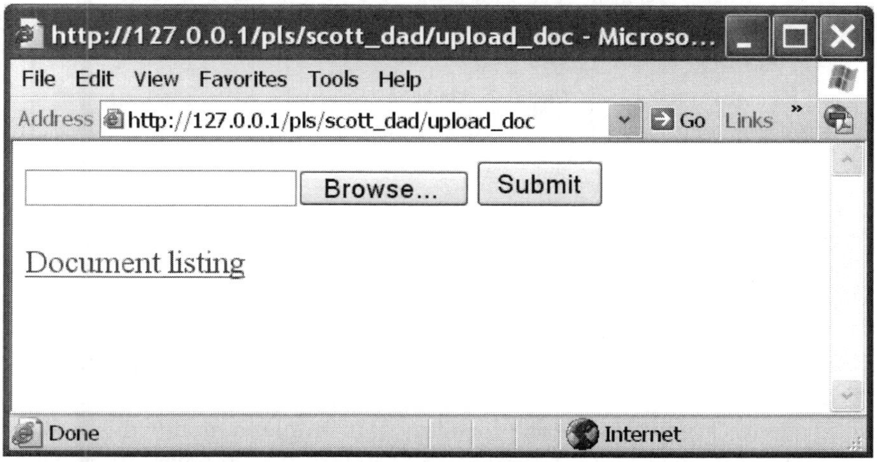

Figure 9-2. Document upload form

A special procedure, WPG_DOCLOAD.DOWNLOAD_FILE, can be used to extend this simple Web interface to also permit downloading of the content in the document table. Some PL/SQL developers implement the download of a file by selecting the content into a local BLOB variable, using UTL_RAW.CAST_TO_VARCHAR2 and HTP.PRN to read the content in chunks, and then spitting it out using the Web Toolkit buffer. There are two reasons why we discourage this approach. First, as we discussed earlier, MOD_PLSQL does not stream data back to the client as the client buffer is filled. In fact, the stream from MOD_PLSQL back to the client doesn't commence until the invocation on the server has finished. Thus, if you are downloading a 1GB file, the user won't be prompted to download until all 1GB of content is populated in the Web Toolkit buffer. The WPG_DOCLOAD.DOWNLOAD_FILE procedure will begin streaming the content immediately. Second, and even more important, there is the potential for character set conversion, especially when operating with content that contains multibyte characters. To successfully transmit binary data regardless of the character set settings for your database or DAD, use the following procedure WPG_DOCLOAD.DOWNLOAD_FILE:

```
create or replace procedure get_file( p_id in number )
as
begin
    for c1 in (select mime_type, blob_content, name
                   from mydocs
                 where id = p_id) loop
        --
        -- Setup the HTTP headers
        --
        owa_util.mime_header( c1.mime_type, FALSE );
        htp.p('Content-length: ' || dbms_lob.getlength( c1.blob_content ));
        htp.p('Content-Disposition: inline ' );
        owa_util.http_header_close;
        -- Then give mod_plsql the BLOB content
        wpg_docload.download_file( c1.blob_content );
        --
        exit;
    end loop;
end;
/
```

Given a document ID, this procedure will emit the stored MIME type in the HTTP header and then immediately stream the content directly back to the requesting client. Given this generic procedure, it is simple to modify the original MY_DOC_LISTING procedure that integrates this download functionality directly into the report. Instead of printing the name of the document in a table cell, we now will generate an HTML anchor for each specific document displayed. This provides an easy mechanism for the user to both see the result listing of all documents and immediately download the document.

```
create or replace procedure my_doc_listing( p_name in varchar2 default null )
as
begin
    htp.htmlOpen;
    htp.bodyOpen;
    if p_name is not null then
        htp.bold('Document ' || p_name || ' successfully uploaded!');
    end if;
    htp.tableOpen;
    htp.tableRowOpen;
    htp.tableHeader('Name');
    htp.tableHeader('Size');
    htp.tableRowClose;
    --
    for c1 in (select id, name, doc_size
                 from mydocs
               order by name) loop
        htp.tableRowOpen;
        htp.tableData( htf.anchor( 'get_file?p_id=' || c1.id, c1.name));
        htp.tableData( c1.doc_size );
        htp.tableRowClose;
    end loop;
    --
    htp.tableClose;
    htp.anchor('upload_doc','Upload a new document');
    htp.bodyClose;
    htp.htmlClose;
end;
/
```

Using just three simple procedures in an Oracle database, we have implemented a poor man's document management system that permits upload and download of content via any Web browser. Keep in mind that this is only an example and is completely devoid of security. Providing a wide-open procedure such as GET_FILE, which can be used to access any document stored in the document table, should be avoided on production systems until other security measures are put into place.

Managing Tables Through the Web

Beyond reading data in Oracle tables and providing reports in a Web application, it's very simple with the PL/SQL Web Toolkit to create a complete set of procedures to create, edit, and delete data as well. Fundamentally, the operations performed are no different than a user issuing INSERT, UPDATE, and DELETE statements from SQL*Plus. But Web-enabling these types of operations makes access to this data much easier.

Let's begin by creating a table to manage information about our favorite stocks and mutual funds as follows:

```
create table my_investments(
     ticker            varchar2(10)    primary key,
     name              varchar2(4000)  not null,
     type              varchar2(20)    not null );
```

Then, like the example in the previous section, we create a simple report.

```
create or replace procedure investment_rpt
as
     l_count number := 0;
begin
     htp.htmlOpen;
     htp.bodyOpen;
     htp.tableOpen;
     htp.tableRowOpen;
     htp.tableHeader('Ticker');
     htp.tableHeader('Name');
     htp.tableHeader('Type');
     htp.tableRowClose;
     --
       -- Display information about each row in the my_investments table
       --
     for c1 in (select ticker, name, type
                   from my_investments
                   order by ticker) loop
         htp.tableRowOpen;
         htp.tableData( c1.ticker );
         htp.tableData( c1.name );
         htp.tableData( c1.type );
         htp.tableRowClose;
         l_count := l_count + 1;
     end loop;
     --
```

```
        htp.tableClose;
        htp.p( l_count || ' rows found');
        htp.bodyClose;
        htp.htmlClose;
end;
/
```

Running this procedure with no rows in the MY_INVESTMENTS table will produce the result shown in Figure 9-3.

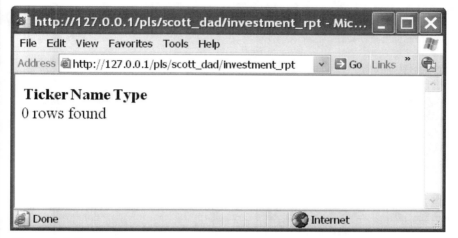

Figure 9-3. Investment report

The next step in the process is to create a procedure that will permit us to
insert a new row into the MY_INVESTMENTS table. To do this we will create an HTML
form with text form fields that will ultimately post the input values back into the
INVESTMENT_RPT procedure.

```
create or replace procedure investment_modify
as
    l_count number := 0;
begin
    htp.htmlOpen;
    htp.bodyOpen;
    --
    -- Open an HTML form which will POST to our main reporting procedure
    --
    htp.formOpen( curl => 'investment_rpt', cmethod => 'POST' );

    htp.tableOpen;
```

```
        --
        -- Generate a text field and label for each column in the table
        --
        htp.tableRowOpen;
        htp.tableData( calign => 'RIGHT', cvalue => 'Ticker:');
        htp.tableData( calign => 'LEFT',
                          cvalue => htf.formText( cname => 'p_ticker' ));
        htp.tableRowClose;

        htp.tableRowOpen;
        htp.tableData( calign => 'RIGHT', cvalue => 'Name:');
        htp.tableData( calign => 'LEFT',  cvalue => htf.formText( cname => 'p_name' ));
        htp.tableRowClose;

        htp.tableRowOpen;
        htp.tableData( calign => 'RIGHT', cvalue => 'Type:');
        htp.tableData( calign => 'LEFT',  cvalue => htf.formText( cname => 'p_type' ));
        htp.tableRowClose;

        --
        -- Generate and HTML form submission button
        --
        htp.tableRowOpen;
        htp.tableData( calign      => 'RIGHT',
                       cattributes => 'colspan="2"',
                       cvalue      => htf.formSubmit(cvalue => 'Submit' ));
        htp.tableRowClose;

        htp.formClose;
        htp.bodyClose;
        htp.htmlClose;
end;
/
```

In this procedure, a few more features of the Web Toolkit have been exploited. The HTP.FORMOPEN and HTP.FORMCLOSE procedures generate the appropriate tags to open and close an HTML form, the HTF functions generate the appropriate HTML and are used as values in other Web Toolkit procedures, and an HTML table cell column span is specified as an attribute in TABLEDATA. When invoked from a browser, this form should look as shown in Figure 9-4.

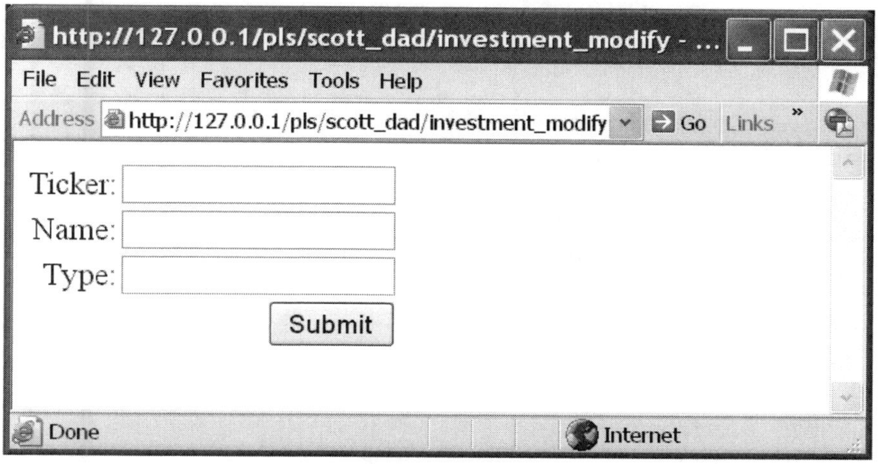

Figure 9-4. Investment modification form

Clicking the Submit button posts the data values by name in each of the form fields to the Oracle HTTP Server. In this case, the data values are posted to the procedure INVESTMENT_RPT, as specified in the HTP.FORMOPEN statement. However, without further modification, clicking the Submit button will generate an error. At runtime, when posted, MOD_PLSQL will look for a procedure named INVESTMENT_RPT with input parameters P_TICKER, P_NAME, and P_TYPE. Because the procedure will not be found, the resulting page will also not be found, and an error will be written to the Oracle HTTP Server error log.

To make this work, modify the definition of the INVESTMENT_RPT procedure to accept the following input parameters:

```
create or replace procedure investment_rpt(
    p_ticker   in varchar2,
    p_name     in varchar2,
    p_type     in varchar2 )
as..
```

After re-creating the INVESTMENT_RPT procedure with the input parameters, we can now click the Submit button on the HTML form and display our original investment report. Keep in mind, though, that we haven't done anything really constructive yet. No data will be inserted into our table because the logic to do this must be placed inside the procedure INVESTMENT_RPT and *not* in the INVEST-MENT_MODIFY procedure. This is because the actual data values posted by the user aren't accessible until they're submitted to the INVESTMENT_RPT procedure.

How do we know when to display the report in procedure INVESTMENT_RPT and not issue an INSERT statement? We could achieve this by checking for non-null values in P_NAME, P_TICKER, and P_TYPE. However, it's usually better to be explicit so we'll add a P_ACTION parameter to both procedures and include it as a hidden form element to be posted by the INVESTMENT_MODIFY procedure.

```
create or replace procedure investment_rpt(
    p_ticker  in varchar2 default null,
    p_name    in varchar2 default null,
    p_type    in varchar2 default null,
    p_action  in varchar2 default 'DISPLAY' )
as
    l_count number := 0;
begin
    if p_action = 'INSERT' then
        insert into my_investments( ticker, name, type )
        values( p_ticker, p_name, p_type );
        commit;
    end if;

    htp.htmlOpen;
    htp.bodyOpen;
    htp.tableOpen;
    htp.tableRowOpen;
    htp.tableHeader('Ticker');
    htp.tableHeader('Name');
    htp.tableHeader('Type');
    htp.tableRowClose;
    --
    for c1 in (select ticker, name, type
                 from my_investments
                order by ticker) loop
        htp.tableRowOpen;
        htp.tableData( c1.ticker );
        htp.tableData( c1.name );
        htp.tableData( c1.type );
        htp.tableRowClose;
        l_count := l_count + 1;
    end loop;
    --
    htp.tableClose;
    htp.p( l_count || ' rows found');
    htp.bodyClose;
    htp.htmlClose;
end;
/
```

```
create or replace procedure investment_modify(
    p_action  in varchar2 default 'INSERT' )
as
    l_count number := 0;
begin
    htp.htmlOpen;
    htp.bodyOpen;
    --
    -- Open an HTML form which will POST to our main reporting procedure
    --
    htp.formOpen( curl => 'investment_rpt', cmethod => 'POST' );


    --
    -- Include a hidden field to indicate our action when POSTed
    --
    htp.formHidden ( cname=> 'p_action', cvalue=> p_action );

    htp.tableOpen;
    --
    -- Generate a text field and label for each column in the table
    --
    htp.tableRowOpen;
    htp.tableData( calign => 'RIGHT', cvalue => 'Ticker:');
    htp.tableData( calign => 'LEFT',
                   cvalue => htf.formText( cname => 'p_ticker' ));
    htp.tableRowClose;

    htp.tableRowOpen;
    htp.tableData( calign => 'RIGHT', cvalue => 'Name:');
    htp.tableData( calign => 'LEFT',  cvalue => htf.formText( cname => 'p_name' ));
    htp.tableRowClose;

    htp.tableRowOpen;
    htp.tableData( calign => 'RIGHT', cvalue => 'Type:');
    htp.tableData( calign => 'LEFT',  cvalue => htf.formText( cname => 'p_type' ));
    htp.tableRowClose;

    --
    -- Generate and HTML form submission button
    --
    htp.tableRowOpen;
    htp.tableData( calign      => 'RIGHT',
                   cattributes => 'colspan="2"',
```

```
                        cvalue        => htf.formSubmit(cvalue => 'Submit' ));
        htp.tableRowClose;

        htp.formClose;
        htp.bodyClose;
        htp.htmlClose;
end;
/
```

We can now call the INVESTMENT_MODIFY procedure from the Web browser and enter the data values shown in Figure 9-5.

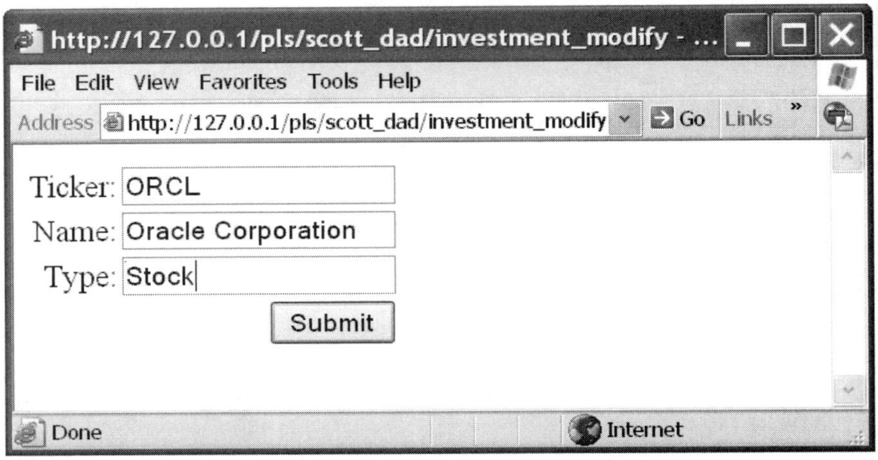

Figure 9-5. Entering a new investment

When the data is submitted, the resulting page should look as shown in Figure 9-6.

Given their simple design, it is easy to extend these procedures to accommodate updates as well as inserts. First, we need to add a new parameter to the procedure INVESTMENT_MODIFY. This new parameter, P_ACTION, will be used to determine whether the action is INSERT or UPDATE in the procedure. Then, because the form should display the current values for the specified investment when editing, we'll also need to fetch those values from the table and display them in our edit form. This is again determined by the value of the P_ACTION parameter. (Obviously, if we're creating a new investment, there are no values to fetch from the table and this query should not be performed.) From the main investment report listing, it would be convenient to display an HTML anchor in the rows of the report itself so a user could immediately click the link to edit the attributes of the investment. To link these two procedures, we simply modify the display of the ticker symbol column to render as an HTML anchor using the

PL/SQL Web Toolkit function HTF.ANCHOR. The target of the anchor is the INVEST-MENT_MODIFY procedure. Note how the P_ACTION parameter is hard-coded to UPDATE in the anchor, and the value of the ticker parameter is generated dynamically based on the value of the ticker column for the particular row.

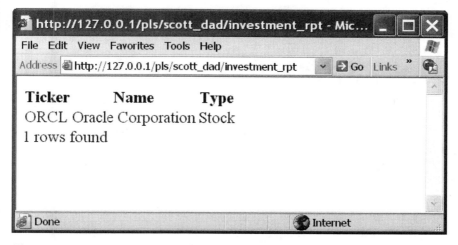

Figure 9-6. Investment report after entering new investment

```
create or replace procedure investment_rpt(
    p_ticker  in varchar2 default null,
    p_name    in varchar2 default null,
    p_type    in varchar2 default null,
    p_action  in varchar2 default 'DISPLAY' )
as
    l_count number := 0;
begin
    if p_action = 'INSERT' then
        insert into my_investments( ticker, name, type )
        values( p_ticker, p_name, p_type );
        commit;
    elsif p_action = 'UPDATE' then
        update my_investments
           set name = p_name,
               type = p_type
         where ticker = p_ticker;
        commit;
    end if;

    htp.htmlOpen;
    htp.bodyOpen;
    htp.tableOpen;
```

```
        htp.tableRowOpen;
        htp.tableHeader('Ticker');
        htp.tableHeader('Name');
        htp.tableHeader('Type');
        htp.tableRowClose;
        --
        for c1 in (select ticker, name, type
                     from my_investments
                    order by ticker) loop
            htp.tableRowOpen;
            htp.tableData(
                htf.anchor(
                    curl => 'investment_modify?p_action=UPDATE&p_ticker=' ||
c1.ticker,
                    ctext => c1.ticker) );
            htp.tableData( c1.name );
            htp.tableData( c1.type );
            htp.tableRowClose;
            l_count := l_count + 1;
        end loop;
        --
        htp.tableClose;
        htp.p( l_count || ' rows found');
        htp.br;
        htp.anchor( curl => 'investment_modify?p_action=INSERT',
                    ctext => 'Create New' );
        htp.bodyClose;
        htp.htmlClose;
end;
/


create or replace procedure investment_modify(
    p_ticker  in varchar2 default null,
    p_action  in varchar2 default 'INSERT' )
as
    l_count number := 0;
    l_row    my_investments%rowtype;
begin
    --
    -- If the action is update, query the values to be
    -- updated from the table
    --
    if p_action = 'UPDATE' then
        select * into l_row
```

```
      from my_investments
    where ticker = p_ticker;
end if;
htp.htmlOpen;
htp.bodyOpen;

--
-- Open an HTML form which will POST to our main reporting procedure
--
htp.formOpen( curl => 'investment_rpt', cmethod => 'POST' );

--
-- Include a hidden field to indicate our action when POSTed
--
htp.formHidden ( cname=> 'p_action', cvalue=> p_action );

htp.tableOpen;
--
-- Generate a text field and label for each column in the table
--
htp.tableRowOpen;
htp.tableData( calign => 'RIGHT', cvalue => 'Ticker:');
htp.tableData(
    calign => 'LEFT',
    cvalue => htf.formText( cname => 'p_ticker',
                            cvalue => l_row.ticker ));
htp.tableRowClose;

htp.tableRowOpen;
htp.tableData( calign => 'RIGHT', cvalue => 'Name:');
htp.tableData(
    calign => 'LEFT',
    cvalue => htf.formText( cname => 'p_name', cvalue => l_row.name ));
htp.tableRowClose;

htp.tableRowOpen;
htp.tableData( calign => 'RIGHT', cvalue => 'Type:');
htp.tableData(
    calign => 'LEFT',
    cvalue => htf.formText( cname => 'p_type', cvalue => l_row.type ));
htp.tableRowClose;

--
-- Generate and HTML form submission button
```

```
    --
    htp.tableRowOpen;
    htp.tableData( calign      => 'RIGHT',
                   cattributes => 'colspan="2"',
                   cvalue      => htf.formSubmit(cvalue => 'Submit' ));
    htp.tableRowClose;

    htp.formClose;
    htp.bodyClose;
    htp.htmlClose;
end;
/
```

Running these procedures in a browser and adding a few of your favorite values should result in a page like the one shown in Figure 9-7.

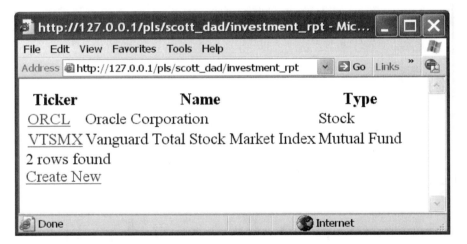

Figure 9-7. Investment report with links

Note that to complete the example, an additional HTML anchor is added at the bottom of the INVESTMENT_RPT procedure, which permits easy creation of a new investment and links to the INVESTMENT_MODIFY procedure with a hard-coded action of INSERT.

This example demonstrates that once the basic methods are implemented, it becomes quite easy to extend the functionality. Additionally, with the simplicity of linking pages in a Web application, it becomes rather simple to link together multiple PL/SQL procedures into what appears to be one cohesive application.

HTTP from the Database

Although not formally a part of the PL/SQL Web Toolkit, the Oracle database includes native PL/SQL packages that can be used to make HTTP requests directly from an Oracle database. This package, UTL_HTTP, can be used to access resources over the HTTP protocol in a very similar fashion to the way in which GET and POST requests are made to a Web server over HTTP.

> **NOTE** HTTP is nothing more than a standard communication protocol. People often intermingle the acronyms HTML and HTTP, but requests over HTTP do not have to be visual in nature.

Using UTL_HTTP, you can write a Web application that renders a page by invoking a PL/SQL stored procedure via MOD_PLSQL. Furthermore, *within* that MOD_PLSQL request, you make one or more HTTP requests emanating directly from the database. As easily as someone can make a request to a Web site to fetch specific HTML content, the same type of Web request operation can be done directly in a PL/SQL stored procedure. Although at first glance you might scratch your head and wonder why you would ever want to do that, there are countless uses for this type of processing.

It is quite simple to write a PL/SQL stored procedure that can fetch the HTML of the home page of the Yahoo! Web site. Rather than author and maintain the infrastructure for a stock quotes Web site, you could easily post a page to one of numerous Web sites that already provide this service and then use the native facilities of Oracle XDB (XML Database) to parse through the results.

A significant issue behind parsing HTML is that HTML can change frequently. If your "host" Web site changed their look and feel, the stolen functionality would no longer work. Integration to a Web site where HTML determines the structure of the results is fraught with problems. This is where XML combined with Web Services is a very elegant solution. XML can be used to convey the structure and semantic elements of a document and Web Services are a convenient infrastructure to send requests and fetch results of this nature.

People often refer to XML and Web Services as the holy grail of computing. Although this assessment is overblown in our opinion, Web Services are a marvelous way to integrate heterogeneous systems. All of a sudden, for certain integration challenges, you don't have to wire gateways together, write automated batch jobs that send files at midnight, or glue together pieces of a solution that can break at any step of the process. Moreover, with Web Services, you are not concerned with where the Web Service is hosted nor what the ultimate source of the data in the response is.

The examples in the following sections work with versions 9*i* of the database and later.

Fetching HTML

Let's start with a simple example using UTL_HTTP. We will write a generic procedure that would simply print the HTML fetched when provided a URL. The specification of function UTL_HTTP is as follows:

```
utl_http.request(
    url                in varchar2,
    proxy              in varchar2 default null,
    wallet_path        in varchar2 default null,
    wallet_password in varchar2 default null ) return varchar2;
```

Ignoring the last two passwords related to wallet management of certificates, this function is extraordinarily simple. You simply provide a URL and an optional HTTP proxy server, and that URL can be fetched directly within the database. For example

```
create or replace procedure print_web_site( p_url in varchar2 )
is
begin
    htp.p( utl_http.request( url => p_url ));
end;
```

You can use this PRINT_WEB_SITE procedure to fetch the contents of any URL and immediately print the results back to the requesting client. If you were to execute this from a browser, assuming you created this in a schema that had a DAD mapped to it, you would invoke it with the URL http://<host>:<port>/pls/<dad>/print_web_site?p_url=www.yahoo.com. In the following example, we will retrieve the page of a popular Internet Web site directly from SQL*Plus.

```
SQL> exec owainit;

PL/SQL procedure successfully completed.

SQL> exec print_web_site( p_url => 'www.yahoo.com' );

PL/SQL procedure successfully completed.

SQL> exec owa_util.showpage;
```

```
Content-type: text/html
Content-length: 1998
<html><head>

<title>Yahoo!</title>...
```

If you execute this example, you'll see that the HTML page from the sample Web site is incomplete or truncated. This is a limitation of the request function because it will only read the first 2,000 bytes of content retrieved. To ensure all the data from the request is retrieved, we'll need to use the function UTL_HTTP.REQUEST_PIECES, shown as follows:

```
utl_http.request_pieces(
    url             in varchar2,
    max_pieces      in natural default 32767,
    proxy           in varchar2 default null,
    wallet_path     in varchar2 default null,
    wallet_password in varchar2 default null ) return html_pieces;
```

The REQUEST_PIECES function is almost identical to the UTL_HTTP.REQUEST function, but instead of being limited to 2,000 bytes per request, REQUEST_PIECES will return a PL/SQL table, with each entry in the PL/SQL table containing up to 2,000 bytes. The following is an example using UTL_HTTP.REQUEST_PIECES, which permits us to download a very large document from a URL.

```
create or replace procedure print_web_site( p_url in varchar2 )
is
    l_pieces utl_http.html_pieces;
begin
    l_pieces := utl_http.request_pieces( url => p_url );
    --
    for x in 1..l_pieces.count loop
        htp.p( l_pieces(x) );
    end loop;
end;
```

With the rewritten PRINT_WEB_SITE procedure, you can fetch the content of any URL up to 62.5MB. It should be apparent that once you have a PL/SQL table of all the content, you could exploit the power of PL/SQL to quickly convert it to a CLOB, use XDB to parse it, and so on.

A Web Service Client Using UTL_HTTP

The Simple Object Access Protocol (SOAP) is an XML-based protocol that is often mentioned in the same breath as Web Services. In essence, SOAP is simply the standard protocol to describe a request and the results of that request. SOAP requests are most often transmitted over HTTP (although this is not a requirement).

Using SOAP, you can easily make Remote Procedure Call (RPC) style requests across the building or across the country. With a standards-based SOAP server acting as a front-end to the data sources, the problem of easily integrating functionality across a wide variety of systems has been significantly simplified. This section shows how easy it is to invoke a Web Service directly from within a PL/SQL stored procedure using nothing but the UTL_HTTP package.

This section uses the following procedures and functions in the UTL_HTTP PL/SQL package:

- **SET_HEADER**: sets values in the HTTP request header

- **BEGIN_REQUEST**: initiates a new HTTP request

- **WRITE_TEXT**: writes text in the HTTP request body

- **GET_RESPONSE**: fetches the HTTP response

- **READ_TEXT**: reads the text in the HTTP response body

- **END_RESPONSE**: terminates the HTTP response

The purpose of our example is to author a PL/SQL stored procedure that will take a U.S. ZIP code as input and display the current temperature in Fahrenheit for that ZIP code area. On the Web, there are a host of publicly accessible SOAP servers that provide this functionality. Our task is to connect the Oracle database to this Web Service. The SOAP envelope for this request is as follows:

```
<?xml version="1.0" encoding="UTF-8" standalone="no"?>
<SOAP-ENV:Envelope xmlns:SOAP-ENV="http://schemas.xmlsoap.org/soap/envelope/"
    xmlns:tns="http://www.xmethods.net/sd/TemperatureService.wsdl"
    xmlns:xsd="http://www.w3.org/1999/XMLSchema"
    xmlns:soap="http://schemas.xmlsoap.org/wsdl/soap/"
    xmlns:xsi="http://www.w3.org/1999/XMLSchema-instance"
    xmlns:SOAP-ENC="http://schemas.xmlsoap.org/soap/encoding/">
    <SOAP-ENV:Body>
        <mns:getTemp xmlns:mns="urn:xmethods-Temperature"
```

```
            SOAP-ENV:encodingStyle="http://schemas.xmlsoap.org/soap/encoding/">
                <zipcode xsi:type="xsd:string">43065</zipcode>
            </mns:getTemp>
        </SOAP-ENV:Body>
</SOAP-ENV:Envelope>
```

In this entire XML document, the only piece that will ever vary is the ZIP code element. Unless the target Web Service changes, everything else in this SOAP envelope will remain consistent.

This SOAP envelope needs to be sent as a request to a SOAP server. The SOAP server will host this Web Service, and our request will be sent over HTTP to this server. Then we will read the response from the same site to fetch our results.

```
create or replace procedure temp_from_zip( p_zip in varchar2)
as
    l_soap_envelope varchar2(4000);
    l_http_request   utl_http.req;
    l_http_response utl_http.resp;
    l_piece            utl_http.html_pieces;
    l_response        varchar2(4000);

begin
    --
    -- Create a SOAP envelope containing the supplied ZIP parameter
    --
    l_soap_envelope := '<?xml version="1.0" encoding="UTF-8" standalone="no"?>
        <SOAP-ENV:Envelope
          xmlns:SOAP-ENV="http://schemas.xmlsoap.org/soap/envelope/"
            xmlns:tns="http://www.xmethods.net/sd/TemperatureService.wsdl"
            xmlns:xsd="http://www.w3.org/1999/XMLSchema"
            xmlns:soap="http://schemas.xmlsoap.org/wsdl/soap/"
            xmlns:xsi="http://www.w3.org/1999/XMLSchema-instance"
            xmlns:SOAP-ENC="http://schemas.xmlsoap.org/soap/encoding/">
            <SOAP-ENV:Body>
<mns:getTemp xmlns:mns="urn:xmethods-Temperature"
  SOAP-ENV:encodingStyle="http://schemas.xmlsoap.org/soap/encoding/">
                    <zipcode xsi:type="xsd:string">';
    l_soap_envelope := l_soap_envelope || p_zip;
    l_soap_envelope := l_soap_envelope || '</zipcode></mns:getTemp>
                        </SOAP-ENV:Body>
                        </SOAP-ENV:Envelope>';

    --
```

```
      -- Start a new request to the target SOAP server, and POSTing our request
      --
      l_http_request := utl_http.begin_request(
          url => 'http://services.xmethods.net:80/soap/servlet/rpcrouter',
          method => 'POST' );
                                 method => 'POST' );
      utl_http.set_header(l_http_request, 'Content-Type', 'text/xml');
      utl_http.set_header(l_http_request, 'Content-Length', length(l_soap_enve-
lope));
      utl_http.set_header(l_http_request, 'SOAPAction', 'getTempRequest');

      --
      -- Write the envelope as part of the request
      --
      utl_http.write_text(l_http_request, l_soap_envelope);

      --
      -- Immediately get the response from our request
      --
      l_http_response := utl_http.get_response(l_http_request);
      utl_http.read_text( l_http_response, l_response );
      utl_http.end_response(l_http_response);
      htp.p( l_response );
end;
/
```

The entire process is fairly straightforward. You simply take an XML document, post it with your own argument values to a specific server, read the response, and end the HTTP request. The purpose of the final HTP.P in the procedure is to review the results returned from the SOAP server.

Running the following code in SQL*Plus will produce some interesting results.

```
SQL> exec owainit;

PL/SQL procedure successfully completed.

SQL> exec temp_from_zip(43065);

PL/SQL procedure successfully completed.

SQL> exec owa_util.showpage;
Content-type: text/html
Content-length: 466
```

```
<?xml version='1.0' encoding='UTF-8'?>
<SOAP-ENV:Envelope
xmlns:SOAP-ENV="http://schemas.xmlsoap.org/soap/envelope/"
xmlns:xsi="http://www.w3.org/2001/XMLSchema-instance"
xmlns:xsd="http://www.w3.org/2001/XMLSchema">
<SOAP-ENV:Body>
<ns1:getTempResponse xmlns:ns1="urn:xmethods-Temperature"
SOAP-ENV:encodingStyle="http://schemas.xmlsoap.org/soap/encoding/">
<return
xsi:type="xsd:float">71.0</return>
</ns1:getTempResponse>

</SOAP-ENV:Body>
</SOAP-ENV:Envelope>
```

It becomes obvious that the result of the request is also a response enclosed in a SOAP envelope. In this example, the temperature in Fahrenheit for ZIP code 43065 is 71.0 degrees. It would be extraordinarily useful to convert this procedure to a function and have it return nothing but the temperature value. This is where Oracle XDB can be exploited.

Although a full explanation of Oracle XDB is beyond the scope of this chapter, it is easy to understand and exploit Oracle XDB for the purpose of our example. Because the return value of the SOAP request is an XML document, we would like to parse the XML document and extract only the return value.

To convert the existing procedure to this function requires the following short steps:

1. Change the procedure to function and add a return type of varchar2

2. Define a local variable called l_xml with a datatype of l_xml

3. Parse the SOAP response and extract just the return value

The finished example looks as shown here.

```
create or replace function temp_from_zip( p_zip in varchar2)
return varchar2
as
    l_soap_envelope varchar2(4000);
    l_http_request  utl_http.req;
    l_http_response utl_http.resp;
    l_piece         utl_http.html_pieces;
```

```
        l_response          varchar2(4000);
        l_xml               xmltype;
begin
    --
    -- Create a SOAP envelope containing the supplied ZIP parameter
    --
    l_soap_envelope := '<?xml version="1.0" encoding="UTF-8" standalone="no"?>
        <SOAP-ENV:Envelope
            xmlns:SOAP-ENV="http://schemas.xmlsoap.org/soap/envelope/"
            xmlns:tns="http://www.xmethods.net/sd/TemperatureService.wsdl"
            xmlns:xsd="http://www.w3.org/1999/XMLSchema"
            xmlns:soap="http://schemas.xmlsoap.org/wsdl/soap/"
            xmlns:xsi="http://www.w3.org/1999/XMLSchema-instance"
            xmlns:SOAP-ENC="http://schemas.xmlsoap.org/soap/encoding/">
            <SOAP-ENV:Body>
<mns:getTemp xmlns:mns="urn:xmethods-Temperature"
 SOAP-ENV:encodingStyle="http://schemas.xmlsoap.org/soap/encoding/">
                    <zipcode xsi:type="xsd:string">';
    l_soap_envelope := l_soap_envelope || p_zip;
    l_soap_envelope := l_soap_envelope || '</zipcode></mns:getTemp>
                        </SOAP-ENV:Body>
                        </SOAP-ENV:Envelope>';

    --
    -- Start a new request to the target SOAP server, and POSTing our request
    --
    l_http_request := utl_http.begin_request(
        url => 'http://services.xmethods.net:80/soap/servlet/rpcrouter',
        method => 'POST' );
                            method => 'POST' );
    utl_http.set_header(l_http_request, 'Content-Type', 'text/xml');
    utl_http.set_header(l_http_request, 'Content-Length', length(l_soap_enve-
lope));
    utl_http.set_header(l_http_request, 'SOAPAction', 'getTempRequest');

    --
    -- Write the envelope as part of the request
    --
    utl_http.write_text(l_http_request, l_soap_envelope);

    --
    -- Immediately get the response from our request
    --
    l_http_response := utl_http.get_response(l_http_request);
```

```
    utl_http.read_text( l_http_response, l_response );
    utl_http.end_response(l_http_response);

    --
    -- Parse the response into a variable of XMLType and then
    -- extract just the return value using XPath syntax
    --
    l_xml := xmltype.createxml( l_response );
    return l_xml.extract('//return/child::text()').getStringVal();
end;
```

With the following modification, we will have a function accessible from SQL that can invoke a Web Service directly from an Oracle database.

```
SQL> select temp_from_zip(43065) from dual;

TEMP_FROM_ZIP(43065)
-------------------------------------------------------
71.0

SQL> select temp_from_zip(20500) from dual;

TEMP_FROM_ZIP(20500)
-------------------------------------------------------
70.0
```

Because SQL is accessible by a variety of tools and technologies, providing this functionality as a SQL function broadens the reach of possible applications that can be addressed. Although there may be forthcoming facilities from Oracle to natively invoke and manage Web Services from an Oracle database (so you don't have to "roll your own"), this section demonstrated how truly powerful the Oracle database can be simply by employing the native UTL_HTTP package.

Summary

With all the Web technologies available—from Java Server Pages to Active Server Pages to Python to PHP—why would you consider authoring a Web application using PL/SQL?

For manipulating an Oracle database, there is nothing easier to use nor closer to the database than PL/SQL itself. Writing a cursor for loop in PL/SQL seems almost trivial compared to the hoops you have to go through in other technologies to achieve the same result. One only has to do the math and count the number of layers between your application and the database: with PL/SQL there is one layer.

Another benefit of authoring applications using PL/SQL Web packages is that the applications are extremely portable. Regardless of platform, you are virtually guaranteed that what is authored on Oracle on one operating system will work without a single modification on Oracle on another operating system. It truly is a "write it once and run it virtually anywhere" type of language and framework.

Finally, when building an application in PL/SQL, you have direct access to all the native rich functionality inside an Oracle database. If you want to add full-text indexing, Oracle Text is at your full disposal. If you need DES encryption, reach for the DBMS_OBFUSCATION_TOOLKIT. If you are considering authenticating your users against an LDAP directory, glance at the DBMS_LDAP package. If you want to build your own custom data warehouse front-end on top of your operational database, look at the OLAP functionality native to the Oracle database. Chances are, if you need to do it, Oracle has already provided a facility to do it in the database.

CHAPTER 10

PL/SQL Debugging

DEVELOPERS KNOW THAT CODE debugging can be a large part of their job. I don't know any developer who gets it right the first time, every time, and never makes a mistake, so developers must employ debugging tips and techniques along the way. PL/SQL developers are no different—we face those same challenges.

In this chapter we'll explore how to effectively debug PL/SQL. We'll cover a range of debugging techniques, from just printing messages to the screen, to logging messages to tables and files, to building your own custom debugging utility.

When you've finished reading this chapter, you should have a solid foundation in and knowledge of the tools out there that can help make you a more effective PL/SQL developer. To start, we'll discuss some principals that may potentially help you avoid the need to debug your code at all or at least will make it easier if errors and bugs crop up.

Defensive Coding

Defensive coding is all about avoiding debugging or at least making your debugging endeavors easier. Of course, you can save yourself a lot of pain by employing some of the good PL/SQL coding practices discussed elsewhere in this book—for example, use of the %TYPE and %ROWTYPE variable attributes to insulate your PL/SQL code from underlying changes to datatype definitions, as discussed in Chapter 4.

In this part of the chapter, we'll discuss a few other techniques that we use to make PL/SQL debugging unnecessary in some cases or at least to make some debugging less painful.

Exceptions

Proper exception handling is important for debugging. Effective handling of exceptions can make the difference between spending a few minutes and spending a few hours searching for the error in your code. In this section, we'll explore briefly how exceptions work and then look at how to use them effectively to aid in debugging.

Handling Exceptions

Exceptions can be handled at the end of any BEGIN-END block. When an exception is raised, processing stops at the offending statement and goes immediately to the end of the current block, searching for an exception handler. If one is found, and the matching exception is indeed handled there, processing proceeds on from the exception block. If no exception handler if found in the current BEGIN-END block, Oracle looks for a matching exception handler in the parent BEGIN-END block, and that continues until either the exception is handled or you reach the outermost block, in which case the processing stops and ends with that unhandled exception. In the following example, we cause a ZERO_DIVIDE error with the statement l_ratio := 1/0; in BEGIN-END block 3:

```
begin   -- block 1
  -- statement
  begin   -- block 2
    -- more statements
    begin   -- block 3
      -- yet more statements
      l_ratio := 1/0;
    end;
    -- these statements are skipped
  exception
    when VALUE_ERROR then
-- handle specific exception
  end;
  -- these statements are also skipped
exception
  when ZERO_DIVIDE then
    l_ratio := 0;
end;
```

Block 3 has no exception handler, so processing continues out to the next outer exception handler, skipping any statements that haven't yet been executed in block 2. Because there are no exception handlers in block 2 to handle the error, processing continues to block 1 (again skipping all the statements yet to be executed in block 1), where finally we find the ZERO_DIVIDE exception handler. Processing continues on from there normally.

Many times, once you've handled an exception, processing can continue. In the previous example, once we set L_RATIO equal to zero in block 1, processing could continue. Other times, you may want to note that the exception happened, but then propagate the exception to an outer block, which may or may not handle it. The following code demonstrates the use of the RAISE command:

```
declare
  L_ratio number;
begin
  L_ratio := 1/0;
exception
  when ZERO_DIVIDE then
    -- log the fact that we encounter the exception
    raise;
end;
```

Notice that we have a RAISE command without any exception name. We simply reraise the exception that is currently being handled. This allows us to log the fact that the exception happened, right when and where it happened, but then allows the exception to continue to bubble up to where an outer BEGIN-END block may know better how to actually handle and fix the exception.

System Exceptions

PL/SQL has 20 predefined exceptions. They are defined in the STANDARD package and are accessible in all PL/SQL routines, in the same manner as built-in functions such as TO_CHAR() and SUBSTR(). Each exception is associated with a SQLCODE error number (we'll come back to this topic later). You've already seen the ZERO_DIVIDE error, which has a SQLCODE error number of 1476. If you check that SQLCODE, you can see that it is in fact the "divisor is equal to zero" error message. On Unix and Linux you can use the OERR utility:

```
[clbeck@clbeck-tecra clbeck]$ oerr ora 1476
01476, 00000, "divisor is equal to zero"
// *Cause:
// *Action:
```

Just supply any SQLCODE and it will, at a minimum, give you the error text. Usually, it also supplies a CAUSE and ACTION, which will help you determine the error and fix it. On Windows, you can do the following:

```
C: >echo msgtxt rdbms ora 1476 | oratclsh

DBSNMP for 32-bit Windows: Version 9.2.0.1.0 - Production on 28-OCT-2003
18:25:23

Copyright (c) 2002 Oracle Corporation.  All rights reserved.

oratclsh[1]- ora-1476: divisor is equal to zero
oratclsh[2]-
```

> **NOTE**   You can find free Perl scripts on the Web that will mimic the Unix and
> Linux OERR command, supplying the CAUSE and ACTION information as well.

If you want to see all of the Oracle defined exceptions, you can look in the
STANDARD specification, which is located in $ORACLE_HOME/rdbms/admin/stdspec.sql.

User-Defined Exceptions

Now that you've seen how Oracle defines exceptions, you may want to define
some of your own:

```
declare
   my_exception exception:
begin
   If some_condition = really_bad then
     raise my_exception:
   end if;
exception
   when my_exception then
     -- make all good
end;
```

Now that you have an exception, you can raise it at any time as long as it's
within the scope of its declaration block. You can define exceptions in a package
specification and then refer to them as PACKAGE.EXCEPTION_NAME, just like global
variables in package specifications.

I would suggest that you use user-defined exceptions sparingly. I believe that
an exception shouldn't be used as a GOTO, but only when a situation arises within
your code that requires special handling. If you find code that employs user-
defined exceptions as a means to break out of loops and subprocedures, then I
would say that that is poorly written code. Execution of code should, for the most
part, proceed logically from the beginning to the end and only jump to a special
handler if something unexpected happens. Now, this isn't to say that you should
never use user-defined exceptions—just use them in those cases in which there is
no other way to accomplish in code what you're trying to do.

As mentioned before, Oracle associates certain exceptions with common
SQLCODE errors that arise during execution. You can, if you so choose, associate
your user-defined exception with a SQLCODE using the pragma EXCEPTION_INIT:

```
declare
  table_space_exists exception:
  pragma exception_init( table_space_exists, -1534 );
begin
  execute immediate 'create tablespace system....';
exception
  when table_space_exists then
--handle error
end;
```

Here we defined an exception, `TABLE_SPACE_EXISTS`, and associated it with `SQLCODE` 1543, which just happens to be as follows:

```
[clbeck@clbeck-tecra clbeck]$ oerr ora 1543
01543, 00000, "tablespace '%s' already exists"
// *Cause: Tried to create a tablespace which already exists
// *Action: Use a different name for the new tablespace
```

Now, if you have a procedure that accepts a tablespace name and attempts to create it via PL/SQL, you can first check to make sure that the tablespace doesn't already exist. There is a possibility that, between the time you check and the time you actually create the tablespace, someone else will create a tablespace with the same name. It's not likely, but it's possible. That is a perfect example of when to use exceptions. Use them to handle the unlikely events.

RAISE_APPLICATION_ERROR()

Just as you can assign your own exception to an Oracle `SQLCODE`, so can you define your own error messages for exceptions that you raise. Using the `RAISE_APPLICATION_ERROR` function, you can raise exceptions and give them meaningful error messages. To call this function, use the following syntax:

```
raise_application_error(error_number, message[, {TRUE | FALSE}]);
```

The `RAISE_APPLICATION_ERROR` parameters are as follows:

- **ERROR_NUMBER:** Any negative integer between –20000 and –20999.

- **MESSAGE:** The error message displayed. It can be up to 2,048 characters long.

- **An optional Boolean parameter:** A value of `FALSE`, which is the default, replaces all previous errors on the error stack. If set to `TRUE`, the error is added to the error stack.

RAISE_APPLICATION_ERROR can be used to raise exceptions in the same manner as RAISE <NAMED_EXCEPTION>. For example:

```
begin
  if salary < expenses then
    raise_application_error( -20001, 'I need more money' );
  end if;
end;
```

A developer can handle these raised exceptions only if she uses the EXCEP-TION_INIT pragma, explained earlier, and binds a user-defined exception to the ERROR_NUMBER used in the RAISE_APPLICATION_ERROR.

The OTHERS Exception Handler

Cases arise in code in which you just have no idea what may happen (or you just don't care!). You just know that if something unexpected happens, you want to handle it. So far, all the exception blocks you've seen have used named exceptions. The OTHERS exception handler acts as a sort of catchall for any exception that might occur in the BEGIN-END block:

```
declare
  l_num number;
  l_char varchar2(10);
begin
  select col1/col2, col3
    into l_num, l_char
  from my_table
  where id = 1;
exception
  when NO_DATA_FOUND then
    -- handle when no rows are returned
  when TOO_MANY_ROWS then
    -- handle when more than one row is returned
  when OTHERS then
    -- handle any other error.
end;
```

There are two important points to note here. First, an exception block can handle multiple exceptions, each with its own WHEN <EXCEPTION>. Second, the catchall exception case of WHEN OTHERS will handle any other exception that may arise that wasn't previously handled with a named exception handler.

In our example, we explicitly handle the NO_DATA_FOUND and TOO_MANY_ROWS exceptions, which are the two standard exceptions that developers think of when using SELECT…INTO statements. But in our case, we have two other possible exceptions that could arise. We could get the ZERO_DIVIDE exception from the col1/col2 division, and we could get a VALUE_ERROR exception if the length of col3 is greater than ten characters. Of course, the correct way to obviate that last potential error is to use the %TYPE variable attribute, but the point here is that many exceptions can arise.

Be warned that misuse of WHEN OTHERS can be detrimental to debugging. If all you ever use are WHEN OTHERS handlers, then it can be hard to know where in your code the problem lies. A poorly placed WHEN OTHERS could catch an exception that you've specifically handled in an outer BEGIN-END block, thus rendering useless your error handling of that exception.

Exceptions are very powerful and useful constructs of the PL/SQL language. They allow developers to catch and handle the unexpected gracefully. They also allow developers to raise their own exceptions with informative messages and halt processing. Proper exception handling is essential for aiding in the debugging process. However, overuse and misuse of some of the features of exceptions, namely WHEN OTHERS and user-defined exceptions, can hinder your debugging efforts. By all means, use exceptions, but use them correctly.

Instrumenting Your Code

Debug information is essential to the developer who is trying to fix a broken piece of code. The more information that is available to him, the better chance he has of locating the offending code and fixing it quickly.

Often, however, when code is stamped "production code," the debugging and logging calls are stripped out. The argument behind this is that it will increase performance if you remove all that erroneous development code. We would argue that leaving that code in is paramount to ensuring efficient and smooth-running production code that can be debugged when it breaks without changing it.

Of course, you don't want to be logging debug information during normal operation of your application, but you definitely want to be able to flip a switch and turn that feature on if a bug does rear its ugly head. If you can't, then you're left trying to duplicate the situation that caused the error in your development environment, which may not always be possible. All this time, your production application is down and your customers are getting angry.

This advice applies to all software developers, not just PL/SQL developers. The Oracle database itself, which is tuned to run as fast as possible, has the capability to log all kinds of debug information if the need arises. Even though the database goes through test after test to ensure that it is 100-percent bug free, unforeseen errors crop up. With Oracle support's help, you can "flip the switch" and a vast range of debug information can be generated. This information is vital to help you get your database running quickly. Imagine if Oracle's development staff had to try to mimic the customer's environment in order to replicate each and every error that occurred in the database. Well, let's just say that that isn't even feasible.

Later on in this chapter, we'll discuss how you can implement debugging and logging in PL/SQL so that during normal operation, no debug information is generated, but by "flipping a switch" you can generate all the debug information you need.

Documentation

I don't know a developer who likes writing documentation. You often hear developers jokingly say, "My code is self documenting" or "I purposely don't document my code because it guarantees my job security." I know that I find it bothersome to do, but I also know how important it is to do it. I don't know how many times I have to revisit some piece of code I wrote, or worse, someone else wrote months ago. When this happens, I seem to spend half my time scratching my head and saying, "What is going on in this procedure?" or "What was the developer thinking when he wrote this?" A lot of this head scratching can be avoided if you take the time to document your code. All that is needed is a brief explanation, a few lines, explaining the logic in plain English.

Of course, the more documentation, the better, and in a perfect world, everything would be fully documented. In the real world, however, time constraints and project deadlines (and sometimes just laziness) preclude developers from documenting. But know this: Taking a few minutes to briefly explain your code when you write it will later save you hours—or even days—of code tracing and head scratching.

Tools

Now that we've reviewed some of the techniques for minimizing code debugging time, let's take a look at the tools available to us when we actually have to roll up our sleeves and do it.

DBMS_OUTPUT

DBMS_OUTPUT is an Oracle-supplied package that allows developers to return text messages to any client that is DBMS_OUTPUT aware.

> **NOTE** You can view the file containing the package specification at `$ORA-CLE_HOME/rdbms/admin/dbmsotpt.sql`.

Think of this package like `printf()` in C or `System.out.println()` in Java. It's the simplest way to debug your PL/SQL, but it does have some limitations.

Specification

If you describe the `DBMS_OUTPUT` package, you'll notice that there are only a few procedures exposed:

```
SQL> desc dbms_output
PROCEDURE DISABLE
PROCEDURE ENABLE
 Argument Name                    Type                    In/Out Default?
 ------------------------------   ---------------------   ------ --------
 BUFFER_SIZE                      NUMBER(38)              IN     DEFAULT
PROCEDURE GET_LINE
 Argument Name                    Type                    In/Out Default?
 ------------------------------   ---------------------   ------ --------
 LINE                             VARCHAR2                OUT
 STATUS                           NUMBER(38)              OUT
PROCEDURE GET_LINES
 Argument Name                    Type                    In/Out Default?
 ------------------------------   ---------------------   ------ --------
 LINES                            TABLE OF VARCHAR2(255)  OUT
 NUMLINES                         NUMBER(38)              IN/OUT
PROCEDURE NEW_LINE
PROCEDURE PUT
 Argument Name                    Type                    In/Out Default?
 ------------------------------   ---------------------   ------ --------
 A                                VARCHAR2                IN
PROCEDURE PUT
 Argument Name                    Type                    In/Out Default?
 ------------------------------   ---------------------   ------ --------
 A                                NUMBER                  IN
PROCEDURE PUT_LINE
 Argument Name                    Type                    In/Out Default?
 ------------------------------   ---------------------   ------ --------
```

Argument Name	Type	In/Out	Default?
A	VARCHAR2	IN	
PROCEDURE PUT_LINE			
A	NUMBER	IN	

DBMS_OUTPUT is only useful for relatively small debugging tasks, because the buffer (where the text messages are cached) is only 1,000,000 bytes long, and each line is only 255 characters in length. The package works by buffering your text messages into an array of VARCHAR2(255). Then a DBMS_OUTPUT-aware client (for our examples, we use SQL*Plus) will print that information when your PL/SQL routine has completed.

SQL*Plus needs to know that you want it to print those messages back, so you need to issue the following command:

```
SET SERVEROUTPUT ON [SIZE <BUFFER_SIZE>]
```

Without this command, your messages will remain in the cache and you won't see them. Eventually, the cache will fill up and you'll find yourself in the ironic situation of your debugging code causing an error in the code!

Using DBMS_OUTPUT with SQL*Plus

Let's look at a few examples of how to use DBMS_OUTPUT. The first one is very basic. Anyplace you want to print out a message, just include the call to the PUT_LINE procedure, and that message will be printed:

```
SQL> set serveroutput on
SQL> begin
  2     dbms_output.put_line( 'foo' );
  3     dbms_output.put_line( 'bar' );
  4   end;
  5   /
foo
bar

PL/SQL procedure successfully completed.
```

If you want to programmatically control whether or not messages are cached for display, you can use the ENABLE and DISABLE procedures:

```
SQL> set serverout on
SQL> begin
```

```
2    dbms_output.disable;
3    dbms_output.put_line( 'one' );
4    dbms_output.put_line( 'two' );
5    dbms_output.enable;
6    dbms_output.put_line( 'three' );
7  end;
8  /
three

PL/SQL procedure successfully completed.
```

Notice the first two messages were ignored by DBMS_OUTPUT and only the text message, THREE, was printed. Use of ENABLE and DISABLE will allow you to instrument your code and leave the debug messages in when it goes to production. When you need to debug, just issue DBMS_OUTPUT.ENABLE prior to running the application and your messages will magically appear. One thing to note is that, as the following code demonstrates, any cached messages will be purged if you issue DBMS_OUTPUT.DISABLE:

```
SQL> begin
 2    dbms_output.disable;
 3    dbms_output.put_line( 'one' );
 4    dbms_output.put_line( 'two' );
 5    dbms_output.enable;
 6    dbms_output.put_line( 'three' );
 7    dbms_output.disable;              -- flushes and disables cache
 8    dbms_output.put_line( 'four' );
 9    dbms_output.put_line( 'five' );
10    dbms_output.enable;              -- enables caching of messages
11    dbms_output.put_line( 'six' );   -- only message printed
12  end;
13  /
six

PL/SQL procedure successfully completed.
```

Only the messages cached after the last DBMS_ENABLE are displayed.

Caveats

When you use DBMS_OUTPUT, there are a couple of "gotchas" of which you should be aware, which we describe in the following sections.

Non-DBMS_OUTPUT-Aware Clients

You can only get the messages back from a routine that is called from a DBMS_OUT-PUT-aware client. Otherwise, you need to "pull" the messages programmatically, from within your application. What this means is that if your procedure is executed as part of a Web application (or a Pro*C or Java application), then the DBMS_OUTPUT messages won't be displayed unless you explicitly code their retrieval.

Character Limit on PUT and PUT_LINE

The PUT and PUT_LINE procedures have a hard line length of 255 characters:

```
SQL> exec dbms_output.put_line( rpad( '*', 255, '*' ) );
**************************************************************************
**************************************************************************
**************************************************************************
**************
PL/SQL procedure successfully completed.

SQL> exec dbms_output.put_line( rpad( '*', 256, '*' ) );
BEGIN dbms_output.put_line( rpad( '*', 256, '*' ) ); END;
*
ERROR at line 1:
ORA-20000: ORU-10028: line length overflow, limit of 255 chars per line
ORA-06512: at "SYS.DBMS_OUTPUT", line 35
ORA-06512: at "SYS.DBMS_OUTPUT", line 133
ORA-06512: at line 1
```

Therefore, if you need to print a lot of text, you'll have to ensure that you have only 255 characters per line. One solution to this problem is to use the SUBSTR function to clip any message you send to DBMS_OUTPUT to the first 255 characters, and just lose the remaining text:

```
SQL> exec dbms_output.put_line( substr( rpad( '*', 500, '*' ), 1, 255 ) );
**************************************************************************
**************************************************************************
**************************************************************************
**************
PL/SQL procedure successfully completed.
```

Alternatively, you can write a wrapper routine that will chunk up your message into 255-character lines, and then send each chunk off to DBMS_OUTPUT. You then use that procedure instead of DBMS_OUTPUT.PUT_LINE to display all your messages:

```
SQL> create or replace
  2    procedure my_put_line( p_line varchar2 ) as
  3      l_offset number := 1;
  4    begin
  5      loop
  6        exit when substr(p_line, l_offset, 255 ) is null;
  7        dbms_output.put_line( substr(p_line, l_offset, 255 ) );
  8        l_offset := l_offset + 255;
  9      end loop;
 10    end my_put_line;
 11  /
Procedure created.

SQL> exec my_put_line( rpad( '*', 500, '*' ) );
********************************************************************************
********************************************************************************
********************************************************************************
**************
********************************************************************************
********************************************************************************
********************************************************************************
*****
PL/SQL procedure successfully completed.
```

Buffer Limit

DBMS_OUTPUT stores your messages in a buffer of a fixed size. That buffer can be no larger than 1,000,000 characters. By default the buffer limit is 2,000 characters. You can increase it to 1,000,000 by issuing this:

```
SET SERVEROUTPUT ON SIZE 1000000
```

or programmatically with this:

```
DBMS_OUTPUT.ENABLE( 1000000 );
```

This setting is session based, so you'll need to reinitialize it for every new database session from which you're debugging. If you try to put more characters into the buffer than it can hold, you'll get an error:

```
SQL> set serveroutput on size 1000000
SQL> begin
  2      for i in 1 .. 5000 loop
```

```
 3        dbms_output.put_line( 'line: ' || i || ' ' || rpad( '*', 240, '*' ) );
 4    end loop;
 5  end;
 6  /
line: 1
****************************************************************************
****************************************************************************
****************************************************************************
line: 2
****************************************************************************
****************************************************************************
****************************************************************************
<--- Lots and lots of output omitted --->
line: 3500
****************************************************************************
****************************************************************************
****************************************************************************
begin
*
ERROR at line 1:
ORA-20000: ORU-10027: buffer overflow, limit of 1000000 bytes
ORA-06512: at "SYS.DBMS_OUTPUT", line 35
ORA-06512: at "SYS.DBMS_OUTPUT", line 198
ORA-06512: at "SYS.DBMS_OUTPUT", line 139
ORA-06512: at line 3
```

Do not rely exclusively on DBMS_OUTPUT for generating debug messages. The line-size restriction and the relatively small buffer size do not make it a great solution for large-scale application debugging. However, for simple small procedures and quick message retrieval from the SQL*Plus client, it works just great.

SQLCODE and SQLERRM

SQLCODE and SQLERRM are built-in functions that return the error code and the error message of the last raised exception. These two functions are extremely useful when you're using the WHEN OTHERS catchall exception and you want to log what exactly caused each exception. Let's look at an example of how you might use them:

```
SQL> set serverout on
SQL> declare
  2    n number;
  3  begin
```

```
 4    n := 'a';
 5  exception
 6    when OTHERS then
 7      dbms_output.put_line( 'SQLCODE = '|| SQLCODE );
 8      dbms_output.put_line( 'SQLERRM = '|| SQLERRM );
 9      raise;
10  end;
11  /
SQLCODE = -6502
SQLERRM = ORA-06502: PL/SQL: numeric or value error: character to number
conversion error
declare
*
ERROR at line 1:
ORA-06502: PL/SQL: numeric or value error: character to number conversion error
ORA-06512: at line 9
```

Notice that the output that SQLCODE and SQLERRM provide is the same error code and message that SQL*Plus returns. Instead of printing it out, you could log the error to a table or file. You'll see examples of logging errors in this manner a little later on.

DBMS_UTILITY.FORMAT_CALL_STACK

We covered this function in the "Code Path Tracing Made Easy" section of Chapter 2, so we'll just briefly recap it here. Basically, the DBMS_UTILITY.FORMAT_CALL_STACK function returns a formatted text string of the current call stack. You can use this information to find out exactly how you arrived at the line of code you're executing. Let's see it in action. We create three procedures: A, B, and C:

```
SQL> create or replace
  2  procedure a as
  3  begin
  4    dbms_output.put_line( dbms_utility.format_call_stack );
  5  end a;
  6  /
Procedure created.

SQL> create or replace
  2  procedure b as
  3  begin
  4    a;
```

```
  5   end b;
  6   /
Procedure created.

SQL> create or replace
  2   procedure c as
  3   begin
  4      b;
  5   end c;
  6   /
Procedure created.
```

Procedure A calls and displays the output of DBMS_UTILITY.FORMAT_CALL_STACK. Procedure B just calls procedure A and procedure C calls procedure B. When we execute procedures A and C, we see the following results:

```
SQL> set serverout on
SQL> begin
  2      a;
  3   end;
  4   /
----- PL/SQL Call Stack -----
  object        line   object
  handle      number   name
66C50624           3   procedure CLBECK.A
66BB7EB8           2   anonymous block

PL/SQL procedure successfully completed.

SQL> begin
  2      c;
  3   end;
  4   /
----- PL/SQL Call Stack -----
  object        line   object
  handle      number   name
66C50624           3   procedure CLBECK.A
66BC5E20           3   procedure CLBECK.B
66BC230C           3   procedure CLBECK.C
66B9E6C4           2   anonymous block

PL/SQL procedure successfully completed.
```

Notice the results are nicely formatted and easy to read. It's easy to determine that both were initiated with an anonymous block, but the second result has the extra step of procedure C calling procedure B, which then calls procedure A. This information is valuable to anyone debugging a large PL/SQL program.

DBMS_APPLICATION_INFO

DBMS_APPLICATION_INFO is a package supplied by Oracle to allow developers to register information about procedures and functions that are currently executing. This information is then immediately available to other sessions in the database without requiring the session currently running to commit any changes. Remember, any information that you spool via DBMS_OUTPUT is only displayed when the process completes. This information is available to view as soon as it is set. Let's take a look at a couple of examples.

> **NOTE**   You can view the specification for DBMS_APPLICATION_INFO at $ORACLE_HOME/rdbms/admin/dbmsapin.sql.

The three main procedures to look out for in this package are as follows:

- SET_MODULE

- SET_ACTION

- SET_CLIENT_INFO

The following simple example demonstrates their usage:

```
SQL> create or replace
  2   package PKG is
  3     procedure DO_WORK;
  4   end;
  5   /

Package created.

SQL> create or replace
  2   package body PKG is
  3     procedure DO_WORK is
```

```
 4        v_emp_cnt number;
 5     begin
 6       dbms_application_info.set_module(module_name=>'PKG.DO_WORK',
 7                                     action_name=>'commencing count');
 8       select count(*)
 9       into   v_emp_cnt
10       from   emp;
11       dbms_application_info.set_action('finished count');
12       for i in 1 .. 1000 loop
13         dbms_application_info.set_client_info('Deleting employee '||i);
14         delete from emp where empno = i;
15       end loop;
16     end;
17   end;
18   /
```

Package body created.

What is the significance of the terms MODULE, ACTION, and CLIENT_INFO? Virtually nothing. They simply represent three character fields into which you assign values while executing your PL/SQL programs. The MODULE can be up to 48 characters, the ACTION up to 32 characters, and the CLIENT_INFO up to 64 characters. In the preceding example, we have recorded the procedure name DO_WORK as our "module," plus some meaningful text for the action indicating the task about to be performed. In a similar fashion, as 1,000 employees were being deleted, we tracked the progress using the SET_CLIENT_INFO procedure.

But the real beauty of the DBMS_APPLICATION_INFO package is where the MODULE, ACTION, and CLIENT_INFO fields are exposed. All three values are viewable from the V$SESSION fixed view:

```
SQL> desc V$SESSION
 Name                          Null?    Type
 ---------------------------   -------- ----------------
 SADDR                                  RAW(4)
 SID                                    NUMBER
 SERIAL#                                NUMBER
    ...
 MODULE                                 VARCHAR2(48)
 ACTION                                 VARCHAR2(32)
 CLIENT_INFO                            VARCHAR2(64)
    ...
```

Thus, from any account that has privileges to query this view, we can observe the execution of the PKG.DO_WORK procedure via V$SESSION:

```
SQL> select module, action, client_info
  2  from v$session
  3  where client_info is not null;


MODULE                  ACTION                  CLIENT_INFO
--------------------    --------------------    ----------------------
PKG.DO_WORK             finished count          Deleting employee 1000
```

Similarly, the MODULE and ACTION are also recorded within the V$SQL view. Thus, it becomes possible to match SQL statements executed on the database to the values set for MODULE and ACTION. For example, after running the PKG.DO_WORK procedure, you can see what SQL statements were executed within that procedure, knowing that the MODULE was set to PKG.DO_WORK:

```
SQL> select sql_text, buffer_gets, executions
  2  from v$sql
  3  where module = 'PKG.DO_WORK';
SQL_TEXT                                    BUFFER_GETS EXECUTIONS
----------------------------------------    ----------- ----------
SELECT count(*)    from    emp                        3          1
DELETE from emp where empno = :b1                   3000       1000
```

Remember, the information from this package is available to view as soon as it is set. Consider the following procedure:

```
SQL> create or replace
  2  procedure test1 as
  3  begin
  4    dbms_application_info.set_action( 'Procedure TEST1' );
  5    for i in 1 .. 10 loop
  6      dbms_application_info.set_client_info( 'Loop number ' || i );
  7      dbms_lock.sleep( 5 );
  8    end loop;
  9  end test1;
 10  /
Procedure created.
```

NOTE You may have to grant execute on DBMS_LOCK to your user.

Now, leaving the previous session running, start a second session and run the following query. If you're the only one in the database, then you should see the following:

```
C:\temp>sqlplus clbeck/clbeck

SQL*Plus: Release 9.2.0.1.0 - Production on Mon Aug 18 20:43:05 2003
Copyright (c) 1982, 2002, Oracle Corporation.  All rights reserved.

Connected to:
Oracle9i Enterprise Edition Release 9.2.0.1.0 - Production
With the OLAP and Oracle Data Mining options
JServer Release 9.2.0.1.0 - Production

SQL> col module for a10
SQL> col action for a20
SQL> col client_info for a20
SQL>
SQL> select module, action, client_info
  2     from v$session
  3  where module is not null
  4  /

MODULE      ACTION               CLIENT_INFO
---------- -------------------- --------------------
SQL*Plus
SQL*Plus
```

Now switch back to the first session and execute the procedure TEST1:

```
SQL> begin
  2     test1;
  3  end;
  4  /
```

The procedure won't immediately return because the program is sleeping for 5 seconds for each loop iteration.

Now switch back to the second session and rerun the same query. Notice now that you can see the information that was written from the first session without the first session committing any work:

```
SQL> /

MODULE      ACTION               CLIENT_INFO
----------  -------------------  --------------------
SQL*Plus    Procedure TEST1      Loop number 1
SQL*Plus
```

Wait 5 seconds and rerun the query yet again. The CLIENT_INFO column is again updated:

```
SQL> /

MODULE      ACTION               CLIENT_INFO
----------  -------------------  --------------------
SQL*Plus    Procedure TEST1      Loop number 2
SQL*Plus
```

And if you wait until the procedure completes, you'll see this:

```
SQL> /

MODULE      ACTION               CLIENT_INFO
----------  -------------------  --------------------
SQL*Plus    Procedure TEST1      Loop number 10
SQL*Plus
```

There is a second view, V$SESSION_LONGOPS, that developers also have access to. The view is defined as follows:

```
SQL> desc v$session_longops
 Name                                      Null?    Type
 ----------------------------------------- -------- ------------------
 SID                                                NUMBER
 SERIAL#                                            NUMBER
 OPNAME                                             VARCHAR2(64)
 TARGET                                             VARCHAR2(64)
 TARGET_DESC                                        VARCHAR2(32)
 SOFAR                                              NUMBER
 TOTALWORK                                          NUMBER
 UNITS                                              VARCHAR2(32)
 START_TIME                                         DATE
 LAST_UPDATE_TIME                                   DATE
 TIME_REMAINING                                     NUMBER
```

```
ELAPSED_SECONDS                           NUMBER
CONTEXT                                   NUMBER
MESSAGE                                   VARCHAR2(512)
USERNAME                                  VARCHAR2(30)
SQL_ADDRESS                               RAW(4)
SQL_HASH_VALUE                            NUMBER
QCSID                                     NUMBER
```

You can set and view the information in this view in the same way as with V$SESSION, but this time you use the procedure SET_SESSION_LONGOPS in the DBMS_APPLICATION_INFO package to set the values:

```
PROCEDURE SET_SESSION_LONGOPS
  Argument Name                Type                    In/Out    Default?
  --------------------------   ---------------------   ------    --------
  RINDEX                       BINARY_INTEGER          IN/OUT
  SLNO                         BINARY_INTEGER          IN/OUT
  OP_NAME                      VARCHAR2                IN        DEFAULT
  TARGET                       BINARY_INTEGER          IN        DEFAULT
  CONTEXT                      BINARY_INTEGER          IN        DEFAULT
  SOFAR                        NUMBER                  IN        DEFAULT
  TOTALWORK                    NUMBER                  IN        DEFAULT
  TARGET_DESC                  VARCHAR2                IN        DEFAULT
  UNITS                        VARCHAR2                IN        DEFAULT
```

You would use this view to advertise information about long-running PL/SQL processes. Periodically, your long-running application or process would update the information in this view, thus allowing others, including such tools as Oracle Enterprise Manager, to report on its status. This helps in the debugging process by allowing developers to keep tabs on where in the process the application currently is. But the information stored in the view is only as good and as useful as the developer who coded the application makes it.

The first two parameters of DBMS_APPLICATION_INFO are RINDEX and SLNO. The procedure uses RINDEX to determine which row within the V$SESSION_LONGOPS view to update. Initially, you set RINDEX to the value of the constant DBMS_APPLICATION_INFO.SET_SESSION_LONGOPS_NOHINT. The procedure returns an internal ID via the OUT parameter that would be used in subsequent calls to modify that same row. The SLNO parameter is for the internal use only and you shouldn't modify it at all.

The rest of the parameters are there for you to store the information that you want to disseminate through the view. You're free to populate the remaining columns through the procedure with any information that you choose, as long as it's of the correct datatype and size for that column. An example would be the parameter OP_NAME. It's suggested that you store the procedure or application name in that field, but there's nothing stopping you from populating it with the current test run name or the user who is executing the code. As long as it's meaningful and helpful for your debugging purpose, store anything you want.

In the following example we loop 20 times, representing the total work that we have to accomplish. After each iteration, we pause for 3 seconds to simulate doing real work and so we can actually see how subsequent calls to SET_SES-SION_LONGSOPS affect what we see when we query the V$SESSION_LONGOPS view:

```
SQL> declare
  2     l_rindex binary_integer;
  3     l_slno binary_integer;
  4     l_totalwork number;
  5  begin
  6     l_rindex := dbms_application_info.set_session_longops_nohint;
  7     l_totalwork := 20;
  8     for i in 1 .. l_totalwork loop
  9       dbms_application_info.set_session_longops(
 10         rindex => l_rindex,
 11         slno => l_slno,
 12         op_name => 'testing session longops',
 13         target => null,
 14         context => null,
 15         sofar => i,
 16         totalwork => l_totalwork,
 17         target_desc => 'This is a test showing how longops works',
 18         units => 'looping with sleep 3' );
 19       dbms_lock.sleep( 3 );
 20     end loop;
 21  end;
```

Now, what is so neat about this is that if we update SET_SESSION_LONGOPS on each iteration, and the sofar and totalwork parameters' values are valid, then the TIME_REMAINING column will show Oracle's best guess on when this procedure will complete. Also, the ELAPSED_SECONDS column will be continually updated to represent how long, in seconds, the procedure has been running.

If approximately 5 seconds after running the preceding routine we run the following query from a second session, then we should see this:

```
SQL> select opname,
  2          username,
  3          sofar,
  4          elapsed_seconds,
  5          time_remaining
  6  from v$session_longops;
```

OPNAME	USERNAME	SOFAR	ELAPSED_SECONDS	TIME_REMAINING
testing session long ops	CLBECK	2	3	27

Notice that the view is reporting that the process is in the second iteration of the loop, that it has been running for 3 seconds, and that it will complete in 27 seconds' time. We know that this isn't possible. The process is going to loop 20 times and pause for 3 seconds during each loop (a total of 60 seconds). But remember that Oracle had only one iteration of the loop to come up with its guess. Issuing the same query 15 seconds later may yield this:

OPNAME	USERNAME	SOFAR	ELAPSED_SECONDS	TIME_REMAINING
testing session long ops	CLBECK	7	18	33

Now the process is in the seventh iteration, has been running for 18 seconds, and Oracle has calculated that it will finish in 33 seconds' time. Considering that it has only been running for 18 seconds, this is again not correct, but it's closer. If we run the query for a third time 15 seconds later, the results may be as follows:

OPNAME	USERNAME	SOFAR	ELAPSED_SECONDS	TIME_REMAINING
testing session long ops	CLBECK	12	34	23

This time Oracle estimates that our long-running process will be finished in 23 seconds' time, and it has currently been running for 34 seconds, giving a total run time of 57 seconds, which is a pretty good estimate.

The longer the process ran, the better Oracle was at estimating when it would complete. Imagine a routine that updated millions and millions of rows. If we use DBMS_APPLICATION_INFO.SET_SESSION_LONGOPS correctly, not only can we keep tabs on how far along the process is, but also Oracle will give us its best guess on when it will complete based on how long it has already taken. This information is extremely valuable when attempting to debug these long-running processes.

Autonomous Transactions

We've discussed autonomous transactions at several points in this book, but it's worth taking a look at them again in the context of debugging. Basically, they make it possible for you to log all the information you want to into a database table, make it immediately available to other sessions, and have it remain in the table, even if the session that logged the information rolled back any or all of its work.

Imagine how useless logging information to a database table would be if the transaction logging the information encountered an error and rolled back its work. Well, without autonomous transaction, the act of logging said information was part of the work it did and it too would have been rolled back, effectively erasing all the debug information.

In many of the previous examples, the possibility of logging information such as SQLCODE and SQLERRM, or DBMS_UTILITY.FORMAT_CALL_STACK, was mentioned but never fully discussed. So now let's look at how you can log debugging information to a database table:

```
SQL> create table log_table(
  2     d date,
  3     message clob
  4  )
  5  /
Table created.
```

```
SQL> create table test_table(
  2     v varchar2(10)
  3  )
  4  /
Table created.
```

Here we created two tables, one to do work in and one to log information to. Next we'll create our LOG_IT package and a test routine to use it:

```
SQL> create or replace
  2  package log_it as
  3
  4     procedure put_line( p_message varchar2 );
  5
  6  end log_it;
  7  /
Package created.
```

```
SQL> create or replace
  2  package body log_it as
  3
  4     procedure put_line( p_message varchar2 ) is
  5     pragma autonomous_transaction;
  6     begin
  7        insert into log_table
```

```
  8        values ( sysdate, p_message );
  9          commit;
 10      end put_line;
 11
 12   end log_it;
 13   /
Package body created.

SQL> create or replace
  2   procedure test_log_it p_value varchar2 ) as
  3   begin
  4     log_it.put_line( 'Starting procedure test_log_it' );
  5     insert into test_table values ( p_value );
  6     log_it.put_line( 'Success' );
  7     commit;
  8   exception
  9     when others then
 10       log_it.put_line( 'Exception when inserting ' || p_value );
 11       log_it.put_line( SQLCODE || ' == ' || SQLERRM );
 12       rollback;
 13   end test_log_it;
 14   /
Procedure created.
```

Notice that we call LOG_IT once when we begin the procedure and then again after the INSERT statement. If an exception is raised, we roll back and log the error. Now let's see what happens when we run it:

```
SQL> exec test_log_it( 'ABCDE' );
PL/SQL procedure successfully completed.

SQL> exec test_log_it( 'ABCDEFGHIJKLM' );
PL/SQL procedure successfully completed.
```

Because we used the OTHERS handler and didn't reraise the exception, it appears that everything works fine. However, while we would expect there to be two rows in TEST_TABLE, on inspection we see only one:

```
SQL> select * from test_table;

V
----------
ABCDE
```

Luckily, we've logged some information in the LOG_TABLE table, so we see what happened:

```
SQL> select to_char(d,'DD-MON-YYYY HH24:MI:SS') d, message
  2     from log_table
SQL> /


D                              MESSAGE
-----------------------------  ---------------------------------------
18-AUG-2003 21:36:38           Starting procedure test_log_it
18-AUG-2003 21:36:38           Success
18-AUG-2003 21:38:55           Starting procedure test_log_it
18-AUG-2003 21:38:55           Exception when inserting ABCDEFGHIJKLM
18-AUG-2003 21:38:55           -1401 == ORA-01401: inserted value too
                                 large for column
```

Even though the second time we executed the procedure we caused an error and rolled back any work, the logged information remained in the table because it was part of an autonomous transaction and wasn't affected by it parent transaction. This method of debugging is very useful. It lets you capture as much debug information as you want, and this information will remain even if the transaction is rolled back.

An added benefit here is you can leave the LOG_IT.PUT_LINE code in your production code. All you need to do is replace the LOG_IT.PUT_LINE procedure with a NULL body and any call to it will be a NOOP. Because it's a procedure within a package and all you're doing is recompiling the package body, it won't invalidate any of your code. Then, at any time, you can again compile the functional version of LOG_IT.PUTL_LINE into the database and again collect debug information. This is an example of instrumenting your code. Leave the ability to easily debug the code—just disable that feature until needed.

UTL_FILE

UTL_FILE is another very useful Oracle-supplied package. It allows you to write to a file on the file system from within a PL/SQL stored procedure. Just as when you used an autonomous transaction to write to a database table, once you write the line to a file, committing or rolling back won't affect it.

I usually prefer to debug my information to a file for a couple of reasons. First, it's easier to review and read as lines in a file, as opposed to columns in a table. Second, I can tail my debug files while the process is running so that I get to see the debug messages generated in real time, using the following command:

```
tail -f debugfile.txt
```

If I were debugging to a table, I would have to keep rerunning the query to fetch the new rows.

> **NOTE** Those of you on Windows may not have the TAIL command, but a quick search of the Web should locate many implementations of TAIL for Windows. We suggest that you acquire one, as it makes monitoring log files much easier.

The TAIL command prints the last *x* lines of a file to the screen. The -F parameter tells it to continue to print the last lines as they're added to the file.

> **NOTE** You can view the specification for UTL_FILE at $ORACLE_HOME/rdbms/admin/utlfile.sql.

There is one downside to debugging to a file. Oracle can only create the file on the database server, and there are many times that developers don't have access to the server. In those cases, you'll probably want to debug to a log table.

Opening a File

To open a file on the file system, you use the FOPEN() function:

```
FUNCTION fopen(location     IN VARCHAR2,
               filename     IN VARCHAR2,
               open_mode    IN VARCHAR2,
               max_linesize IN BINARY_INTEGER DEFAULT NULL) RETURN file_type;
```

Here are the parameters you supply to define the file you wish to open:

- **LOCATION:** This defines the directory in which the file will be opened. You supply either the name of a directory object that you've already created with the CREATE DIRECTORY command or the actual directory. If you supply the actual directory, then that directory must be defined in the database's init.ora file as a value for the parameter UTL_FILE_DIR.

- **FILENAME:** This is the name of the file that you're using.

- **OPEN_MODE:** This is a string defining how you want to open the file, either in write (W), read (R), or append (A) mode.

- **MAX_LINESIZE:** This optional parameter defines the maximum character per line including the newline character. Valid values are 1 through 32767.

If the call to FOPEN is successful, then a handle to the file will be returned. You use this handle to access the file and manipulate it.

Writing a Line

Once you have a valid file handle, you can write to it using the PUT_LINE procedure:

```
PROCEDURE put_line(file    IN file_type,
                   buffer IN VARCHAR2,
                   autoflush IN BOOLEAN DEFAULT FALSE);
```

You supply the following parameters:

- **FILE:** This is the handle of the file that you received when you called FOPEN.

- **BUFFER:** This parameter is the test that you want to write to the file.

- **AUTOFLUSH:** This directs Oracle to flush the buffer to the file straight away or not. The default action is FALSE.

You can make repeated calls to PUT_LINE once you've opened the file. There is no need to open the file before each write.

Closing the File

Lastly, once you've finished writing to the file, you should close it, freeing any resources in use maintaining the open file:

```
PROCEDURE fclose(file IN OUT file_type);
```

To close the file, just pass in the valid handle you've been using.

Using UTL_FILE

Let's look at an example of using UTL_FILE to debug. We'll modify our existing LOG_IT package:

```
SQL> create or replace
  2  directory TEMP_DIR as 'c:\temp'
  3  /
Directory created.

SQL> create or replace
  2  package body log_it as
  3
  4    procedure put_line( p_message varchar2 ) is
  5      l_file utl_file.file_type;
  6    begin
  7      l_file := utl_file.fopen( 'TEMP_DIR',
  8                                'debugfile.txt',
  9                                'a',
 10                                32767 );
 11      utl_file.put_line( l_file,
 12                         to_char( sysdate, 'DD-MON-YYYY HH24:MI:SS' ) ||
 13                         ' ' || p_message );
 14      utl_file.fclose( l_file );
 15    exception
 16      when others then
 17          null;
 18    end put_line;
 19
 20  end log_it;
 21  /
Package body created.
```

Now we again execute the same two calls to the procedure TEST2:

```
SQL> delete from test_table;
1 row deleted.

SQL> commit;
Commit complete.

SQL> exec test_log_it( 'ABCDE' );
PL/SQL procedure successfully completed.
```

```
SQL> exec test_log_it( 'ABCDEFGHIJKLM');
PL/SQL procedure successfully completed.

SQL> select * from test_table;

V
----------
ABCDE
```

This time our debug messages were written to the file c:\temp\debugfile.txt. In another window we were running a TAIL -F on the debug file and received the following output:

```
C:\temp>tail -f debugfile.txt
18-AUG-2003 22:20:16 Starting procedure test_log_it
18-AUG-2003 22:20:16 Success
18-AUG-2003 22:20:37 Starting procedure test_log_it
18-AUG-2003 22:20:37 Exception when inserting ABCDEFGHIJKLM
18-AUG-2003 22:20:37 -1401 == ORA-01401: inserted value too large for column
```

Now all our messages are spooled to this window in real time, and they're also saved in the debug file for later review.

Real-Time Debugging with Pipelined Functions

As we've discussed, when using DBMS_OUTPUT the output isn't available until the entire process completes. For years, developers have been frustrated when testing their code with the DBMS_OUTPUT facilities because:

- The output wasn't available until the call ended.

- Not many tools beside SQL*Plus supported retrieval of its output.

In the previous UTL_FILE section, we talked about use of the TAIL command to stream debug messages back to a file in "real time." An alternate means of getting these real-time debugging messages is to use pipelined functions (discussed in detail in Chapter 5).

Because pipelined functions stream their rows (or their output) back to the calling environment in "real time," it should be possible to pipe debugging output back to the developer as well. Consider a procedure that cycles through five significant tasks and that outputs some message at the conclusion of each task:

```
procedure NIGHTLY_BATCH is
begin
  dbms_output.put_line('Starting task 1');
  TASK_1;
  dbms_output.put_line('Starting task 2');
  TASK_2;
  dbms_output.put_line('Starting task 3');
  TASK_3;
  dbms_output.put_line('Starting task 4');
  TASK_4;
  dbms_output.put_line('Starting task 5');
  TASK_5;
end;
```

First, we'll need a collection for the output, because pipelined functions must return a collection. Keeping things simple, we'll just output a large VARCHAR2:

```
SQL> create or replace
  2  type output is table of varchar2(1000);
  3  /
```

Type created.

Next, we'll create some procedures to simulate the tasks in the NIGHTLY_BATCH procedure—in our case, they'll simply sleep for 5 seconds. We'll use a little dynamic SQL to generate five procedures, TASK_1 to TASK_5:

```
SQL> begin
  2  for i in 1 .. 5 loop
  3    execute immediate
  4    'create or replace procedure TASK_'||i||
  5    ' is begin dbms_lock.sleep(5); end;';
  6  end loop;
  7  end;
  8  /
```

PL/SQL procedure successfully completed.

```
SQL> select object_name
  2  from user_objects
  3  where object_name like 'TASK%'
  4  /
```

OBJECT_NAME

```
--------------------------------------
TASK_1
TASK_2
TASK_3
TASK_4
TASK_5
```

Now the NIGHTLY_BATCH procedure can be recast as a pipelined function, and the DBMS_OUTPUT calls can be replaced with the PIPE ROW command:

```
SQL> create or replace
  2   function NIGHTLY_BATCH return output pipelined is
  3   begin
  4     pipe row ('Starting task 1');
  5     TASK_1;
  6     pipe row ('Starting task 2');
  7     TASK_2;
  8     pipe row ('Starting task 3');
  9     TASK_3;
 10     pipe row ('Starting task 4');
 11     TASK_4;
 12     pipe row ('Starting task 5');
 13     TASK_5;
 14     return;
 15   end;
 16   /

Function created.
```

With a pipelined function, we now only need to query our pipelined function to see the output. Unfortunately, conveying what happens next in print is somewhat difficult, but to run the NIGHTLY_BATCH and see the output we ran this:

```
SQL> select * from table(nightly_batch);
```

< 25 seconds elapsed>

```
COLUMN_VALUE
--------------------------------------------------
Starting task 1
Starting task 2
Starting task 3
Starting task 4
Starting task 5
```

537

The output got deferred until the procedure completed! There's nothing wrong with the code—it's SQL*Plus that's causing the problem here. By default, the array size in SQL*Plus is set to 15 (and array fetching is a good thing in most circumstances, as you've already seen in many examples throughout this book), so SQL*Plus won't display any output until 15 rows are piped back to it from the NIGHTLY_BATCH procedure. Setting the array size back to 1 resolves the problem:

```
SQL> select * from table(nightly_batch);

COLUMN_VALUE
---------------------------------------------------
Starting task 1
< 10 seconds elapsed>
Starting task 2
Starting task 3
< 10 seconds elapsed>
Starting task 4
Starting task 5
```

This is the best that we can do because of the prefetch optimization discussed in Chapter 3, but it's a significant improvement on DBMS_OUTPUT. Whereas DBMS_OUTPUT is limited to a 255-character output, the only limitation for using a collection as output is the developer's imagination. For example, in a client application written in Oracle Forms, you could use a pipelined function to send "progress indicators" back to the calling environment as a long-running process takes place.

Of course, in a more realistic scenario, our TASK_*n* procedures would be doing a lot more than just sleeping for 5 seconds. Let's alter the task procedures to perform some DML on a table T and see if our pipelined streaming output still works as expected:

```
SQL> create table T ( x ) as select 1 from dual;

Table created.

SQL> begin
  2    for i in 1 .. 5 loop
  3      execute immediate
  4       'create or replace procedure TASK_'||i||
  5       ' is begin update t set x = x + 1; end;';
  6    end loop;
  7  end;
  8  /

PL/SQL procedure successfully completed.
```

And now let's rerun our pipelined `NIGHTLY_BATCH` procedure:

```
SQL> select * from table(nightly_batch);

COLUMN_VALUE
----------------------------------------------------------
Starting task 1
ERROR:
ORA-14551: cannot perform a DML operation inside a query
ORA-06512: at " TASK_1", line 1
ORA-06512: at " NIGHTLY_BATCH", line 4
```

This isn't a problem with pipelined functions per se—the issue here is that we can't perform DML whenever we perform a `SELECT` statement. The solution is to use an autonomous transaction, as discussed earlier, so that the `NIGHTLY_BATCH` procedure runs within its own transaction:

```
SQL> create or replace
  2  function NIGHTLY_BATCH return output pipelined is
  3      pragma autonomous_transaction;
  4  begin
  5     pipe row ('Starting task 1');
  6     TASK_1;
  7     pipe row ('Starting task 2');
  8     TASK_2;
  9     pipe row ('Starting task 3');
 10     TASK_3;
 11     pipe row ('Starting task 4');
 12     TASK_4;
 13     pipe row ('Starting task 5');
 14     TASK_5;
 15     commit;
 16     return;
 17  end;
 18  /

Function created.
```

Now, because the `NIGHTLY_BATCH` function (and the tasks within it) runs in a transaction separate from our calling environment, no errors are encountered:

```
SQL> select * from table(nightly_batch);
```

```
COLUMN_VALUE
-----------------------------------------------------
Starting task 1
Starting task 2
Starting task 3
Starting task 4
Starting task 5
```

A Custom DEBUG Utility

So far I've discussed tools and utilities that are available from Oracle. I talked about the different supplied packages and built-in functions, and how to use them. Let's now shift gears a bit and talk about a custom package written for debugging purposes. This package has been invaluable to me and my colleagues in debugging our PL/SQL applications. I call the package DEBUG. In this section, I'll briefly cover how the package is constructed and the key procedures.

A full description of DEBUG, along with complete code listings, is deferred to Appendix A so that we may focus the discussion on how to use this package effectively. To run the examples in this chapter, simply download and install the DEBUG utility from the Downloads section of the Apress website (http://www.apress.com), and also run the DEBUG_DB script to create the necessary databases objects.

DEBUG uses many of the features and techniques described previously in the chapter. It prints its debug information to a file, although alternatively you could create a log table with the NOLOGGING option, so as not to task the database with unneeded writes and redos. The true power of DEBUG lies in its capability to debug individual procedures or packages within your application.

Requirements

Imagine for a second you have a PL/SQL application with a large number of procedures, functions, and packages, and an error is encountered. If you've followed some of the recommendations in this chapter, you've instrumented your code with calls to a debugging routine. These debug statements may produce thousands and thousands of lines of output when enabled. From a developer's perspective, these lines can be cumbersome and sometimes difficult to review. But as the developer, you probably have a good idea where the error is or, better yet, you've isolated the error to a particular PL/SQL package or procedure, so you're only interested in the debug messages from that particular package or procedure. All the techniques described earlier in this chapter are all or nothing: Either you get all the debug information or none of it. And either every run of the application produces debug or no run does. The central idea behind the development of the DEBUG package was to give developers much finer control over who generates messages and what debug is actually generated, without making any changes to the application.

Based on this central idea, the core requirements for the DEBUG tool were broken down as follows:

- Useable in any PL/SQL

- No limit on the amount of debug that can be generated

- No limit on the length of a line of debug

- Real-time feedback

- Self-aware (i.e., it knows what line and package it is in)

- Capability to turn on and off easily

- Capability to selectively debug packages/procedures/functions

- Acts differently depending on who runs the process

- Stores messages to a file

- Easy to use

Now that we've outlined what we require of our DEBUG tool, let's begin to look at how to create it.

Database Design and Setup

The SQL script Debug_DB.sql contains all the code for the required database objects for our DEBUG tool. This script is fully described in Appendix A and is freely available for download from the Apress website. In short, it contains code to do the following:

- Create a schema to house the DEBUG utility.

- Create a table, DEBUGTAB, that stores profile information for each DEBUG user, so that it will act according to how each user has set up his environment.

- Create a trigger, BIU_FER_DEBUGTAB, to validate the format of the profiling data.

- Create a directory object to which DEBUG will write messages.

Package Layout

Let's now explore what the DEBUG package looks like. There are four main procedures that the DEBUG package must implement:

- Initialize the profile.

- Generate debug messages.

- List the current debug profile.

- Clear the profile.

The initialization procedure INIT() should take in all the options that we can set for the debug profile:

```
procedure init(
    p_modules      in varchar2 default 'ALL',
    p_dir          in varchar2 default 'TEMP',
    p_file         in varchar2 default user || '.dbg',
    p_user         in varchar2 default user,
    p_show_date    in varchar2 default 'YES',
    p_date_format  in varchar2 default 'MMDDYYYY HH24MISS',
    p_name_len     in number   default 30,
    p_show_sesid   in varchar2 default 'NO' );
```

The procedure F() that will generate the debug message should take in the parameterized message and a list of the variables to substitute:

```
procedure f(
    p_message in varchar2,
    p_arg1     in varchar2 default null,
    p_arg2     in varchar2 default null,
    p_arg3     in varchar2 default null,
    p_arg4     in varchar2 default null,
    p_arg5     in varchar2 default null,
    p_arg6     in varchar2 default null,
```

```
    p_arg7     in varchar2 default null,
    p_arg8     in varchar2 default null,
    p_arg9     in varchar2 default null,
    p_arg10    in varchar2 default null );
```

We're sure a few of you have noticed that we have a hard limit for the number of substitutions into the debug message. There are two options if you wish to get around this limitation. You can use either || to build the debug string (giving you an unlimited number of values to substitute in) or the DEBUG.FA() routine, whose specification is as follows:

```
emptyDebugArgv Argv;

  procedure fa(
    p_message in varchar2,
    p_args    in Argv default emptyDebugArgv );
```

In Appendix A we fully explain what the ARGV type is and how you use it. Suffice to say here that it removes the ten-parameter limitation of the F() implementation. Once the profile is set, we need a way to review it. We need a status routine:

```
  procedure status(
    p_user in varchar2 default user,
    p_dir  in varchar2 default null,
    p_file in varchar2 default null );
```

And finally we need a way to clear our debug profile when we no longer want to generate debug messages:

```
  procedure clear(
    p_user in varchar2 default user,
    p_dir  in varchar2 default null,
    p_file in varchar2 default null );
```

Both STATUS() and CLEAR() take in P_USER, P_DIR, and P_FILE. Remember, the primary key to the debug profile consists of all of those values. The user will need to supply them both to access the correct record. As a shortcut, we allow P_FILE and P_DIR to be passed in as NULL. In that case, all debug profiles for the supplied USER will be affected.

Implementation

Appendix A provides the full implementation details of all the procedures in DEBUG. In addition to the four procedures in our specification, as described previously, some private procedures in the DEBUG package body are implemented as well:

- **DEBUG_IT():** This procedure is the coordinator of the debug package. Both F() and FA() call it, and it in turn calls the following four private procedures.

- **WHO_CALLED_ME():** This procedure determines from what line of code in what procedure the debug message was called. It uses the Oracle-supplied function DBMS_UTILITY.FORMAT_CALL_STACK(), described earlier in this chapter, to get the call stack.

- **BUILD_IT():** This procedure builds and returns the header of the debug message. The header contains all the information about the call to DEBUG, formatted according to the debug profile set up with INIT().

- **PARSE_IT():** This procedure allows us to parse and modify the message itself. Substitutions of %s to appropriate values are also carried out.

- **FILE_IT():** With the header and message parsed, formatted, and ready for display, we use the FILE_IT procedure to attempt to write the information to the desired file.

Basic Operation

In the following sections we'll run through some of the very basic features and functionality of DEBUG, starting with how to initialize it.

Initializing

The first step when using DEBUG (after we've properly installed it, of course) is to initialize it:

```
PROCEDURE INIT
  Argument Name                 Type                 In/Out   Default?
  ----------------------------  -------------------  ------   --------
  P_MODULES                     VARCHAR2             IN       DEFAULT
  P_DIR                         VARCHAR2             IN       DEFAULT
  P_FILE                        VARCHAR2             IN       DEFAULT
  P_USER                        VARCHAR2             IN       DEFAULT
  P_SHOW_DATE                   VARCHAR2             IN       DEFAULT
  P_DATE_FORMAT                 VARCHAR2             IN       DEFAULT
  P_NAME_LEN                    NUMBER               IN       DEFAULT
  P_SHOW_SESID                  VARCHAR2             IN       DEFAULT
```

This is the INIT procedure of DEBUG. A call to this procedure will set up the proper environment to debug. The main parameters we're interested in at the moment are P_MODULES and P_DIR.

- **P_MODULES:** A list of the packages/procedures we want to debug

- **P_DIR:** The name of the DIRECTORY object to which we are debugging

- **P_FILE:** The name of the file to write the debug information to

Now we make a call to INIT:

```
SQL> execute debug.init( 'ALL', 'TEMP', 'debug.dbg' );
PL/SQL procedure successfully completed.
```

When we inspect that file, we should see this:

```
Debug parameters initialized on 07-SEP-2003 16:03:40
          USER:  UTILITY
       MODULES:  ALL
     DIRECTORY:  TEMP
      FILENAME:  debug.dbg
     SHOW DATE:  YES
   DATE FORMAT:  MMDDYYYY HH24MISS
   NAME LENGTH:  30
SHOW SESSION ID:  NO
```

This is just a listing of our current DEBUG environment. For the user UTILITY, all debug messages will be generated and written to the file debug.dbg.

Using STATUS

We can use the procedure STATUS() from the SQL*Plus command prompt to see the current profile enabled:

```
SQL> exec debug.status
Debug info for UTILITY
----------------------
USER:               UTILITY
MODULES:            ALL
DIRECTORY:          TEMP
FILENAME:           myDebug.dbg
SHOW DATE:          YES
DATE FORMAT:        MMDDYYYY HH24MISS
NAME LENGTH:        30
SHOW SESSION ID:    NO

PL/SQL procedure successfully completed.
```

Generating Messages

Now let's make a call to DEBUG.F():

```
SQL> exec debug.f( 'my first debug message' );

PL/SQL procedure successfully completed.
```

Pretty anticlimactic, wasn't it? There was no indication that anything happened. Go check line 8 of the debug file:

```
10282001 213953(UTILITY.ANONYMOUS BLOCK    1) my first debug message
```

There it is! There's our message. But what is all that extra stuff? It's the header information that was created and added to the message.

- The first set of numbers is the date in the format MMDDYYYY, and the second set of numbers is the time in the format HH24MISS. The date format is just as the profile says it should be.

- The next piece of information is the owner and object that initiated that call. We see that it says that the anonymous block owned by the user UTIL-ITY made the call, and it was at line 1 of that object.

The WHO_CALLED_ME() procedure parsed that information from the call stack and this is where it becomes very useful.

Modifying Our Profile

Let's change our profile and generate another message:

```
SQL> begin
  2      debug.init( p_dir => 'TEMP',
  3                      p_file => 'myDebug.dbg',
  4                      p_date_format => 'HH:MI:SSAM',
  5                      p_name_len => 20 );
  6   end;
  7   /
PL/SQL procedure successfully completed.

SQL> exec debug.f( 'another message' );
PL/SQL procedure successfully completed.
```

Inspecting the debug file reveals the following:

```
Debug parameters initialized on 28-OCT-2003 21:51:04
               USER: UTILITY
            MODULES: ALL
          DIRECTORY: TEMP
           FILENAME: myDebug.dbg
          SHOW DATE: YES
        DATE FORMAT: HH:MI:SSAM

        NAME LENGTH: 25
    SHOW SESSION ID: NO

    09:53:19PM(UTILITY.ANONYMOUS BLOCK  1) another message
```

We now have a new date format and the name length is shorter. You can play with the formatting until it's right for you. I like the default myself, so I'm going to put it back.

```
SQL> begin
  2      debug.init( 'all', 'TEMP', 'myDebug.dbg' );
  5   end;
  6   /
PL/SQL procedure successfully completed.
```

Let's now explore how the substitution works. Recall that the DEBUG utility allows the caller to pass in a string and values to be substituted into it. For every %s found in the message, DEBUG will try and substitute the next parameter. If we execute the following:

```
SQL> exec debug.f( '%s %s!', 'hello', 'world' );
```

the resulting debug message will be this:

```
10282001 224317 (UTILITY.ANONYMOUS BLOCK     1) hello world!
```

Using FA()

Using F() is only good when you have ten or fewer parameters. If you have more than ten parameters, you can use the FA() call. Recall that this procedure takes in a message and a user-defined type, ARGV. Here's an example of calling it:

```
SQL> exec debug.fa( 'The %s %s %s', debug.argv( 'quick','brown','fox' ) );
```

The result is as follows:

```
10282001 225121(UTILITY.ANONYMOUS BLOCK     1) The quick brown fox
```

> **NOTE** ARGV can take any number of values, so now you have a facility to pass in an unlimited number of values to substitute.

Formatting the Debug File

We can also use \N and \T to format the message:

```
SQL> exec debug.f( 'The %s\n%s fox', 'quick', 'brown' );
```

Again, here's the resulting message:

```
10282001 225630(UTILITY.ANONYMOUS BLOCK      1) The quick
                                                   brown fox
```

Removing the Profile

When we're done debugging, we can remove our profile using the following call to DEBUG.CLEAR():

```
SQL> exec debug.clear;

PL/SQL procedure successfully completed.

SQL> exec debug.status

Debug info for UTILITY
No debug setup.

PL/SQL procedure successfully completed.
```

Any subsequent calls to DEBUG.F() or DEBUG.FA() won't generate debug messages for the user BOOK.

Making the Package Executable by PUBLIC

To make the DEBUG package executable by PUBLIC, execute the following:

```
SQL> grant execute on debug to public;

Grant succeeded.
```

Now we'll connect as another user, SCOTT, and use the DEBUG package. We need to prefix all references to DEBUG's procedures with UTILITY.DEBUG:

```
SQL> connect scott/tiger
Connected.
SQL> exec utility.debug.init( 'all', 'TEMP', 'MyDebug.dbg');

PL/SQL procedure successfully completed.

SQL> exec utility.debug.status;
```

```
Debug info for SCOTT
--------------------
USER:                   SCOTT
MODULES:                ALL
DIRECTORY               TEMP
FILENAME:               MyDebug.dbg
SHOW DATE:              YES
DATE FORMAT:            MMDDYYYY HH24MISS
NAME LENGTH:            30
SHOW SESSION ID:        NO


PL/SQL procedure successfully completed.
```

Let's move on to the really impressive feature of DEBUG: its capability to selectively display debug messages depending on what procedure it's called from.

Selective Debugging

This is where you can see the real power of DEBUG. The first thing we'll need is a few procedures to debug. Let's switch back to the UTILITY user:

```
SQL> create or replace
  2 procedure a as
  3 begin
  4 debug.f( ' AAAAAAA ' );
  5 dbms_output.put_line( ' AAAAAAA ' );
  6 end a;
  7 /
Procedure created.


SQL> create or replace
  2 procedure b as
  3 begin
  4 a;
  5 debug.f( ' BBBBBBB ' );
  6 dbms_output.put_line( ' BBBBBBB ' );
  7 end b;
  8 /
Procedure created.


SQL> create or replace
  2 procedure c as
  3 begin
```

```
  4 b;
  5 debug.f( ' CCCCCCC ' );
  6 dbms_output.put_line( ' CCCCCCC ' );
  7 end c;
  8 /
Procedure created.

SQL> create or replace
  2 procedure d as
  3 begin
  4 c;
  5 debug.f( ' DDDDDDD ' );
  6 dbms_output.put_line( ' DDDDDDD ' );
  7 end d;
  8 /
Procedure created.

SQL> create or replace
  2 procedure e as
  3 begin
  4 d;
  5 debug.f( ' EEEEEEE ' );
  6 dbms_output.put_line( ' EEEEEEE ' );
  7 end e;
  8 /
Procedure created.
```

Here we have five procedures that call each other, and each has debugging code compiled into it. We included calls to both DEBUG and DBMS_OUTPUT so we can demonstrate the power of the DEBUG package.

Normally using DBMS_OUTPUT, we would just enable SERVEROUTPUT and spool the debug messages to the screen:

```
SQL> set serverout on size 1000000
SQL> exec E;
AAAAAAA
BBBBBBB
CCCCCCC
DDDDDDD
EEEEEEE

PL/SQL procedure successfully completed.
```

As we explained earlier, it's an all or nothing venture—we see either the entire debug log or none of it. What if we just want to get some debug information? With the DEBUG package, we can do just that.

Now we initialize DEBUG and re-execute procedure E:

```
SQL> execute debug.init( 'ALL', 'TEMP', 'debug.dbg' );
PL/SQL procedure successfully completed.

SQL> exec E;
PL/SQL procedure successfully completed.
```

Looking in the debug file we should see this:

```
09072003 160540(              UTILITY.A    3)   AAAAAAA
09072003 160540(              UTILITY.B    4)   BBBBBBB
09072003 160540(              UTILITY.C    4)   CCCCCCC
09072003 160540(              UTILITY.D    4)   DDDDDDD
09072003 160540(              UTILITY.E    4)   EEEEEEE
```

The five lines of debug information are now there. You're probably thinking that this isn't so impressive—you can accomplish this with UTL_FILE. But notice the information that is there. It has the date and time that the debug information was generated, which is very useful when debugging. Then notice that it lists which OWNER.PROCEDURE generated the message and at which line number. This helps you know exactly where each message is coming from. And lastly, it prints the message itself.

If that was all that DEBUG did, it would be a great improvement over DBMS_OUTPUT or UTL_FILE. Now let's see the real power of this utility. Let's reinitialize DEBUG but supply just a few procedures to debug:

```
SQL> execute debug.init( 'A,B,D', 'TEMP', 'debug.dbg' );
PL/SQL procedure successfully completed.

SQL> execute E;
AAAAAAA
BBBBBBB
CCCCCCC
DDDDDDD
EEEEEEE
PL/SQL procedure successfully completed.
```

No difference in the DBMS_OUTPUT output. But if we look back in the debug.dbg file, we should see this:

```
Debug parameters initialized on 07-SEP-2003 16:14:16
              USER:  UTILITY
           MODULES:  A,B,D
         DIRECTORY:  TEMP
          FILENAME:  debug.dbg
         SHOW DATE:  YES
       DATE FORMAT:  MMDDYYYY HH24MISS
       NAME LENGTH:  30
   SHOW SESSION ID:  NO


09072003 161418(                    UTILITY.A    3)   AAAAAAA
09072003 161418(                    UTILITY.B    4)   BBBBBBB
09072003 161418(                    UTILITY.D    4)   DDDDDDD
```

Only the procedures A, B, and D generated debug messages. The call to DEBUG.F that procedures C and E made generated no information. In this small example, eliminating two lines of debug information doesn't necessarily help you, but imagine instrumenting your code with DEBUG.F calls and then, when necessary, enabling just the debug from a particular procedure. That is very powerful.

When you're done debugging, you can just uninitialize your debug with a call to DEBUG.CLEAR and no more messages will be generated. And all this without changing a single line of your production code!

I've used this method in many applications and it just works. It's simple and noninvasive. It's easy to use and when it's not enabled it produces almost no overhead on the application. I've gotten calls from users saying they've encountered an error in an application that I wrote a year prior. I don't remember exactly every line of code or how everything was done, but I do know that I used DEBUG. All I do is enable the DEBUG for that user and review the generated file, and I can usually pinpoint relatively quickly where the error is. Remember, DEBUG generates the procedure name and line number where the debug message was executed. That information alone with verbose messages should be more than enough for you to begin looking in the right place.

Debugging In-Production Code

Once we've completed the development process and want to move the application into production, we may well still have hundreds and hundreds of lines of debug. We want to avoid the overhead of calling DEBUG to maximize performance. Although working through each message and removing them all will do the trick, there is an alternate solution. All we need to do is modify the F() and FA() procedures, adding return; as the first line of each. This way, when either is called, it immediately returns, doing no work whatsoever. It's true that there is still a bit of overhead with this method, but the benefit outweighs that overhead.

To test the timing of calls to DEBUG.F(), we can use a simple PL/SQL procedure, such as the following. In this case, we default the test to perform 1,000 DEBUG.F() calls, sending in three substitution variables for each call. We do that 20 times and then calculate the average time it took for 1,000 calls:

```
create procedure debug_timer(
   p_test_cnt number default 20,
   p_iterations number default 1000 ) as
--
   l_start timestamp;
   l_end timestamp;
   l_timer number := 0;

begin
   for i in 1 .. p_test_cnt loop
     l_start := current_timestamp;
     for j in 1 .. p_iterations loop
       debug.f( 'A %s C %s E %s G', 'B', 'D', 'F' );
     end loop;
     l_end := current_timestamp;
     l_timer := l_timer +
                 to_number( substr( l_end-l_start,
                            instr( l_end-l_start, ':', -1 )+1 ));

   end loop;
   dbms_output.put_line( 'In ' || p_test_cnt || ' tests ' );
   dbms_output.put_line( 'it took an average ' ||
                       l_timer/p_test_cnt || ' seconds' ||
                       '/' || p_iterations || ' calls to f().');
end debug_timer;
```

NOTE This procedure will only work in Oracle9*i* and higher. We use the new datatype TIMESTAMP, which measures subsecond time, to a default precision of six decimal places.

Timing Debug Statements

Now let's run this procedure and see the results:

```
SQL> exec debug_timer
In 20 tests
it took an average 1.83848415 seconds/1000 calls to f().

PL/SQL procedure successfully completed.
```

As you can see, in this case it took on average 1.83 seconds to perform 1,000 DEBUG.F() calls. Of course, your results will vary depending on your processor.

Let's now run the same test against the modified version of DEBUG. All we do is add a return; as the first line of F() and FA(), as follows:

```
procedure fa(
    p_message in varchar2,
    p_args    in Argv default emptyDebugArgv ) is
  begin
    return;
    debug_it( p_message, p_args );
  end fa;

procedure f(
    p_message in varchar2,
    p_arg1    in varchar2 default null,

    p_arg2    in varchar2 default null,
    p_arg3    in varchar2 default null,
    p_arg4    in varchar2 default null,
    p_arg5    in varchar2 default null,
    p_arg6    in varchar2 default null,
    p_arg7    in varchar2 default null,
    p_arg8    in varchar2 default null,
    p_arg9    in varchar2 default null,
    p_arg10   in varchar2 default null ) is
  begin
    return;
    debug_it( p_message,
              argv( substr( p_arg1, 1, 4000 ),
                    substr( p_arg2, 1, 4000 ),
                    substr( p_arg3, 1, 4000 ),
                    substr( p_arg4, 1, 4000 ),
                    substr( p_arg5, 1, 4000 ),
```

```
                          substr( p_arg6, 1, 4000 ),
                          substr( p_arg7, 1, 4000 ),
                          substr( p_arg8, 1, 4000 ),
                          substr( p_arg9, 1, 4000 ),
                          substr( p_arg10, 1, 4000 ) ) );
    end f;
```

Now let's rerun the timing test and look at the results:

```
SQL> exec debug_timer
In 20 tests
it took an average .04530185 seconds/1000 calls to f().

PL/SQL procedure successfully completed.
```

Forty-five thousandths of a second on average to execute 1,000 calls to DEBUG.F() is not very much time. So it would seem that leaving the debug calls in your production application isn't going to dramatically impair performance.

> **NOTE**   These figures are simply for comparison and do not constitute absolute debug timing. The figures you get back in performing these tests will naturally vary depending upon how your system is configured.

A further benefit is that you can remove RETURN; from the two procedures and debug your production application at any time. We all know that errors come up in production applications that are difficult or impossible to reproduce in a development environment. Leaving the calls to DEBUG in your code gives you the ability to witness the error in real time, and quickly track down and fix the problem.

Where Is DEBUG Useful?

There are many places you can use DEBUG:

- You can use it in any PL/SQL application. Just sprinkle calls to F() and FA() wherever you want. And when you want them to become active, initialize a debug profile. When you aren't debugging an application, just clear your profile and the calls to DEBUG won't produce any output.

- Consider a PL/SQL application or routine that isn't called from SQL*Plus. How about a Forms application that calls some server-side PL/SQL? How can you easily get any feedback from your code? You can't. You need DEBUG.

- If you're familiar with row-level security (RLS) in Oracle, then you know about the policy procedure you need to implement to enable that feature. But that procedure can't be called directly. Oracle calls it itself when a SELECT is performed on the table with RLS enabled. Good luck getting feedback from that without using DEBUG.

- A trigger is another example of a PL/SQL routine that isn't directly called by a user or an application, and DEBUG is a great way to monitor what the trigger is doing.

- Using the timestamp of each debug message, you can determine how long it takes to get from debug messages to debug messages in your code. This can help you find performance bottlenecks in your code. If you have the following:

```
...
debug.f( 'before calling my_proc' );
my_proc;
debug.f( 'after calling my_proc' );
...
```

and the time between messages is long, you know that the procedure MY_PROC() is taking a significant amount of time to execute, and you might want to look into increasing its performance.

I suggest that every PL/SQL developer get a copy of the DEBUG package and give it a try. You can download it from the Downloads area of the Apress website (http://www.apress.com). If you're interested in complete information about and a code listing for the DEBUG package, see Appendix A.

Summary

As you've learned, there are many, many debugging facilities available to you as a PL/SQL developer, from the simplest DBMS_OUTPUT, to simple table and file logging, to a fully functional DEBUG utility. We didn't have sufficient time and space in this chapter to explore all debugging options available to you. For example, JDeveloper offers a full-featured PL/SQL debugger with the capability to set breakpoints in your routines, step through your code line by line, and examine variable values at each step. It's not just for Java developers. If you're interested

in trying out JDeveloper, you can download a free copy of it from
`http://otn.oracle.com/products/jdev/content.html`.

As PL/SQL developers, we've used all of the techniques described in this chapter and continue to use all of them. Each is useful in certain circumstances. There isn't just one correct way to debug. A combination of performing defensive coding, using effective exception handling, and employing the tools described in this chapter will enable you as a developer to quickly and efficiently track down problems and fix your applications.

APPENDIX A

Building DEBUG

IN THIS APPENDIX, WE present a code listing for the custom debugging utility, DEBUG, which we used in Chapter 10. This code is freely downloadable from the Apress website at http://www.apress.com.

Database Design and Setup

Because DEBUG is a PL/SQL utility, it lives in the database, and we'll need to have a schema to own it. This schema can be owned by any user granted the CONNECT, RESOURCE, and CREATE PUBLIC SYNONYM roles. I suggest that you create a schema to hold this DEBUG package and grant EXECUTE on the DEBUG package to PUBLIC. That way, you have one copy of the package and everybody shares it. In my database, I usually have a schema called UTILITY that owns utilities such as DEBUG, so I will use UTILITY in this example:

```
SQL> create user utility identified by utility;
User created.

SQL> grant connect, resource, create public synonym to utility;
Grant succeeded.
```

Now we're ready to create the schema objects we'll need to support the DEBUG utility.

Tables

What we want to do now is set up the DEBUG package so that it will act according to how each user has set up his or her environment. Instead of storing that information in the environment, we'll store it in a database table called DEBUGTAB. The code to create this table is as follows:

```
create table debugtab(
  userid      varchar2(30),
  dir         varchar2(32),
  filename    varchar2(1024),
```

```
modules      varchar2(4000),
show_date    varchar2(3),
date_format  varchar2(255),
name_length  number,
session_id   varchar2(3),
--
-- Constraints
--
constraint debugtab_pk
  primary key ( userid, dir, filename ),
constraint debugtab_show_date_ck
  check ( show_date in ( 'YES', 'NO' ) ),
constraint debugtab_session_id_ck
  check ( session_id in ( 'YES', 'NO' ) )
)
/
```

As you can see by the column names, we store all the information for each user who wants to use DEBUG. Options such as which procedures generate debug messages, what the date/timestamp format is, and whether or not to show the session ID are all stored in this table.

Indexes and Constraints

There is only one index on this table, namely the primary key DEBUGTAB_PK. It was created in the CREATE TABLE statement. We use the USERID, DIR, FILENAME combination to uniquely identify a record. That might seem a bit strange, because you might think that USERID would be sufficient. However, consider applications in which every user connects as the same login, and the user's true identity is retrieved by some other means (such as cookies in the case of a Web-based application, for example). If we had only used USERID as the primary key, then one debug profile would have had to suffice for the entire application. That would not be very friendly, or useful, especially if you have several developers working on the application simultaneously.

The check constraints on the DEBUGTAB table ensure that the values entered are correct, and when reading data out of the DEBUGTAB table, we can assume those columns will only have YES or NO as their value.

Triggers

We use a trigger on the DEBUGTAB table to ensure that the profile data is formatted correctly when entered:

```
create or replace
trigger biu_fer_debugtab
before insert or update on debugtab for each row
begin
  :new.modules := upper( :new.modules );
  :new.show_date := upper( :new.show_date );
  :new.session_id := upper( :new.session_id );
  :new.userid := upper( :new.userid );
```

Here the trigger formats the data, uppercasing the values supplied:

```
declare
  l_date varchar2(100);
begin
  l_date := to_char( sysdate, :new.date_format );
exception
  when others then
    raise_application_error(
      -20001,
      'Invalid Date Format In Debug Date Format' );
end;
declare
  l_handle utl_file.file_type;
begin
  l_handle := utl_file.fopen(
                location => :new.dir,
                filename => :new.filename,
                open_mode => 'a',
                max_linesize => 32767 );
  utl_file.fclose( l_handle );
exception
  when others then
    raise_application_error(
      -20001,
      'Cannot open debug dir/file ' ||
      :new.dir || '/' ||
      :new.filename );
  end;
end;
/
```

This portion of the trigger validates the date format supplied. It attempts to create a string with the supplied mask. If the mask is invalid, an application error is raised and the insert is aborted. It then makes sure that the directory and filename supplied are valid and that Oracle has the ability to write to it.

This simplifies the coding of the DEBUG package because we can assume that all the data in the DEBUGTAB table is valid.

DIRECTORY Object

UTL_FILE used to work by supplying an actual directory name. In later versions of the database (9 and up), you could supply a DIRECTORY object name instead of setting the UTL_FILE_DIR parameter of the database. This version of DEBUG has been updated to use that DIRECTORY object. To create an object, you need to execute the following:

```
create or replace directory TEMP as '/some/directory/writable/by/Oracle'
```

Package Layout

Let's now explore what the DEBUG package looks like. The DEBUG package must implement four main procedures:

- Initialize the profile.

- Generate debug messages.

- List the current debug profile.

- Clear the profile.

The initialization procedure, INIT(), should take in all the options that we can set for the debug profile:

```
procedure init(
    p_modules      in varchar2 default 'ALL',
    p_dir          in varchar2 default 'TEMP',
    p_file         in varchar2 default user || '.dbg',
    p_user         in varchar2 default user,
    p_show_date    in varchar2 default 'YES',
    p_date_format  in varchar2 default 'MMDDYYYY HH24MISS',
    p_name_len     in number   default 30,
    p_show_sesid   in varchar2 default 'NO' );
```

The procedure, F(), that will generate the debug message should take in the parameterized message and a list of the variables to substitute:

```
procedure f(
  p_message in varchar2,
  p_arg1    in varchar2 default null,
  p_arg2    in varchar2 default null,
  p_arg3    in varchar2 default null,
  p_arg4    in varchar2 default null,
  p_arg5    in varchar2 default null,
  p_arg6    in varchar2 default null,
  p_arg7    in varchar2 default null,
  p_arg8    in varchar2 default null,
  p_arg9    in varchar2 default null,
  p_arg10   in varchar2 default null );
```

We're sure a few of you have noticed that we have a hard limit for the number of substitutions into the debug message. There are two options if you wish to get around this limitation. You can use either || to build the debug string (giving you an unlimited number of values to substitute in) or the DEBUG.FA() routine. Its specification is as follows:

```
emptyDebugArgv Argv;

  procedure fa(
    p_message in varchar2,
    p_args    in Argv default emptyDebugArgv );
```

We'll explain later what the ARGV type is and how you use it. Suffice it to say that it removes the ten-parameter limitation of the F() implementation. Once the profile is set, we need a way to review it. We need a status routine:

```
procedure status(
  p_user in varchar2 default user,
  p_dir  in varchar2 default null,
  p_file in varchar2 default null );
```

And finally we need a way to clear our debug profile when we no longer want to generate debug messages:

```
procedure clear(
  p_user in varchar2 default user,
  p_dir  in varchar2 default null,
  p_file in varchar2 default null );
```

Both STATUS() and CLEAR() take in P_USER and P_FILE. Remember, the primary key to the debug profile is both of those values. The user will need to supply

them both to access the correct record. As a shortcut, we allow P_FILE to be
passed in as NULL. In that case, all debug profiles for the supplied user will be
affected.

Implementation

Now it's time to start coding. We'll need to implement the four procedures in our
specification, but there are some private procedures in the DEBUG package body
that need to be implemented as well. Let's break up the private debug processes
into logical units of work. We need to do the following:

- Determine what code called DEBUG, using WHO_CALLED_ME().

- Build the debug header information, using BUILD_IT().

- Parse the debug message and perform substitutions, using PARSE_IT().

- Write the debug message to a file, using FILE_IT().

We'll write a private procedure/function for each of these. Let's start, though,
with the public interfaces used to generate a debug message: F(), FA(), and
DEBUG_IT().

F()

The procedure F() is the most commonly used procedure in the DEBUG package.
You can use this procedure anywhere in your code to generate a message to a file
and so allow yourself to see (in real time) what is going on. Its implementation is
quite simple:

```
1    procedure f(
2      p_message in varchar2,
3      p_arg1    in varchar2 default null,
4      p_arg2    in varchar2 default null,
5      p_arg3    in varchar2 default null,
6      p_arg4    in varchar2 default null,
7      p_arg5    in varchar2 default null,
8      p_arg6    in varchar2 default null,
9      p_arg7    in varchar2 default null,
10     p_arg8    in varchar2 default null,
11     p_arg9    in varchar2 default null,
12     p_arg10   in varchar2 default null ) is
```

```
13     begin
14       debug_it( p_message,
15                   argv( substr( p_arg1, 1, 4000 ),
16                         substr( p_arg2, 1, 4000 ),
17                         substr( p_arg3, 1, 4000 ),
18                         substr( p_arg4, 1, 4000 ),
19                         substr( p_arg5, 1, 4000 ),
20                         substr( p_arg6, 1, 4000 ),
21                         substr( p_arg7, 1, 4000 ),
22                         substr( p_arg8, 1, 4000 ),
23                         substr( p_arg9, 1, 4000 ),
24                         substr( p_arg10, 1, 4000 ) ) );
25     end f;
```

As you can see, it does nothing but repackage the ten P_ARGS into an ARGV and pass it to a routine called DEBUG_IT().

The ARGV Type

ARGV is a type that we define in the DEBUG specification. It is defined as follows:

```
type argv is table of varchar2(4000);
```

We created the ARGV type to support the FA() implementation. Using this ARGV type, we can pass in any number of parameters into a procedure. Consider it as an array.

The procedure F() was included for simplicity, whereas the procedure FA() was included for completeness. It is much easier to type this:

```
l_var varchar2(5) := 'World';
debug.f( 'Hello %s', l_var );
```

than to call this:

```
l_var varchar2(5) := 'World';
debug.fa( 'Hello %s', debug.argv( 'World' ) );
```

Also, in terms of how it is called, DEBUG.F() is closer to the C printf() function than DEBUG.FA(), and we were trying to mimic printf().

If you have over ten variables you need to substitute, you can use either FA() or ||.

FA()

The FA() implementation is even simpler than F():

```
1    procedure fa(
2      p_message in varchar2,
3      p_args     in Argv default emptyDebugArgv ) is
4    begin
5      debug_it( p_message, p_args );
6    end fa;
```

As you can see, it makes a straight call to DEBUG_IT() without doing any work at all. You might wonder why we didn't have F() call FA() and have FA() do the work. That will become clear later on. For now, we'll just say that it has something to do with calculating who called the DEBUG routine.

DEBUG_IT()

This procedure is the coordinator of the DEBUG package. Both F() and FA() call it, and it in turn calls the four private procedures that we mentioned briefly earlier. Anytime we have a package like DEBUG (a package with multiple entry points to common functionality), we should make a private controlling procedure to do all the real work. That way, if we need to make a change to the logic of the package, we make it in one place. All the entry points, F() and FA() in this case, stay synchronized in terms of their common functionality.

Let's take a look at the implementation of the coordinator of the DEBUG package:

```
1    procedure debug_it(
2      p_message in varchar2,
3      p_argv     in argv ) is
4    --
5      l_message long := null;
6      l_header long := null;
7      call_who_called_me boolean := true;
8      l_owner varchar2(255);
9      l_object varchar2(255);
10     l_lineno number;
11     l_dummy boolean;
12   begin
13
```

We knew by the way F() and FA() called DEBUG_IT() that it took in the debug message string and the ARGV type. We've also set up a few local parameters.

The first thing we want to do is to check whether the current user has DEBUG enabled. That is accomplished by selecting out any records in the DEBUGTAB table in which the USERID is the current user. In this case, we check it against the pseudo-column USER, which is set to the username of the user currently executing the procedure:

```
14      for c in ( select *
15                    from debugtab
16                    where userid = user )
17      loop
18
```

Next, we need to make a call to the first of our four private procedures, WHO_CALLED_ME(). The call is wrapped in the IF-THEN structure for performance reasons. If there are two records with the same USERID and different FILENAMES, then there is no reason to call WHO_CALLED_ME() the second time through the loop (because it will come up with the same results). This reduces CPU processing time.

```
19        if call_who_called_me then
20          who_called_me( l_owner, l_object, l_lineno );
21          call_who_called_me := false;
22        end if;
23
```

Now we want to check if the L_OBJECT variable returned by WHO_CALLED_ME() is in the comma-delimited list of object names that are currently being debugged:

```
24        if instr( ',' || c.modules || ',',
25                   ',' || l_object || ',' ) <> 0 or
26           c.modules = 'ALL'
27        then
28
```

Finally, if it's determined that the debug message should be written, we call the other three private procedures, which will handle the work:

```
29          l_header := build_it( c, l_owner, l_object, l_lineno );
30    l_message := parse_it( p_message, p_argv, length(l_header) );
31          l_dummy := file_it( c.dir, c.filename, l_header || l_message );
32
33        end if;
```

```
34        end loop;
35
36    end debug_it;
```

Notice that we don't check the return value from FILE_IT(). That's because there is nothing we can do if the message has failed. We don't want to stop execution of the application just because DEBUG could not write the message. We'll have to troubleshoot why no messages are being written (see the "Troubleshooting DEBUG" section later on).

Searching for Matches in Strings

Another thing you might be wondering is why both search strings in the INSTR() on lines 24 and 25 are padded with commas. That was done to ensure that no mistaken debugging of a routine takes place. Consider the case of two procedures, A() and AA(). If the developer only wanted to debug the procedure AA(), and a debug call was initiated from the A() procedure, then without the addition of the commas, the debug message would be printed mistakenly. Let's look at how the INSTR() function works:

```
SQL> select instr( 'Samantha', 'man' ) position from dual;

   POSITION
----------
        3
```

INSTR() looks for the second parameter within the first parameter and if it finds it returns the index of it. In this example, INSTR() found the string MAN in the string SAMANTHA starting at position 3.

Getting back to the example of the two procedures A() and AA(), the string A is in the string AA, but we don't want to debug A(), so we put a comma on each side of the strings and now search for ,A, within the string ,AA,. Because there's no match, no debug is generated, which is the desired effect. Here's an example to show this point:

```
SQL>  declare
  2      debug_procedure_name long := 'A';
  3      list_of_debuggable_procs long := 'AA';
  4   begin
  5      if instr( list_of_debuggable_procs,
  6                   debug_procedure_name ) <> 0 then
  7        dbms_output.put_line( 'found it' );
  8      else
```

```
 9        dbms_output.put_line( 'did not find it' );
10     end if;
11     if instr( ',' || list_of_debuggable_procs || ',',
12                    ',' || debug_procedure_name || ',' ) <> 0 then
13        dbms_output.put_line( 'found it' );
14     else
15        dbms_output.put_line( 'did not find it' );
16     end if;
17 end;
18 /
found it
did not find it
```

WHO_CALLED_ME()

The first of the four procedures that we encounter in the DEBUG_IT() procedure is WHO_CALLED_ME(). This procedure will determine from what line of code in what procedure the debug message was called. What we want to do in this procedure is use the Oracle-supplied function DBMS_UTILITY.FORMAT_CALL_STACK() to get the call stack.

The *call stack* is the listing of the procedures and function that we've recently traversed. If we initially called procedure A() and it in turned called procedure B(), which called procedure C(), the call stack indicates where we are currently in the code and what procedure(s) we went through to get to that point. It also includes other information such as current line numbers.

We can then use the string manipulation functions, SUBSTR(), INSTR(), LTRIM(), and RTRIM(), to parse out the information we're interested in. Let's take a look at how that will work.

The first part of the code defines the procedure and the local variables. Notice the three OUT parameters. Because this procedure needs to return multiple pieces of information, we need to use OUT parameters instead of making this a function (which could return only a single value):

```
1    procedure who_called_me(
2      o_owner  out varchar2,
3      o_object out varchar2,
4      o_lineno out number ) is
5    --
6      l_call_stack long default dbms_utility.format_call_stack;
7      l_line varchar2(4000);
8    begin
9
```

Included in the comments (lines 10 through 19) is an example of what the output for `DBMS_UTILITY.FORMAT_CALL_STACK()` might look like. The first three lines are heading information. Each subsequent line is a line in the call stack. The information in each line includes the owner, object name, and line number, among other things. It is those three pieces of information that we'll need to parse out and return.

```
10      /*
11        ----- PL/SQL Call Stack -----
12          object        line  object
13          handle      number  name
14        86c60290          17  package body UTILITY.DEBUG
15        86c60290         212  package body UTILITY.DEBUG
16        86c60290         251  package body UTILITY.DEBUG
17        86aa28f0           1  procedure OPS$CLBECK.A
18        86a9e940           1  anonymous block
19      */
20
```

The primary task that `WHO_CALLED_ME()` needs to carry out is to skip the first six lines of the call stack. The first three lines, we know, are just the heading information and the next three are calls from inside the `DEBUG` package itself. Those three calls in the debug stack are, in reverse order, as follows:

- The call to `F()` or `FA()` (line 16)

- The call to the controller procedure `DEBUG_IT()` (line 15)

- The call to the procedure `WHO_CALLED_ME()` (line 14)

If we have `F()` call `FA()` and then have `FA()` do the work of `DEBUG_IT()`, the stack would have a different number of levels depending on which of the two we called, making it much harder to write `WHO_CALLED_ME()`. Let's consider the next section of code:

```
21      for i in 1 .. 6 loop
22        l_call_stack := substr( l_call_stack,
23                            instr( l_call_stack, chr(10) )+1 );
24      end loop;
25
```

Now the local variable `L_CALL_STACK` starts with the line we're interested in. For ease of use, let's set a local variable to just that line, ignoring anything after it:

```
26        l_line := ltrim( substr( l_call_stack,
27                               1,
28                               instr( l_call_stack, chr(10) ) - 1 ) );
29
```

If the call stack looks like the preceding example, then L_LINE will look like this:

```
86aa28f0          1    procedure OPS$CLBECK.A
```

Now let's begin to parse L_LINE. First we remove the object handle, 86aa28f0, by reassigning L_LINE to equal the SUBSTR() of itself starting at the first whitespace. This is wrapped within an LTRIM() that removes all leading whitespace:

```
30        l_line := ltrim( substr( l_line, instr( l_line, ' ' )));
31
```

L_LINE now looks like this:

```
1    procedure OPS$CLBECK.A
```

Now L_LINE starts with the line number of the code where this occurrence of DEBUG.F() or DEBUG.FA() was called from. We want to save that information and include it in the debug message, so that the developer can easily find exactly where in the code this message originated from. We assign it to the OUT parameter O_LINENO, and then strip it from L_LINE:

```
32    o_lineno := to_number(substr(l_line, 1, instr(l_line, ' ')));
33    l_line := ltrim(substr(l_line, instr(l_line, ' ')));
34
```

> **NOTE** We use the same technique to remove the next word from L_LINE as we did to remove the object handle in the previous step.

Next, we want to remove the kind of object that called DEBUG. The tricky part here is that there may be either one or two words to strip off. If DEBUG was called from

- A procedure or function in a package body

- A member routine in a type body

- An anonymous block

then we need to remove the word body or block from L_LINE too, using the following code:

```
35    l_line := ltrim( substr( l_line, instr( l_line, ' ' )));
36
37    if l_line like 'block%' or
38       l_line like 'body%' then
39      l_line := ltrim( substr( l_line, instr( l_line, ' ' )));
40    end if;
41
```

Now the only thing left in the line is the OWNER.OBJECT_NAME. We now set the other two OUT parameters to the appropriate values using all four of the string manipulation functions:

```
42    o_owner := ltrim( rtrim( substr( l_line,
43                                1,
44                                instr( l_line, '.' )-1 )));
45    o_object  := ltrim( rtrim( substr( l_line,
46                                instr( l_line, '.' )+1 )));
47
```

Finally, if DEBUG was called from an anonymous block, the call stack doesn't supply an OWNER.OBJECT_NAME, so the assignment of O_OWNER and O_OBJECT causes them to be set to NULL. We check to see if O_OWNER is NULL. If it is, then we need to set O_OWNER to equal the user connected in the current session and set O_OBJECT equal to ANONYMOUS BLOCK:

```
48    if o_owner is null then
49      o_owner := user;
50      o_object := 'ANONYMOUS BLOCK';
51    end if;
52
53    end who_called_me;
```

BUILD_IT()

Once we determine that this call to DEBUG should generate a debug message, we call the second internal package procedure, BUILD_IT(), to build and return the header of the debug message. The header contains all the information about the call to DEBUG, formatted according to the debug profile set up with INIT(). It may include the timestamp of when it was called, the owner and object name from which it was called, and the line number of that object. We determined that information in WHO_CALLED_ME() and forwarded it to BUILD_IT(), along with other information for formatting the header:

```
1     function build_it(
2        p_debug_row in debugtab%rowtype,
3        p_owner      in varchar2,
4        p_object     in varchar2,
5        p_lineno number ) return varchar2 is
6        --
7        l_header long := null;
8     begin
9
```

There are just three steps in BUILD_IT(). First, we want to check and see if we should include the SESSION_ID in the header information. If so, we assign the global variable, G_SESSION_ID, to the local variable, L_HEADER. We use a global here for performance reasons. The session doesn't change once this DEBUG package is instantiated, so we don't need the overhead of getting the session ID on every call. Instead of this, we can simply set the global variable once in the instantiation block of DEBUG and then just reference it when necessary. We'll show you what that looks like later on—for now, just assume that G_SESSION_ID is set correctly.

```
10       if p_debug_row. session_id = 'YES' then
11          l_header := g_session_id || ' - ';
12       end if;
13
```

Next, we want to determine if the message formatting wants to include the date and time. If so, we append the correctly formatted timestamp to L_HEADER:

```
14       if p_debug_row.show_date = 'YES' then
15          l_header := l_header ||
16                       to_char( sysdate,
```

```
17                              nvl( p_debug_row.date_format,
18                                   'MMDDYYYY HH24MISS' ) );
19       end if;
20
```

Finally, we append the owner, object name, and line number to L_HEADER and return it to the caller DEBUG_IT():

```
21       l_header :=
22         l_header ||
23         '(' ||
24         lpad( substr( p_owner || '.' || p_object,
25             greatest( 1, length( p_owner || '.' || p_object ) -
26             least( p_debug_row.name_length, 61 ) + 1 ) ),
27             least( p_debug_row.name_length, 61 ) ) ||
28         lpad( p_lineno, 5 ) ||
29         ') ';
30
31       return l_header;
32
33     end build_it;
```

There is some tricky stuff here with GREATEST(), LEAST(), and SUBSTR() used to size the owner and object name correctly. The reason we allow the developer to control the size of the name display is that if we always use the maximum space to display the OWNER.OBJECT, then there is usually quite a bit of whitespace in it. Identifiers in Oracle can be a maximum of 30 characters, meaning that the OWNER.OBJECT can be as large as 61 characters. Because this isn't usually the case, though, we give developers a way to control that display length.

Another thing to note is the parameter type of P_DEBUG_ROW(DEBUGTAB%ROW-TYPE). Because we call this routine from within a CURSOR FOR loop in DEBUG_IT(), and the query for that loop is a SELECT * query, we can pass the entire row to the BUILD_IT() routine in one variable. This makes defining the procedure cleaner, which in turn makes the call to it shorter.

PARSE_IT()

Once the message header is complete, we may need to modify the message itself. In PARSE_IT() substitutions of %s to appropriate values are carried out. We need to pass not only the message string, but also the values to substitute into it (in the form of the ARGV type) and the length of the header string to PARSE_IT():

```
1      function parse_it(
2        p_message         in varchar2,
3        p_argv            in argv,
```

```
4        p_header_length in number ) return varchar2 is
5        --
6        l_message long := null;
7        l_str long := p_message;
8        l_idx number := 1;
9        l_ptr number := 1;
10   begin
11
```

NOTE   You'll see why we need the header length later on.

The first thing to do is check if anything needs substituting. If a % or a \ isn't found in the message, then we can just return the P_MESSAGE unaltered:

```
12       if nvl( instr( p_message, '%' ), 0 ) = 0 and
13          nvl( instr( p_message, '\' ), 0 ) = 0 then
14         return p_message;
15       end if;
16
```

Now we loop, looking for instances of %, and exit the loop when no more are found:

```
17       loop
18
19         l_ptr := instr( l_str, '%' );
20         exit when l_ptr = 0 or l_ptr is null;
```

If a % is found, then we append all characters prior to it to the local variable L_MESSAGE:

```
21           l_message := l_message || substr( l_str, 1, l_ptr-1 );
22           l_str :=  substr( l_str, l_ptr+1 );
23
```

Next, we examine the character immediately following the %. If it is an s, then we've found where a substitution needs to happen and carry it out:

```
24          if substr( l_str, 1, 1 ) = 's' then
25             l_message := l_message || p_argv(l_idx);
26             l_idx := l_idx + 1;
27             l_str := substr( l_str, 2 );
28
```

If the character immediately following the % is another %, we add one % to L_MESSAGE and continue. In Oracle, if you have two single quotes together in a string, the first one escapes the second one and only one is displayed. That same logic is true here for percent symbols:

```
29          elsif substr( l_str,1,1 ) = '%' then
30             l_message := l_message || '%';
31             l_str := substr( l_str, 2 );
32
```

Or else if the character immediately following the % we initially found was not s or %, then it's just a % in the string and should be appended to L_MESSAGE so it will be displayed:

```
33          else
34             l_message := l_message || '%';
35          end if;
36
37       end loop;
38
```

Now we make a second pass over the message to look for \N and \T. Those familiar with coding in C or Java know that to put a new line or a tab into a printed string, you use \N and \T, respectively. Because we're copying the C style of using %s for placeholders in variable substitution, we include the new line and tab formatting also. The logic here is exactly the same as in the previous loop. First, we reset the local variables:

```
39       l_str := l_message || l_str;
40       l_message := null;
41
```

Now we loop, looking for a \ and exit when no more are found:

```
42       loop
43
44          l_ptr := instr( l_str, '\' );
45          exit when l_ptr = 0 or l_ptr is null;
```

If a \ is found, we append everything prior to it to L_MESSAGE:

```
46          l_message := l_message || substr( l_str, 1, l_ptr-1 );
47          l_str :=  substr( l_str, l_ptr+1 );
48
```

Now we examine the character immediately following the \. If it is an n, then we add a new line to the message, which is where the length of the debug header comes into play. We want the new line to start right below where the first line did, which is immediately following the header. So the new line must be padded with spaces the length of the header to line up properly:

```
49          if substr( l_str, 1, 1 ) = 'n' then
50             l_message := l_message || chr(10) ||
51                           rpad( ' ', p_header_length, ' ' );
52             l_str := substr( l_str, 2 );
53
```

If the next character is a t, we append the tab character to L_MESSAGE:

```
54          elsif substr( l_str, 1, 1 ) = 't' then
55             l_message := l_message || chr(9);
56             l_str := substr( l_str, 2 );
57
```

If the next character is another \, we handle it just as we did previously, with the double percent signs:

```
58          elsif substr( l_str, 1, 1 ) = '\' then
59             l_message := l_message || '\';
60             l_str := substr( l_str, 2 );
61
```

Or else it is just a \ and we print it:

```
62          else
63             l_message := l_message || '\';
64          end if;
65
66       end loop;
67
```

All that is left to do is return the parsed and formatted string:

```
68        return l_message || l_str;
69
70    end parse_it;
```

There is nothing extremely hard about this procedure. The only thing to watch is that, in using SUBSTR() and INSTR(), you don't lose a character in the process.

FILE_IT()

Finally, the header and message are parsed and formatted, and are ready for display. We can now attempt to write the information to the desired file using the fourth and final private function in the DEBUG package: FILE_IT(). Its definition and local variables are pretty straightforward. This function will return TRUE or FALSE, depending on whether or not it was successful in writing the message to the file.

```
1    function file_it(
2      p_file     in debugtab.filename%type,
3      p_dir      in debugtab.dir%type,
4      p_message in varchar2 ) return boolean is
5      --
6      l_handle utl_file.file_type;
7    begin
8
```

Notice that we define P_FILE as DEBUGTAB.FILENAME%ROWTYPE. This ensures that the data types for this variable stay in sync with the table DEBUGTAB. If you recall, FILE_IT() is called with the filename stored in the database, and that information is retrieved using a CURSOR FOR loop in DEBUG_IT(). To avoid a type mismatch, we define this parameter as type DEBUGTAB.FILENAME%TYPE, which will keep the input parameter the same type as the column filename in the table. The same applies to P_DIR.

We use the Oracle-supplied package UTL_FILE to open the file:

```
9        l_handle := utl_file.fopen(
10                   location => p_dir,
11                   filename => p_file,
12                   open_mode => 'a',
13                   max_linesize => 32767 );
14
```

Then we write the message into the file:

```
15      utl_file.put( l_handle, '' );
16      utl_file.put_line( l_handle, p_message );
```

And then we close the file and return TRUE:

```
17      utl_file.fclose( l_handle );
18
19      return true;
20
```

You might think it would be easier and more efficient if we left the file open and only wrote the message each time, and you would be right. But because we don't know when the last call to DEBUG is going to be made, we can't know when to finally close the file. So, yes, opening and closing the file is a performance hit, but it's a necessary one.

NOTE   Remember, DEBUG is normally used during the development phase of your application, so a slight performance increase is fine. We'll show you later on how to remove most of the overhead of DEBUG during deployment without changing a single line of your application code.

The last block of code is the exception handler for FILE_IT():

```
21   exception
22      when others then
23        if utl_file.is_open( l_handle ) then
24          utl_file.fclose( l_handle );
25        end if;
26
27        return false;
28
29   end file_it;
```

We use the UTL_FILE package and so need to catch and handle any exceptions that may be raised. UTL_FILE can throw many different exceptions, and any one of them will leave us unable to write the message. We don't want DEBUG to cause the routine calling it to fail, so we capture all exceptions with the WHEN OTHERS clause, and quietly close the file and return FALSE, never having written the debug message.

> **NOTE** This can cause confusion for the developer who is expecting debug information to be generated. See the section titled "Troubleshooting DEBUG" for the most common problems you'll encounter when using DEBUG.

INIT()

Now we've finished all the code for writing the debug message to a file, but we haven't given the developer a way to initialize DEBUG. This is where the INIT() procedure comes into play. It takes in as parameters all the attributes that a developer can set in his or her debug profile. All the parameters are defaulted, so you can just call DEBUG.INIT() to set up your profile:

```
0    procedure init(
1       p_modules      in varchar2 default 'ALL',
2       p_dir          in varchar2 default 'TEMP',
3       p_file         in varchar2 default user || '.dbg',
4       p_user         in varchar2 default user,
5       p_show_date    in varchar2 default 'YES',
6       p_date_format  in varchar2 default 'MMDDYYYY HH24MISS',
7       p_name_len     in number    default 30,
8       p_show_sesid   in varchar2 default 'NO' ) is
9    --
10      pragma autonomous_transaction;
11      debugtab_rec debugtab%rowtype;
12      l_message long;
13   begin
14
```

The first thing to do is delete any profiles that conflict with the one that we'll insert:

```
15      delete from debugtab
16       where userid = p_user
17         and filename = p_file
18         and dir = p_dir;
```

Now we perform the insert, using the `RETURNING-INTO` clause of the `INSERT` statement to capture the values that were inserted:

```
19      insert into debugtab(
20         userid, modules, dir, filename, show_date,
21         date_format, name_length, session_id )
22      values (
23         p_user, p_modules, p_dir, p_file, p_show_date,
24         p_date_format, p_name_len, p_show_sesid )
25      returning
26         userid, modules, dir, filename, show_date,
27         date_format, name_length, session_id
28      into
29         debugtab_rec.userid, debugtab_rec.modules,
30         debugtab_rec.dir, debugtab_rec.filename, debugtab_rec.show_date,
31         debugtab_rec.date_format, debugtab_rec.name_length,
32         debugtab_rec.session_id;
33
```

Remember that we created a trigger, `BIU_FER_DEBUGTAB`, on the `DEBUGTAB` table that could change the data on the way into the table. The trigger uppercases a few of the columns. We might have supplied yes as the value for `SESSION_ID`, but the trigger will uppercase the value and store `YES`. We want to know exactly what the row that was inserted looked like, and so we return its values. We store those returned values in `DEBUGTAB_REC`, which is defined as a `DEBUGTAB%ROWTYPE`, so we know the types will match.

Next, we want to write to the debug file the current debug profile settings. To do this, we build up a message string that includes all the values inserted into the `DEBUGTAB` table:

```
34      l_message := chr(10) ||
35                    'Debug parameters initialized on ' ||
36      to_char( sysdate, 'dd-MON-yyyy hh24:mi:ss' ) || chr(10);
37      l_message := l_message || '         USER: ' ||
38         debugtab_rec.userid || chr(10);
39      l_message := l_message || '       MODULES: ' ||
40         debugtab_rec.modules || chr(10);
41      l_message := l_message || '     DIRECTORY: ' ||
42         debugtab_rec.dir || chr(10);
43      l_message := l_message || '      FILENAME: ' ||
44         debugtab_rec.filename || chr(10);
45      l_message := l_message || '     SHOW DATE: ' ||
46         debugtab_rec.show_date || chr(10);
47      l_message := l_message || '   DATE FORMAT: ' ||
```

```
48        debugtab_rec.date_format || chr(10);
49      l_message := l_message || '    NAME LENGTH: ' ||
50        debugtab_rec.name_length || chr(10);
51      l_message := l_message || 'SHOW SESSION ID: ' ||
52        debugtab_rec.session_id || chr(10);
53
```

Finally, we attempt to write the message by calling FILE_IT(). This time we do care about the return code from FILE_IT(), because, in the event of our being unable to write to the file, there is no reason why we should allow the initialization to occur. If FILE_IT() is unsuccessful, we roll back the insert and raise an application error:

```
54      if not file_it( debugtab_rec.filename, l_message ) then
55        rollback;
56        raise_application_error(
57          -20001,
58          'Can not open file "' ||
59          debugtab_rec.filename || '"' );
60      end if;
61
```

Otherwise, we commit and return:

```
62      commit;
63
64    end init;
```

You might think that it's a bad thing to commit or roll back in this procedure because it could affect open transactions. But remember line 10:

```
pragma autonomous_transaction;
```

This makes the INIT() procedure run in its own transaction space. Committing or rolling back in it will have no effect on the transaction that called it.

CLEAR()

Having generated a way to create a debug profile, we need to create a way to remove it as well. CLEAR() is that procedure, and it's very simple. It just deletes from the DEBUGTAB table any record that matches the inputted parameters. Again, we use the PRAGMA AUTONOMOUS_TRANSACTION directive to ensure the commit called won't affect the calling transaction:

```
1    procedure clear( p_user in varchar2 default user,
2                        p_dir  in varchar2 default null,
3                        p_file in varchar2 default null ) is
4      pragma autonomous_transaction;
5    begin
6      delete from debugtab
7       where userid = p_user
8         and dir = nvl( p_dir, dir )
9         and filename = nvl( p_file, filename );
10      commit;
11    end clear;
```

NOTE   In this procedure, if the caller doesn't supply a filename and DIR, all the profiles for the specified user will be deleted.

STATUS()

Lastly, we supply a procedure called STATUS to display the current debug profile. Just like CLEAR(), the user supplies the username and an optional filename. Because STATUS displays its output using DBMS_OUTPUT.PUT_LINE, you need to call it from SQL*Plus or some other DBMS_OUTPUT-aware client.

```
1    procedure status(
2      p_user in varchar2 default user,
3      p_dir  in varchar2 default null,
4      p_file in varchar2 default null ) is
5    --
6      l_found boolean := false;
7    begin
8
```

Now we print the header of the listing and display the output using DBMS_OUTPUT.PUT_LINE:

```
9      dbms_output.put_line( chr(10) );
10     dbms_output.put_line( 'Debug info for ' ||
11                              p_user );
```

Then we loop over any rows that satisfy the CURSOR FOR loop query:

```
12      for c in ( select *
13                     from debugtab
14                     where userid = p_user
15                       and dir = nvl( p_dir, dir )
16                       and nvl( p_file, filename ) = filename )
17      loop
18        dbms_output.put_line( '--------------' ||
19                       rpad( '-', length( p_user ), '-' ) );
```

We set a local Boolean variable, L_FOUND, to TRUE so that we know that we found at least one matching record:

```
20        l_found := true;
```

Next, we use DBMS_OUTPUT.PUT_LINE to write the output to the developer's screen:

```
21        dbms_output.put_line( 'USER:              ' ||
22                       c.userid );
23        dbms_output.put_line( 'MODULES:           ' ||
24                       c.modules );
25        dbms_output.put_line( 'DIRECTORY:         ' ||
26                       c.dir );
27        dbms_output.put_line( 'FILENAME:          ' ||
28                       c.filename );
29        dbms_output.put_line( 'SHOW DATE:         ' ||
30                       c.show_date );
31        dbms_output.put_line( 'DATE FORMAT:       ' ||
32                       c.date_format );
33        dbms_output.put_line( 'NAME LENGTH:       ' ||
34                       c.name_length );
35        dbms_output.put_line( 'SHOW SESSION ID:   ' ||
36                       c.session_id );
37        dbms_output.put_line( ' ' );
38      end loop;
39
```

Finally, if we don't find any records, we notify the caller of that fact with this message:

```
40      if not l_found then
41        dbms_output.put_line( 'No debug setup.' );
42      end if;
43
44    end status;
```

Finishing Touches

The only code that we haven't yet shown you is the instantiation code of DEBUG. If you recall, we used a global variable called G_SESSION_ID to store the session ID. We told you that we populated that value once on the first call to DEBUG. The variable is defined as follows:

```
package body debug as

  g_session_id varchar2(2000);
```

and the code that initializes it is this:

```
begin
  g_session_id := userenv('SESSIONID');
end debug;
```

There you go—the entire DEBUG utility. You can see the utility in action in Chapter 10.

Troubleshooting DEBUG

You saw that DEBUG was coded to quietly fail if it couldn't write the message to the file. This section presents some things to look for if you aren't getting messages from DEBUG or you're getting errors initializing your profile.

You Get an Error Initializing the Profile: File Does Not Exist

Check to see if Oracle has the privilege to write to the directory. You can accomplish this by logging into SQL*Plus as a DBA and running the following:

```
SQL> show parameter utl_file_dir
```

NAME	TYPE	VALUE
utl_file_dir	string	/tmp

Verify that the value is the same as the directory that you're passing in. This value is case sensitive on Unix, so double-check to ensure it's an exact match.

An alternative way to check is to review the INIT.ORA file and see what the value is set to. Remember, even though it says one thing in the INIT.ORA file, the value may be different because the value may have been changed after the database was started.

NOTE Values in the INIT.ORA file are only read at startup.

You Get an Error Initializing the Profile: File Exists

Check the privileges on the file. The Oracle process owner needs write permission on the file.

No Message Is Written to the Debug File

Check the following items:

- Verify that your debug profile for the appropriate user is in fact enabled by using DEBUG.STATUS().

- Verify that the Oracle process owner has write permission to the directory specified in the profile. It's true that, when the profile was initialized, the directory and file were valid but things might have changed since then.

- Verify that the Oracle process owner has write permission on the file itself. Again, things may have changed since the profile initialization.

- Verify that the directory is still a valid value of the INIT.ORA parameter UTL_FILE_DIR.

Index

Symbol and Numbers

: (colon), appearance in alert logs, 378
10053 event optimizer trace, examining, 281
10520 event, explanation of, 75

A

ACCESS_PARAMETERS of external table, purpose of, 383–384
ACTION field, exposing in DBMS_APPLICATION_INFO package, 522–523
ADD_A_COACH procedure, relationship to delayed processing solution for triggers, 331–332
ADD_COLUMN procedure
altering to wrap call to RUN_DLL, 220–221
creating, 219–220
ADDRESS column in V$SQL, using with invoker rights procedures, 243–244
ADD_ROW procedure, adding to TEN_BYTE_COLUMN table, 197–198
"administrator database trigger" privilege, granting, 363
after and before DML row triggers, performance of, 312–314
after-statement trigger, firing, 311
alert file package
errors messages in, 368
exceptions in, 380–382
location of, 368
and notification life cycle, 382–384
obtaining code for, 370
overview of, 368–369
sample extract of, 368–369
structure of, 369–370
alert files
controlling size of, 384–385
displaying lines from, 373
as external tables, 371–375
history naming options for, 386–387
and ORA-01555 errors, 389–391
preventing duplicate roll overs in same day, 387–388
processing, 375–380
reading, 371
reading lines from, 374–375
reviewing contents of, 393–394

rolling over, 384–387
scheduling and concurrency of, 387–389
structure of, 370–371
and unreported errors, 391–393
alert messages
identifying, 377–378
saving with notification package, 398–399
ALERT_FILE_EXT external table, creating, 372–373
ALERT_SID.LOG alert file name, standardization of, 368
ALL_OBJECTS view
bulk collecting rows from, 193
copying, 29–30
fetching single row from, 181
Alpha package, implementing, 434–437
AMATCH function, purpose of, 384
analytic functions in SQL, benefits of, 44–45
AND operations, handling with PL/SQL, 28
annual_review_candidates cursor, purpose of, 64–65
anonymous PL/SQL blocks
calculating maximum salaries in, 136–137
versus definer rights programs, 416–417
relationship to calling PL/SQL dynamically, 283
relationship to NOCOPY compiler hints, 209–210
role in demonstrability example, 11–12
Application Context, using with logon triggers, 449
APPLICATION_TYPES package, centralizing datatype control with, 151–152
archive log destination, checking free space in, 402–404
ARGV type
example of, 543
passing values with, 548
array fetching, example of, 142–143
array of snapshots, processing for use with RS package, 170–171
array processing example, replicating using DBMS_SQL, 179

587

ERROR_MSG_ARRY collection variable, using with alert files, 377
ERRS table, creating, 226
ETL (extract, transform, load), explanation of, 245
exception handling
using cursor attributes for, 129–130
using OTHERS exception handler, 510–511
exceptions
advantages of, 511
in alert file package, 380–382
defining in package specifications, 508
handling, 506–507
obtaining comprehensive list of, 508
raising, 508, 509–510
system exceptions, 507–508
user-defined exceptions, 508–509
EXECUTE IMMEDIATE versus DBMS_SQL, 303
EXECUTE privileges, relationship to packages, 432–433
execution times, capturing when using varchar2 associative arrays, 87–88
existence checks, relationship to cursors, 128–129
EXPLAIN PLAN tool, advisory about, 14
explicit cursors
example of, 120–126
versus implicit cursors, 117–119, 132
iterating, 119–120
relationship to dynamic SQL, 299–300
relationship to top-n processing, 130–132
using for existence checks, 128–129
using with bulk collection, 183
external tables
alert files as, 371–375
alert files as external tables, 382–383
querying, 373–374

F

F() procedure in DEBUG package, example of, 542–543
FA() calls, using with DEBUG package, 548
fetching
array fetching, 142–143
CGI environment variables, 471
HTML, 496–497
rows in bulk, 181–185
single row fetching, 119–126
FGA (fine-grained auditing), using, 447–448, 450

fields, sequencing in record-based DML, 260–262
file handles, writing to, 533
FILE_IT() procedure in DEBUG package, description of, 544
files
closing after writing to, 533
debugging to, 531–532
managing, 478–483
opening file systems, 532–533
filler tables, generating result sets of data with, 29–30
FOPEN() function, opening files on file systems with, 532–533
FOR keyword, converting to FORALL for use with bulk binding, 188
FOR loops, fetching rows in, 126–130, 187
FORALL statements, using SAVE EXCEPTIONS keyword with, 190–191
%FOUND cursor attribute, example of, 129
free space
checking in archive log destination, 402–404
monitoring in databases, 404–405
FRENAME procedure in UTL_FILE package, using with alert files, 385
FUD factor, explanation of, 162
function-based indexes, precreating values with, 280–282
function calls
reducing, 274–280
from SQL, 267–268, 270–271, 274
functions
defining as view columns, 270
registering information about while executing, 521–528
viewing source code for, 453–456

G

GET procedure, relationship to invoker rights, 239
GET_GENDER_NAME function, relationship to exposing data model, 269
GET_MY_PROGRAM function, using invoker rights with, 419
GET_RESPONSE procedure in UTL_HTTP package, description of, 498
glob context, creating, 82
global variables, 78–80, 89
adding, 81
adding to initialization section, 88–89
referencing, 80

forums.apress.com

JOIN THE APRESS FORUMS AND BE PART OF OUR COMMUNITY. You'll find discussions that cover topics of interest to IT professionals, programmers, and enthusiasts just like you. If you post a query to one of our forums, you can expect that some of the best minds in the business—especially Apress authors, who all write with *The Expert's Voice*™—will chime in to help you. Why not aim to become one of our most valuable participants (MVPs) and win cool stuff? Here's a sampling of what you'll find:

DATABASES

Data drives everything.

Share information, exchange ideas, and discuss any database programming or administration issues.

INTERNET TECHNOLOGIES AND NETWORKING

Try living without plumbing (and eventually IPv6).

Talk about networking topics including protocols, design, administration, wireless, wired, storage, backup, certifications, trends, and new technologies.

JAVA

We've come a long way from the old Oak tree.

Hang out and discuss Java in whatever flavor you choose: J2SE, J2EE, J2ME, Jakarta, and so on.

MAC OS X

All about the Zen of OS X.

OS X is both the present and the future for Mac apps. Make suggestions, offer up ideas, or boast about your new hardware.

OPEN SOURCE

Source code is good; understanding (open) source is better.

Discuss open source technologies and related topics such as PHP, MySQL, Linux, Perl, Apache, Python, and more.

PROGRAMMING/BUSINESS

Unfortunately, it is.

Talk about the Apress line of books that cover software methodology, best practices, and how programmers interact with the "suits."

WEB DEVELOPMENT/DESIGN

Ugly doesn't cut it anymore, and CGI is absurd.

Help is in sight for your site. Find design solutions for your projects and get ideas for building an interactive Web site.

SECURITY

Lots of bad guys out there—the good guys need help.

Discuss computer and network security issues here. Just don't let anyone else know the answers!

TECHNOLOGY IN ACTION

Cool things. Fun things.

It's after hours. It's time to play. Whether you're into LEGO® MINDSTORMS™ or turning an old PC into a DVR, this is where technology turns into fun.

WINDOWS

No defenestration here.

Ask questions about all aspects of Windows programming, get help on Microsoft technologies covered in Apress books, or provide feedback on any Apress Windows book.

HOW TO PARTICIPATE:

Go to the Apress Forums site at **http://forums.apress.com/**.

Click the New User link.